EUROPEAN MONETARY UNION

To Ekaterini Pilioura-Karaveli for her unending and unfailing encouragement.

**The author's royalties shall be offered to charitable
institutions concerned with abandoned children.**

European Monetary Union

An application of the fundamental principles of monetary theory

GEORGES CARAVELIS
European Parliament

Avebury

Aldershot · Brookfield USA · Hong Kong · Singapore · Sydney

© Georges Caravelis 1994

Published by
Avebury
Ashgate Publishing Limited
Gower House
Croft Road
Aldershot
Hants GU11 3HR
England

Ashgate Publishing Company
Old Post Road
Brookfield
Vermont 05036
USA

British Library Cataloguing in Publication Data

Caravelis, Georges
European Monetary Union: An Application of
the Fundamental Principles of Monetary
Theory
332.494

ISBN 1 85628 885 4

Library of Congress Cataloging-in-Publication Data

Caravelis, Georges, 1949-
European monetary union : an application of the fundamental
principles of monetary theory / Georges Caravelis.
    p. cm.
Rev. version of author's thesis (Ph.D. -- University of London).
Includes bibliographical references.
ISBN 1-85628-885-4
1. European Monetary System (Organization) 2. European currency
unit. 3. Monetary policy--European Economic Communtiy countries.
4. Money--European Economic Community countries. I. Title.
HG930.5.C32   1994
332.4'566'094--dc20   94-8707
                                                            CIP

Printed and Bound in Great Britain by
Athenaeum Press Ltd, Newcastle upon Tyne.

Contents

List of abbreviations

AU$	Australian dollar
B	Belgium
BFR	Belgian franc
BIS	Bank for International Settlements
CEPR	Centre for Economic Policy Research
COM	Commission of the European Union
D	Republic of Germany
DI	Divergence Indicator
DK	Denmark
DKR	Danish krone
DM	Deutsche mark
DR	Greek drachma
E	Spain
ECB	European Central Bank
ECOFIN	Economic and Finance Ministers
ECSC	European Coal and Steel Community
ECU	European Currency Unit
EEC	European Economic Community
EFA	European Fiscal Authority
EIB	European Investment Bank
EMCF	European Monetary Cooperation Fund
EMI	European Monetary Institute
EMF	European Monetary Fund
EMS	European Monetary System
EMU	Economic and Monetary Union
ERDF	European Regional Development Fund
ERM	Exchange Rate Mechanism
ESC	Portuguese escudo

ESCB	European System Central Banks
EU	European Union
EUA	European Unit of Account
EUR 12	European Community of 12 Member States
F	France
FF	French franc
FRS	Federal Reserve System
GDP	Gross Domestic/National Product
GFCF	Gross Fixed Capital Formation
GR	Greece
HFL	Dutch guilder
I	Italy
IMF	International Monetary Fund
IR	Ireland
IRL	Irish punt
L	Luxembourg
LFR	Luxembourg franc
LIT	Italian lira
MFA	Medium Financial Assistance
Mio	Million
Mrd	1 000 million
NL	The Netherlands
OCAs	Optimum Currency Areas
P	Portugal
PPP	Purchasing Power Parity
PTA	Spanish peseta
SFR	Swiss franc
STMs	Short-Term Monetary Support
TUE	Treaty on European Union
UK	United Kingdom
UKL	Pound sterling
USA	United States of America
USD	US dollar
VSTF	Very-Short-Term-Facility
YEN	Japanese yen

List of tables

Acknowledgements

This monograph is the product (an external economy to me, a diseconomy to those associated with it) of an effort of not less than twelve years, carried out at McGill, Cambridge and London Universities. During this period, the help and support, advice and counsel, encouragement and its opposite as well as knowledge that I have received and gained, are due to teachers, supervisors and friends, who are too numerous to mention.

I feel obliged to express my gratitude to my first supervisor, Jack R. Weldon of McGill University, who first taught me that examining monetary institutions 'without a good theory of money' would be a futile exercise. The last time we met was on 19 September 1986. It was he who had said that 'the original idea of the five hypotheses had to be carried out without much compromise'. I have followed his advice, for it has been shown to be a precious guide.

To my second supervisor at McGill, Athanasios Asimakopulos, I am also indebted, not so much for his encouragement of my research, but mainly for his method which I have adopted in justifying everything for logical consistency and for his insightful comments on methodology.

There is one supervisor whose support no other student could have had: Victoria Chick of University College London. Not only am I indebted to her intellectually for the final version of this book but also materially for her undertaking to enrol me in the University of London as external student at a time when Tom Asimakopulos, due to serious illness, had to give up his supervisory role. She has been a model supervisor.

Two friends, Omar Hamouda of York University at Toronto and Geoff Harcourt of Cambridge University, have given precious encouragement. Omar has commented on almost all chapters and influenced its direction; he has been forthcoming whenever needed. Geoff invited me twice to Cambridge University and accorded me the status of a *visiting scholar*, not because of my research but because of my employment at the European Parliament. To these dear friends, I owe a special debt.

Two great economic thinkers, Robert Triffin and James Meade, have been supportive. R. Triffin received me warmly at UCL at Louvain-la-Neuve and discussed chapter 3 at length and, in his last letter to me, approved of my interpretation of the Triffin hypothesis. J. Meade also approved the direction of chapter 6 on money being an externality. I have been honoured to have been able to meet these two great men.

During my two stays at Cambridge University, I had the good luck to have met Alistair and Sheila Dow, Paul Wells, Yoshinori Shiozawa, Bob Rowthorn and its graduate students. I have profited from their argument.

I have benefited greatly from the penetrating questions and comments of my two examiners: Laurence Harris of London University (internal) and Sheila Dow of Sterling University (external). Their recommendation to go ahead with the publication of the thesis as originally presented with minor changes has compensated me for the effort involved in this book. I am deeply indebted to both for their encouragement.

I am grateful to a number of people for commenting on individual chapters or for discussing the logic of the book. I should mention Wolfgang Heislitz, Bernard Schmidt, Claude Gnos, Alessandro Roncaglia, Niels Thygesen, Thomas Rymes, Sergio di Stefanis, Betty Price, my colleagues of the secretariat and rapporteurs of the economic committee of the European Parliament.

Patricia Brulant has read the manuscript, corrected the mistakes and helped improve the style. Véronique Kaboha has been an efficient proof-reader. Anna Sakellari helped me use the Wordperfect programme and corrected the bibliography. The library staff of McGill and Cambridge Universities, of the Commission's DGII and of the European Parliament have been helpful.

My debt to the literature cited is far larger than the footnote and bibliography references. I risk failure not to have included it all for I have re-written this book at least three times; the duration of its research and writing is too long to keep track of all sources consulted.

Finally, I owe a special debt of gratitude to two dear persons: my wife, Ekaterini Pilioura-Karaveli, who has remained a constant and engaging support to my research and re-writing of this book *and* to my brother, Nicholas Karavelis, who has been a father-figure during all these years.

Preface

This book is a revised version of my PhD thesis submitted to the University of London. Its initial argument has been retained intact but the numerous references have been relegated to notes at each chapter.

The argument is about a monetary-theoretic approach to the origin, transformation and evolution of monetary institutions. It consists of five hypotheses, the realism and logic of which are geared to economic history. It is applied to Economic and Monetary Union and is intended to provide answers to five questions relating to *why* EMU was agreed on, *when* it would be realised, *how* its monetary unit would be established, *which* means should be used to implement it and *what* purpose it would serve.

These five hypotheses are meant to frame formerly unresolved problems in the theory of money as well as to act as tools for the appraisal of the Utility theory of money through a reconsideration of Walras's *Elements*, and of the State theory of money via a restatement of Keynes's *General Theory*. Both are found to be inadequate; the first, because of the logical inconsistency entailed in its theoretical construction; the second, because of its limited explanatory power and suggestive capacity.

An alternative approach to money is offered, aiming at suggesting new answers to the basic questions about money. It starts from the premise that the asset which internalises a sufficient number of money externalities is capable of becoming money. For this to happen, certain conditions embodied in the hypotheses ought to be satisfied. If the postulate: *money is an externality* is applied to EMU, it is found that EMU's institutional arrangement is defective.

1   Introduction and summary

How could one explain the origin, evolution and transformation of monetary institutions? Why should an exercise of this kind require a new approach to money and monetary theory? These two questions are the subject-matter of this book. They are inevitably linked with the traditional monetary questions about the origin, nature and functions of money and with the explanation and suggestion of an alternative monetary-theoretic approach that claims to say something useful about the institutional arrangement proposed for the European monetary union.

The monetary institutions to which our own approach is to be applied, are those of the Treaty on European Union (TEU) and, in particular, the amendments to the EEC Treaty establishing Economic and Monetary Union (EMU).[1] The decision of the European Council of Maastricht is the most important in the history of the European Community; it is also a milestone in the management of monetary institutions. It is essentially a strategy to achieve European monetary integration, not later than 1999. The TEU is also about a new institutional balance between Community institutions: Council, Commission, Parliament and Courts, and the acquisition of additional competence in new or existing fields by the Community.[2]

EMU is the single, most important yet voluntary transfer of monetary sovereignty from Member States to the Community since the establishment of the European Economic Community (EEC) by the Rome Treaty. The process has been evolutionary, difficult and at times painful.[3]

EMU is an institution in its own right, not only because it consists of monetary institutions that evolve as the stages of EMU evolve, but because it calls for the transformation of existing monetary institutions in Member States, in particular, the national central banks. Consequently, the objective of this book is not merely to explain the origin, evolution and transformation of EMU's institutions but also to suggest why different stages of economic and

1

monetary integration call for a different institutional arrangement.

An assessment of EMU with tools of received theory boils down to a single point: 'which Member States will fulfil the four convergence criteria stated in Article 109j of the TEU?'. Or, given the current economic stagnation due to zero growth, record high unemployment, volatility of asset prices, fragile markets and low level of effective demand, coupled with serious transformations in Europe, will the political commitment be sustained until the start of the third stage?

Yet an extreme interpretation of convergence is based on a logic (leaving aside the political intention). The *logic* says: 'replace the anchor currency of a system by the anchor of the *expected rate of inflation*'. National monetary policies will be co-ordinated, during the second and, possibly, third stage of EMU to ensure convergence of expected inflation rates. No anchor currency is needed but an anchor of nominal convergence. In other words, the gold standard system, having the pound sterling as its anchor currency, the Bretton Woods system, having the US dollar as its anchor or the EMS with the D-mark established by the markets as its anchor, have been *theoretically deficient*. This convergence logic is both ahistorical and lacks theoretical content. It is ahistorical because there has not been a single monetary experience similar to it. However, this would have been of no particular interest if there had been a theory behind it.

If an alternative approach to monetary theory is followed, the above preoccupations become *secondary*. The central issue then becomes the appropriateness of the institutional setting of EMU. This exercise calls for a reconsideration of the fundamental questions about the design of institutions and demands a re-examination of the basic questions about money, which are still unresolved. Hence, the success of EMU would depend on resolving the above issues in an economic context that is not what it used to be. The process of globalisation of markets and production processes has changed everything.

It is paramount to understand that EMU as an institution raises fundamental monetary questions to which tentative answers should be given before it becomes fully operational:

a) *What* is EMU and what differentiates EMU from the EMS?
b) *Why* has EMU been proposed and established?
c) *When* could one realize EMU?
d) *How* could such a project be made possible?
e) *Which* means are available for the realization of EMU?
f) *What* is the end-purpose of EMU?

Question a) is treated in detail in chapter 2 with tools of traditional theory while constantly using the framework of questions b) to f). In fact, questions b) to f) correspond to five hypotheses intended to frame formerly unresolved problems and to constitute a systematic body of thinking providing new answers to the basic monetary questions.

Chapter 2 gives a detailed analysis of the provisions of EMU and of its economic logic. EMU is founded on traditional bases. It entails objectives such as the promotion of sustainable and non-inflationary growth respecting the environment, a high degree of convergence of economic performance, economic and social cohesion and solidarity among Member States, etc. All these objectives should be consistent with the primary objective: *price stability*.

These objectives are to be achieved in accordance with certain principles, such as 'subsidiarity', which takes the form of Member States retaining the management of economic policy, *and* 'indivisibility', which requires the transfer of control over monetary and exchange rate policy from Member States to the ECB. The principle of an open market economy with free competition is further reinforced by the liberalisation of capital movements and of payments, not only between Member States but also with respect to non-Community countries.

The second stage of EMU started on 1 January 1994 with the creation of the European Monetary Institute (EMI). During stage two, the freeing of capital and payments, the prohibition of monetizing public debt and of privileged access to financial institutions for the financing of public deficits, the independence of national central banks, the freezing of the composition of the ECU basket, nominal convergence and reduction of public deficits, are supposed to be completed.

The third stage of EMU *may* begin in 1997 but, according to Article 109j of the TEU, not later than on 1 January 1999. It will entail the fixity of exchange rates leading to the adoption of a single currency, the European Currency Unit (ECU); a single monetary policy will be pursued by the European System of Central Banks (ESCB), containing an independent European Central Bank (ECB); a single exchange rate policy will be determined by the Council of Ministers and the ECB.

The passage from one stage of EMU to another is made possible because the institutional structure will evolve and because its monetary unit will change its character. As the institutional structure changes, responsibility for economic, monetary and exchange rate policy and prudential supervision, will change.

Economic policy, even in the final stage, rests with Member States, at least on paper. We argue in chapter 7 that this cannot be preserved once the monetary unit of EMU internalises a number of money externalities necessary for its establishment as a currency in its own right. However, the provisions of EMU stipulate national sovereignty over this matter, provided that excessive deficits are avoided in stage three of EMU; otherwise, sanctions shall be imposed on any Member State failing to comply with measures for the deficit reduction.

Monetary policy is set to evolve as the institutional structure evolves. Of special interest is the start of the third stage of EMU. The establishment of the ESCB and the ECB marks the beginning of the third stage and will be followed by a period of 'irrevocably fixed exchange rates' before it leads to the introduction of a single currency. This evolutionary process entails a serious transfer of monetary control from national central banks to the ECB. The ESCB is assigned the task of defining and implementing the monetary policy of the Community; the task has to be performed with the objective of price stability.

Exchange rate policy will become a shared responsibility in the third stage. The decision on the exchange rate policy with respect to third countries' systems will be shared between the ESCB and the Council. The latter will adopt an exchange rate system with fixed exchange rates against non-Community currencies only by virtue of a unanimous decision; this is an unlikely event in the Community of the Twelve and an impossibility in a Community of perhaps Sixteen in 1996. Otherwise, a recommendation has to be made by the ECB or the Commission and, then the Council, by a qualified majority, can adopt, adjust or abandon agreed parities consistent with the objective of price stability.

EMU's institutional change of policy-making could be assessed by reference to the efficiency of the policy. This becomes clearer when the monetary policy instruments available at each stage are examined. The TEU lists all the traditional instruments. However, will this do if the traditional theories of money are shown to be inadequate to explain the origin, transformation and evolution of money upon which EMU's instruments are based? Are traditional instruments effective when global finance and capital markets are present?

The above questions preoccupy us in the examination of the economic logic of EMU and of the legally stated nature of its monetary unit, the ECU. The ECU's character changes as the stages of EMU unfold. In the first stage, the ECU remained a basket currency, composed of fixed amounts of the twelve currencies. After ratification of the Maastricht Treaty, 'the currency composition of the ECU basket shall not be changed' (art. 109g). This 'frozen ECU' would coincide with the second stage of EMU. From the start of the third stage, 'the value of the ECU shall be irrevocably fixed', leading to establishing the 'ECU as the currency in its own right' (art. 1091(4)).

The freezing of the currency composition coupled with the removal of the obstacles to the use of the ECU, is assumed to give further impetus to both official and private ECU to be established in money and foreign exchange markets as a means for the settlement of debts. The underlying idea is to establish the ECU as a 'parallel currency' in a step-by-step process. This legalistic approach to the ECU is challenged in all subsequent chapters. How does one explain the origin, monetary nature and change in the character of the ECU? Is there a role for the ECU? Why has the ECU been chosen to serve as the centre of the system? What will the implications be for monetary and

4

exchange rate policies and for prudential supervision? Will financial stability be assured?

The strategic question is whether the proposed structure of EMU is appropriate for fulfilling its main objectives. This assessment calls for a theory of money capable of answering the *basic questions* of monetary theory: What is money? What causes a money to become established? What criteria should an asset satisfy in order to be used as money? What are the costs and benefits of the existence of money? Who should control the money supply? What are the characteristics of a money economy?

For these basic questions, received monetary theory has no ready answers. To these questions, one should add questions b) to f) raised earlier, which seek to explain the origin, evolution and transformation of monetary institutions. Taken as a whole, these questions amount to a reconstruction of the argument about an alternative theory of money.

An approach of this kind is proposed in **Chapter 3**. There we synthesise *five hypotheses* drawn from the existing body of monetary theory into an alternative monetary-theoretic approach. We claim that this approach of analysis has considerable *explanatory power* and a high degree of *suggestive capacity*. Explanation and suggestion are the elements embodied in the five hypotheses we propose and which are meant to answer the questions b) to f).

The hypotheses are these: H1: The Hicksian proposition of historical contingency which asserts that *monetary theory belongs to monetary history and arises out of monetary disturbance*. In other words, a monetary disturbance, like the great depression, acts as a spur to formulating a theory, as Keynes's *General Theory*, so as to understand its causes and to form proper policies and thus create the appropriate institutions that may mitigate it. For example, the birth of the EMS could be understood if one explained the monetary disturbance that had given rise to the theoretical debate on the fixed vs flexible exchange rates or on the institutional approach and the policies that have followed since then. The same applies to EMU. The monetary disturbance relates to the aggravation of the 'redundancy problem' caused by the globalisation of finance, capital, trade and investment. To this, one should add the new orthodoxy: 'achieve price stability'.

The *redundancy problem* refers to the loss of the theoretical independence of the control of money supply; it mainly stems from the liberalisation and instability of financial markets following the completion of the single market and increasing globalisation. It has also to do with the erosion of monetary sovereignty due to the application of the banking directive, which means harmonised criteria for the right of establishment for banks and other financial institutions; it concerns, too, the resulting problem of banking supervision and the management of the lender of last resort function. Finally, it touches the problem of the erosion of national autonomy in controlling the exchange rate in a global financial market.

5

H2: The Aristotelian notion of evolving money asserts that *it is the stage of economic development of a given economic area, which determines the nature of money and invents a medium of exchange or a means of settlement*. In other words, pure exchange does not necessarily give rise to a medium of exchange; it is the degree of the division of labour and specialisation, the level of technological advance, the scale and depth of the market and capital accumulation that would invent money to facilitate exchange.

In this evolutionary setting, money is not static, nor abstract, nor imaginary. It *evolves* as the stage of development of a society *evolves*. Four stages of development are identified: Autarky, Primary, Middle and Modern stage. Each stage is defined by reference to its characteristic money, customs, laws and economic development.

Applying H2 to the ECU, it is found that the ECU is appropriate to the Middle stage. First, the ECU has no independent existence; its origin stems from the fact that an initial supply of ECU by the European Fund for Monetary Cooperation (EFMC) has been made against a deposit of 20% of gold and 20% of dollar reserves. Second, the ECU does not have an independent value because it is a basket of twelve currencies and its value changes as the exchange rates of its components change.

There is an additional explanatory function of the Aristotelian notion of evolving money. It concerns the degree of interdependence of open economies which increases as one moves from the Primary stage to the Modern one. Community interdependence has been accentuated by increased trade, factor mobility and transfer of technology. This has rendered devaluations ineffective.

H3: The Cipolla thesis of the essential properties of monetary systems states that *no international or national monetary system ever existed or lasted long without having its own money*. An international currency requires the fulfilment of three conditions for its emergence:
a) highly stable value,
b) high confidence,
c) the support of a sound, strong and open economy.

These three criteria contain varying degrees of explanatory power and suggestive capacity, because the roles played by and the importance attached to them have varied as the development stages evolved.

High confidence, highly stable value and *a strong economy* suggest that if one identifies the forces that would induce the three criteria to be met, one would find a way to introduce a monetary unit acceptable to markets. Given no institutional restrictions, this money would become dominant.

There is a second pillar to the Cipolla thesis. It has to do with the political commitment of the responsible body, government or monetary authority, to allow or promote its money in international markets.

6

H4: The Triffin postulate of the determinants of monetary reforms asserts that *reforms of the international and national monetary systems have mainly been determined by the private sector rather than by governments.*

H4 entails two explanatory functions. First, studies of economic history support the view that a currency becomes internationally or nationally established only if it is widely utilised by the private sector. Second, the private sector is the source of innovation in monetary instruments. When we come to explaining the ECU's development and the innovations brought about in commercial banking, we find that both stem mainly from the private use of the ECU.

The Triffin postulate suggests another approach to viewing reforms. The nature of a monetary institution is correlated with the nature of its monetary unit. So, if one wishes to change or modify a monetary institution, one could do it more efficiently through the change or modification of its money; acceptability by the private markets is the test. If markets are receptive to the modification, the change in the character of money will be evolutionary. Causality runs from the nature of money to the nature of its institution, not the other way.

H5: The Essentiality criterion on the nexus of monetary causality is an economical way of stating three inseparable ideas: *the nexus of causality in monetary theory, the reason why money is essential and the welfare aspects of money.* As to the first idea, we schematically state the nexus of causality as follows:

$$origin \; --> \; nature \; --> \; functions \; --> \; rate \; of \; interest$$

As to the term origin, traditional monetary theory identifies four doctrines. Chartalism claims that money originates in the State's will. Nominalism asserts that money originates in social conventions. Commodity theory holds the view that money originates in the saleability of a good. Utility theory believes that money circulates only because of the utility, direct or indirect, of the money-stuff. In chapters 6 and 7, we demonstrate that the origin of money should be sought in the internalisation of money externalities.

As to the term nature, received monetary theory seeks to give substance to it in a circular argument. Money is either defined by its functions: money is what money does, *or* by its origin. We approximate nature with the *form* money has taken over time: *its transformation from pure commodity to paper and credit.* We argue in chapter 6 that *money is essentially an externality* whose form is not measurable; we say that the internalisation of different money externalities at each Aristotelian stage has given rise to a different kind of money.

Our central argument is that all monetary aspects - that is to say the type of asset functioning as a means of settlement of debt or of exchange or of store of value, the type of monetary policy, the kind of power (economic, financial

7

or political) money entails, the substitutability of currencies or currency convertibility and the monetary institutions that would be created to accommodate the needs and requirements of the issue, control and distribution of money - all the above can be reduced to one question: *the nature of money*.

The second idea of H5: why money is essential in an economy, says that a well specified economic model should be consistent with our five hypotheses and should be instrumental in integrating value and monetary theories. This would require, inter alia, an exact specification of the influence of money on production, exchange, distribution and consumption decisions and also an analysis of the likely changes that would follow, if demand for or supply of money changed.

Such a specification of money introduces welfare considerations, consistent with the third idea of H5, and necessitates an alternative definition of a social welfare function.

H5 should be seen in the context of three states of nature: *uncertainty*, *maximisation principle* and *free entry*. These three states constitute the underlying logic of all five hypotheses.

H1 to H5 serve as tools for a re-examination of received monetary theories. We attempt to discover whether these theories contain an explanation of how the present status of the ECU will develop *or* a suggestion of what course of action should be undertaken for the systematization of the final stage of EMU.

Applying H1 to H5 to the Utility theory is the task of **Chapter 4**. The monetary status of the ECU in stages one and two of EMU resembles that of Walras's paper money in the *Elements*. Walras's paper money is conceived as a *parallel* currency, which is the ECU in stage two. Yet are Walras's paper money and the ECU of the second stage money or investment instruments? We examine this question in the context of Walras's *Elements* because this theory is the most complete model of its kind conforming to the stylised facts about EMU. The stylised facts concern the characteristics of Walras's model and the fulfilment of the conditions entailed in H1 to H5.

All Neo-Walrasian proposals to either reform the EMS (such as the UK proposal on the 'hard ECU') or to define the ECU as 'Europa', 'frozen ECU', 'hardened ECU', 'commodity standard ECU', or to define a new monetary order based on the elimination of government monopoly in issuance of money, derive their theoretical inspiration from Walras's monetary theory. Hence, one cannot understand the parallel currency proposals for the transitional period unless one grasps their theoretical foundations which are Walras's theory of money.

Does Walras's paper money meet H5 on the nexus of monetary causality and H2 on the Aristotelian notion of evolving money? Answering these two questions effectively means re-stating Walras's monetary theory. Yet understanding Walras's theory demands the understanding of Walras's vision of economic process which presupposes an understanding of the six assumptions underlying the *Elements* as well as the method of introducing money in the *Elements*.

Walras's monetary theory has, we argue, been much misunderstood. We therefore re-state it, paying attention to the role assigned to his paper money and to the logic of the services rendered by the circulating capital. Walras's money originates in the concept of the *service of availability* and is part of the circulating capital fund whose prices are determined in the services market. We pay particular attention to the motives for holding cash for we believe that there is no rationale for the derivation of the price of money without the prior establishment of a reason for the existence of money.

While the circulating fund enabled Walras to introduce money alongside stocks, the very idea of the fund undercut the *raison d'être* of paper money, as the role played by the paper money could equally be performed by any component of the circulating fund. Yet there is another inconsistency. Walras's economic agent in his theories of exchange, production and capital formation is rational, for he adheres to assumptions of perfect competition, certainty, full knowledge of all opportunities and static context where no changes in the data are allowed.

These four assumptions constitute the base for Walras's maximisation principle. In the theory of money, this rationality does not hold. For if these assumptions hold, then Walras's economic agent is irrational, since he holds cash balances and thus incurs a loss equal to the interest foregone. This is so for two reasons; firstly, he knows the equilibrium prices established in the groping phase and secondly, he knows the role of the fund of circulating capital. Thus, the conceptual vision of the *Elements* strips paper money of any essential role.

We therefore conclude that the marginal utility theory, if applied to paper money, does not explain the origin, nature or role of money. Nor can it derive its value from the demand side of an economy, since it gives opposite results. Hence Walras's monetary theory and, by analogy, all neo-Walrasian proposals, cannot predict the necessary transformation of the ECU in its final phase.

However, Walras's bimetallic system suggests useful modifications to the second stage of EMU and to the EMI. We elaborate on these suggestions to establish the ECU as the co-anchor to the system during the second stage of EMU.

Chapter 5 is spent discussing the State theory of money, whose father is Plato but gained respect because of Knapp and, in particular, because of Wicksell's *Lectures*. The true representative of the State theory is Keynes's *General Theory* (GT). We concentrate on the GT because it brings to the surface something new. This new element is Keynes's view that the capitalist system is subject to crises of confidence which, in turn, lead to crises of expectations resulting in a normally low level of effective demand and hence in high unemployment. These crises result from a system of decentralised

9

decision-making in a state of uncertainty which is accentuated by the monetary nature of production and which makes the system inherently unstable. The instability stems from three states of nature: uncertainty, incomplete knowledge and individual freedom.

Keynes proposed a two-fold cure for structural instability. The first was to regulate the monetary system so that organised markets would restrain individual freedom from hoarding or lending money at will, which might not be desirable. The second was to use the monetary system in order to influence the long-term rate of interest by influencing expectations about the prospective yield of capital.

Keynes assigned to the money rate of interest an important role. It integrates value and monetary theories via its effects on quantities and, in particular, on the rate of new investment. This is the essence of the second idea of H5. Yet his original conception was negated by Keynes, himself, when he came to a contrary conclusion: "For my own part I am now somewhat sceptical of the success of a merely monetary policy directed towards influencing the rate of interest" (GT: 164).

The Post Keynesian school of thought, an extension of Keynes's underlying principles, is also examined with reference to its assumption of the endogeneity of money supply, its financial instability hypothesis and its proposal to reform the international monetary system. The criticism applied to Keynes's Clearing Union having the bancor as its anchor, applies to Post Keynesian thinking.

Contrary to the views surveyed which have money acting as the standard of the system, Keynes accepted the money-wage as being more *sticky* than the value of money. Such a choice entails an inherent circularity: 'an asset to be accepted as a means of payment requires that its value must be more stable than the value of other assets'. The consequence of such reasoning is that Keynes's money cannot meet Cipolla's thesis requiring that the anchor currency of the system should have a highly stable value. It is this property of money that enhances confidence in an asset to be accepted as money and it is this characteristic of money that implies *liquidity*.

Keynes's theory of money cannot predict the transformation of a monetary system, for it fails H2, which is concerned with an evolving theory of money. This is so because his theory of the rate of interest is developed within the context of a particular stage of the evolution of banking and financial institutions, which is impossible since the integration of money into the economic system cannot be demonstrated at all times.

However, Keynes has provided us with significant and insightful observations as to the role of money at a particular monetary stage although, he has not provided us with a theory suggesting how one could make the ECU, a money in its own right. Keynes's theory of money fails our H2, partly H3 and H4.

Unsatisfied with the explanatory power and suggestive capacity of existing monetary theories in demonstrating the role of money in an economy and in explaining the monetary transformations over time, in **chapter 6**, we offer an alternative approach to money. In order to argue that money originates in the market, which must be at a certain stage of development (i.e. H2 on the notion of evolving money), it is imperative to settle the question relating to the *nature proper* of money as stated in the H5 on the Essentiality criterion. Only then could we define its properties, show its essential monetary role and say how money affects and is affected by the institutional structure and how it may stimulate output or alter relative prices.

If the question of the nature of money is settled, we will know what causes an asset to become established as money or fall into disuse. Consequently, it should suggest the transformation of the ECU proper for the second and third stage of EMU. Equally, if the nature of money is known, the appropriate monetary instruments for pursuing a consistent monetary policy could be identified.

Should the above context be accepted, then an alternative approach would be imperative. Our basic premise is: *Money is essentially an externality.* Our premise calls for a definition of money externalities. We take account of the salient features of the institution of money and of a money process, and give the following definition:

> *In a money process defined as Money-Commodity-Money (M-C-M*), a money economy (or diseconomy) is an event realised in the market, which confers an appreciable benefit (or inflicts an appreciable damage) on some person(s), transactor(s) or institution(s) who were not fully consenting parties or active participants in reaching the decision(s) that led directly or indirectly to the event in question.*

We assume a money economy, characterised by a money process (M-C-M*) which is interwoven with a number of systems, such as information centres, satellite communications, security and above all banking and financial intermediaries, regarded as interdependent and inseparable. Hence any externality generated in one system will enter into the utility or cost function of more than one independent decision-maker.

The argument is expounded using a *taxonomic approach* to the economic forces that generate money externalities or the processes that capture money externalities. For example, capturing of transaction cost, of learning and technological and of seigniorage externalities would lead to the establishment of an asset as money. Yet its continuance as money would depend on confidence and price level externalities.

Having thus specified our taxonomy, we go back to economic literature from which we draw information for stating our alternative approach. Money externalities are not purely market phenomena but are manifested in the market when rational choices are made. They may be grouped in five categories, each containing a number of individual externalities. The five categories of money externalities are shown in Table 1.1.

Table 1.1
Categories of money externalities

I	Transaction Costs Externalities
II	Price Level Externalities
III	Confidence Externalities
IV	Learning and Technological Externalities
V	Seigniorage Externalities

Under the *transaction costs externalities*, we have assembled all market organisation cost conditions leading to real-income and distributional externalities. They are associated with the transmission of information, existent in the market but internalised by the currency used for the settlement of debt. They are shared variables in nature entering the utility and cost functions.

Under the *price level externalities*, we denote the notion that any act of a user or of a producer of money which affects either directly or indirectly the general level of prices would cause a 'price level externality'. A change in the price level induces a series of interrelated money externalities which essentially establish a redistribution mechanism.

Under the *confidence externalities*, we refer to those external economies or diseconomies generated by the institutional structure necessary to support a monetary system and its money. They are mainly associated with the producer of money but are internalised and reflected in the choice of the users. Confidence externalities have to do with a set of conditions that mould the preferences of the users of money, necessary for the continuance of a currency in the market.

Under the *learning and technological externalities* category, on the assumption that economic man is capable of learning and of communicating, we refer to the internalisation of all non-pecuniary externalities which are due to the use of the same currency. Both learning and communicating contribute to the growth of knowledge resulting in invention and technological innovation. The greater the market, the greater the social economies of scale, the greater the internalised external economies.

Under the heading of *seigniorage externalities*, we refer to the creation of seigniorage in the banking system internalised by the means of managing deposits and to the relevant internalisation of externalities captured by different forms of monetary institutions. The sources of seigniorage are found in the role of banks and financial intermediaries, or simply banking system. This category of externalities is responsible for financial instability.

Our alternative approach seeks to demonstrate the nexus of causality of H5, which in fact resolves the circular argument of the traditional theory, via a reformulation of the basic monetary questions, such as what is money, what causes a money to be established, what is the role of money, what does it affect and what is it affected by. It has arrived at two conclusions:

> *A)   Any asset, financial or not, that has the single property which internalises the money externalities generated in the economic spheres of exchange, of production, of accumulation and of distribution, is capable of becoming money.*

> *B)   The five categories of money externalities induced by the institution of money causes money to be 'super-non-neutral'.*

In **Chapter 7**, we explore the implications of the above two conclusions for: a) the social welfare function, which has to be modified; b) the perfectly competitive model, which does not apply to money; c) the IS-LM model, whose assumption of the exogeneity of money supply cannot be retained. The results of such an enterprise are disturbing for the traditional theory and new answers to formerly unsolved monetary problems are suggested.

H1 to H5 are also re-examined under the premise that money is an externality and the discussion leads to a third conclusion:

> *C)   As money evolves so would its monetary system.*

The money externalities internalised by the ECU are examined and the conditions for an electronic ECU are specified.

The important implication of our alternative approach for EMU is that its institutional arrangement is found to be defective. Capturing of the liability management and risk externalities by the ECB necessitates the internalisation of *systemic risk*, the principal cause of financial instability. If this conclusion is accepted, the traditional function of central banks of lender of last resort ceases to apply and becomes a function of *last resort of managing risk*. Hence, prudential supervision should be assumed by the ECB.

Yet this will not remedy the deficiency. A single European Fiscal Authority should be created at the start of the third stage; this will prevent structural instability and compensate for the money externalities internalised by the ECB. This will occur at the expense of national central banks, which formerly internalised the same money externalities and at the expense of Member States, who will lose real resources through the movements of banking and financial services.

Notes

1. The Treaty on European Union (TEU) was agreed, at the European Council of Maastricht on 9-11 December 1991, and it was signed at Maastricht on 7 February 1992. The TEU provides for amendments to all existing Treaties: the European Economic Community (1958), the European Coal and Steel Community (1952) and the European Atomic Energy Community (1958). The European Council of Edinburgh, on 11-12 December 1992, agreed to interpretive texts relating to subsidiarity, transparency, enlargement and foreign relations, economic recovery, future financing of the Community until 1996 and to the exemptions granted to Denmark. Following ratification by all Member States in accordance with their constitutional provisions and the favourable ruling of the German Federal Constitutional Court, the TEU entered into force on 1 November 1993.

2. The new fields of Community competence cover common foreign and security policy (art. J to J.11) and justice and home affairs cooperation (art. K to K.9) as well as the amendments to the EEC Treaty covering the citizenship of the Union (art. 8), culture (art. 128), public health (art. 129), consumer protection (art. 129a), trans-european networks (art. 129b to 129d), industry (art. 130), and cohesion fund (art. 130a to 130e). Community competence is further strengthened in the areas of research and development (art. 130f to 130p), environment (art. 130r to 130t), development cooperation (art. 130u to 130y) and common commercial policy (art. 110 to 116).

3. The process began in 1968 with the Customs Unions resulting in a common external tariff and necessitating the coordination of economic policies and monetary cooperation as outlined in the orientations stated in the "Barre Memorandum" (1969). It continued with the "Werner Report" (1970) and the decision of the Council of Ministers in 1971 to realise EMU by stages in a decade but the international currency crisis prevented its implementation. Instead, the "Snake" was formed in March 1972 so as to keep EEC currencies within +/- 2.25% fluctuation margins. In March 1979, the European Monetary System was established with its three mechanisms: Exchange Rate, Credit and Intervention coupled with a monetary unit, the ECU. The EMS's final objective, the creation of a European Monetary Fund, never materialised.

2 Treaty on economic and monetary union

2.1 Introduction

The articles of the Treaty on European Union (TEU) relevant to EMU are examined under our premise that states: *monetary institutions provide the incentive structure of a monetary economy*. As the incentive structure evolves, the direction of economic change is shaped. Money, as an institution, and the economic laws of traditional theory define exchange, investment, production and distribution. The probability of engaging in one or another activity is largely determined by the institution of money (section 2.10).

The above economic logic defines our task in examining the evolution of the European Union (EU) from a customs union to the snake, to the EMS which is now being transformed into EMU. The principles underlying the TEU are examined with tools of traditional monetary theory in the context of capital and payments liberalisation (sections 2.2 and 2.3). Hence, the monetary rule of the ECB to maintain price stability calls for an examination of the likely avenues that might affect its potency in the determination of real income (section 2.4). If fiscal policy, as a counter-cyclical instrument, has lost its strength because its primary objective is to reduce excessive budgetary deficits (sections 2.5 and 2.6), it is of interest to know if the exchange rate policy is to retain its effectiveness as an anti-inflationary policy or in promoting a stable environment for growth (section 2.7).

The convergence criteria will entail a cost of adjustment if a degree of homogeneity in performance is to be attained (section 2.8). Yet the nominal convergence criteria are challenged because they are in essence dependent on the *expected rate of inflation* and because they do not take account of the convergence potential of an economy. We alternatively propose an EMU convergence potential index (section 2.9).

Who will bear the cost of adjustment? What will the likely benefits be? Is the institutional design capable of dealing with financial instability? Does the independence of the ECB suffice for preserving price stability when global markets could feed systemic risk endangering thus the solvency of banking and financial institutions?

These are the questions we raise as the EMU institutions are analyzed (sections 2.10 to 2.13). These themes are part and parcel of the anchor of the system, the ECU. Its origin, nature, functions and value are interlinked with the mechanisms of the EMS, which shall change in character as the character of the ECU changes. The basket ECU will become a frozen ECU, then a hardened ECU and lastly a currency in its own right (section 2.14). The method by which the ECU would be established in the private sector as a means for the settlement of debt, is nowhere stated. The relatively autonomous growth of the private ECU has set in motion a parallel currency. However, a parallel currency raises all the basic questions of monetary theory: What is money? Where does money originate? etc. (sections 2.15 to 2.16).

Our concern to examine the appropriateness of the institutional set-up of EMU stems from our interest in an approach that seeks to explain the origin, evolution and transformation of monetary institutions. As we review the approaches to EMU (section 2.17), we ask the questions:

a) Why has EMU been proposed and established?
b) When could one realize EMU?
c) How could such a project be made possible?
d) Which means are necessary for the realization of EMU?
e) What is the end-purpose of EMU?

2.2 Principles

The TEU sets out the principles governing the conduct of economic and monetary policies. For the former, close coordination must be sought, the completion of the internal market should be achieved and the definition of common objectives must be consistent with the principle of an open market economy with free competition.

As to monetary policies, the activities of the Community should aim at irrevocably fixing of the exchange rates leading to the introduction of a single currency, the ECU. They should also lead to the definition and conduct of a single monetary and exchange rate policy. The primary objective of both of these shall be to maintain price stability and have a secondary objective: 'support the general economic policies'.

The guiding principles for economic and monetary policies would be stable prices, sound public finances, stable monetary conditions and a sustainable balance of payments. They must promote a harmonious and balanced development of economic activities, a sustainable and non-inflationary growth respecting the environment, a high degree of convergence of economic performance, a high level of employment and social protection, the raising of the standard and of the quality of living, cohesion and solidarity among Member States (Art. 2).

These principles are general and not unique to EMU. Other industrial countries have used similar principles in their constitutions.[1] The major difference between the Maastricht Treaty and the Rome Treaty is the principle of subsidiarity (Art. 3b):

> In areas which do not fall within its exclusive competence, the Community shall take action, in accordance with the principle of subsidiarity, only if and in so far as the objectives of the proposed action cannot be sufficiently achieved by the Member States and can therefore, by reason of the scale or effects of the proposed action, be better achieved by the Community.[2]

The principle of subsidiarity finds support in the economic logic of EMU. Traditional monetary theory holds the view that, from the institutional point of view, monetary policy can be *divorced* from economic policy. Such a view could be supported if and only if the nature, role and functions of money are considered to be insignificant in an economy. This *divorced* economic logic is fully adopted by the TEU. Monetary policy is centralised in the ECB while economic policy remains within the competence of the Member States.

A second aspect of the principle of subsidiarity is the undefined responsibility over prudential supervision, according to which, Member States retain responsibility for the activities of the banking and financial institutions, while the ECB shall contribute to the smooth conduct of policies pursued by the national authorities (Art. 105(2)). The question of systemic risk, the main cause of financial instability, is not treated because traditional monetary theory prescribes that the body authorizing the activities of banks and financial institutions should be *divorced* from the body responsible for their supervision.

2.3 Capital and payments: globalisation

If the principles of an open market economy with free competition coupled with the free movement of goods, persons, services and capital, were applied to capital and payments, it would mean that all restrictions on the movement of capital and on payments between Member States and between Member States and third countries would be prohibited (Art. 73b to 73g).[3] Two countries, Greece and Portugal, by derogation, are allowed to maintain such restrictions until the end of 1995 (Art. 73e).

Safeguard measures against third countries are allowed if movements of capital to and from third countries cause or threaten to cause serious difficulties for EMU. Equally, for serious political reasons, if the Council has not taken the necessary measures on capital movements and payments, a Member State may take urgent measures on its own initiative. Thus capital controls are retained on exceptional grounds.

Capital controls have so far played a dual role in the EMS. Realignments of exchange rates have been without excessive cost *and* management of demand has been eased. Both have worked through the mechanism of the interest rate. If exchange rates were expected to change, holders of a currency considered to be a candidate for devaluation had to be convinced to hang on to it by higher interest rates to cover the expected devaluation. With capital controls preventing holders switching out to another currency, a smaller rise would do. Thus potential speculation has been limited through exchange controls rather than by raising domestic interest rates.[4]

Member States have also been able to keep domestic interest rates above equilibrium levels in order to discourage demand. If capital controls had been removed, the high interest rates would have attracted inward capital and the exchange rates would have appreciated, putting pressure on the parities of the EMS; the alternative would have been to lower interest rates, encouraging demand that would cause a deficit in the current account.[5]

Capital and payments liberalisation has ended the effectiveness of the above mechanisms. Yet this should be seen in the context of global markets that have been the *principle feature of the 1980s*. Innovation, technology, deregulation and the increasing role of institutional investors have dissolved the national boundaries between national financial frontiers. There has begun to emerge a global capital market whose consequences the traditional monetary theory is not capable of analyzing.

By the term *globalisation* or *global markets*, Crook (1992: 5) takes account of "...expanding international trade, the growth of multinational business, the rise in international joint ventures and increasing interdependence through capital flows". Looking at Table 2.1, one is astonished by the growth of global finance.

The statistics are staggering. International bank credit in 1981 was $1040 billion but in 1992 reached $3710 billion, an increase by a 3,4 multiple. The stock of international bank lending (cross-border lending plus domestic lending in foreign currency) has increased from $324 billion in 1980 to $7.5 trillion in 1991; if expressed as percentage of OECD GDP, it increased tenfold. The total of international bonds outstanding was $259 billion in 1982 but in 1991 reached $1.65 trillion.

Whereas portfolio investment (bonds and equities) and direct investment in 1981 were in near equilibrium (both in terms of outflows and inflows), in 1992, the portfolio investment in outflows was about 1,7 times higher than outflow direct investment of the industrial countries (IC); in terms of inflows, portfolio investment was about 3,5 times higher than inflow direct investment.

18

The same trend is found for the securities transactions (bonds and equities) with foreigners of the major world economies: US, Japan and Germany. It should be noted that "[b]etween 1980 and 1990 the volume of worldwide cross-border transactions in equities alone grew at a compound rate of 28% a year, from $120 billion to $1.4 trillion a year" (Crook, 1992: 9).

Table 2.1
Global market for capital and finance
(in billion US $)

	1981	1986	1989	1992
International bank credit (1)	1040.0	1900.0	2905.0	3710.0
as % of OECD GDP (3)	4%	a)	a)	44%
Portfolio investment (IC):				
Outflows (2)	30.5	182.3	267.3	254.4
Inflows (2)	50.6	180.7	304.2	313.4
Bonds as % of OECD GDP (3)	3%	a)	a)	10% *
Assets as % of GDP: US (3)	9%	a)	a)	93% *
J (3)	7%	a)	a)	119% *
D (3)	8%	a)	a)	58% *
Foreign exchange turnover**(4)	a)	206.0	663.0	967.0 *
Derivatives of which: (5)				
Exchange-traded instruments	a)	583.0	1762.0	3518.0 *
Over-the-counter instruments	a)	500.0	2402.0	4449.0 *
Direct investment (IC):				
Outflows (2)	49.2	89.9	205.3	149.7
Inflows (2)	41.0	62.8	159.9	89.6

Source: (1) BIS Report 1993 and Int. Banking Statistics: 1991
(2) IMF Balance of Payments Statistics
(3) BIS, reported in The Economist, 19.09.1992
(4) Group of Ten (1993)   a) not available
(5) Group of Thirty (1993)   * 1991   ** per day

The growth of derivative financial instruments, such as interest rate futures or swaps and options or currency futures or swaps and options, have almost doubled at the end of 1991 if compared to at the end of 1989. In fact, exchange rate instruments were of the order of $583 billion in 1986 and grew to $3 518 billion in 1991. An even greater growth was recorded in the over-the-counter instruments; they were $500 billion in 1986 but reached $4449 billion in 1991. The size of the market and its phenomenal growth give an indication of their potential in terms of benefits and of their inherent systemic risks.

Derivatives, according to currency experts and international organisations, are the result of the hedging needs stemming from the volatility of interest rates and currency turbulence. They are instruments suitable for spreading risk or sharing risk and supporting liquidity, especially in unsettled times. Yet, given the concentration of business in a few financial institutions, the unregulated nature of the market and lack of transparency, derivative instruments have the potential of being a source of systemic disturbance, leading not only to the volatility of asset prices but also to a number of external economies and diseconomies.

A tentative conclusion from the evolution of portfolio investment is that bonds and equities have assumed an important role in world markets. The volume of international bonds outstanding in terms of the GNP of industrialised countries has reached a very high proportion.

Equally, international trade has increased significantly since the beginning of the 1980s but it stabilised at the level of 1987 in early 1990s. Yet the level of international trade among industrialised countries in very high and if world growth is re-established, trade is expected to expand.

Even direct investment in industrial countries has multiplied in the last twelve years; outflows have multiplied by more than three times while inflows by more that two times. For example, foreign direct investment outflows from US, Japan, Germany, France and Britain increased, on average between 1986 and 1990, from $61 to $156 billion *per year*. The global stock of foreign direct investment is estimated to be $1.7 trillion, with 35 000 transnational corporations and 147 000 foreign affiliates.

The principal characteristic of the 1980s is the role of financial institutions, such as pension funds, insurance companies, mutual funds, trust funds and hedge funds. The IMF study (1993: 2) gives a measure of their significance by referring to the size of the portfolio investment managed by institutional investors: "Total assets of U.S. institutional investors rose from $2 trillion (66 percent of GNP) in 1981 to $6.5 trillion (133 percent of GNP) in 1990. Similarly, the total assets of U.K. institutional investors climbed from £130 billion (52% of GNP in 1980) to £550 billion (108 percent of GNP) in 1990. U.S. and European fund managers alone now control over $8 trillion in assets. ... Thus investment decisions are becoming increasingly concentrated in the hands of professional fund managers". Institutional investors in Europe and Japan, according to the G 10 Report, hold about 20% of their securities assets in foreign securities while those in the US correspond to a smaller percentage (about 7%). The trend of foreign securities holdings in the US, Japan and Europe has been on the increase.

The indicator that shows the quantitative importance of international capital transactions and payments, is the rapid growth in foreign exchange trading.

The daily average of net foreign exchange turnover was about $206 billion in 1986 but increased to $967 billion in April 1992 for only the ten main market centres. The IMF study estimates that the worldwide net turnover in 1992 could have reached the $1 trillion *a day*. Its size could be compared with the total foreign reserves of all industrial countries, which were $555.6 billion at the end of April 1992. Its importance could also be shown by comparing it to world trade. In 1989, for example, global foreign exchange trading was about $660 billion daily; this figure was almost *forty times* the average daily value of world trade.

The world's largest financial market is the foreign exchange market (including the global stock of the principal derivatives). In its recent survey on international capital markets, the IMF (1993: 1) stated:

> It is the only truly global financial market: currencies are traded in financial centres around the world, connected by communication systems that allow nearly instantaneous transmission of price information and trade instructions. The market has grown rapidly over the last decade as a result of the liberalization of cross-border capital flows and the relaxation of regulatory constraints on institutional investments.

What does the above statistical evidence mean? The G 10 Report (1993: ii), quoting Mr Brady, former US Secretary of the Treasury, stated the fear: "The latest survey of foreign exchange markets indicates daily turnover approaching $1 trillion, which is roughly double the official reserves of our countries. In these circumstances, even small changes in capital flows, let alone the massive speculation we have just witnessed, can have profound effects on our economies".

There are benefits and costs of global markets. The former are familiar and concern competition, flexibility and efficiency in the allocation of resources. Costs for borrowers have declined, markets have gained depth and width, and earnings of investors have risen. Yet the financial markets have become more fragile.

The instability of the market was tested in September 1992 and in July 1993 with the European exchange markets experiencing the dire consequence that a wave of speculation triggered off; serious movements of capital brought about serious disadvantages, such as uncertainty in investment and trade, loss of control of money supplies and of exchange rate movements and volatility of asset prices.

A number of policy issues involved need commentary. The indicators of Table 2.1 point to a direction; if globalisation continues, international financial interdependence will increase to the point that the financial centres of North America, Western Europe and Japan, will become global in their trade, investment and finance markets. What are the likely effects of interdependence

21

on key macroeconomic variables?

Theoretically, financial and monetary instability and loss of macroeconomic control are considered as costs by the traditional monetary theory because its instruments are rendered impotent. Globalisation of capital markets affects interest rates, government budgets, public debts and exchange rates. The financial transformation of the 1980s has increased banking competition and lowered profits; but it has also increased interdependence of financial institutions and increased *systemic risk*. This interdependence might be shown to contribute to financial stability or to financial collapse, depending on the institutions designed to regulate the global system.[6] If capital flows are completely liberalised and unregulated and banking and financial markets are integrated, interest rates will be equalised and cannot be used as tools of demand management or of exchange rate determination. The burden of adjustment will be shifted onto fiscal policy.

The most important aspect of globalisation of capital and finance is that it has put an end to Keynes's (1944) vision about their role in the context of Bretton Woods and made the IMF's clause on controls of capital transfers inoperative.[7] We return to this matter under the Hicksian proposition in chapter 3 but also in all subsequent chapters.

What has globalisation meant to the four policy variables: money supply, interest rate, exchange rate and fiscal policy, and financial stability? The heated debate over the institutional, political and financial *independence* of national central banks or of the ECB becomes of *secondary* importance if the theoretical independence of a monetary institution associated with the *control of money supply is lost*.

Let us take an example drawn from the case of derivatives. Have derivatives altered the channels of influence of monetary policy? "First, much of the transmission process operates in the first instance, through the impact of monetary operations on financial intermediaries, particularly banks. How have derivatives altered banks' liquidity and interest rate management practices, and might these alterations affect the transmission process? Second, has the improved ability of corporations to hedge interest rate and exchange rate risks altered the sensitivity of their investment decisions to interest rate and exchange rate movements?" (McDonough, 1993: 2).

Hence the problem of EMU: Can its institutional structure cope with globalisation? Will its monetary policy be able to attain price stability? Are traditional monetary instruments upon which EMU relies for open market operations appropriate in the absence of capital controls? Does deregulation promote speculation? These questions preoccupy us in all subsequent chapters and are not only relevant to EMU but also to all monetary systems, domestic or international.

2.4 Monetary policy

Monetary policy is based on three commitments: pursuit of price stability, independence of the ECB and establishment of a single currency, the ECU. The credibility of these three commitments will depend on the efficiency of institutional structures required to face global markets *and* will determine the quality of monetary policy.

In accordance with the principles of TEU, the third stage will start with the irrevocable locking of the exchange rates between currencies. This will lead to the introduction of the ECU, as the single currency; it will replace national currencies in due course. From then onwards, the ESCB will assume its full powers.

The primary objective of the ESCB is stated in the TEU: 'to maintain price stability and, without prejudice to the objective of price stability, to support the general economic policies with a view to contributing to the achievement of the objectives of the EU' (Art. 105(1)).

As to the purpose of EMU (i.e. price stability, balanced growth, converging living standards, high employment and external equilibrium), EMU does not differ from the objective of the USA's Federal Reserve System, which was assumed to foster monetary and credit conditions favourable to 'the maintenance of a high level of employment, stable values, and a rising standard of living' (FRS, 1947: 1).

Four basic tasks for the ESCB are stated in Article 105(2):
a) define and implement the monetary policy of the Community,
b) conduct foreign exchange operations consistent with the exchange rate policy provisions,
c) hold and manage the foreign reserves of the Member States,
d) promote the smooth operations of payment systems.

In addition, the ECB shall have the exclusive right to authorise the issue of bank-notes within the Community and shall *only* contribute to the national policies relating to the prudential supervision of credit institutions and the stability of the financial system.

In essence, the evolution from the EMS to EMU depends on a simple fact. The EMS, which is a de facto hegemonic semi-fixed exchange rate system with Germany maintaining an independent monetary policy and the others fixing their currencies to the D-mark, is to be transformed into another entity. This entity is federal in nature and the formulation of its monetary policy is made by all countries participating in the third stage. As the EMS has developed, with markets establishing the DM as the anchor of the ERM, Germany has conducted policies appropriate to maintain the external value of the DM or competitiveness via managed floating, while the rest have stuck to fixed rates with respect to the DM. Hence the transfer of hegemonical monetary policy from the Bundesbank to the ESCB is the crucial issue in the transition to the third stage.

Price stability as an objective of the ESBC might be considered comparable to Wicksell's concern, see *Lectures II*, of the stable value of money. The two, though, differ fundamentally. The ESBC's objective will provide the framework for monetary cooperation among twelve Governors of national central banks and six members of the ECB Executive Board to preserve irrevocably fixed exchange rates until the adoption of the ECU as a single currency. In the case of Wicksell, it is not fixed exchange rates which, through domestic and international competition in goods and services, will force a convergence of inflation rates but it is the monetary policy that will preserve a common inflation rate *as if* inflation is a purely monetary phenomenon. Once the single currency is established, the ESCB will pursue a monetary policy consistent with price stability as Wicksell has prescribed it.

This return to monetary orthodoxy should be seen in the context of the experience of the Community with inflation in the 1970s and 1980s and the change in theoretical perception of the relative efficiency of monetary policy and rules for its conduct. There is a voluminous literature on the cost of anticipated and unanticipated inflation and on the benefits of price stability to which we return below.

A second important aspect is the economic logic of EMU. It is about what determines real income. It could be summarised in one sentence: *real income is wholly determined by whatever determines the stock of money*. This is only possible if two laws of one price exist. The first law concerns the prices of freely tradeable commodities and the second concerns the one interest rate.

The 1992 single market is about establishing the conditions for the free movement of goods, services, capital and persons and about measures that will strengthen market mechanisms and competition policy. The prices of freely tradeable commodities will tend to be equalised and only transaction costs and taxes may account for price differences.

In integrated money and financial markets, interest rates can only differ if national currencies are not considered close substitutes. If the requirement (fixity of exchange rates) for monetary union held, then national currencies would become close substitutes and interest rates would converge. If so, then, the law of one interest rate would be established and Mundell's (1962) model would hold: 'monetary policy is ineffective and only fiscal policy matters'. A deviation from this law would be possible if markets viewed the credit worthiness of Member States differently and if fiscal policy created divergence in economic performance giving rise to differential returns on assets and thus produced less than perfect substitutability between assets.

The interesting thing to know is that under fixed exchange rates, where monetary policy is ineffective and only fiscal policy is effective, the latter is effective only *because of an accommodating monetary policy*. How is this possible? Assume an increase in government spending which could increase both income and interest rates temporarily. The rise in interest rates would attract capital flows which would put pressure on the exchange rates to appreciate. Fixity of the exchange rates would require intervention by the monetary authorities to sterilise the capital inflows; it would thus increase reserves resulting in an increase of the money supply.

Theoretically, the same logic is applied to budget deficits. Because deficits are financed by increases in the stock of money, deficits cause inflation. If *binding rules* on upper limits are set, it will minimise increases in the money stock. But deficits could be financed by external borrowing. Hence a rule on 'external borrowing' has to be found in order to monitor the increase or decrease of the stock of money.

Limiting the recourse to external borrowing in non-Community currencies is a means aimed at controlling the financing of public sector deficits and at monitoring the total growth of money and credit from external sources. Hence, intervention in non-Community currencies in the third stage will be made mainly by the ECB or by the national central banks, subject to 'approval by the ECB in order to ensure consistency with the exchange rate and monetary policies of the Community' (ESCB Statute, Art. 18 and 31.2).

It is this economic logic that has led the TEU to decide on *binding rules*. National economic policies are geared to a single rule: 'avoid excessive public deficits'. The transition from the second to the third stage is about satisfying four nominal criteria which themselves depend on one: *convergence of expected inflation rates*. And a single rule governs the conduct of monetary policy: *price stability*.

The debate on 'Rules versus Discretion' is old but has not ended.[8] Three arguments for constraints to be placed on central banks have been put forward. First, Friedman (1948) argued that central banks lacked the necessary knowledge and information for successful discretionary policy. Forecasting the future path of the economy would be difficult and fine tuning impossible since variable time lags would discredit all efforts. Thus a constant rate of monetary growth would be preferable.

The second argument for rules is due to the rational-expectations camp (Lucas, 1972). Its argument is that changes in monetary policy have no effect on output and employment because economic agents, in forming their inflationary expectations based on the correct theory, take account of policy changes. Anticipation of higher inflation is transformed into higher wage demands leaving output and employment unchanged. Hence, a constant rate of monetary growth would minimise uncertainty about inflation.

The third argument is based on policy credibility. Kydland and Prescott (1977) argued that rules can become 'time-inconsistent' if they are not binding. Time inconsistency occurs when a policy which seemed optimal to policy-makers at the start, no longer seems desirable when the time comes to take action. Without a binding commitment holding policy makers to the original plan, they have the discretion to switch to another policy which appears better.

Variants of these three arguments have stressed that rules on monetary policy enhance the predictability of policy and hence improve the ability to make informed resource allocation decisions; or that rules are a mechanism for imposing discipline on economic policy makers who might otherwise manipulate the instruments for their own benefit and to the detriment of the public.[9]

It should be noted that the above mentioned arguments in favour of rules on monetary policy or on central banks' behaviour are set within a Neo-Walrasian context which is a derivative of the monetary vision of the utility or commodity theory of money (we return to it in chapter 4). The Neo-Walrasian logic presupposes two conditions: a) the ECB will be able to control the supply of money and b) a stable relationship between the supply of and demand for money in the economy exists. In chapter 7, we demonstrate that if money is an externality, the supply of money cannot be controlled by a single central authority; more importantly, financial innovation in the presence of global markets coupled with increased systemic risk, does not support a stable relationship between demand for and supply of money.

However, the underlying philosophy of the Treaty's insistence on a single monetary policy, defined and implemented by a single institution, is found in the Delors report. Recognition of the consequences stemming from the Council Directive 88/361/EEC on freeing capital movements,[10] from the second Council Directive 89/647/EEC on a single banking licence,[11] and the ineffectiveness of monetary policy if integrated money and financial markets establish one interest rate, have led the Delors report to propose the centralisation of monetary policy: "The responsibility for the single monetary policy would have to be vested in a new institution, in which centralized and collective decisions would be taken on the supply of money and credit as well as on other instruments of monetary policy, including interest rates" (§ 24).

We argue in chapter 3 that the case for the centralisation of monetary policy could be made persuasive if the analysis were to be cast in the context of global markets. Global financing has undermined Member States' interest rate policies because the mobility of capital sensitive to an interest rate differential has led to appreciation or depreciation of exchange rates which are assumed to be semi-fixed under the EMS rules. Limiting movements in exchange rates implies that the interest rate target set by money supply is no longer within the reach of national central banks but is estimated by speculators.

However, the success or failure of EMU partly rests with this new institution, the ESCB which embodies the ECB. The structure of the ESCB, the primary and secondary tasks of the ECB, the economic and political independence of the ECB and the instruments available to the ESCB may determine the success or the failure of the EMU.

2.5 Economic policy

The TEU does not refer to the economic policy of the EU but to the conduct of national economic policies. This stems partly from the economic logic of traditional monetary theory, which finds support in the principle of subsidiarity and from the logic of deficits. The broad guidelines of the economic policies of Member States and the Community will be concluded by the European Council on the basis of a report by the Council, following a recommendation from the Commission (Art. 103(2)). This procedure has entered into force from the start of the second stage.

The coordination of economic policies and convergence of economic performance will be ensured by the mechanism of 'multilateral surveillance'. On the basis of information, such as convergence programmes, forwarded by the Member States, the Commission shall submit reports to the Council. Then the Council shall 'monitor the economic development in each of the Member States' (Art. 103(3)). If the economic policy of a Member State is not consistent with the broad guidelines, the Council can make recommendations to the state concerned and make them public, if necessary.

Convergence programmes have been adopted by most Member States, except France, Luxembourg and Denmark which would submit theirs in due course. The common characteristic of all the programmes has been fiscal consolidation. The concern of monetary policy has been to achieve and preserve a high degree of price stability. Yet the current recession has led to zero growth, rapidly rising unemployment and widening budget deficits since fiscal policy has had to play the bigger role in accommodating the recession.

Community financial assistance is provided for under Article 103a(2) 'where a Member State is in difficulties or is seriously threatened with severe difficulties caused by exceptional occurrences beyond its control'. Article 103a, as drafted, may cause different interpretations. Its first paragraph states that 'the Council may, acting unanimously on a proposal from the Commission, decide upon the measures appropriate to the economic situation, in particular if severe difficulties arise in the supply of certain products'. Severe difficulties are expected to arise with the excessive government deficits. Yet are deficits covered by Article 103a?

Community financial assistance should be seen in a complementary context of the TEU concerned with 'economic and social cohesion'. It will be endowed with a Cohesion Fund (Art. 130a to 130e) and financial assistance in cases of balance of payments difficulties, applicable to stage two and to Member States with a derogation in stage three (Art. 109h and 109i). The Cohesion Fund is mainly intended to finance projects in the fields of environment and trans-European networks, principally in the area of transport infrastructure. The beneficiaries of this Fund shall be Greece, Ireland, Portugal and Spain.

2.6 Rules on excessive deficits

Member States are held responsible for the excessive government deficits (Art. 104c). The Commission is entrusted with an additional task in monitoring the development of the budgetary situation and of the stock of government debt of each Member State.

Budgetary discipline is defined by reference to two reference values of two criteria stated in a protocol on excessive-deficits:

a) 3% for the ratio of the planned or actual government deficit to GDP at market prices,
b) 60% for the ratio of government debt to GDP at market values.

These criteria, as stated in Article 104c(2), allow certain flexibility of judgement in taking account of the evolution of these ratios. For example, the deficit/GDP ratio would be assessed by reference to its trend, i.e. whether it has declined substantially and continuously; or if the excess over the reference value is exceptional and temporary. The debt/GDP ratio would be assessed by reference to whether this 'ratio is not sufficiently diminishing and not approaching the reference value at a satisfactory pace'.

If a Member State does not fulfil the requirements under *one* of these criteria, the Commission shall prepare a report. This report shall also take into account another criterion: whether government deficit exceeds government investment expenditure as well as other factors such as the medium term economic and budgetary position.

If, after a Council recommendation to a Member State concerned, the latter's excessive deficit persists, *sanctions* will be imposed, from the beginning of stage three, under Article 104c(11):

a) the issuing of bonds and securities by the State concerned would require additional and approved information,
b) the EIB might have to reconsider its lending policy towards the State concerned,
c) a non-interest-bearing deposit with the Community might be required of the State concerned,
d) the imposition of fines.

Sanctions play a dual role. They can enhance the credibility of a policy but can hinder the development efforts of a country. Take the case of Portugal in 1991. Its GDP per head was 56.3 of the Community's average: 100; it had a real GDP growth of 2%, an inflation rate of about 11%, a debt/GDP ratio of 67.4%, a deficit/GDP ratio of 6.4% and its long-term interest rate of 17.1%. Portugal embarked on a development programme with the highest GFCF during the period 1986-91 and had a good export performance. Real unit labour costs and the current balance were kept within manageable limits.

Any imposition of sanctions would doubly penalise Portugal. For example, declaring Portugal ineligible to receive financing from the EIB would imply cutting down on projects in telecommunications, energy or transport. Requiring Portugal to make a non-interest bearing deposit with the Community, because of its excessive deficit/GDP ratio of 6.4% (instead of 3%), will mean the poorest Member State subsidises the richer Member States.

The monetary financing of deficits stemming from the activities of Central Governments, regional or local authorities, public authorities, other bodies governed by public law, either directly through the ESCB or via national banks is banned under Article 104.

Privileged access by Community institutions or bodies, central governments, regional, local or other public authorities, other bodies governed by public law or public undertakings of Member States to financial institutions, for the purpose of financing of deficits, is also banned under Article 104a.

These two prohibitions are further strengthened by a *no bail-out* clause under Article 104b which makes both the Community and Member States not responsible for the commitments of Governments and of all other public bodies (i.e. authorities or undertakings).

It should be noted that the ban on the monetary financing of deficits, the prohibition of granting overdraft and other credit facilities to public institutions, the denial of privileged access to the financial markets and the ban on assuming liability for commitments of individual Member States, are effective from the start of stage two of EMU. To this effect, secondary legislation has been adopted by the Council in December 1993.

All the above constitute *binding rules* in the budgetary field. The underlying logic of and the consequent need for such binding rules are stated in the Delors report (§ 30):

> firstly, impose effective upper limits on budget deficits of individual member countries of the Community,... secondly, exclude access to direct central bank credit and other forms of monetary financing while, however, permitting open market operations in government securities; thirdly, limit recourse to external borrowing in non-Community currencies.[12]

The economic logic of fiscal rules is based on three fears. First, a fiscally irresponsible Member State, accounting for a serious proportion of the total debt, could push up interest rates in the Community. Second, given the ban on bail-outs and limited coercive effect exercised by markets, solidarity would mean the ECB having to intervene and inject more liquidity in order to rescue a Member State. Consequently, the goal of price stability would be compromised. Third, a Member State on the brink of bankruptcy would send the value of its securities 'tumbling', a fact which could quickly spill over into a full-scale financial crisis affecting the financial institutions holding its debt. Hence unsustainable borrowing could trigger financial instability.

If the financing of such deficits is limited by eliminating the access to bank credit, governments will have to cut down expenditure in order to preserve the monetary union. Otherwise, accumulated deficits in the Community would raise the level of interest rates, with undesirable effects on exchange rate policy vis-à-vis third countries, not to speak of the effects on investment, on debt servicing and on economic growth.

There is a second economic rationale with deficits. To prevent the ECB having to monetize the debt of some single member and thus allowing one country to levy the inflation tax on the rest, binding rules governing the size and the financing of budget deficits should be set. The odd thing is that binding rules are not proposed on surpluses and an asymmetry is thus entailed in EMU.

A more interesting aspect of deficits is the case where capital is borrowed by one country regardless of the rate of return it can earn. The lending country could end up with a smaller domestic capital stock than it would otherwise have had, provided that the rate of return in the borrowing country is higher. Thus the equity share becomes problematic.

Neo-Walrasians who advocate rules for monetary policy are proponents of a fiscal policy discipline imposed by the market. Such discipline would work via two mechanisms. The first has to do with higher cost of borrowing which is the result of fiscal laxity; markets would exact an increasing default premium or higher risk associated with lower expected repayment or markets could refuse lending altogether. The second market mechanism could work via pressures for tax harmonisation. If a government spends a lot, it will have to tax a lot; higher taxes though would induce economic agents to move to places with lower taxes. Declining tax revenues would create pressure for competitive tax harmonisation resulting in cuts in spending or higher borrowing.

For market discipline to work, certain conditions need to be satisfied. Frankel and Goldstein (1991) identified five: a) the market must have accurate information on the size and composition of the debtor's obligations; b) there must not be any implicit or explicit guarantee of a bail-out; c) the financial system must be strong so that a given debtor is not regarded as likely to fail; d) the borrower's debt should not be monetized by central banks; e) there must be neither high costs of mobility nor provision of public services that compensate for tax differentials. In the case of EMU, condition e) is not satisfied and a) is only partly satisfied.

Yet market discipline is not symmetric. Compare the situation of the USA, having its dollar serving as an anchor, with that of Mexico, having a currency linked to the US dollar. Dismantling capital controls in the 1980s helped the USA to finance its fiscal deficit. The fiscal expansion of the Reagan administration, together with the monetary tightening of the Federal Reserve, caused interest rates to rise to a record high in the US. High interest rates of an anchor currency have always attracted capital inflows. As a consequence and in large part, they financed the US budget deficit at an interest rate lower than if capital controls had been in place. On the other hand, Mexico's debt was rendered unsustainable under high interest rates; when it threatened to default, market discipline worked. Borrowers stopped all new financing and Mexico could not borrow at any price. Capital liberalisation for some developing countries has meant a sanction that has taken the form of capital flight.

Critics of fiscal rules from the federal camp argue that, given the fact that two national policy instruments: exchange rate and monetary policy, have been given up, fiscal policy becomes an adjustment mechanism. In the face of low labour mobility due to linguistic and cultural barriers, fiscal policy also assumes the role of a shock absorber. But what kind: National or Community? Goodhart (1991: 169) says: "First, so long as the shocks are asymmetrical across the regions of the Community, a federal system provides a degree of insurance, via diversification to the constituent regions. Second, in a national system, the balance between accepting a higher fiscal deficit and higher future taxes on the one hand and/or less complete stabilisation of the national economy will be automatically stabilized by overspills through the current account to other countries".

The federal camp is not necessarily against rules. They rely on one: 'governments should not be able to finance deficits' (i.e. Art. 104c). Cooper (1990: 280) went further in arguing that the Community should assume the Member States' debts:

> To create a level fiscal playing field at the time when a European currency union is created, all existing European public debt ought to be consolidated as a given data in Brussels. The consolidated debt would become the future obligation of the European Community as a whole, and the national capitals would be relieved of it.

It has been argued that fixed exchange rates provide fiscal discipline. Under conditions of perfect capital mobility and asset substitutability a deficit could be financed by inward capital. Suppose fiscal policy is expansionary, thus creating a positive interest rate differential. The higher interest rate would attract capital, creating a balance of payments surplus. Sterilisation of inward capital would help finance the fiscal expansion. How long can this financing last? Schinasi (1989: 405) argues that it will depend on "...the productivity of the government's expenditures (the rate of return on public investment projects,

31

for example) and the credibility of the government to service such borrowing without resorting to inflationary monetary policies".

The advocacy or criticism of binding rules on deficits and debt could have been more persuasive, had it been examined under an alternative approach which claims that *money is an externality*. Even with traditional tools of monetary analysis, the justification for rules on fiscal and monetary policy is the theoretical premise that 'money on the whole is neutral'. In the context of EMU, this is another variant of neo-Walrasian thinking clothed in institutional language.

Traditional economic theory holds the view that demand management or stabilisation is not needed if: a) all markets work with perfect flexibility; this means that relative prices and real wages would adjust so as to restore equilibrium in all markets; b) labour mobility is high; c) Member States' economies are symmetrical. Under such circumstances, monetary policy and exchange rate instrument could be desirably centralised. This is what the EMU has done; it has centralised monetary policy with a single currency and a single interest rate instrument since, directly, it does not have any real effects on the economy while, indirectly, it can affect real income only if monetary policy is accommodating. Consequently, money is truly neutral at all times and Hume's world is born. Fiscal policy assumes the burden of stabilisation.

Yet at the EU level, the Community budget is likely to remain a very small part of total public sector spending and fiscal harmonisation is pursued because fair competition requires that indirect and direct taxes should not distort competition in tradeable commodities. The fiscal constraints are increasing but the adjustment process, when the fiscal policy acts as a shock absorber in the face of a supply shock (oil-shock, wage settlements), is relatively slow,[13] and does not necessarily entail the same cost for all countries.

However, there is a direct relationship between the rate of growth of GDP (y), of budget deficit (b_d) and of debt (d). The rate of growth of d cannot exceed the rate of growth of y and at the same time maintain constant the rate of growth of the b_d/y. Hence,

$$d/y = (b_d/y)/y \qquad (1)$$

Healey and Levine (1992: 32) estimated equation (1) and found that if price stability is maintained, "...a budget deficit equal to 3 per cent of GDP is only consistent with a long-run debt to income ratio of 60 per cent provided that a growth rate of 5 per cent per annum is sustained". Given the bleak estimates by the Commission that economic growth in the Community will not exceed 1.2% in 1994 and 2% in 1995, both deficit and debt of all Member States will increase.

How could one bring down the d/y ratio? There are three ways: a) tax increases and/or expenditure cuts, b) surprise inflation that wipes out the real value of the debt if the latter is not indexed, c) default. Given that option b) cannot be used since the ECB pursues price stability and option c) is not warranted under Article 104b on 'no bail-out', only option a) is available. Suppose option a) is used so drastically in order to sustain the d/y ratio. Given the increasing cost of debt servicing, sustainability implies a primary budget surplus.

This can be demonstrated with the help of equation (1). Suppose the ratio of interest cost to GDP is r(d/y) and the primary budget deficit is defined as deficit less interest cost:

$$PD = b_d - rd \qquad (2)$$

By dividing equation (2) by y and by substituting equation (1) into (2) for b_d, we have:

$$PD/y = (y - r) \ (d/y) \qquad (3)$$

Hence the primary budget surplus required to stabilise the debt/GDP ratio is proportional to the difference between the real interest rate and the GDP growth (y) as well as the debt level (d/y).

Equation (3) has been estimated by Healey and Levine (1992: 33): "...solvency requires that, with a growth rate of 3 per cent and a real interest rate of 6 per cent, the primary balance must be brought to a surplus of 1.8 per cent of GDP to stabilise the debt to income ratio at 60 per cent of GDP".[14] If the average growth until 1996 is 2% as the Commission (1993a) predicts, the 60% ratio of debt/GDP could be sustained provided that the real interest is 8% and the budget surplus 3.6% of GDP.

If one applies the logic of Sargent and Wallace (1981) to EMU, which states that central banks, independent or not, are forced by circumstances to monetise public debt, then, the ECB will not be able to resist pressure and hence will monetise excessive debt. Two channels are possible. First, if growth and employment are bleak, budget deficits will increase. This will exert pressure on the interest rate. If price stability is maintained, the higher interest rate will cause a shift in the composition of the GDP; public consumption will increase and private investment will decrease. The rate of GDP growth will be reduced, which will oblige the ECB to interpret Article 103a as legal means for monetising public debt. Article 103a calls for Community financial assistance to a Member State faced with 'severe difficulties arising in the supply of certain products'.

A second channel for forcing the ECB to intervene, despite Article 104b on 'no bail-out' clause, concerns the notion of 'solidarity' called for in Article 2 of the TEU. For at least four countries: Belgium, Greece, Ireland and Italy, the debt/GDP ratio has by far exceeded the 60% limit, reaching the mark of above 100%. If capital markets refuse to make further loans, two options are open; either the Member State concerned becomes insolvent or Article 103a is reinterpreted to mean that the Member State is faced with severe difficulties and debt monetisation is undertaken by the ECB.

The case against binding fiscal rules has been made by the Centre for Economic Policy Research (1991). Its argument is centred on the ineffectiveness of rules to reduce deficits and debts, especially when hidden debts via publicly owned agencies are taken into account. The cost to be incurred in a period of recession and the relationship of equation (3) are two additional reasons. It proposes, as an alternative, the strengthening of market discipline, coupled with two requirements. The first concerns a new regulation on systemic risk and payments system; the second relates to the prudential protection of banks and financial intermediaries.

2.7 Exchange rate policy

During the period of capital controls and flexible exchange rates, the variables: money supply, fiscal policy, interest rate and exchange rate, could be regarded as independently exogenous policy instruments. Then trade flows or current account imbalances mainly determined the exchange rates. Various policy measures and instruments, such as taxation, reserves and interest rates, influenced the direction of the exchange rates. Even then, a decision to fix the exchange rate narrowed the choice on interest rate.

With capital liberalisation since the early 1980s and managed exchange rates since the breakdown of Bretton Woods, only two instruments can be chosen as exogenous: interest rates and fiscal policy. Yet the expansion of global finance has tied monetary policy and exchange rate together via interest rates. Assume a tight monetary policy to fight inflation; it will raise interest rates, which then will attract capital flows and thus the exchange rate will appreciate rendering exports uncompetitive. Hence global capital markets have meant that expectations coupled with interest rate differentials largely determine exchange rates and monetary policy; interest rate and exchange rate have become one policy instrument.

Since fiscal policy, at least on paper and subject to the reservations raised in chapter 7, rests with Member States, the question of 'who controls the external value of the ECU in stage three' is paramount. Price stability will be difficult to achieve if the exchange rate is decided by a body other than the ECB, since the latter will have to support the agreed exchange rate.

Given the provisions of Article 109 on concluding formal agreements on an exchange rate system for the ECU vis-à-vis non-Community currencies, there are two possibilities. The first concerns a unanimous decision by the ECOFIN Council to do so. For this formal agreement, the Council will need to consult 'the ECB in an endeavour to reach a consensus consistent with the objective of price stability' (Art. 109(1)). Since unanimity is not easy to attain, the second option is more likely.

The second option concerns the absence of a formal agreement. By a qualified majority, the Council may formulate general orientations for exchange rate policy vis-à-vis non-Community currencies, based on a recommendation from the ECB or on a recommendation from the Commission after consulting the ECB. 'These general orientations shall be without prejudice to the primary objective of the ESCB to maintain price stability' (Art. 109(2)). This second option, therefore, amounts to a shared responsibility for the agreement on the exchange rate of the ECU.

The formulation of Article 109 is a compromise of two schools of thought. The first holds the view that monetary and exchange rate policies are indivisible. So the institution which is responsible for setting the interest rate should also be responsible for setting the exchange rate since a decision to raise interest rates in order to maintain price stability is, other things being equal, a decision to strengthen the currency via the inward capital flows.

The second school holds the view that one can divorce monetary policy from exchange rate policy because their interdependence is not strong. The orientations on a single exchange rate policy vis-à-vis third countries could be adopted by a separate body, such as the ECOFIN Council, and, in the context of such guidelines, the ECB could implement the agreed orientations.

The two schools differ in their theories of exchange rate determination. The 'indivisibility' school follows the asset market theory where the exchange rate would be mainly influenced by global capital markets. The 'divorce' school follows the Keynesian view that the exchange rate is likely to be influenced by productivity of a country and its relative elasticities of imports and exports.

The empirical literature on the subject has not settled the question of a *good* theory of exchange rate determination.[15] Hence the TEU opted for a compromise. Reaching a consensus that would be consistent with the objective of price stability would mean creative conflicts between Ministers and the ECB. Unless price stability were not to be the *sole* objective of ECB, and via the instrument of exchange rate policy, other objectives would be pursued.

Two issues associated with fixed exchange rates should be examined. The first is about the balance of payments. The second concerns the future exchange rate of ECU/US dollar and of ECU/Yen.

Traditionally, for a given growth rate and unemployment level in a Community of 12 Member States and 12 currencies, if imports exceeded exports of goods and services, there were two options: foreign borrowing or exchange rate change. With the creation of a single currency by 1999, the inter-country balance of payments disequilibria would become inter-regional disequilibria. For a country with chronic balance of payments difficulties, the single currency would do away with payments problems. There will be no exchange rate to defend and foreign exchange reserves will become irrelevant.

The single currency does not really deal with 'what makes tradeable goods and services competitive'. Nor does it say anything on whether inter-regional borrowing would still be needed if imports continued to outbalance exports. In fact, exports are vital for the strength of aggregate demand, the growth prospects of a region/country and employment. After all, exchange rates have been used in the past for growth purposes and, in some instances when labour mobility has been difficult, a change in exchange rate aided exports.[16]

Neither would the inter-regional borrowing disappear with a single currency; it might even aid it. This is so because one way of improving productivity of a region is to compete in capital markets for investment funds. That would mean, if the region is discriminated against (i.e. Mexico), higher interest costs to attract capital.

As to the second issue, one should recognise that, although the EU has so far had a balanced current account, there is no compelling reason for it to remain so. Prices, investment and terms of trade have evolved at different rates. Consider prices.

Productivity gains are reflected either in lower prices or higher profits. The price trend is a way of improving the competitiveness of exportable goods and services. For the average periods of 1971-80 and 1981-90, the price deflator in the Community declined from 11% to 6,8%; in the US, from 7.4% to 4.2%; and in Japan, from 7.6% to 1.4%. In other words, both the USA and Japan did better in the field of competitiveness than the EU.

Table 2.2
Shares in world exports, 1980-88

	1980	1981	1983	1984	1985	1986	1987	1988
EC: M	26,7	25,6	25,3	24,6	24,9	24,7	24,3	23,1
TG	25,5	25,2	24,4	23,7	24,0	24,2	23,8	22,5
US: M	16,2	17,6	16,1	16,2	15,6	13,5	13,2	14,4
TG	17,7	18,9	17,3	17,6	16,6	14,4	14,5	16,0
J: M	12,3	14,9	14,4	16,6	16,4	16,3	15,1	15,2
TG	10,8	12,8	13,1	14,3	14,3	14,7	13,6	13,9

Source: Commission (1991a)   M=manufacturing   TG=total goods

Consequently, the shares of the EU, USA and Japan in the world export market changed over the period 1980-88 (see Table 2.2). Both the EU and the USA exports in third markets showed a modest performance. Their shares have declined continuously: from 25.5% in 1980 to 22.5% in 1988 for the EU and from 17.7% in 1980 to 14.4% in 1986 and small recovery in 1986 (i.e. 16%)

for the US. In contrast Japan's market share showed an opposite trend: from 10.8% in 1980, it rose to 14.7% in 1986 and fell slightly in 1988 (i.e. 13.9%). Interpreting the trend, the Commission (1991a: 143) stated: "The relatively poor performance of the Community exports during most of the 1980s is largely related to changes in the relative competitiveness of its manufacturing sector, which dominates EC merchandise exports".[17]

The loss of exchange rate as a policy instrument has been assessed. Aizenman and Frankel (1982) argued that the loss depends on whether the real shock is industry-specific or country-specific. If there is diversified industrial structure, the loss of exchange rate is less costly. If shocks are country-specific, difficulties are greater.

Vinals (1990) stressed that the 1992 single market would strengthen market mechanisms and competition. Such a set-up would increase the downward flexibility of money wages and prices. Hence the need to change exchange rates in order to change wage cost is not needed.

As to the automatic adjustment mechanisms, Sachs and Sala-I-Martin (1989) calculated, for the USA federal system, the automatically adjusted taxes and transfer payments in the event of country-specific shocks. They estimated that these automatic mechanisms would offset roughly 40% of region-specific income shocks.

If we transpose these three factors to the EU of 1994, we find that the EU has a sufficiently diversified industrial structure and, therefore, industry-specific shocks would not create particular difficulties. But country-specific shocks are still possible and would require a flexible fiscal policy. Wage moderation has already occurred, not so much because of the single market but, because of high unemployment rates expected to reach 11% in 1994. Giersch (1989) believed that labour markets would be more flexible if growth prospects were realised in the 1992 post-period. For this, competition is the clue, because automatic fiscal absorbers do not exist in the Community budget, nor are they foreseen in the TEU.

2.8 Rules on passage to third stage

The most difficult aspect of EMU is credibility; credibility as to the commitment of Member States to willingly transfer monetary sovereignty to a supernational institution; credibility as to the welfare maximisation of EMU; credibility as to the equity question and allocative efficiency.

Article 109j of the EMU Treaty seeks to bolster credibility as to the commitment of ten out of twelve countries (UK and Denmark are not obliged to join the third stage) to move to third stage by 1 January 1999. The transition presupposes fulfilment of four criteria, according to which, one may assess the degree of sustainable convergence. The protocol states:

1) an average rate of inflation (consumer price index), over a period of one year before the examination, should not exceed that of, at the most, the three best performing Member States by more than 1.5% points;
2) no excessive budget deficit (defined in section 2.6);
3) respect of the normal fluctuation margins of ERM for at least two years without severe tensions and without devaluing against any other Member State currency;
4) an average nominal long-term interest rate observed over a period of one year, that does not exceed by more than 2% points that of at most the three best performing Member States in terms of price stability.

Secondary criteria such as integration of markets, balance of payments on current account, unit labour costs, etc, would be taken into account in the reports of the Commission and of the EMI to be submitted to the ECOFIN Council. The Council shall assess and recommend to the Heads of State or Government: a) which Member States fulfil the necessary conditions for the adoption of a single currency, and b) whether a majority of the Member States fulfils the necessary conditions for the adoption of a single currency. Upon the Council's recommendation, the Heads of State or Government, not later than 31 December 1996, acting by a qualified majority, shall decide on a) and b) and thus set a date for the beginning of the third stage.

Member States that do not satisfy the convergence criteria may apply for a derogation. Article 109k is concerned with provisions of the status of Member States. A derogation implies the suspension of voting rights at the Council on matters concerning excessive deficits and sanctions; exclusion of the governors concerned in matters over the ESCB primary objective and tasks, prudential supervision and authorization of bank notes or ECB opinions and recommendations; no right for the Member States with a derogation at Councils to decide on exchange rate policy and appointment of ECB's Executive Board. The Member States concerned will not be exempt from multilateral surveillance. Yet how will a Member State with a derogation link its currency to the ECU is not specified. The proposal by the Commission to abrogate a Member State's derogation is to be examined once every two years by the Heads of State or of Government.

The principles for the transition are three: a) no obligation to participate, b) no Member State may oppose the transition to third stage but certain Member States may, where they so request and taking account of their specific situation, be granted longer time-limits enabling them to meet the conditions of EMU, c) no Member States may be excluded from third stage.

The UK and Denmark opted to exercise principle a). Two protocols annexed to the TEU contain the legal provisions relating to the UK's 'opting out' and Denmark's 'exemption' clause. The opting out applies to the UK and is not a general clause. It recognises that the 'UK shall not be obliged or committed

38

to move to the third stage of EMU without a separate decision to do so by its government and parliament'. In the case of Denmark, it is recognised that the 'Danish Constitution contains provisions which imply a referendum in Denmark prior to Danish participation in the third stage of EMU'. The Edinburgh European Council of 11-12 December 1992 agreed that 'Denmark will not participate in the single currency, will not be bound by the rules concerning economic policy which apply only to Member States participating in the third stage of EMU, and will retain its existing powers in the field of monetary policy according to its national laws and regulations, including powers of the National Bank of Denmark in the field of monetary policy'. The implication of the special status for UK and Denmark means that their voting rights at the Council will be suspended on matters related to a single monetary policy.

The strict nominal convergence criteria and rules of voting at the Council [18] would complicate the passage to third stage. The 'opting out' clause for the UK and Denmark, plus the fact that Greece would not easily satisfy the criteria, could create a blocking minority of 23 votes. It would still require a qualified majority of 54 votes out of a total of 76, entailing at least eight Member States. The real test would be Italy. Only Article 104c(6) which stipulates that it is the Council that decides 'whether an excessive deficit exists', could save the case. Otherwise the EMU would be stalled.

The more important provision of EMU is stated in Article 109j(4) because it entails an element of *automaticity* :

> If by the end of 1997, the date for the beginning of the third stage, has not been set, the *third stage will start on 1 January 1999*. Before 1 July 1988, the Council, meeting in the composition of Heads of State or of Government,..., shall, acting by a qualified majority,..., confirm which Member States fulfil the necessary conditions for the *adoption of a single currency* [stress added].

In theory, the third stage could start even with two countries but, in such a case, the whole edifice of the EU would collapse. Equally, in theory, at the latest on 1 January 1999, the third stage will *automatically* begin. Yet the German Federal Constitutional Court, in its judgement relating to EMU, rejected the automatic course for EMU and insisted on the legally binding nature of the convergence criteria.

Let us examine the convergence criteria in the context of received theory. They all depend on *the expected rate of inflation.* Expected inflation convergence would mean adjustment in the face of capital liberalisation' and loss of policy instruments, serious deflationary measures while in recession, and an unfavourable world situation associated with major economic transformations.

The *nominal interest rate* is approximately the sum of real interest rate (which is equal to interest rate minus inflation) and the expected inflation rate. Hence, if expected rates of inflation are likely to converge, so would the nominal interest rates.

Devaluations are monetary phenomena when capital mobility and asset substitutability are high. If that is the case, in the long-run, the purchasing power parity (PPP) would hold and devaluations would depend on the expected rate of inflation.

Equally, excessive budget deficits are dependent on *debt servicing*. For example, the ratio of interest payments/GDP in 1991 was: Belgium 10.9%; Denmark 7.4%; Germany 2.7%; Greece 13.2%; Spain 3.6%; France 3.2%; Ireland 8.3%; Italy 10.2%; Luxembourg 0.6%; Netherlands 5.9%; Portugal 8.5% and U.K. 3.2%. The countries with the highest deficits have also the highest debt servicing. But debt servicing depends on long-term interest rates, the latter dependent on inflation, and thus, indirectly, on expected inflation.

Price stability is considered by the current orthodoxy as prerequisite for medium-term growth because it contributes to an efficient allocation of resources and because it is needed if fixed exchange rates are to be preserved. A low inflation rate is also needed to avoid the competitiveness gap between Member States in tradeable goods which create higher regional unemployment if labour mobility is low or require downward wage and price adjustment. Yet if the cause of inflation is not monetary but structural, then substantial price differentials are inevitable within a monetary union.

However, if elimination of expected inflation were the only economic objective, it would be easy to attain it. A tight monetary policy would raise interest rates to a record high, rendering companies in cyclical industries bankrupt and thus reducing the productive stock of capital with a serious fall in real wages and incomes. The induced inflow of capital would cause an appreciation of the currency and hence render exports uncompetitive. As a result of both causes, the level of effective demand would fall, leading to a check of capital accumulation and to a record high unemployment rate. But elimination of expected inflation at all cost is not the end-objective of EMU. Consequently, the crux of the matter is 'what policy to pursue for the convergence criteria to be fulfilled without a disruption to real economic activity'.

For the control of expected inflation, the instruments have varied. Interest rates and fiscal policy have been used with some success. Incomes policy and credit controls have fallen out of favour. Various definitions of money supply have been offered and monetary targets have been followed without good results. Credit controls had the same fate. A combination of an exchange rate target, combined with target ranges of money supply (such as M1 or M3 or M0 in the UK) or money demand has been tried. All that under the received monetary theory of *what determines real income*, associated with the

40

assumption that the *money supply is an independent exogenous policy instrument*. The latter assumption is the more important for EMU for it is related to the question of 'what is money'.

It is of interest to examine the nominal criteria in view of the protocol on convergence criteria and the recent experience shown in Table 2.3.

Table 2.3
Estimates of nominal convergence indicators

	Public debt (% of GDP)		Borrowing (% of GDP)		Inflation (annual %)		Long-term interest rate	
	1991	1993	1991	1993	1991	1993	1991	1993
B	129.5	138.4	6.6	7.4	2.9	2.8	9.3	7.3
DK	71.7	78.5	2.2	4.4	2.5	1.4	10.1	8.9
D	41.9	50.2	3.2	4.2	3.8	4.3	8.6	6.3
GR	100.9	113.6	16.3	15.5	18.4	13.7	-	-
E	45.5	55.6	5.2	7.2	6.2	4.7	12.4	10.2
F	35.5	44.9	2.1	5.9	3.0	2.3	9.0	6.8
IRL	95.9	92.9	2.0	3.0	2.3	2.3	9.2	7.7
I	101.4	115.8	10.2	10.0	6.9	4.4	13.0	11.3
L	6.2	10.0	1.0	2.5	2.9	3.6	8.2	6.9
NL	79.0	83.1	2.5	4.0	3.4	2.1	8.9	6.7
P	67.4	69.5	6.4	8.9	11.1	6.7	17.1	12.4
UK	41.0	53.2	2.7	7.6	7.2	3.4	9.9	7.9
E12	58.0	66.4	4.6	6.4	4.5	3.8	10.2	8.1

Source: Commission (1993b)

2.8.a) *Price stability criterion*

As to price stability, in 1993, the three best performing were Denmark with 1.4%, the lowest inflation rate, the Netherlands with 2.1% and France with 2.3%, the third best performing. The reference range based on 1,5 percentage price differential, could be calculated by taking the third best performing country or the average of the three or the lowest inflation rate. If we take the third best performing country, then the reference range will be 3.8%, which incidently was the EU average. Seven countries satisfied the inflation criterion: Belgium, Denmark, France, Ireland, Luxembourg, the Netherlands and the UK. Very close to the reference range were Germany, Spain and Italy while Greece had the highest inflation followed by Portugal. Yet Portugal made an effort in bringing down its inflation rate from 11.1% in 1991 to 6.7% in 1993.

All indices are subject to theoretical scrutiny. The question of 'what should the basket of consumer goods contain' is not easy. Should indirect taxes that affect mainly retail prices be excluded? Should only labour costs of tradeables be considered? Should mortgage costs be included? Should variations in consumption be maintained? How could one allow for differences relating to the prices of services, which are linked to productivity rather than to income and price? Will the Balassa effect (1964) be taken into account?[19]

Crawford (1993: 181) maintains that non-tradeables will not slow down as fast as tradeables because: "(1) cost-plus pricing is more prevalent in business that are sheltered from foreign competition; (2) services (whose costs are mainly labour and capital) do not experience the same external price discipline as goods in general...(3) prices charged by public utilities...exacerbate the slower convergence of retail prices".

If one takes account of the above methodological difficulties, one may be inclined to propose the 'labour costs per unit' as a more reliable indicator of 'expected inflation'. This is what we propose for our convergence potential index below.

An issue that has raised interest is the inflation tax or seigniorage. Phelps (1973) considered seigniorage in terms of differential taxation. Tobin (1986: 11) defined it: "The ability of the government to finance expenditure by issuing money is the seigniorage associated with its sovereign monetary monopoly". Spaventa (1989: 560) measured it as "as a rate of inflation times the ratio of money balances to GDP".

In chapter 6, we argue that, in so far as the change in monetary balances causes changes in the price level, this monetary monopoly creates *price level externalities* which are broader than a form of taxation. Yet seigniorage is not associated with the monetary monopoly. Any asset established in the market as money or near-money would create *seigniorage externalities* that have nothing to do with inflation.

There is a camp of economists, which argues that, for fiscally weak countries where taxation systems are inadequate, it might be optimal to favour a relatively high inflation associated with higher seigniorage. Although seigniorage from money creation may have implications for savings, capital accumulation and long-run solvency, these weak countries have no other more efficient mechanism to raise taxes; the distortions induced by inflation ought to be traded off with those induced by taxes.

Giavazzi (1989) estimated the government revenue generated via the seigniorage attached to money creation in the Community by employing the 'cash flow measure of seigniorage'; this method looks at the additional money balances the public demands per year, given the reduced real value of balances it holds. Giavazzi (1989: 85) arrived at two conclusions:

The data show that the countries where seigniorage revenue is the highest are also the countries where the revenue from other forms of taxation is the lowest. Seigniorage still accounts for 7 per cent of total government revenue in Greece, 5 per cent in Spain, around 4 per cent in Italy and Portugal; these are also the countries where the share of tax revenue (net of seigniorage) in GDP is the lowest. Low tax revenues often reflect the structure of the economy; it is not clear that they could be raised very fast. They are often associated with a narrow tax base, rather than with lower-than-average tax rates.

The method used by Giavazzi (1989) was employed by Gros and Thygesen (1992: 179) who arrived at a different result: "...the inflation tax has been most important in the two non-EMS members Portugal and Greece. Among the EMS members it is important mainly for Spain and Italy; however, even in these two cases seigniorage revenues have already declined to less than 1 percent of GDP in 1988-9". When the opportunity cost definition of seigniorage (which is equal to the interest rate on public debt times the total amount of cash and required reserves) was used, Gros and Thygesen (1992: 180) found that "...during the EMS period seigniorage revenues were reduced by about 1-1.5 per cent of GDP in Italy and about 0.5 per cent in Spain. No reduction is apparent in Greece. ... Portugal experienced a reduction of about 1.5% per cent of GDP".

Where does this debate leave us? Cobham (1991: 377) concluded that "...the issue of seigniorage as an argument against entering the EMS (or EMU) is probably forgotten". The real issue is not the confusion between anticipated and surprise inflation that Cobham has criticised, but the question of *what is optimum* and this depends on the nature and role of money. A neutral money would only affect the inflation rate and thus the optimum rate may be chosen. If money is non-neutral and works via the interest rate it would affect all nominally fixed assets. Then anticipated inflation, being a tax on money balances, would affect the entire portfolio. If money is super-non-neutral (generating and internalising externalities) then, the consumption, production and welfare functions would be changed. Consequently, the optimum has to be re-worked anew.

A more relevant issue for the *fiscally weak* countries is the adjustment cost, associated with the effort to bring down inflation rates to those experienced in more developed Member States. This is stressed by Fotopoulos (1990 and 1991). The cost is relevant because the causes of inflation in the two groups are different. In the advanced countries, two factors played a significant role in the determination of inflation rates in the period 1971-80: the welfare state and commitment to near full employment. The average inflation rates for these countries were: Germany and Holland, about 7.5%; the UK 14%; France 9.9%. Once these two factors played a less significant role, their inflation rates fell

43

to 2.6%, 6.5% and 6.3% respectively.

The peripheral countries, which are also fiscally weak, face a different cause of inflation; it is mainly caused by structural imbalances arising from obsolete methods of production and consumption patterns. The peripheral countries had never committed themselves to full employment nor developed a welfare state. On the other hand, the inflation rates of Greece and Portugal for the same periods: 1971-80 and 1981-90 increased from 13.7% to 18.1% for Greece and from 16.1% to 17.9% for Portugal.

In principle, changes in the competitiveness within the Community largely reflect differences in the price performance between Member States. Whereas, in the group of advanced countries, prices have fallen and made their tradeables competitive, in the group of peripheral countries, prices have risen and made their exports. From this uncompetitive position, the peripheral countries are required to bring their inflation rates down to about 4% in the next five years. The policy options are either an anti-inflationary policy via an incomes policy, coupled with an investment programme that would regenerate their manufacturing sector, or become permanent Member States with a derogation.

2.8.b) Excessive budget deficit criterion

According to Table 2.3, the general government net borrowing increased to more than 6.4% for the EU in 1993. Only two Member States, Ireland and Luxembourg, satisfied the 3% ratio of deficit/GDP. With reference to 1991, the fiscally sound countries of Denmark, Germany, France, the Netherlands and the UK, were turned into fiscally weak in 1993. Save for Germany whose unification cost was higher than had been estimated, the rest took fiscal measures to mitigate the effects of economic recession. In Spain and Portugal, previous efforts at fiscal consolidation were reversed. The stabilisation programmes of Belgium and Italy have not been aided by the unfavourable economic environment of high interest rates and zero growth. Greece has remained the laggard with the highest deficit/GDP ratio.

The worsening of the deficit/GDP ratio is partly due to cyclical factors. The Commission (1993b: 13) estimated the cyclical component of the deficit by taking account the reference path for GDP and by estimating a mean trend for GDP over the cycles. The change in the cyclical component measures the budgetary impact of changes in the output gap relative to trend. The cumulative change from 1990 to 1993 was calculated to be 4.6% of which the cyclical component was 2.2%.

As to the debt/GDP criterion, five countries: Germany, Spain, France, Luxembourg and the UK, still had a ratio below the reference value of 60% in 1991. Yet in the last three years, these five have experienced a deterioration of their debt/GDP ratios. In fact, there is not a single Member State, except

44

Ireland, that has not experienced an increase in its debt/GDP if 1991 is taken as the reference year. The debt/GDP ratio for Belgium, Greece and Italy stands at above 100% and is still rising.

A serious issue with debt statistics, shown in Table 2.3, is what is included or excluded in its calculation. For example, in the case of Belgium, Portugal and Luxembourg, social security debt is excluded from the consolidated central and local government debt. The short-term liabilities of the Danish government is also not included. Similarly, certain liabilities of Länder are not included in the German government debt expressed at nominal value. Equally, the French government debt excludes trade credits and accounts payable. Greece's central bank's direct advances also are excluded. All these categories are *hidden State debt* since they are public sector liabilities. If one adds to it the unfunded public sector pension liabilities, the ratio of debt to GDP will double.[20]

2.8.c) Long-term interest rate criterion

Our theoretical point made earlier that there is a close correlation between inflation and long-term interest rate, is confirmed by the data. In all Member States, the long-term interest rates measured by the 10 year government bonds fell, on average, from a 15% in 1981 to about 8.1% in 1993 and this trend is in line with the corresponding inflation reduction.

In terms of the TEU criterion of 2% points divergence between a Member State and the three best performing Member States in terms of inflation, we find that, in 1993, on the base of Table 2.3, the best performing were Denmark, France and the Netherlands. Hence a reference range is given between 8.7% to 10.9%. Spain, Greece (if its 5 year government bonds are taken as a proxy), France, Italy and Portugal do not satisfy this criterion; the rest do.

Two remarks should be made when examining long-term interest rates. First, a comparison between countries is not easily made because there is no comparable data. Table 2.3 is based on different national definitions; in some cases, central government bonds were taken while in others, public sector or state bonds were used. Second, the period 1991-93 was still one with relatively stable exchange rates under the ERM discipline. The widening of the fluctuation margins to +/-15% since August 1993 would make predictions of the evolution of long-term interest rates less plausible.

This convergence criterion is judged by a number of people[21] as unnecessary if inflation rates have converged by the launch of the single currency. The theoretical case for this convergence criterion is found in Walters (1986). He argued that under fixed exchange rates of the EMS and stable expectations, nominal interest rates should be the same. But if there are different rates of inflation, the real interest rate in the low-inflation, due to the design of the EMS, will be higher than that in the high-inflation rate. This is an asymmetry of the system; countries with the high-inflation rate should have a higher real interest rate in order to control its inflation.

If we compare Germany's ex-post real long-term interest rates and its inflation between 1985-89 with that of others, we find that, on average, Germany had the lowest inflation (2.1%) and real interest rate (4%) among ERM participants. The UK had an inflation rate of 5% and a real interest rate of 4.3%. The countries that had lower real interest rates than Germany were Greece (1.9%) and Portugal (2.1%), yet both recorded the highest inflation rate (about 16%) and did not participate in the ERM.

2.8.d) No-devaluation criterion

As to the no-devaluation criterion, it should be noted that it was conceived within the mechanics of the exchange rate mechanism (ERM) of the EMS, leading to a system of no realignments. From the late 1980s and onwards, the circumstances favoured such an idea because Spain in June 1989, the UK in October 1990 and Portugal in April 1992 had joined the ERM, leaving only Greece outside the system. The Scandinavian countries and Austria had also pegged their currencies to the ECU.

However, two monetary disturbances: globalisation of markets since mid-1980s and the tightened monetary policy from mid-1991 by the Bundesbank having its DM as the anchor currency for the ERM, fuelled strains within the system. The Danish 'No' to the TEU in the June 1992 referendum, the narrow 'Yes' of the French September 1992 referendum, the lengthy political process of ratification in the UK and the challenging of the TEU before the German Federal Constitutional Court further fuelled uncertainty and speculation.

To the above, one should add the following fact; growth had began slipping below trend, budgetary balances had deteriorated rapidly coupled with the inappropriate 'policy-mix', the unification cost of Germany had resulted in an asymmetric demand shock leading to higher inflation than expected and subsequently, to high interest rates which, in turn, set in train a real appreciation of the DM. The fact also that the private sector with the emergence of institutional investors, had become more powerful than national central banks, searching for protection against devaluation risks, all these factors contributed to shaking confidence in the ability of Member States to defend their exchange rates. The result of all these strains was severe pressure on ERM currencies, leading to a sequence of adjustments within the ERM. The UK sterling and the Italian lira withdrew from ERM in September 1992. Five realignments involving four currencies took place. In the end, the temporary widening of the ERM fluctuation margins from +/-2.25% or 6% to +/-15% was decided on 2 August 1993. Hence a system of managed floating has set in.

Commenting on the above system, the Commission (1993b: 23) said: "The weakening of exchange-rate discipline within the ERM represents a setback to the integration process within the Community as previously envisaged but, in the present circumstances, wider ERM bands are the most pragmatic response to the recurrent tensions on the foreign-exchange markets". What is often forgotten by the Commission is that the *real* cause of the tension in the ERM and its subsequent collapse is the *inconsistent trinity* stemming from a system that seeks to hold together fixed exchange rates, free capital movements and independent national monetary policies. We take up these themes and examine them in greater detail in the next chapter.

However, a legalistic approach would argue that while devaluations must be avoided for two years, this does not preclude a general realignment of exchange rates during the period. But there is a wider issue. The CEPR report (1991) favours only one criterion: unchanged parities within the narrow ERM bands for two years. It favours this criterion coupled with the non-monetisation of deficits clause on grounds that their macro-economic cost may permanently endanger the commitment to price stability; it also finds inflation and interest rate convergence insufficient. Exchange rate stability will aid convergence of inflation and interest rates and force countries with high deficits to reduce them. Fixity of parities for two years would also eliminate active speculation. The question is whether this option under the present circumstances is still valid.

2.9 Convergence criteria reconsidered

Gros and Thygesen (1992) constructed an EMU indicator, shown in Table 2.4, based on five macroeconomic variables assumed to measure the health of an economy. It resembles the convergence criteria of EMU with a difference; the exchange rate stability and long-term interest rate criteria have been replaced by the unemployment rate and current account balance.

Table 2.4
EMU indicator for 1991

B	DK	D	GR	E	F	IRL	I	L	NL	P	UK
23.2	11.7	12.8	51.8	26.2	12.5	24.9	30.2	-	11.6	21.7	16.4

Source: Gros and Thygesen, 1992, Table 14.2.1

Gros and Thygesen (1992: 469) interpreted the values of Table 2.4: "A high value of the EMU indicator indicates that the country needs a great deal of adjustment before it can join a 'virtuous' EMU". A first group of Denmark, Netherlands, France, Germany (and Luxembourg, not included), is rather homogeneous and scores the lowest indicator. A second group consists of Portugal, Belgium, Ireland and Spain requiring some adjustment if compared to the first group. The UK, with a value of 16.4, is closer to the first group. Italy and Greece with the highest indicator, belong to the third group in need of major adjustment.

The Gros-Thygesen EMU indicator is supposed to suggest something different from the EMU criteria by concentrating on what is the state of an economy. Yet it simply confirms the present situation described by the TEU's convergence criteria and confirmed by Table 2.3. A more interesting indicator would have been an *index of convergence potential*.

2.9.a) Index of convergence potential

This convergence potential index would show the degree of adjustment needed in order to create a rather homogeneous group, taking account of past and current efforts to build an economy which can sustain the pressure of competition, innovation and external shocks. We have chosen five variables to construct the EMU convergence index of economic potential. The five indicators are: public debt, gross fixed capital formation, current account balance, compensation of employees and unemployment rate. The public debt is shown in Table 2.3 while the other four indicators are shown in Table 2.5.

The *debt* variable is chosen for three reasons. First, it is related to both deficit and economic growth via equation (3) and thus takes account of deficits or surpluses. Second, the debt's components, such as interest cost or expenditure on investment, determine its trend. Third, public debt is a form of redistribution of income between the public and private sectors. Any government bond denominated in domestic money for a 10-year period is a mechanism by which private savings in period t are transferred to government in expectation that in period t+10 the government will honour its promise to redeem to the holder the face value of the bond plus the yearly interest earned.

Current theoretical thinking may accept the distributional effects of public debt but holds the view that debt neutrality has general validity. The debate over the effects of debt has flourished since Barro's (1974) paper on the so-called Ricardian-equivalent-hypothesis, which holds the view that if the private and public sectors have equal access to financing, are homogenous and borrow at the same interest rate, private or public debt is alike and thus *debt neutrality* holds.

Barro's hypothesis of debt neutrality would hold only if certainty, perfect foresight and correctly anticipated growth were assumed. Otherwise, debt matters not because of speculation or of different views held by the private or public sectors about future consumption but because of income distribution. In this sense both the private and public debt matter because the one cannot have general validity without reference to the other.

Our view is sound because income distribution has both micro and macro effects. "In a model in which different agents have different utility functions, or propensities to consume, or different access to credit, and these differences are not completely offset by direct linkages (bequests and transfers), the economy cannot simply operate as if it were just one individual (as in representative-agent models). The distribution among different individuals of some crucial variables (income, credit,....) will have a macro-impact, irrespective of rational expectations, forward-looking behaviour, and the like" (Vaciago, 1993: 350).

Table 2.5
Estimates of convergence potential indicators

	G F C F as % of GDP		Curr. balance as % of GDP		Compensation of empl. in %		Unemployment rate in %	
	1991	1993	1991	1993	1991	1993	1991	1993
B	19.8	18.6	1.7	1.3	6.6	4.5	7.5	9.5
DK	16.9	14.9	1.4	2.8	3.8	2.6	8.9	10.5
D	23.2	22.7	-0.6	-1.2	5.8	3.4	5.1	6.8
GR	18.2	17.1	-5.1	-3.7	15.1	11.8	7.7	7.8
E	24.0	20.4	-3.8	-2.7	7.9	7.3	16.3	21.2
F	20.9	18.6	-0.5	0.6	4.4	3.1	9.5	10.8
IRL	16.8	15.5	2.0	3.4	4.7	5.7	16.2	18.4
I	19.8	17.7	-1.8	-0.1	8.7	3.1	10.0	11.0
L	29.0	29.2	28.0	25.2	4.4	5.9	1.6	2.6
NL	20.5	19.8	3.6	3.0	4.3	3.5	7.0	8.2
P	26.0	25.9	-2.9	-2.1	17.2	8.1	4.1	5.2
UK	16.7	15.0	-1.8	-2.9	8.9	3.5	8.8	10.4
E12	20.8	19.3	-1.1	-0.4	7.0	3.8	8.8	10.6

Source: Commission (1993a and 1993b)

Since Ricardo's *Principles* (1817: preface), the principle problem of political economy has been one: "To determine the laws which regulate this distribution [rent, profit, and wages]...". In Keynes's (1923) world, debt servicing is a transfer of income from taxpayers to the holders of bonds and this transfer is the cause of depression because the latter class does not consume or invest it all. In other words, income distribution is the principle problem because it is correlated with investment, capital accumulation and production.

The theoretic interest in the *Gross Fixed Capital Formation* indicator stems from the fact that income distribution depends on the rate of investment. Investment is a primary determinant of output, employment and distribution. Consequently, the investment capacity of the public sector, given the relationship between growth, budget deficit and debt as expressed in equations (1) to (3), will be limited by its level of debt. Debt, debt servicing and investment are correlated. In general, "...[the share of profits to income] (π/Y) would always depend on [the capitalists's propensity to consume] c_c, suggesting, of course, that the profit share and rate of profit depend on the consumption/saving behaviour of those who live off capital" (Arestis, 1992: 136).

The GFCF is assumed to stand for commitments of investment (private and public) and is the source of economic growth, capital accumulation and welfare. Efforts of countries to build a sustainable economic base will be reflected in the ratio of GFCF/GDP; its effects will be shown on reducing budgetary deficits. Table 2.5 shows the development of GFCF expressed as percentage of GDP. The EU's 19.3% in 1993 was higher than the USA's 15.8% but lower than Japan's 29.7%.

The *compensation of employees* stands as a proxy of expected inflation. The choice of this variable is justified by the cost structure of Community GDP. Compensation of employees accounts for about 52% of GDP. Service, the more labour intensive sector of the EC economy, accounted for about 61% of civilian employment in 1990 while in some Member States: Belgium, Denmark, Netherlands and UK, the service sector accounted for about 68%. It is this sector's wage settlements that determine those of industry and of agriculture and which influence the expected inflation rate.

At a theoretical level, the compensation of employees is the single most important indicator, plus investment, of the *supply side* performance of a country. "Wage developments have a pivotal role to play not only in the process of convergence and in sustaining macro-economic stability but also in revitalizing an employment-creating growth trend in the Community at the present time" (Commission, 1993b: 29).

As Table 2.5 shows, wage moderation has meant the decline in the rate of compensation of employees in the EU from 7% in 1991 to 3.8% in 1993. With an 11% unemployment rate in 1993, wage increases have been slowed down and expected to remain below the rate of inflation. This wage moderation is reflected in the evolution of real unit labour costs (an amalgam of real wage and productivity). According to the Commission (1993b), the decline in real unit costs has contributed strongly to profitability of capital in almost all Member States.

The *balance of current account* is chosen because it mirrors the real factors influencing the performance of a country, the structural changes and its competitiveness; the evolution of the individual items is the mirror of an economy. This is so despite the fact that the financing of current account deficits is not an external constraint due to fully liberalised capital movements. Given the functional relationship of exports being a function of the rate of exchange, that of imports being a function of disposable income and that of capital flows being a function of the rate of interest, a deficit or surplus need not be a good or bad development. Suppose high unemployment is to be dealt with by policies geared to favouring inward foreign investment; an initial surplus may be shown; it would also alleviate the constraint imposed on the level of investment by the level of saving. But as activity increases and disposable income rises, imports will increase and the initial surplus would be self-correcting.

According to Table 2.5, a current account surplus emerged in those Member States where demand was depressed resulting in high unemployment rate, such as Belgium, Denmark, Ireland, Luxembourg and the Netherlands. Sustained deficits were recorded in the same period in Greece, Spain, Portugal and the UK, reflecting partly the real appreciation of their currencies due to an economic upswing. The case of Germany is interesting; unification transformed a surplus into a deficit because of income transfers and wage increases in East Germany.

Lastly, the *unemployment rate* is by far the more reliable indicator of economic activity and a test for the potency of policy instruments. As Table 2.5 shows, within three years (1991-93), the unemployment rate has risen from 8.8% to 10.6%, which was as high as in 1985. There was no uniform rate of unemployment in the EU and large differences were prevailing. The highest rates in 1993 were recorded in Spain and Ireland with 21.2% and 18.4% respectively while the lowest in Luxembourg (2.6%) followed by Portugal (5.2%). The trend, however, was the same; unemployment increased in all Member States.

From Tables 2.3 and 2.5, we have constructed the EMU potential convergence index of economic activity for 1993 shown in Table 2.6.

Table 2.6
EMU convergence potential index for 1993

B	DK	D	GR	E	F	IRL	I	L	NL	P	UK
113	53	25	104	24	18	61	90	-41	56	49	34

Source: Tables 2.3 and 2.5

Some qualifications about our EMU convergence index of economic potential should be made. For computational purposes, GFCF is subtracted from debt on the assumption that all GFCF is financed by government bonds. The current account deficit/surplus is added to/ subtracted from debt because it represents the need for more borrowing if in deficit and the possibility of paying back part of debt if in surplus. Compensation of employees is added to debt because higher wages cause an increase in inflation and in interest rates which lead to higher debt servicing. The unemployment rate is subtracted from debt because it causes moderation of wages and thus lowers inflation leading to lower interest rates and lower debt servicing.

The EMU convergence potential index is not an objective indicator; its strength rests with its suggestive capacity; it recommends to the countries with a high value of EMU convergence potential index, the type of adjustment necessary before the third stage. It avoids the strictness of the EMU nominal criteria and the backward-looking feature of the Gros and Thygesen indicator. Our index is offered as an alternative in discussing 'what should be done today for convergence tomorrow'. The ranking of Member States is also arbitrary although, they are clustered around distinct values.

Three distinct groups could be formed from Table 2.6. The first consists of France, Germany, Spain and Luxembourg (which has an -41 reflecting its very low debt/GDP, not representative of the EC); the index of this group rages between 18 and 25 points. This group differs from that of Gros and Thygesen; the Netherlands and Denmark are excluded because of their high debt/GDP ratios and low GFCF/GDP ratios. Spain is included because of its low debt/GDP and high GFCF/GDP ratio.

The second group includes those Member States that have an index falling within the bounds of 34 to 60; these are: the UK, Portugal   Denmark, Netherlands and, almost, Ireland. This group retains its dynamism but needs adjustment. It differs from the second group of Gros and Thygesen because Belgium is relegated to the third group, due to its very high debt/GDP ratio.

The third group consists of laggards: Belgium, Greece and Italy, they all have an index above 90. All three have below average GFCF/GDP ratios, while two of them, Belgium and Italy are rather competitive, Greece is not and has an unemployment rate below the EEC average. The effort of adjustment required for these countries is herculean.

2.10 Institutions

The underlying premise of this thesis is that the design, the internal structure, the decision-making bodies and the objectives of monetary institutions are more important factors in determining the path of growth or stagnation than the division of labour and specialisation. In this context, we accept North's (1991: 97) postulate:

Institutions are the humanly devised constraints that structure political, economic and social interaction. They consist of both informal constraints (sanctions, taboos, customs, traditions and codes of conduct) and formal rules (constitutions, laws, property rights). Throughout history, institutions have been devised by human beings to create order and reduce uncertainty in exchange.

It is of importance therefore to know whether EMU's institutions would reduce uncertainty in exchange and investment and thus create an economic environment that would induce increasing productivity.

EMU provides for two consultative bodies, a Monetary Committee[22] and an Economic and Finance Committee, as well as two institutions: EMI and ECB. In a forthcoming report by the European Parliament (1994), the role, independence and accountability of these institutions are to be examined. It will suffice here to concentrate on the EMI and ECB.

2.11 European Monetary Institute (EMI)

What differentiates stage one from stage two is the creation of the EMI on 1 January 1994. This will mean that the Committee of governors of national central banks would be dissolved and that the EMI, with its own legal identity, would take over the credit mechanisms and the tasks of the European Monetary Cooperation Fund.

There are, for any monetary institution, three constituent parts of *real power*: internal structure, independence and tasks. As to the internal structure of the EMI, its members are the national central banks and its governing administrative body is the Council.

As to the independence, Article 109e(5) makes compulsory the adoption of legislation by Member States to lead to the independence of their central banks and to make their statutes compatible with the statute of the ECSB. France has completed the parliamentary process of granting independence to its central bank. Belgium, Italy and Portugal have adapted their central bank laws. Spain is in the process of reforming its central bank act. Luxembourg and Greece are to submit to their Parliaments the required reforms.

In the same logic, the EMI Council must not seek or take instructions from Community bodies or governments.

As to the tasks, responsibility for monetary policy remains with national authorities. The EMI shall strengthen the cooperation between national central banks and the coordination of the monetary policies, thus ensuring price stability; it shall monitor the functioning of the EMS, facilitate the use of the ECU and oversee the development and smooth functioning of the ECU clearing system; it shall hold consultations with national central banks on issues affecting financial stability and the use of monetary policy instruments. The EMI shall be consulted by national central banks on monetary policy.

Another task of EMI would be to prepare the third stage by designing the instruments and procedures for carrying out a single monetary policy, by harmonising the compilation and distribution of statistics, by promoting the efficiency of EC cross-border payments and by supervising the technical preparation of ECU bank-notes.

Two factors limit this seemingly real power of EMI. First, the opinions or recommendations of EMI have no binding force (Art. 15.2 of EMI protocol). Second, the EMI is entitled to hold and manage foreign exchange reserves as an agent for and at the request of national central banks, but cannot use these reserves in ways that impair the monetary and exchange rate policies of any national monetary authority (Art. 6.4 of EMI protocol). Taking over the EMCF and administering the VSTF mechanism, STM support mechanism and MTF assistance does not entitle EMI to own reserves.[23]

2.12 European Central Bank (ECB)

What differentiates stage two from three is the establishment of the ECB. As soon as the ECB is established, the EMI shall go into liquidation; EMI's claims and liabilities will be settled with the national central banks in accordance with the key for the ECB capital subscription. The EMI's functions would be taken over by the ECB.

2.12.a) ECB instruments

The exclusive right to authorise the issue of bank-notes within the EU is conferred upon the Governing Council of the ECSB. Both the ECB and national central banks may issue such notes. The legal tender status within the EU will be carried only by bank-notes issued by the ECB and national central banks.

A second instrument of control available to the ECB is to require credit institutions established in Member States to hold minimum reserves in accounts with it and with national central banks. The calculation of the required minimum reserves shall be established by the Governing Council. In cases of non-compliance, the ECB shall levy penalty interest or impose other sanctions.

A third instrument of the ECB is open market operations. The general principles are established by the ECB. Both the ECB and national central banks may operate in the financial markets by buying and selling outright (spot and forward) or under repurchase agreement, by lending or borrowing claims and marketable instruments, in Community or non-Community currencies and in precious metals. They may also conduct credit operations with credit institutions and other market participants.

Quantitative credit controls, measures to regulate lending or interest rates or other instruments are considered incompatible with open and competitive markets.

There is a serious difference between effective policy making and imposition of strict operational rules for the ECB. As to the effective policy making, the ECB has been endowed with all possible power. But operational rules have not been stated in its statute. In the opinion of Crockett (1991: 8) "...the ESCB should operate without reserve requirements or, at the very least, should pay a market rate of interest on whatever reserves it requires banks to hold". Hall (1990: 283) expressed a similar view: "There is much to be said for using an interest instrument rather than a monetary-quantity instrument...If the bank pays higher interest on reserves, the demand for reserves rises and there is deflationary pressure. To stimulate the European Economy and raise prices, the central bank would increase the differential and decrease the demand for reserves". The same sentiment had been expressed by Ciampi (1989: 230), even for the second stage of EMU: "The ESCB could then carry out its monetary policy by focusing on the level of interest rate".

The choice of interest rates as an instrument of monetary policy is the recognition that the earlier practice relying on 'monetary aggregate targets' and on control via reserves had failed. Fry (1991: 494) attributed the failure to the unstable relationships between monetary aggregates and macroeconomic variables and between monetary aggregates and reserve money and added: "Financial innovation and liberalization appear to have eroded the stability of these relationships in most EC countries".

2.12.b) ECB independence

The legal independence of ESCB is guaranteed: 'neither the ECB, nor a national central bank, nor any member of their decision-making bodies shall seek or take instructions from Community institutions or bodies, from any Government of a Member State or from any other body' (Art. 107). The ECB 'shall enjoy in each of the Member States the most extensive legal capacity accorded to legal persons under their laws'.

"Political independence is defined as the ability of a Central Bank to autonomously choose her economic policy objectives without constraints or influence from government" (Alesina and Grilli, 1991: 11). Alesina and Grilli (1991) devised an index based on 8 factors: Governor and Executive not appointed by government, Governor and Executive Board appointed for more than 5 years, no mandatory government representative on Executive, no government approval of policy decision, statutory requirement to pursue price stability, no explicit conflicts between central bank and government. They arrived at the following conclusion: "...the ECB, according to this statute, will be as independent from national and European political institutions as the Bundesbank. In fact, the proposed statute is in many respects quite similar to that of Bundesbank" (p. 31).

Economic independence is defined by Alesina and Grilli (1991: 14) as "...the ability to use, without restrictions, monetary policy instruments to pursue monetary policy goals. Specifically, the most important and common constraint to the daily management of monetary policy derives from the Central Bank's obligations to finance public deficits". The index devised by Alesina and Grilli contained 8 factors of which four are related to government *credit* from the Central Bank: no automaticity, at market rate, for temporary period only, and limited in amount; two factors concern absence of government *controls* on quantitative and qualitative commercial bank lending; another two concern unsold government *bonds* not bought by central bank and *discount rate* set by central bank. Their conclusion for the ECB was: "...its level of independence will be high and, thus, its ability to credibly pursue its objectives should be guaranteed" (p. 15). In fact, it is as high as the Bundesbank's.

Why such an interest in the independence of ECB? The literature is rich. Three themes have been analyzed and measured: central bank independence and inflation, unemployment and inflation and growth and inflation. Cukierman, Webb and Neyapti (1992: 383) looked at the first theme for all members of the World Bank and found that: a) "Legal independence is an important and statistically significant determinant of price stability among industrial countries, but not among developing countries", b) "An inflation-based index of overall central bank independence...contributes significantly to explaining cross-country variations on the rate of inflation", c) "There seems to be a vicious circle between inflation and the lack of central bank independence, which deserves fuller investigation". These results confirm those by Alesina and Grilli (1991: 15): "...independent Central Banks have out-performed more dependent ones. In particular, independent Central Banks appear to have been quite successful in maintaining a low inflation rate without high costs in terms of output stabilisation or growth".

Neumann (1991), the Commission (1990), the Bank of England (1992) and many others have estimated various measures of the Phillips curve. The endogenous adjustment of inflationary expectations, it is argued, has destroyed the stable trade-off between inflation and unemployment. The Bank of England estimated the Phillips curve by taking the unemployment rate as an independent variable and inflation as dependent, and found for the period of 1950-91, a weak positive correlation.

Alesina and Summers (1990), Gros and Thygesen (1992), among many, have examined the relation between economic growth and inflation. The Commission (1990: 90) estimated it for the OECD countries and concluded that 'there is a strong negative relationship between income and inflation for the period 1975-85', and 'there is no statistically significant relationship between growth and inflation for the period 1955-85'.

However, there is an issue at stake here. Constitutional guarantees of independence do not automatically ensure price stability. A second element is needed and this has to do with the benefits organised interest groups derive from price stability. Yet organised interest groups differ substantially between less developed countries and more advanced ones. Historical experiences with hyperinflation resulting in destruction of assets do not explain *why* inflation is resisted in one society but not in another, although the two had experienced the same dire effects of inflation.

A possible reliable explanation rests with our premise that institutions, being the expression of organised interests, would resist inflation because otherwise their fundamental incentive to exist would be shaken and their benefits would diminish. In such a context and if our money process (M-C-M*), see chapter 6, is accepted, the financial sector plays an important role. The structure of financial systems would give an additional support to an anti-inflation bias. However, the structure of financial systems consists of banking (universal or not), width and depth of financial market and prudential supervision.

2.13 Prudential supervision

Two of the most important banking roles of a Central Bank: lender of last resort and prudential supervision, are missing.[24] Received central bank theory argues that the lender of last resort is about providing liquidity at times of distress in order to prevent failures. Hence the integrity of the financial system needs supervision that the central bank should exercise. The statute of the ESCB refers to open market and credit operations which allow the ECB and national central banks to 'conduct credit operations with credit institutions and other market agents' (Art. 18). This amounts to a secondary responsibility that does not even meet Bagehot's lender of last resort rule.

The half-commitment of the ECB to prudential supervision should be noted: 'The ECB may offer advice to and be consulted by...on the scope and implementation of Community legislation relating to prudential supervision of credit institutions and to the stability of the financial system' (ECB Statute, Art. 25). Even if the Council were to confer on the ECB 'specific tasks' in this matter, the same article states that prudential supervision will cover 'credit institutions and other financial institutions except insurance undertakings'. Hence the ECB is limited to the task of counsellor and monitor.

Neither is it clear if the present situation is to be maintained. Of the twelve national central banks, three Member States: Belgium, Denmark and Germany have a separate body responsible for supervision; the rest have retained the old central banks' supervisory role. Article 14.4 of the ECB Statute provides national central banks with the option of performing 'functions other than those specified'. However, this can only be done if these *new tasks* do not 'interfere with the objectives and tasks of the ESCB'. Hence there would *not* be a clear responsibility for prudential supervision.

The CEPR report (1991: 105) proposed the centralisation of banking supervision on the grounds that financial integration increases the exposure of banks in one country to those in another and liquidity shortfalls is transmitted via the payment systems to other countries: "The principle of subsidiarity therefore requires that responsibility for regulation be transferred to a central body when either European financial integration is well advanced or the single currency is introduced". Prate (1992: 15) went further: "Within the regulatory domain, one can imagine creating...a "Prudential Committee", bringing together the responsible parties from the national regulatory bodies, representative from the Commission and, as from 1994, also form the [EMI], and eventually the [ECB]".

In chapter 7, where we examine the money externalities internalised by the ECB, we argue that the two roles of lender of last resort and prudential supervision have merged into one: *last resort of systemic risk*. Systemic risk (defined as a bank-run that stems from the fear of one bank failure leading to a mass withdrawal of funds from many banks and causing a collapse of the entire system) could be dealt with by recognising that it is an endogenous feature of global capital and financial markets. It is induced by the internalisation of money externalities generated by the unregulated cross-border netting schemes and payment systems. In this sense, systemic risk is *institutional*. It is the main cause of financial instability to which we return in chapter 7.

2.14 The European Currency Unit (ECU)

The theoretical anchor of the system is the ECU and an important article of the TEU is 109g:

> The currency composition of the ECU basket shall not be changed. From the start of the third stage the value of the ECU shall be irrevocably fixed in accordance with Article 109l(4).

This article is the most important for at least four reasons. First, it links the EMS with the second stage of EMU. Second, the ECU links the three mechanisms of EMS: exchange rate, intervention, and credit with EMU. Third, behind the words: 'fixity of the composition of the ECU basket and of the value of the ECU', all traditional monetary theory of money is hidden. Fourth, Article 109l(4) specifies the method of establishment of the ECU as a single currency of the system.

The official ECU is defined dually: a) by its composition and b) by its functions. Pursuant to the Resolution of the European Council establishing the EMS (hereafter 'Resolution'),[25] the value and the composition of the ECU is identical with the value of the European Unit of Account (EUA).[26] At the day of entry of the EMS on 13 March 1979, the ECU was defined as the sum of 'fixed' amounts of nine Community currencies.[27] On 17 September 1984, the Greek drachma and on 21 September 1989, the Spanish peseta and the Portuguese escudo were included.[28] The fixed amounts and weights of currencies of the ECU basket were changed as the EMS evolved.[29] The revised composition and relative weights are shown in Table 2.7.

Table 2.7
Composition of the ECU basket

	a) 13.3.79		b) 17.9.84		c) 29.9.89	
	Amount	Weight	Amount	Weight	Amount	Weight
DM	0,828	32.98	0,719	32.1	0,6242	32.00
FF	+1,15	19.83	+1,31	19.1	+1,332	19.29
HFL	+0,286	10.51	+0,256	10.2	+0,22	9.48
BFR	+3,66	9.27	+3,71	8.2	+3,301	8.08
LFR	+0,14	0.36	+0,14	0.3	+0,13	0.20
LIT	+109	9.50	+140	10.1	+152	10.23
DKR	+0,217	3.06	+0,219	2.7	+0,197	2.59
IRL	+0,0076	1.15	+0,0087	1.2	+0,0086	1.11
UK	+0,0885	13.34	+0,0878	14.8	+0,0878	12.06
DR			+1,15	1.3	+1,44	0.95
PTA					+6,885	5.15
ESC					+1,393	0.81
	=1 ECU		=1 ECU		=1 ECU	

Source: Council Regulations 3180/78, 2626/84, 1971/89

All EMS currencies have two values: a *central rate* and a *market rate*. The official *central rates* would remain constant as long as there are no currency realignments and as long as the fixed amounts of the basket remain constant. The *market values* of all EMS currencies for one ECU are computed directly by taking into account the actual market rates of each ECU component quoted by commercial banks given the value of one ECU. It follows that the 'market value' of one ECU or of all EMS currencies is dependent on the relative weights of each currency component *and* on the respective value of the fixed amounts as evaluated in the market. Hence they vary in line with the daily exchange rate movements.

The weight of the amount of each currency in the ECU basket plays an important role.[30] Currencies with large weight tend to move the ECU more than the small ones. The ECU market value of currency i would stand at a premium or discount against its ECU central rate depending on whether currency i appreciates or depreciates in the exchange market at that time. ECU-central rate and ECU-market rate are identical for currency i when it is at a par with each of the other currencies in the ECU basket.

There are at least five ways in which a fixed-weight basket or constant-value ECU could be achieved. Each of them corresponds to a definition of the ECU and each of them corresponds to a version of monetary theory. The first is the current 'composite currency ECU'; the second is the 'frozen ECU' as stated in Article 109g of the EMU Treaty; the third is the Spanish/German 'hardened ECU'; the fourth is the UK's 'hard ECU' and the fifth is the 'constant-value ECU'.

Freezing the composition of the ECU means no further additions to the number of currencies that make up the basket and abolition of the five yearly recomposition.

The *hardened ECU* maintains the basket ECU but insists that the ECU be redefined every time a realignment occurs so that the ECU exchange rate of the strongest currency be stable. The German proposal (1991) proposed to do it by increasing the basket amount of the currency or currencies which had appreciated most or by simultaneously reducing the amount of depreciating currencies, or both. The Spanish proposal (1991) ensured the ECU's parity against the strongest currency at times of realignment by increasing the individual currency components of the devalued currencies.

The *hard ECU* proposed by the UK (1990) retains its basket nature but attaches a condition to it: 'it will not be allowed to devalue against any national currency in a realignment'. For example, the quantities of the weaker currencies are added automatically in the same proportion as they depreciate whereas the amounts of the appreciating currencies remain unchanged.

There are various ways by which one could maintain the average value of the *ECU constant*. One is to have an 'inflation-proof ECU'. Another is to define it with respect to a basket of commodities, or through competitive monetary policies, or by fixing the percentage weights in the ECU basket.

We analyze the frozen and hardened ECU in the subsequent sections and the hard and constant-value ECU in chapter 4. If we see the ECU in the context of Article 109g and Article 109l, we should notice that the value of the frozen ECU, with the gradual convergence of prices, will be stabilised; it will be transformed into a hardened ECU at the start of stage three when the exchange rates of national currencies with respect to the ECU is to be irrevocably fixed. The full-fledged EMU will begin the moment the ECU ceases to have its characteristics of a basket currency and becomes a currency in its own right, as long as the external value of the ECU is maintained. During stage three, the Council of the Member States in stage three shall, by unanimity, decide how the national currencies will be replaced by the ECU. Only then will the European Currency Unit become the *ecu*, the single currency of the system. As to the value of the ECU with respect to the dollar or Yen or Sraffa's (1960) imaginary standard commodity, it cannot be held constant unless the internalisation of money externalities by the ECU is maintained fixed or a stationary state is established. This is the theoretical essence of the provisions of the EMU.

Yet the provisions of the TEU have taken over all mechanisms defined in the Resolution on the EMS. The functional definition of the ECU is also stated in the EMS Resolution. The ECU is used as:

a) the denominator for the exchange rate mechanism;
b) the basis for a divergence indicator;
c) the denominator for the intervention and credit mechanisms;
d) a means of settlement between monetary authorities of the EC.

As the denominator for the exchange rate mechanism (ERM), the ECU is used to construct the bilateral central rates and intervention limits for each currency.[31]

As to the divergent indicator, both the central and market rates of the ECU are relevant. "The divergence indicator (DI) measures the degree of movement of a specific currency against its maximum divergence spread" (Commission, 1979: 87). Reviewing the performance of the DI, the Commission (1984: 12) said:

> It has lost much of its significance, and has often failed to give the expected signal for two main reasons: first, its technical short-comings, due to the impossibility of taking full and accurate account of different weights in the ECU, and of entirely eliminating the influence of component currencies that are not subject to the narrow band; and secondly, the bias introduced because certain bilateral relations within the system have been considered, in practice, more important than others.

As to the third function of the ECU, i.e. denominator for the intervention mechanism, "[w]hen a currency crosses its 'threshold of divergence', this results in a presumption that the authorities concerned will correct this situation by adequate measures, namely: i) diversified intervention; ii) measures of domestic monetary policy; iii) changes in central rates; iv) other measures of economic policy" (EMS Res., A. § 3.5).

The Resolution is not explicit on the nature of the four adjustment measures.[32] It was left to the Governors of national central banks to work out the operating procedure and rules in a form of an 'Agreement' between the central banks; it was agreed out on 13 March 1979 and stipulates the governing procedures for the mechanisms of the EMS.[33]

The nature of intervention policies depends on the size of intervention resources. This mechanism incorporates the credit mechanisms under the snake system: a) Very-short-Term-Facility (VSTF), b) Short-Term Monetary Support (STMS), c) Medium Financial Assistance (MFA).[34]

Whereas the ECU represents the liability side of the EMCF, the credit mechanisms represent its asset side. Whereas the exchange rate and intervention mechanism represents the tensions created in such an arrangement, the credit mechanisms represent the means by which tensions among participating currencies are relieved.

Expressing debts and credits in terms of ECU implies a burden-sharing of an exchange rate risk for both creditor and debtor, in the event of a realignment of central rates; this is so because if one central rate is adjusted, all the others follow suit. Suppose France swaps FF for DM for a loan assumed to be repaid in DM. If in the meantime, the franc parity is realigned downward, France would lose by buying back DM at a higher rate. If France borrows ECUs which Germany has deposited, the loss to France equals the ECU-franc depreciation. This will be less than the FF/DM fall.[35]

2.15 European Monetary Cooperation Fund (EMCF)

Since 1 January 1994, the EMI has assumed responsibility for the EMCF. However, the origin of the official ECU resides with the fourth function of the ECU to be realised by the EMCF. "To serve as a means of settlement, an initial supply of ECU's will be provided by the EMCF against the deposit of 20% of gold and 20% of dollar reserves currently held by the central banks" (Res. A.3.8). This is the only supporting element in the Resolution regarding the EMCF, which is neither the managing institution of the credit facilities nor does it own the reserves.

The deposited 20% of gold and 20% of dollars with the EMCF in return for ECUs are in the form of legal contracts for three-month revolving swaps. Thus the gold and dollar portions are then repaid to the central banks, revalued according to a formula based on the recent market prices of gold and dollar, and then deposited again in return for equivalent amount of ECUs. In short, the depositing procedure is merely a book-keeping ritual and no gold or dollar physically leaves the national central banks, which remain responsible for the deposited amounts with the EMCF and earn interest on their dollar deposits. The value of the EMCF reserves is variable; it depends on the daily value of gold; for example, in April 1979, it was equivalent to 165 ECU per ounce but, in April 1982, to 327 *and* the market value of the dollar which is equally variable, since its floating.

The utilisation of the ECU is stated in Art. 18 of the Agreement. ECUs are used for: a) intra-community settlements; b) transfer of ECUs to one another central bank against dollars, EEC currencies, SDRs or gold; c) acquiring dollars against ECU from the EMCF between two periodic adjustments.

There is a remuneration clause: "Central banks whose ECU assets are less than their forward sales of ECUs shall pay interest to the EMCF on the difference between these two aggregates" (Art. 19); there is also a liquidation clause: "... net users of ECU assets shall bring these back up to a level equal to that of their forward sales and central banks that are net accumulators shall transfer to the net users the excess of their ECU assets" (Art. 20).

What do all these institutional provisions amount to? First, the ECU has no existence of its own. "With the current system of three-month revolving swaps, the vast majority of ECU reserves do not have an existence of their own. They simply represent, under a different name, the particular gold and dollars belonging to the central bank concerned ...for at the end of that period if the swaps are unwound, so that all the participants reclaim their original amount of gold and dollars, these ECUs also lose their existence" (Padoa-Schioppa, 1980: 335).

Second, the use of the ECUs is limited. The ECU spot settlements in the ERM for the period 1979-85 amounted to $6.0 billion. "Their attractiveness as an asset is further circumscribed by their limited acceptability...; accumulated creditor positions in ECU are not convertible; and the yield is low (being an average of official discounts rates" (Commission, 1984: 10).

Third, the official ECU can be only held by EC central banks and, since 1985, by other official 'designated institutions'. Holdings by non-EC official institutions, such as BIS and central banks of the Scandinavian countries and Austria, have remained minimal. Until 1985, the official ECU paid no return to the holder. This reluctance was due to the resistance of some national central banks to extend large credits through the VSTF when such ECU holdings could be remunerated at an interest rate between 3 to 4 per cent below the rates paid for similar maturities in the private ECU market. Even after the interest rate of the official ECU was brought close to market rates in 1985, the use of the official ECU did not expand. The fear of a parallel currency that could undermine the monetary target or rule of central bank has made them reluctant.

Fourth, even in the exchange and intervention mechanism, the ECU has not assumed fully its two-fold functions: denominator and calculation of the divergence indicator. "Also, the ECU is not used in practice as the numeraire when there is a realignment of central rates. The consequences for the ECU are deduced from the desired bilateral rate changes rather than vice versa, clearly demonstrating the strong bilateral nature of the system" (Padoa-Schioppa, 1980: 335).

Fifth, the official ECU is purely a *credit instrument*. "In practice, however, the ECU is considered not so much as a reserve asset but as a means of credit that will eventually have to be settled using other assets" (Commission, 1984: 10). This aspect of the ECU is further treated in ch. 4 where we demonstrate the consistency of a parallel currency *only if* it is an investment or credit instrument.

Sixth, the official ECU circulates only among central banks and cannot be exchanged against ECUs held by the private sector. There are, therefore, two separate ECU circuits: one for the central banks with the official ECU and another for the private sector with the private ECU. Linking the official ECU with the private ECU has been opposed by national central banks for fear that it will lead to greater liquidity.

2.16 The private use of the ECU

The private use of the ECU (or private ECU) is a contract between private agents that agree to accept payment obligations in ECU. These contracts are usually based on the 'open-basket ECU' definition.[36] It is called so because it is based on the official composition of the ECU though it changes composition when the official composition changes. Thus, if a ten-year ECU bond was concluded in 1983, it was based on the initial composition of the ECU basket shown in Table 2.7. But when the bond matures in 1993, it will be repaid with ECU containing the drachma, peseta and escudo shown in Table 2.7.

As we argue in chapter 3, the private ECU has made a breakthrough in ECU bond issues, ECU money market and even in ECU derivatives. The private ECU has assumed money attributes such as a financing currency, hedging and trading instrument and an investment currency. It is thus important to explore the implications for and the meaning of the divergence between the actual ECU exchange rate from its theoretical value (i.e. the rates that can be obtained by unbundling the currencies that constitute the ECU) as well as the divergence between the actual rate of interest from its theoretical value.

Until 1990, it was assumed that arbitrage would limit the actual movement of the ECU exchange rate and of the ECU interest rate relative to the theoretical rates. Gros and Thygesen (1992: 218) found:

> Moreover, statistical analysis...shows that until early 1990 there was a strong tendency for the value of the ecu to go back to the value of the basket. After early 1990 this tendency becomes very weak and finally disappears during the year. ...This result suggests that in 1990 the ecu did indeed become independent from the basket.

The same statistical result applies to the rate of interest. Gros and Thygesen (1992: 220) stated:

A statistical analysis of the interest-rate differential (actual minus theoretical) suggests a growing independence for the ecu. Before early 1990 there was a strong tendency for it to return to zero, but after late 1990 this changes and in statistical terms the interest-rate differential becomes also a random walk.

If the *autonomy* of the exchange rate of the private ECU is secured and the ECU interest rate *independence* is established by the markets, then the Triffin postulate (chapter 3) suggests that the ECU as a parallel currency will be established by the private, not the public sector. Thus, we need a monetary theory to analyze the monetary role of a parallel currency and this is Walras's paper money treated in chapter 4.

It should be noted that the international aspect of the ECU might develop at a faster pace than the domestic. The question then is to know if an internationally established ECU could be a better method by which the ECU could transform its basket character into a currency of its own. We examine this theme under the Cipolla thesis in chapter 3.

If, in money and capital markets, the private ECU has set in motion a *parallel currency*, given the dual definition of the ECU by its functions and its frozen composition, it raises all the basic questions of monetary theory, that occupy us in the remainder of this book:
a) What is money?
b) Where does money originate?
c) What assets are likely to be used as money?
d) What are the costs/benefits of the existence of money?
e) By what means does money get established?

2.17 How others have seen EMU

Understanding the economic logic of EMU necessitates a prior understanding of the Delors report (1989) and, in particular, the papers that had been submitted to the Committee entrusted to study and propose concrete stages leading to EMU. The lukewarm position of the Delors report that 'a monetary union does not necessarily require a single currency' is due to Duisenberg (1989). The fixity of exchange rates prior to adopting the ECU as a single currency is due to Pöhl (1989). The federal organisation of the ECB is the work of Thygesen (1989). The fiscal rules on deficits and debt should be sought in Lamfalussy (1989). Campi (1989) should be credited for a new approach to monetary policy restricted by the loss of instruments. The unnecessary centralisation of fiscal policy stems from Baer and Padoa-Schioppa (1989).

What the Werner and Delors reports have achieved could be summarised in a phrase: 'a new academic interest in monetary matters'. This new interest has resulted in a voluminous literature on the Werner and Delors reports, the EMS and EMU; it can be usefully arranged in three approaches: 'exchange rate', 'institutional' and 'parallel currency'.

The *exchange rate approach* has emphasised the pros and cons of the fixed versus flexible exchange rates regimes and has been extended to cover theoretical constructions like Williamson's target zones[37] or McKinnon's tripartite co-ordination of monetary policy.[38] The theoretical logic of such proposals stem from the optimum currency areas literature.[39]

Using the tools of the exchange rate approach, Feldstein (1992) argued against EMU. His opposition is centred on the idea that a single market does not require a single currency because a single currency is likely to reduce intra-European trade. This would result because the EC is not an optimum currency area, since labour and wage rate flexibility is missing.[40] Any fixity of exchange rates will lead to stagnation in poorer countries. Currency volatility does not inhibit trade. Yet price stability, acceptable as an objective, needs a change in public attitudes rather than a monetary rule. Hence Feldstein proposes flexible exchange rates in order to regain the interest rate and exchange rate instruments.

Feldstein's recipe might work provided that his flexible exchange rate is accompanied by capital controls which safeguard it against the globalisation of markets. Otherwise the recipe is misleading because in the presence of mobile capital, monetary policy and exchange rate policy are really one instrument, not two, and that is the interest rate. The expansion of global finance has tied monetary policy and exchange rate policy together, while expectations coupled with interest rate differentials largely determine exchange rates.

The *institutional approach* begins from the premise that the TEU empowers the Community to take action in the monetary field and hence advance to the final stage of the EMU.[41] The theoretical case of this approach rests firmly with the State theory of money. To the extent that EMU is an essentially political undertaking, the logic of this approach could lead one to argue that, since the *means* are given, only the *interests* play a role. Hence, if the interests of those countries that matter are satisfied, EMU could be made a European Federal System reflecting the interests and experience of those countries.

If the appropriate institutions are not there to coordinate monetary and fiscal policies, Meade (1990: 100) believes EMU might prove to be 'unstable'. The Keynesian apparatus that emphasises the interdependence of fiscal and monetary policies is used to state: "Any strategy which implied conducting monetary policy so as to control inflation without regard to its effects on budget balances and of conducting fiscal policies so as to control budget balances without regard to their effect on price inflation, could turn out to be a recipe for economic and monetary instability". Of the four possible paths for a solution only two offer a satisfactory outcome: either 'do not build an EMU' or 'fiscal policy and monetary policy must be centralised'. We return to this matter in chapter 7 and offer a solution to Meade's instability.

The *parallel currency approach* has its roots in Plato (see chapter 5), but the idea that the ECU should be a parallel currency in the EC has as its father, Triffin (1977, 1979, 1980, 1984 and 1986). His writings constitute an approach, which is analyzed under the Triffin Postulate in chapter 3. The postulate asserts that it will be the private sector which first establishes the private ECU in the market. Once established, it will, as it has happened with all previous reforms of monetary systems, force national monetary authorities to adopt it as a single currency.

A variant of the parallel currency approach is that of the Neo-Walrasian camp examined in detail in chapter 4. The idea is to use the market in order to establish the ECU as a common currency which can co-exist as a thirteenth currency. The theoretical case was made by Walras's *Elements* where paper money co-existed with gold and silver. Whether a single currency will ever be established is a matter for the market. Gresham's Law will apply in reverse: good money drives out bad.

2.17.a) Two speed EMU[42]

A variant of the exchange rate approach is the two-speed monetary union. The theoretical case was made by the former President of the Bundesbank, Dr Pöhl (1993). The details have been supplied by the Association for the Monetary Union of Europe (1993) for the second stage of EMU. The essence of the recommendation made by the AMUE is stated in its paragraph 485: "a stability zone forming a broadened anchor for the rest of the countries could at the beginning comprise Germany, France, Belgium, Luxembourg, Holland and Denmark". The choice of these countries is made on two main criteria: 'price stability' and 'exchange rate stability', and a secondary criterion 'interest rate convergence'. It proposes the *formation of a monetary union by five Member States* who fulfil the nominal convergence criteria of the TEU. These five Member States will 'serve as a stable anchor for those countries where further adjustment to convergence is still required'.

The stability zone of these five countries will be endowed with "...an additional unlimited long-term finance facility (extra-facility for short) for foreign exchange market interventions. The asset settlement mechanism for these facilities is indefinitely suspended. Central bank interventions drawing on the facility are not sterilized. Access to the facility is limited, but not automatic, and subject to a number of conditions" (§ 510).

In order to maintain a code of conduct among the five, the EMI will 'survey and monitor each central bank's adherence to the agreement'. The agreement will be something similar agreed upon by the central banks of the EMS, on how to implement the core group's monetary union. Hence the EMI, without power of decision, will be made 'an independent arbitrator'.

Certain conditions are attached to the would-be agreement:a) a non-devaluation clause, conditional on using the extra-finance-facility (EFF), b) a consistency rule for monetary policy: 'Money supply is then to grow in proportion to a commonly agreed nominal (or unavailable) rate of inflation plus the expected growth rate of potential output' (§ 525), c) a no sterilization of reserve flows clause aided mainly by EFF.

It is recognised by the AMUE that its kind of 'Monetary Union of the Five' presupposes autonomous and politically independent central banks as well as additional measures. These additional measures are about 'the voluntary acceptance of a productivity oriented wage rule' (§ 473). This wage rule will form the base of a European approach to an incomes policy.

A second element necessary for the 'MU of the Five' is to form 'an independent group of economic advisers, consisting of economic experts respected across Europe, to draw up an annual 'Report on Economic and Monetary Convergence in the EC" (§ 475). The task of the economic experts will be to act as impartial assessors of what is needed for the formulation of guidelines of the economic policies of the Member States so that economic policies of Member States become coherent and consistent with stability oriented growth.

The AMUE study neither states the assumptions under which its 'MU of the Five' will be possible, nor is it explicit on who gains and who bears the costs. It implicitly assumes that if the 'MU of the Five' succeeds, it will be good for the Community and this will be an external economy to the rest. If one adds to it that the formation of the 'MU of the Five' is associated with economic growth and price stability, then the economic logic rests with the welfare gains shared by the rest.

The AMUE study recognizes that its 'MU of the Five' essentially establishes a two-speed-Community and adds: "The Maastricht Treaty leaves little room for an institutional two-speed approach to EMU, at least after 1996" (§ 481). Yet it justifies its choice on welfare considerations.

The innovation introduced by the AMUE resides with its proposal to reform the present asset settlement rule of the EMS (the latter obliges national central banks to repay all interventions credits with foreign exchange reserves) by suspending the asset settlement rule via the introduction of the EFF.

This reform presupposes:
a) independent central banks,
b) high substitutability of the assets included in the definition of M3,
c) full control of money supplies by each of the five central banks,
d) equal partners within the 'core group',
e) an exogenously given supply of money for each of the five,

f)   the anchor currency is exogenous to the system.

The above six conditions lack realism and are misleading. They could be applicable if two of the conditions of the inconsistent trinity hold.   In the presence of global markets in trade, banking, finance, direct investment and capital, the assumptions of independent central banks, having full control of an exogenous money supply do not hold.

The assumptions of equal partners and of an anchor currency exogenous to the system cannot be made because among the 'MU of the Five' the dominant central bank is the Bundesbank and the anchor-currency to the five is the D-Mark.

The unrealistic assumption of the high substitutability of assets is shown by recalling the broader definition of the money supply, M3 (M3 = currency in circulation + sight deposits with banks + savings deposits + claims on monetary institutions + placements as deposits at statutory notice or with contractual maturity over one year).   For one country only, Germany, in February 1991, M3 was 719 839 mio ECU of which M1 accounted for 261 235 mio ECU.   In other words, about 64 per cent of the total money supply of the anchor currency is fully substitutable with the other partners of the 'MU of the Five'.

If the wage-setting is based on money wage increases being linked to productivity, the AMUE believes that the cost-push inflation will be dealt with and inflationary expectations will wither away;   uncertainty will then be manageable. However, this wage-setting rule does not necessarily conform to the varied practices in the twelve Member States.   If the service sector accounts for a substantial part of GDP, the measurement of productivity becomes difficult, almost impossible.

It is believed by the AMUE that speculation originates in a situation characterised by complete capital liberalisation and integrated finance and capital markets while labour markets are segmented and labour mobility is low.   Hence if the labour market is made flexible by a wage-productivity rule, speculation will be constrained.   This theoretical proposal is contrary to what the G 10 Report has found that global markets account for market instability leading to speculation.

Furthermore, the EFF may dispense with the existing repurchase-clause provided that a high degree of substitutability between assets denominated in various currencies exists. This could be demonstrated to exist *if interest rates have converged*. As Table 2.3 shows, the 'MU of the Five' in 1993, had the lowest long-term interest rate was 6.3% while its highest was 8.9%.

The more serious problem of the AMUE study is that it feeds speculation and encourages competitive devaluations as free-riders, by the countries that are not members of the 'MU of the Five'.   If both phenomena gain momentum, they may lead to the break up of the Single Market.

In short, the AMUE study slightly reforms the EMS; it effectively means reinforcing the dominant position of the Bundesbank whose currency has lost its relative capacity to internalise money externalities. By forming the 'MU of the Five', it maintains the D-Mark at the centre of the second stage of EMU, which will thus continue to internalise confidence externalities and capture seigniorage externalities.

2.18 Concluding remarks

The EU endowed with a single money would mean a new entity in Europe; it would introduce a new organization of economic and monetary affairs; it would shape the behaviour of economic agents and of jurisdictions; it would create new institutions and lay down the foundations for political union. EMU is both feared and needed.

EMU was conceived as a means to deal with the implications stemming from globalisation, for monetary and exchange rate policies, and financial instability. The economic logic of EMU rests with the premise that real income is determined by whatever determines the stock of money. This logic resides in a new orthodoxy, which praises price stability and convergence; yet price stability presupposes full control of the money supply while convergence requires binding rules that confine the limits of economic and monetary policies.

As the stages of EMU unfold so does the evolution of its institutions. We apply to EMU the premise that the design, internal structure and power of decision are more important factors determining the path of growth than, say, specialisation. In such a context, institutional convergence means granting independence to national central banks and voluntary transfer of national monetary sovereignty to the ECB.

The literature on the EMS and EMU[43] could be usefully divided into three approaches: *institutional*, *exchange rate* and *parallel currency*. The first two have treated a purely monetary phenomenon with tools not apt for monetary theory. The third is a case that shows that models inappropriate for analysing EMU are used for purposes other than that of monetary theory. All three approaches undermine the explanatory power of monetary theory. The latter is seen as a systematic body of hypotheses suggested by facts and framed for the purpose of *establishing interesting results*. In our case, it should explain the birth, evolution and transformation of EMU.

EMU could alternatively be examined by raising five questions that correspond to five hypotheses:

H1 Why has EMU been proposed and adopted in its present form? Is there a monetary disturbance that has given birth to EMU? This is the essence of the *Hicksian proposition of historical contingency.*

H2   When should one expect the final stage of EMU to begin? Is the stage of development of the Community appropriate for the introduction of a single money? These are the kind of questions the *Aristotelian notion of evolving money* is required to answer.

H3   How could one ensure the longevity of a monetary system? The *Cipolla thesis of the essential properties of monetary systems* seeks to provide an answer to this question.

H4   Which means are necessary for the transformation of existing or for the establishment of new institutions? The *Triffin postulate of the determinants of monetary reforms* entails an explanatory function to this effect.

H5   What purpose will EMU serve? This is a welfare question on the benefits and costs of such an enterprise. It also asks if allocative efficiency is improved and if equity is distorted. This is the meaning of the *Essentiality criterion on the nexus of monetary causality.*

Our alternative approach to EMU is based on the above five hypotheses and occupy us in the next and subsequent chapters.

Notes

1. See the Federal Reserve Act of 1913 and its evolution as recorded in FRS (1984) and the Committee of Governors (1993) for a comparative analysis of the institutional features of national central banks.
2. The European Council of Edinburgh, 11-12 December 1992, adopted an overall approach to the principle of sudsidiarity which lays down the areas of application. This approach has not changed EMU.
3. The TEU has replaced Articles 67 to 73 of the Rome Treaty from 1 January 1994. Consequently, Council Directive on the liberalization of capital movements (88/361/EEC) will cease to apply.
4. See Rogoff (1985), Eltis (1989) and Artis and Taylor (1988) for statistical evidence on onshore-offshore interest differential being more volatile for countries exercising capital controls.
5. See Schinasi (1989) for theoretical arguments to support the imperfect substitutability of assets even with mobile capital.
6. See Tobin (1984) for an early proposal, Summers and Summers(1990) and Steil (1992) for the latest proposals to regulate global markets at world level.
7. IMF's Sec. 3 states: "Members may exercise such controls as are necessary to regulate international capital movements, but no member may exercise these controls in a manner which will restrict payments for current transactions or which will unduly delay transfers of funds in settlement of commitments,...".
8. The debate dates back to Simons's article (1936) and is reviewed by Tobin (1980) who also takes the 'expectations camp' to task.
9. Frankel and Goldstein (1991) surveyed the literature on rules.
10. See OJ L 178, 8.7.1988 and Commission (1987) for an analysis.
11. See OJ No L 386, 30.12.1989 and Zavvos (1989) for an appraisal.
12. The theoretical case for fiscal rules on excessive deficits is made by Lamfalussy (1989) on four arguments: the absence of fiscal coordination, the inefficiency of capital markets in allocating savings, the fear over the price stability objective because fiscal expansion and the preservation of fixed exchange rates.
13. See the study commissioned by Observatoire Français des Conjonctures Economiques in Atkinson et al (1991); a reduction of unemployment rate by 1% could be achieved with a reduction of real wage rate by 0.6% taking ten years to have an effect on growth.
14. See Commission (1990: chapter 5) for similar results.
15. Currie and Hall (1986) and Begg (1989) have provided us with complete surveys on both the empirical literature and theories of exchange rate determination. Both present a picture of general failure. See also Allsop and Chrystal (1989) and Dornbusch (1987).

16. Thygesen (1986) appraised the ten first realignments of EMS and identified the second and the tenth as being successful cases of devaluations that changed the competitiveness of the countries concerned.

17. Frankel and Goldstein (1990) identified three other factors influencing the current account imbalance and thus exchange rates: a) level and composition of government spending, structure of taxes and borrowing standing; b) increased investment financed by foreign borrowing and its rate of return; c) nature of increased consumption associated with the current account imbalance.

18. Pursuant to Art. 148(2) of the Rome Treaty, for the deliberations at the Council, the Member States dispose of the following votes: Germany, France, Italy and UK: 10, Belgium, Greece, Holland and Portugal: 5, Spain: 8, Ireland and Denmark: 3, and Luxembourg: 2. Qualified majority is defined as 54 votes out of a total 76. A blocking minority is 23 votes. If the Council decides on a proposal from the Commission, the 54 votes could be any combination; in all other cases, the 54 votes should comprise at least 8 Member States.

19. The Balassa effect refers to the differences in productivity growth, ceteris paribus, between countries, which would cause substantial increases in prices of non-tradable in the country where productivity is higher; a 3% productivity difference causes a 4,3% GDP deflator difference.

20. See article by S. Brittan, "The harmful myth of hidden state debt", Financial Times, 15.12.1993, which refers to the estimates of the CS First Boston pamphlet on *Employment and Hidden Debt*.

21. See de Grauwe (1992), CEPR report (1991), Crawfort (1993) and Gros and Thygesen (1992)

22. Kees's article (1987) is a reliable source on the role and activities of the Monetary Committee set up in 1958.

23. See EP report (A3-0294/93), which seeks to give additional responsibilities to the EMI so as to reform the EMS.

24. Sarcinelli (1992: 135), concerned with the traditional functions of a central bank, criticised the design of the ECB: "Among the banking functions no longer in the foreground are those of lender of last resort and of guarantor of the proper working of the payment system; even though somewhat linked by their common roots, they are logically distinct".

25. Various sources have reproduced the Resolution of the European Council of 5 December 1978 on the establishment of the EMS and related matters such as Commission (1979), Ludlow (1982) and van Ypersele and Koeune (1985).

26. See Council Regulation (EEC) No. 3180/70 of 18.12.1978 (OJ L 379, 30.12.1978) which simply renamed the EUA as ECU and retained the composition unchanged.

27. There is a voluminous literature on the EMS. See Commission (1979) for the technical aspects of the EMS and for previous efforts of the Community towards economic and monetary union.

28. See Council Regulations (EEC) No. 2626/84 of 15.12.1984 (OJ L 247, 16.9.1984) and No.1971/89 of 19 June 1989 (OJ L 189, 4.7.1989) which modified Council Regulation No. 3180/78.

29. See Commission documents (1982 and 1989) for an appraisal of the system at different stages of its development.

30. Any change in the exchange rate of currency i in terms of the ECU, given the fixed quantity of currency i entering the basket, will change the market value of the ECU. But it will change the parities of all others with respect to their ECU in the opposite direction. The larger the weight of the said currency change, the greater the effect on the rest of the currencies.

31. The ERM's technical aspects are analyzed in the Deutsche Bundesbank (1979), Bank of England (1979). The origin of the ERM and the painful compromises reached are documented in Ludlow (1982). An early appraisal of EMS is found in Masera (1981), Davies (1982), Summer and Zis (ed)(1982), de Cecco (ed)(1983) Ungerer et al (1983), Wood (1983) and Thygesen (1984).

32. See Thygesen (1984) and Commission (1984) for an analysis of the first eight realignments. The ninth to fourteenth realignments have been commented in the annual economic reports of the Commission.

33. The Agreement between the central banks of the Member States of the EEC laying down the operating procedures for the EMS has been reproduced in Commission (1979) and in van Ypersele and Koeune (1986).

34. See Commission (1989) for an analysis of the Basle/Nyborg agreement and Ungerer (1990) for a comprehensive review of the developments and policies in the EMS since its inception up to EMU. Mazas and Santini (1988) analyzed the Nyborg agreement in the context of the accession of sterling to ERM.

35. See Reading (1979) on the risk share in the ERM when two central banks agree to intervene in order to keep their currencies, one at the top of the margin, the other at the bottom, within their bands.

36. Representative analyses of the basket currencies are those of Polak (1979), Thygesen (1980) and Coats (1982); Abraham et al (1984) and Moss (1984) use the theory of financial innovation.

37. Williamson (1983, 1985, 1986) coined the term 'target zones' so as to provide a framework whereby volatility and misalignments of exchange rates come to an end.

38. McKinnon (1982, 1984, 1986) has been insistent on a monetary agreement between the three principal world currencies: dollar, yen and

DM in an effort to end dirty floating and world inflation. McKinnon's blueprint is to return to some fixed exchange rate system amongst the three while Currie (1993) proposes an implicit rule for exchange rates amongst the G 7.

39. See Ishiyama (1975) for a survey on optimum currency areas and Marston (1984) for the case of small countries joining exchange rate unions. The recent contributions to the theory of economic integration are surveyed in Tovias (1991). A case by case application of the different definitions of optimum currency area to the ECU is undertaken by Narassiguin (1992).

40. Bini Smaghi and Vori (1992: 78) compared the EC with the US and found: "First, the economies of the EC countries are more homogenous than those of the US and therefore less likely to experience asymmetric disturbances. Secondly, the exchange rate instrument is less efficient in the EC, because of the higher real wage rigidity and the scarce labour mobility within the EC states. Finally, powerful budgetary tools are available both in the EC and the US to face asymmetric shocks".

41. A representative analysis of the institutional approach is the Delors report (1989), Gros and Thygesen (1988, 1990, 1992), Collignon (1990) and the Commission (1990).

42. This section first appeared in the EP report (A3-0296/93).

43. There are numerous contributions to the debate ranging from the enthusiasts (Emerson, 1990; De Grauwe et al, 1992; Bean, 1992), to neo-Marxists (Fotopoulos, 1991; Bryan, 1992) who see only the deflationary aspects of EMU, to sceptics (Meade, 1989, 1990; Fry 1991; Dornbusch, 1991; Folkerts-Landau and Garber, 1991; Atkison et al, 1992) and many others cited in the subsequent chapters.

3   A monetary-theoretic approach to EMU

3.1 Introduction

Monetary institutions that we have so far considered are interwoven with systems of debts and credits, of claims and obligations, of specialised information and internalised externalities and of banking and financial intermediaries.   They originate, evolve and are transformed because such complex interwound relationships involve considerations of purpose, implicit or explicit. As the purpose changes, so will the structure of such institutions evolve. It is therefore important to know the forces at work that define the purpose and so change the structure.

Reference to examples of monetary unification might provide us with invaluable information but cannot answer *why* the structure changes. EMU seen in such a context should not be regarded as unique in monetary history. Attempts at monetary unification have been made and will continue to be made as long as the underlying forces of monetary development are changing. For example, Germany and Italy in the nineteenth century are interesting cases of monetary unification, demonstrating that *different routes to monetary integration have been followed*; the former case shows economic and monetary integration leading to political unification,[1] whle the latter case shows political and monetary unification preceding economic integration.[2] Relevant also is the case of the Federal Reserve System[3] or of the Bundesbank[4] because of the institutional aspects of federal systems.

The lessons learned from such examples or monetary disturbances are linked in this chapter, to a body of monetary knowledge that claims to be able to explain the origin, evolution and transformation of the monetary institutions or the system. To this effect, we propose the five hypotheses referred to in the preceding chapter. They are intended to be a systematic body of thinking, call it *an approach*, that has succeeded in drawing out some tentative answers to

76

questions relating to the *why, when, how, what means* and *what purpose* of EMU.

It might be claimed that the hypotheses we develop in the next section, boil down to one postulate: 'we need a good theory of money which could explain the Why and the How and entail a degree of suggestion as to When and to What'. However, monetary theory has not advanced significantly. Chick (1978: 37) reviewing the literature, made a serious accusation:

> Though they attracted the attention of Aristotle (and doubtless others before him) and have left a voluminous literature since, the basic questions of monetary theory remain unanswered: What is money? What causes money to become established? What assets are likely to be used as money, and what causes them to fall into disuse? What are the private and social costs and benefits of the existence of money? What are the effects of changes in the quantity of money and how much control does or ought society exercise over the money supply?

A similar sentiment of despair has been expressed by Hahn (1982: 1) in his appraisal of the place of money in the general equilibrium model: "A world in which all conceivable contingent future contracts are possible neither needs nor wants intrinsically worthless money". Unsatisfactory is the state of the arts according to Hicks (1989: 42), who has re-examined monetary theory by restating his 1967 position: "A useful way of introducing the monetary theory...is to begin by calling into question these two assumptions [what is money and who supplies it], asking how far they are justified".

A divergent view is held by Greenwald and Stiglitz (1991: 32) who believe that monetary theory has advanced because of the introduction of informational imperfections into monetary theory. They claim that informational imperfections could explain why "...monetary policy may be ineffective, not because households are willing to hold whatever money the banking system creates, but because banks are unwilling to lend". This is a familiar conclusion dating back to Keynes's *Treatise of Money* (1930) and says nothing new about the basic monetary questions.

The hypotheses (hereafter H1 to H5) of the next section are meant to constitute a framework of logical thinking intended to provide a methodological approach to EMU *and* a systematic appraisal of monetary theory. They should not be seen in the context of Friedman's (1953) methodology, which claims that the 'validity' of a hypothesis stems from its 'predictive capacity'. Nor should H1 to H5 be related to Popper's (1972) 'theorem of refutation' whereby empirical evidence can show that a hypothesis is false.[5]

H1 to H5 do not claim to entail a 'predictive capacity' of the kind proposed by Robbins (1984),[6] but only a *suggestive capacity*. They follow Kaldor's

(1985) method of 'stylised facts' that give rise to constructing a hypothesis and thus entail mainly an *explanatory power*.[7]. As 'stylised facts' we take the experience of monetary institutions in their historical context and the characteristics of monetary phenomena.

H1 to H5 rest on a simple premise: *explanation is the main goal of monetary theory*. However, explanation presupposes an understanding of the history of monetary theory, which is accumulated knowledge of related facts. A second property of monetary theory might be *suggestive capacity* by which we mean the property of a hypothesis to indicate the trend of the course of events or of effects if certain monetary criteria are satisfied; it also implies comparison of trends between competing explanations.

To the extent that H1 to H5 constitute a method of appraisal, they are, in terms of Dow's (1985) mode of thought, neither Cartesian/ Euclidean in their construction, meaning that they establish basic axioms, nor Babylonian in their formulation, implying different strands of argument logically reinforcing each other.[8] In other words, H1 to H5 do not establish basic axioms but only premises that can be valid or not; and they fail the test of coherence if they are not taken as a whole. H1 to H5 share some common features of Kuhn's (1970) paradigms such as consistency in application, broad scope in formulation, simplicity in logic and fruitfulness in explanation.

H1 to H5 are grounded in economic history, not in pure logic. In this sense, we follow Joan Robinson's (1964) view that economics is historical. In order to put flesh on the conceptual world of our hypotheses, we relate them to the evidence coming from monetary history and apply it to EMU. The aim is to uncover causal forces at work.

The logic and realism of H1 to H5 determine the extent of the application of our monetary approach to EMU. H1 to H5 are meaningful statements organized in a consistent way, containing only the elements that make the hypotheses useful tools, designed to serve as partial premises for explaining the forces that would establish the ECU as the anchor of EMU. However, since hypotheses cannot be fully realistic, H1 to H5 in strict logic "...are mere instruments or tools framed for the purpose of *establishing* interesting results" (Schumpeter, 1954: 15).

H1 to H5 are supposed to constitute an apparatus of methodology dealing with monetary institutions and of explaining their origin and evolution. They act as instruments for describing the likely economic effects of monetary disturbances *and* for recommending the formation of proper monetary policies. These two intended purposes aim at saying something useful about the birth, nature and transformation of EMU.

In short, H1 to H5 constitute an approach to money making inferences about the relationship between theoretical concepts and monetary institutions. The aim is to uncover causal forces at work.

3.2 Hypotheses stated and applied to ECU and EMU

3.2.H1 The Hicksian proposition

In his Essay: 'Monetary Theory and History - an Attempt at Perspective', Hicks (1967: 156) advanced the following proposition:

> *Monetary theory is less abstract than most economic theory; it cannot avoid a relation to reality, which in other economic theory is sometimes missing. It belongs to monetary history, in a way that economic theory does not always belong to economic history.*

Hicks (1967: 156) examined the nature of monetary disturbances under which major monetary works had been written and concluded: "So monetary theories arise out of monetary disturbances". In order to support this proposition, he drew examples from Ricardo's monetary writings covering the period of Napoleonic War Inflation, from Keynes's *General Theory*, a book of the Great Depression, or his *Treatise on Money*, a book on how the Restored Gold Standard is to be made to work. Equally, Thornton's *Paper Credit* is on why a credit system must be managed and Mill's *Principles* is influenced by the fear of unmanaged booms.

Hicks (1977: 45) also thought that Wicksell's work stemmed from a single monetary disturbance: "In spite of the relation that undoubtedly exists between Wicksell's monetary theory and his rather 'real' or non-monetary theory, he makes it evident that it was this rather long period of falling prices which was the principal issue he had in mind".

The Hicksian proposition could be applied to Walras's *Elements*, which coincides with a revolution in economics and deals with a different monetary problem. The revolution is the rise of the marginal utility theory of value. The monetary problem is a happy one: 'a spell of prosperity lasting about twenty years'.

The *Elements* coincides with the revival of laissez-faire liberalism. Free trade became the official doctrine for domestic and foreign affairs in Europe, except perhaps in France where a mild protectionist tradition was retained. It is in this context that the *Elements* was conceived. Colonialism expanded in Africa, Asia and Latin America. The balanced budget remained a basic tenet of belief. "Substantially the credo of economic and political liberalism prevailed in the field of monetary policy throughout the period. ... [O]f all the articles of that credo, the gold standard was the last to go" (Schumpeter, 1954: 770).

Why a gold standard and not a silver standard to support Walras's paper money? Schumpeter (1954: 770) reported the unhappy experience of Austria, Italy and Russia with the silver standard and the ensuing continuous depreciation of paper money in terms of silver which had retarded their growth. On the other hand, gold triumphed: "past experience with depreciated currencies had invested the gold standard with a prestige that was for the time being unchallengeable; the unfettered or *automatic* gold currency had become the symbol of sound practice and the badge of honor and decency".

Gold's triumph did not affect Walras. He remained bimetallist overwhelmed by the logic of the quantity theory of money. Walras's chief concern was to show that bimetallism was the only system that could stabilise the price level. The co-existence of paper money in a bimetallic system is based on the guarantee that paper money is quoted in metallic francs; the system entails a 100% metallic coverage.

3.2.a) H1 applied to the EMS and EMU

The Hicksian proposition has two interrelated pillars; the one is related to a monetary disturbance, the other to a monetary theory. The two are inseparable and imply that a monetary disturbance acts as a spur to understanding its causes. In this way, the Hicksian proposition describes a *causality* from monetary disturbance to monetary theory, to formation of policies, to setting up appropriate monetary institutions intended to correct the monetary disturbance.

Why has EMU been proposed in its present form? A satisfactory answer presupposes an understanding of the motives that have given rise to the birth of the EMS and then of EMU. The birth of the EMS could be explained by two monetary experiences; the period of floating exchange rates resulting in high volatility,[9] overshooting,[10] and misalignment[11] *and* the experience of a 'non-system' that allowed active and creeping inflation,[12] instability of credit and unmanaged international debt.[13] The EMS was supposed to act as a cushion against these two monetary disturbances.[14]

Seeing the EMS in historical perspective, it could be argued that it entails features and shares causes similar to the ones experienced by the three major periods of exchange rate floating since the beginning of this century. The first period (1914-1925) was caused by the failure of the 19th century gold standard, a failure mainly due to the First World War, which undermined not only the position of sterling but also London's position as the focus of the international financial system. The second period of floating (1931-1936) was caused by Britain's weakened position in the system, which forced her to go off the gold standard. During this time, exchange rates changed by 20-30% a year against each other; overshooting was equally common and economic fundamentals were a bad guide to exchange rate variability; inflation rose by 60% in France in 1936 and similar trends were experienced in other countries.[15] With the Tripartite Monetary Agreement between Britain, France and the US and with the pegging of the dollar gold price at $35 an ounce currency stability was restored in 1936.

The third period of floating is identified as 'a non-system', meaning that several currencies act as anchor but without a centre determining the rules of conduct. It begun with the breakdown of Bretton Woods; some say that the actual day is 15 August 1971, when the US authorities suspended the dollar's convertibility into gold; others say that the appropriate date is March 1973 when all currencies began floating.

During the third period of floating, the world experienced two oil crises (1973-4 and 1979), high inflation rates, higher unemployment rates than before, slow output growth, trade deficits which reached in 1979 around 2 million ECUs with corresponding surpluses for Japan and OPEC countries and an expansion of international liquidity before official floating was announced. It is estimated that real economic growth was only 60 percent as rapid during 1973-79 as it had been in the preceding seven-year period; unemployment rates in industrialized countries were 50 percent higher and have since remained high.[16]

These results should not be attributed to floating rates alone. "A review of the experience with floating reveals an exchange rate system with a number of weaknesses. ... Yet it is unclear that the alternative systems that have been proposed, such as a return to fixed rates, would be better" (Obstfeld, 1985: 442). The real problem of the EMS has been its *inconsistent trinity*.[17] The inconsistent trinity is a well established monetary theorem which stipulates that it is almost impossible to hold together: a) fixed exchange rates, b) free capital movements, and c) independent national monetary policies.

Experience has shown that countries may have any of the two but not the three at the same time. If a country chooses to have fixed exchange rates and free capital movements, it can not have an independent monetary policy because the latter will have to pursue a policy geared to restraining capital flows. If a country chooses to have an independent monetary policy and no capital restrictions, it will be forced to have a flexible exchange rate because only then can it control its money supply and thus manipulate its interest rate to sterilize capital flows. If a country chooses to have an independent monetary policy and fixed exchange rates, it will have to restrict capital flows for otherwise it may not control its money supply.

On the other hand, fixed exchange rates and perfect capital mobility mean that the dominant central bank, whose currency acts as the anchor, will determine the currency area in which only one rate of interest will prevail. This has been the preferred option of the Bundesbank.

If the monetary disturbance of the pre-EMS period resulted in *misalignments* of the exchange rates for the major currencies, the Hicksian proposition would have us believe that the costs of misalignment were sufficiently high to lead to a *new* monetary theory and the formation of a new monetary institution. However, no new monetary theory was formed. Monetary policy continued using received monetary doctrines. Consequently, the resulting monetary institution, the EMS, was conceived as a means to mitigate the costs of misalignment, which according to Williamson (1983) involved adjustment costs in the tradeable goods sector, a slow-down in the rate of capital formation, pressures for protectionism and an upward push to world inflation.

Of these four costs, the slow-down in the rate of capital formation is the most serious. This was emphasized in the Florence speech of the then President of the Commission, now Lord Jenkins (1978), who held the view that real exchange uncertainty has strong inhibitory effects on investment. Businessmen, he said, hesitate to invest in the prospect of a future depreciation in a European currency.

As to EMU, the monetary disturbance that gave birth to it, is *the globalisation of markets in trade, direct investment, capital and finance*. This globalisation during the 1980s as we said in section 2.3, put an end to the applicability of IMF's legal provision to capital controls. These had fully reflected Keynes's 1944 vision on 'the explicit right to control capital movements'. Keynes (1980: 20) stated his vision while appearing before the UK House of Lords:

> Let me take first...[the issue of] our power to control the domestic rate of interest so as to secure cheap money. Not merely as a feature of the transition, but as a permanent arrangement, the plan accords to every government the explicit right to control all capital movements. What used to be a heresy is now endorsed as orthodox. In my own judgement, countries which avail themselves of this right may find it necessary to scrutinise all transactions, as to prevent evasion of capital regulations. Provided that the innocent, current transactions are let through, there is nothing in the plan to prevent this. In fact, it is encouraged. It follows that our right to control the domestic capital market is secured on firmer foundations than ever before, and is formally accepted as a proper part of agreed international arrangements.

The above quotation of Keynes entails all the ingredients of the post-1944 monetary arrangements of the IMF. Globalisation of markets of capital and finance has radically changed all that and the new orthodoxy is in search of a theory. The traditional monetary policy as an instrument to determine the rate of interest has become impotent; this is due to global markets that has arisen because of innovation, technology and deregulation. Keynes's vision of government having the right to control capital movements, has yielded to looser financial regulation and to liberalisation of all markets.

Keynes's world of direct controls to make monetary policy stick, either by preventing banks offering interest-bearing money to depositors or by sheltering national banks from foreign competition, has now gone. With this disappearance, the traditional function of central banks has changed; it would have to become liability management and risk externalities. As a result of it, the traditional function of central banks of last resort has had to be transformed; it has become 'management of systemic risk'. The elasticity of substitutability between traditional money and near money increased substantially; as deregulation continued, the interest rates paid on these assets were determined by the market and not by the direct controls.

The effects of globalisation on the EC monetary arrangements could be summarised in *two* propositions: a) aggravation of the *redundancy problem* and b) *erosion of national sovereignty* in controlling the money supply and the exchange rate. The redundancy problem is described by Mundell (1968) as the role of the nth country in a well defined region. The first stage of EMU plus the completion of the internal market have so far shown that free capital mobility and n autonomous macroeconomic policies are inoperative. The experience of the currency turmoil of September 1992 and of July 1993 has confirmed this theoretical point. Both have undermined the full autonomy of n macroeconomic policies, rendering semi-fixed exchange rates impossible.[18]

By the notion of *redundancy*, we wish to express a single idea. If finance and capital markets are global, interest rates will have to carry even more of a burden. *One policy instrument - interest rate - is supposed to influence four objectives: boost investment, control inflation, stabilise the exchange rate and increase private savings.* However, these four objectives more often than not, conflict with each other. Boosting investment requires low interest rates but controlling inflation implies high interest rates. Increasing the flow of savings of the private sector means a relative independence of monetary policy to control interest rates but again this may diverge from a policy concerned with the stabilisation of the exchange rate. Let us call this phenomenon: *the conflicting quarter of globalisation.*

The *conflicting quarter of globalisation* is a phenomenon concerned with the impotence of policy instruments stemming from the evolving structures. For example, the single European financial market would further decrease national monetary sovereignty because the application of the second banking directive 89/647/EEC, meaning that the right of establishment for banks and other financial institutions, would not be regulated by the peculiarities of the home regulation but by common rules. Under existing rules of banking supervision, which are neither harmonised among Member States, nor coordinated, the lender of last resort function of national central banks has been further complicated.

The evolving structures due to globalisation have eroded national autonomy in controlling the money supply and the exchange rate in a financial market characterized by free capital mobility. Crook (1992: 29) summarised the case: "Thanks largely to financial innovation and the expansion of global finance, neither of these conditions [governments controlling the money supply and stable relationship between demand for and supply of money] was met in the big industrial economies in the 1980s".

National monetary sovereignty is further eroded by speculative attacks in times when the central bank is running a monetary policy divergent from money demands and at the same time, international capital mobility aids self-fulfilling speculation. "What is the effect of speculation? The analysis of Euro-currency markets at times of turbulence provides a vivid illustration. When realignments of the order of 3-5% are expected to occur, short-term interest rates shoot up to 40-60% in the currencies expected to depreciate" (de Cecco and Giovannini, 1989: 5).

The turmoil of exchange rates due to speculation in September 1992 and the resulting redistribution of reserves from national central banks to speculators, gave ground to the fears that the EMS was vulnerable to speculative attacks. The IMF (1993a: 12-3) concluded:

> Even countries that succeeded in maintaining sound economic fundamentals can find their currencies vulnerable to strong exchange market pressures triggered by currency depreciation in other participating countries...to make it credible that the commitment to exchange rate stability will override domestic economic objectives when conflicts do arise, it is necessary for most countries participating in a pegged exchange rate system to relinquish monetary policy autonomy and subordinate official short-term interest rates to the objective of maintaining exchange rate stability.

The loss of independence of monetary policy in the EU in the context of global finance and integrated markets has had serious consequences for the conduct of monetary policy.[19]   Do traditional assumptions about stable demands for money or intermediate targets used in the conduct of monetary policy hold?   Experience has demonstrated that financial innovations and removal of capital restrictions have altered the *mechanism of transmission*. The velocity of money [defined as V=(Price X Income)/Money stock] is not any longer stable, nor can it be assumed constant. Financial deregulation and innovation plus advanced technology in exchange market dealing have changed the nature of the transmission mechanisms. Monetary policy does not any longer affect or influence directly the real economy via interest rates. It is the structure of assets internalising varying money externalities that affects the portfolio preference via which it influences the real economy.

The traditional definition of money supply of *M3 cannot any longer be assumed stable*. Its definition as 'Currency in circulation + sight deposits with banks + savings deposits + claims on monetary institutions + placements as deposits at statutory notice or with contractual maturity of over one year', may not be appropriate.   Financial innovations, such as interest-bearing cash deposits or bonds with variable interest-rates, have replaced traditional bank loans. Technological advances in tele-communications and computers have lowered information and transaction costs for financial products such as derivatives. Consequently, all *components of M3 are affected by the behaviour of institutional investors.*

According to the report of the G-10, only for the USA, Japan and Europe, total cross-border securities holdings by their residents in 1991 reached the amount of US$ 2,5 trillion. Moreover, the increase in these investments has come from the demand induced by institutional investors, seeking profitable investments and reduced risk.

In other words, the traditional assumption of any country, while being exposed to international competition and being able to control its money supply, cannot be made. Near-money investments outside the banking system has risen to such an extent that the traditional assumption that *liquid assets are a stable component of M3 losses its strength.*

A second issue follows from the above. Under conditions of globalisation, the demand for money with respect to either interest rates or income (or expenditure) or both cannot be assumed stable. If this is so the logic of using monetary aggregates, such as M3, as the base for monetary policy targets and monetary coordination based on specific monetary targets *is undermined.*

A third concern comes naturally. Are asset prices influenced by monetary policy or by the cycle? Falling asset prices in the USA, Japan and EU countries have forced banks to accumulate non-performing loans. This accumulation has had its effects; banks had to restrain their lending activities and to adjust to their deteriorated capital positions. Hence deposits with banks *cannot be assumed reliable* components of M3 and cannot be used as reliable indicators of monetary target for inflation.

A fourth issue of concern has to do with the traditional method of controlling money supply via reserves. The traditional way of exercising an automatic constraint on money creation was the instrument of minimum reserve ratios. Yet with offshore centres and expansion of the Euromarket, the *instrument of minimum reserves has lost its potency.* Countries with high minimum reserve ratios have experienced the phenomenon of seeing its banks tempted to evade their obligation by shifting their business to offshore heavens, where reserve-free subsidiaries have been established.

We may conclude from the above consequences due to globalisation that only the monetary policy of an anchor currency may still be assumed more stable; the rest have become powerless.[20]

The monetary disturbance caused by global markets has coincided with two other events: German monetary unification and the dogma of the 1980s on price stability. The German monetary unification has had profound consequences. These include: abolition of price subsidies raising thus the price level by approximately one third and leading to a price-wage-spiral; a currency unification has been achieved by converting all existing Ostmark into D-mark at a rate of 1:1, which in turn has implied higher unemployment benefits and subsidies and an income transfer to Ostmark holders; a serious fall in productivity leading to high unemployment; a budget surplus in 1989 has been turned into a deficit in subsequent years; a current account surplus also turned into a deficit but accompanied temporarily by a higher growth rate. The cost of unification has meant high real interest rates for a currency acting as the 'anchor' of the system.

This state of affairs points to a serious conclusion: Germany is no longer the model it used to be. Even the might of the Bundesbank is questioned. Such questioning has been induced by the inclusion, in the executive board of the Bundesbank, directors from the five new Lander, who have not the same priority over price stability with respect to growth. To this, one should add the shaky status of DM kept solid by high interest rates; these have attracted capital flows from the rest of the Community. The status of DM as an 'anchor currency' for the first (and possibly the second) stage of EMU could only continue if the fundamental economic imbalances were corrected in time. Otherwise the current money externalities internalised by the DM will disappear.

German unification had another effect; sovereignty was regained. The economic giant of Europe also became a political heavy-weight. What were the options? The first one was that Germany would shift its interest to the disintegrating COMEKON and, in particular, to its immediate neighbours thus creating a new political structure with serious consequences for the Community but also for the whole of Europe. The second option would involve deepening the Community integration via a political union. The TEU adopted a parallel development in both EMU and political union. The latter option for Germany has won.[21]

All the above fears about possible disturbances (monetary, economic and political) have given birth to EMU in its present form. Have they led to a new monetary theory as the second pillar of the Hicksian proposition would have us believe? Attempts have been made and these are reviewed in chapter 4. An alternative is offered in chapters 6 and 7.

3.3.H2 The Aristotelian notion of evolving money[22]

The Socratics (Plato's *Republic* and *Laws*; Xenophon's *Economicus* and *Revenues of Athens*; Aristotle's *Politics* and *Ethics*) held an evolutionary theory of money. Of the three, Aristotle's excelled in clarity and analytical performance. In the *Nicomachean Ethics* and *Politics*, Aristotle developed an evolving theory of money.[23]

There is not a single chapter of Aristotle's two great works devoted exclusively to monetary theory, nor is the phrase *evolving theory of money* anywhere stated. From the texts cited, it would be apparent that we could summarize the Aristotelian notion of evolving money as follows:

Exchange as such does not necessarily devise a medium of exchange. It is the stage of economic development - i.e. the degree of the division of labour and specialization, the level of technological advance and communication, economies of scale and capital accumulation - that would invent money to facilitate exchange. As the stage of economic development evolves so does money's nature.

Aristotle identified four stages of development: a) Autarky, b) Primary, c) Middle and d) Modern. Each stage entails specific characteristics of production, exchange and distribution, depending on the degree of the division of labour and specialization, the level of technological advance and communication, economies of scale and capital accumulation. *Money changes its character as the above factors change the structure of society.* The stuff of which money is made (call it the nature of money) evolves as the stage of development evolves. Money may also assume different functions (or the relative importance of functions may change) in different stages.

A state of autarky is provided for by nature where the division of labour is insignificant, technology is primitive and capital is not accumulated. In such a state of nature,[24] there is no exchange and no need for money.

Nor, in a state of simple form of association or first community, is there need for formalised exchange. "In the primary association therefore (I mean the household) there is no function for trade, but it only arises after the association has become more numerous" (Politics 1257a 18).

In the *Primary stage* associated with simple primitive societies or tribes, indirect exchange is absent, but barter is well developed; "for such tribes do not go beyond exchanging actual commodities for actual commodities, for example giving and taking wine for corn, and so with the various other things of the sort" (Politics 1257a 23).[25]

It is of interest to note that in the *Primary stage*, direct exchange existed in an environment which was non-mercantile, and commodity money co-existed; such a money assumed only the function of 'store of value'. "These first coins were rather large coins, which must have been very valuable - confirming our impression that early metallic money must have been mainly a store of value" (Hicks, 1969: 67).

The *Middle stage* began with the realization that "... all things are produced more plentifully and easily and of a better quality when one man does one thing which is natural to him and does it at the right time and leaves other things" (Plato, Republic III 370). Consequently, the division of labour increased, specialization increased, technology advanced and capital accumulated.[26] As a result of such a process, self-sufficiency diminished, the wants and interdependence of man increased and communication became complex.

This interdependence and complexity could be partly relieved by exchange. "Exchange on these lines is not contrary to nature, nor is it any branch of the art of wealth-getting, for it existed for the replenishment of natural self-sufficiency" (Politics 1257a 29). Hence exchange is natural and, since it is natural, has a purpose.[27]

Nevertheless, indirect exchange became necessary in order to satisfy the diversity of wants due to three economic forces: the division of labour, increased association and easiness in communication. "For when they had come to supply themselves more from abroad by importing things in which they were deficient and exporting those of which they had a surplus, the employment of money necessarily came to be devised" (Politics 1257a 31). Therefore, *money originated in the market-place* with the sole purpose of facilitating exchange. In this sense, it assumed the function of the 'medium of exchange'.[28]

The most interesting economic notion in Aristotle is that money is neither static, nor abstract, nor imaginary. *Money evolves as the stage of development of the optimum size of a polis evolves*. Aristotle was the first to state the evolving nature of money:

> For the natural necessaries are not in every case readily portable; hence for the purpose of barter men made a mutual compact to give and accept some substance of such a sort as being itself a useful commodity was easy to handle in use for general life, iron for instance, silver and other metals, at the first stage defined merely by size and weight, but finally also by impressing on it a stamp in order that this might relieve them of having to measure it; for the stamp was put on as a token of the amount (Politics 1257a 34).

Hence the form or nature of money has evolved. It was first an uncoined commodity, having intrinsic value but easy to handle and defined merely by size and weight. It then became more specific with a stamp representing the quantity and quality of money. As it changed its nature, it assumed other functions and characteristics.

In the *Ethics*, Aristotle was more analytical. In the first place, exchange could only occur if proportionate equality between the products could be established by a 'standard'. "It is to meet this requirement that men have introduced money; money constitutes in a manner a middle term, for it a measure of all things, and so of their superior value, that is to say, how many shoes are equivalent to a house or to a given quantity of food" (1133a 19). Hence the origin of the 'measure of value' function and the exchange process, Commodity - Money - Commodity (C-M-C).

Another important function of money: 'standard of deferred payments' was recognized. "Now money serves us as a guarantee of exchange in the future; supposing we need nothing at the moment, it ensures that exchange shall be possible when a need arises, it meets the requirements of something we can produce in payment so as to obtain the thing we need" (Ethics 1133b 11).

Wicksell, in his *Lectures II*, was mainly concerned with ways and means that would keep the purchasing power of money constant. The same issue had bothered Aristotle long before; he had even proposed a method for its solution. "Money, it is true, is liable to the same fluctuation of demand as other commodities for its purchasing power varies at different times; but it tends to be comparatively constant. Hence the proper thing is for all commodities to have their prices fixed; this will ensure that exchange, and consequently association, shall always be possible" (Ethics 1133b 19). It should be noted that Aristotle's method was conceived to apply to the *Middle stage*.

In the early period of the *Modern stage*, credit co-existed in an economy characterized by a money exchange process where money is recognized as representative wealth. Both had been recognized by Aristotle only to be rejected on the grounds that they were unnatural and without a purpose: "indeed wealth is often assumed to consist of a quantity of money, because money is the thing with which business and trade are employed" (Politics 1257b 8).

Credit money presupposes well-organized markets, which is the main feature of the Modern stage. In this stage, money changes its simple characteristics. The nature of money becomes an art of wealth-getting. Aristotle stated this evolution with clarity:

> So when currency has been invented as an outcome of the necessary interchange of goods, there came into existence the other form of wealth-getting, trade, which at first no doubt went on in a simple form, but later became more highly organized as experience discovered the sources and methods of exchange that would cause most profit (Politics 1257b 1).

Money as representative wealth and money in its credit form used for the purpose of 'usury' were condemned by Aristotle "...because its gain comes from money itself and not from that for the sake of which money was invented...but interest increases the amount of the money itself... consequently this form of the business of getting wealth is of all forms the most contrary to nature" (Politics 1258b 3).

Aristotle's moralist view of usury was not shared by his contemporaries. Demosthenes, for instance, "...considered credit to be of as much importance as money itself in the business world, and declared one who ignored this elementary fact to be a mere know-nothing" (Trever, 1916: 106).[29]

3.3.a) H2 applied to ECU and interdependence

H2 entails two explanatory functions. The first identifies the forces that determine the nature of money in the market. The second describes the effects, resulting from the stage of development, on the interdependence of countries or regions.

H2 ought to be enriched, if only to avoid important characteristics of monetary systems of the Middle and Modern stages being neglected. Only then could Aristotle's analytic intention be justified. Both Hicks (1969) and Chick (1992) have identified characteristics that help better understand Aristotle's insights.

Hicks (1969) talks of three phases: First, Middle and Modern. These correspond to Aristotle's. Aristotle's stage of Autarky and the method to explain 'what money is' and 'what money does' in different stages are neglected. The two stages of interest are the Middle and Modern. In Hicks's Middle phase, we find a mixed system of commodity money and paper money with banks to have developed. This was the period of the classical theories of money when "Money was changing its character, beginning to link up with credit and with finance" (Hicks, 1969: 72).[30]

Stages of development cannot be contained by time periods. It could be argued that Chick's stage 2 of banking development with causality running from increases in reserves to loans and then deposits, corresponds to the banking penetration in Aristotle's Middle stage.[31] The bank deposit multiplier is the control mechanism in Chick's stage 2; so is Walras's system of bimetallism in the *Elements*.

In Hicks's Modern phase, "it is the 'inside' market - the market for (more or less) credit-worthy borrowers - which particularly matters" (Hicks, 1969: 77). Money in this stage has become a statement of debt (or a promise) and is linked with credit and with finance. It is based on two kinds of security which were carried over from the *Middle Stage*. "The first is surety or guarantee. ... A sufficient example of this method is the acceptance of a bill of exchange. The acceptor, in effect, is selling his confidence" (Hicks, 1969: 8). The second refers to the development of financial intermediaries based on the principle of spreading risk, "the so-called 'Law of Large Numbers' which is the basis of Insurance" (Hicks, 1969: 79).

This conforms to Chick's stage 5 where the causal nexus runs from 'changes in loan supply being equal to the change in loans which causes changes in deposits and the latter induce changes in reserves'. In the Modern stage, the driving force is loans and consequently both banks and financial intermediaries engage in aggressive lending activity.

Does the ECU belong to a particular stage? ECU's making was mainly political, partly legal and slightly economic. The official or private ECU status is odd because it stems from a mixed system of a monetary arrangement showing a dependent existence similar to the one found in the Aristotelian or Hicksian Middle phase. In the first stage of EMU, the ECU is neither commodity money nor credit. Hence it belongs to neither the Primary, nor the *Modern stage*.

The ECU belongs to the *Middle stage* for two reasons. First, the EFMC holds, in principle, deposits of 20% of gold and 20% of dollar reserves although, effectively, these reserves are owned by the national central banks. In return an initial supply of ECU was issued against this deposit. Nothing physical has occurred because the operation takes the form of three-month revolving swaps. The issuance of ECUs was made so that the ECU would be able to carry out the function of 'a means of settlement' between the EFMC and national central banks. As we said in the preceding chapter, the ECU has been of limited use in the settlement of national central banks' claims. This is a pure use of a banking system operating on credit, with the assumption that this credit has no independent existence and that its value is derived from the proviso that it is convertible into another entity, such as dollar reserves or gold. So is the mixed system of the Aristotelian Middle stage in which paper money had an existence only by reference to the promise that paper money was convertible into gold.

Second, it is clear that the ECU does not have an independent existence partly because it is a basket of twelve currencies mixed in proportion to the relative size of each participant country and partly because its *essentiality* stems from its legal function as a unit of account in the exchange rate mechanism of the EMS. Had this not been legally stated, any national currency more stable than the ECU could have served the functions conferred on it more efficiently. This is born out by the fact that the markets have established the DM as the anchor of the EMS, and this will continue until the third stage of EMU. As we argue in chapter 7, the ECU only internalises the externalities associated with reduced risks.

The second aspect of the Aristotelian notion of evolving money concerns the interdependence of states or regions that results from the division of labour, technological advance and capital accumulation. The interdependence of the EU has accentuated because of trade, factor and services mobility and transfer of technology.

The Community Members have come to depend heavily on intra EC trade. Intra-EC trade as percentage of GDP, on average, between 1960-67 to 1985-90, has increased from 25% to 43% for Belgium and Luxembourg; 24% to 39% for Ireland; 22% to 32% for the Netherlands; 10% to 22% for Portugal; 8% to 12% for Germany; 3.5% to 11% for the UK; 6% to 12% for Greece; 4.5% to 11% for France; 4% to 10% for Italy and 3% to 9% for Spain.

Another indicator showing the importance of trade independence is to consider the share of intra-EC trade in total trade; in 1992, on average, the EU's imports accounted for 59.3% while its exports for 61.3%. In addition, intra-EU trade was 10 points higher for imports in 1992 than in 1980, and approximately 7 points higher for exports. As a result, trade has grown more quickly than output since the creation of the Community. Trade diversion and trade creation, coupled with a deepening effect, gave a general tonic to investors' confidence.

Labour mobility has been stable. It is expected to increase with the entry into force of the TEU. The EU citizenship (Art. 8 to 8d) coupled with the right of citizens to vote and stand as candidates in municipal elections and European Parliament elections, the equal consular protection, the right to petition and to apply to the Ombudsman and the Protocol on social policy annexed to the TEU concerning the free movement of workers, right of establishment and mutual recognition of diplomas and qualifications, would enhance the mobility significantly.

Technological transfers have taken two forms: direct investment and licensing of know-how. Licensing of know-how has had a better development; the principal recipients have been the less prosperous countries: Ireland, Greece, Spain and Portugal.

Why is interdependence so important?[32] Because it is a condition of the closeness of countries and refers to the degree of two-way influence of one economy on another at the margin. Interdependence, firstly, stems from economic integration, which means that goods and assets in one country become closer substitutes in another and that, under different regimes of exchange rates and mobility of factors of production, the law of one price for goods and assets could be established. Under fixed exchange rates, for example, national monies are almost perfect substitutes. Secondly, no matter what the exchange rate regime, there is a dynamic linkage between current exchange rates and expectations of future exchange rates influenced by the past and current course of policies. Thirdly, the effects of interactions of policies pursued by major countries have an impact on the smaller countries. Hence interdependence means reciprocal dependence.

The main theoretical consequence of high interdependence stems from the product markets. The prices of traded goods will be determined internationally. If product markets are completely integrated, interdependence renders devaluations ineffective. If trade penetration is low, *money illusion* works for the following reason; devaluations influence relative prices, direct resources in traded goods when unemployed factors exist and domestic consumption via *money illusion*.

The extent to which the EU economy is subject to 'state-specific' and 'sector-specific' shocks and the extent to which the exchange rate can modify relative prices will determine the efficiency of the exchange rate. Bini Smaghi and Vori (1992: 86) estimated both: "...for all EC countries except Ireland there is a significant inverse correlation between sector-specific and state-specific factors. ... This would suggest that the exchange rate is a less useful instrument of adjustment in the EC than it would be in the US". This conclusion is the opposite of Eichengreen's (1990). Bini Smaghi and Vori (1992: 89) also estimated the elasticity of nominal wages with respect to prices and to unemployment: "These measures differ among EC countries, but for all responsiveness of wages to prices is higher than to unemployment".

In terms of policies, the consequences for monetary and fiscal policies are diametrically different. Under conditions of perfect capital mobility, the law of one interest rate is established, whereas with fixed exchange rates, only fiscal policy is effective and under flexible exchange rates, only monetary policy works.

Reciprocal dependence leads to a game- theoretic framework, similar to the so-called Stackelberg solution and renders the nth monetary policy redundant unless monetary cooperation is effective.[33].

3.4.H3 The Cipolla thesis

In five lectures on *Money, Prices and Civilization in the Mediterranean World*, Cipolla (1956) arrived at a number of conclusions which will be referred to subsequently. We could summarize them as follows:

> *No international or national monetary system ever existed or lasted long without having its own anchor money. An international money requires two necessary conditions: 'high unitary value' and 'intrinsic stability' and a sufficient condition for its emergence to an international status: 'the support of a sound, strong and open economy'.*

Looking at the international currencies of the Middle Ages, Cipolla (1956) identified four international currencies: the Byzantine 'nomisma', the Moslem 'dinar', the Florentine 'fiorino' and the Venetian 'ducate'. He examined the circumstances that supported their emergence to an international currency and their common features.

Cipolla (1956: 14) makes clear that the Byzantine dominance, the Arab era, the Florentine period and the Venetian influence share similar features: "As late as the nineteenth century no western state enjoyed a complete monetary sovereignty. ... Yet a step was then taken that was important for the achievement of monetary sovereignty: from the middle of the century in each state, only its own national currency circulated. ... Whenever a state organization was rising in strength and efficiency, one hears of its effects to keep out of monetary circulation certain types of foreign coins".

Three common characteristics were identified by Cipolla to assess the success and failure of the international money of the Middle Ages:
a) High unitary value,

b) Intrinsic stability,

c) Support by an economy which was strong, sound and played a pre-eminent role in international exchanges.

Cipolla (1956: 24) attached different weights to a), b), c) and singled out the economic background as being the more significant:

> The triumph of the 'nomisma' would have been completely inconceivable without the industrial and commercial power of the Byzantine Empire in the first part of the Middle Ages. The basic reason for the success of the reform of Abd el Malek and the wide circulation of his coins throughout the world was, with due respect to Allah, the economic significance of the new Moslem Empire and its great role in the system of international exchange of those generations. If one wants to understand the reasons for the triumph of the 'fiorino' of Florence in the second half of the thirteenth century and in part in the fourteenth, one must keep in mind the tremendous expanding force of the Florentine economy at that time and its great impact on international banking and trade. In the same way, the triumph of the 'ducato' would remain incomprehensible if it could not be related to the expansion of the Venetian economy and the role of that city in the system of international transactions during the fifteenth century.

The Cipolla study refers to the beginning of the Aristotelian Middle Stage of a monetary system based on metallic money. The essence of the Cipolla thesis is the introduction of three criteria by which one could evaluate a monetary system. If we substitute for 'high unitary value', *highly stable value of money*[34] and for 'intrinsic stability', *high confidence in money*[35] plus the 'economic background', we have devised a system of assessing all stages.

These three criteria entail varying degrees of explanatory power because the roles they play and the importance attached to them have varied as the stages of economic development have evolved. For example, in the *Primitive stage*, the *highly stable value* was paramount because money was mainly used for its 'store of value' function rather than for its 'medium of exchange' function. Cipolla (1956: 25-6) made a similar observation and took account of the social forces that attributed significance to the one or other criterion:

> In the habit of the Middle Ages of using coins by weight rather than by tale, it was especially the stability in fineness that mattered. ... The importance of high unitary value, which was not as great as that of the other two elements, was based on logical and emotional factors. ... The high unitary value of the dollars of the Middle Ages was important not only for the prestige it gave, but also for the social implications it brought into play.

The suggestion made by the Cipolla thesis is that if one finds the forces that induce the three criteria: *high confidence, highly stable value* and *support of a strong economy* to be fully met, one will find a way to introduce a monetary unit that will be acceptable to markets. The criteria also indicate that, given no institutional restrictions, this monetary unit will become dominant. What economic forces or institutional arrangements are necessary for the fulfilment of these criteria? One is drawn back to the theory of money, capable of explaining and of suggesting the course of the likely effects.

In general theoretical terms, one may say that a *highly stable currency* in the medium-term should be associated with a low inflation rate. The *high confidence* criterion should result in a low real interest rate. The *strong economy engaged in international exchanges* criterion should influence the stability of the exchange rate. These three indicators could guide us in examining the relevant cases.

There is a second pillar to the Cipolla Thesis. This has to do with the political commitment of the government in question to allow or even promote its currency in the international field in order to enjoy prestige, be eagerly demanded and easily accepted. Cipolla refers in detail to the political decision of the Arab rulers, at the time of Abd el Malek, which were designed to promote the 'dinar' internationally when still the Mediterranean was a 'nomisma area' of the Byzantine Empire. The monetary reforms of Abd el Malek ranged from the change of inscriptions on the dinar (from Greek to Arabic) to the imitation of 'nomisma' in gold content, design and weight.

Religion was also used for the dinar's promotion; the Greek words: 'Father, Son and Holy Ghost' were changed to 'Allah is witness that there is no God but Allah'. Given the economic power of the Moslem Empire, these reforms "[m]arked a real turning point in the monetary history of the Mediterranean. The new Moslem coins soon enjoyed a tremendous prestige and although the 'dinar' did not drive out of the Mediterranean area the Byzantine 'nomisma', it broke down the monopoly of the latter as an international currency" Cipolla (1956: 19-20).

3.4.a) Cipolla criteria and the ECU

There is evidence that the EU meets fully the third Cipolla criterion - i.e. economic background.[36] The EU, in 1992, had the largest GDP in the world,[37], although the third largest GDP per head after the USA and Japan. The EU inhabits the second smallest territory, with Japan the first, and has the largest population in the western world.[38]

The EU is the largest trading group in the world and, in 1990, accounted for about 39% of world trade.[39] The EU imports accounted for 23,8% of its GDP while its exports accounted for 22,8% of its GDP. The respective percentages for the USA were: 9,2% and 7,9% and for Japan were: 7,9% and

9,7%, implying a smaller openness for the US and Japan.

The foreign official reserves (convertible currencies and SDRs) of the twelve Member States were about five times greater than the USA's and more than four times greater than Japan's. Similar statistics are found if the IMF quota positions are examined.[40] The financial institutions are well developed in most EU countries and are comparable to those in the USA. The Euromarkets deal with about two-thirds of international loans. In terms of capital movements (direct and portfolio investments), the EU is the leading world actor. It is the first merchant marine power. Its labour force is highly skilled and enjoys the world's highest standard of living, the best health care and social services.

The EU represents a cultural power and influence unequalled in the world, with the making of a world cultural and economic power. Yet this superpower is dependent on the USA for its security and, partly, for its monetary system. It has also twelve governments with whom power still rests.

As to the other two criteria, *highly stable money* and *high confidence*, they could only be applicable to the private ECU, not to the official ECU whose circuit consists of the twelve national central banks plus the central banks of these third countries granted the status of 'other Holder of ECU'. Furthermore, the official ECUs take the form of swaps and are held as reserves. The marketability of the private ECU depends on these two criteria.[41]

The marketability of a *composite currency*[42] such as the SDR or the EC, depends on its technical characteristics. The properties of these composite currencies are the stability of their value and secure income return. The stability property is the result of the averaging method of a basket of national currencies whose exchange rate volatility is offset by the weighted arithmetic mean implicit in the valuation of the ECU. The same applies to the interest rates of these composite currencies, which determine the income return; they represent a blending of national interest rates.

The ERM rules have further contributed to making the ECU basket less volatile.[43] Such an inherent stability ensures the use of the ECU as a hedging instrument because the reduced cost of stabilizing exposures in different currencies minimizes the total cost of hedging. Given that the predictability of the ECU based on the process of averaging is less pronounced by comparison with the predictability of each currency component of the basket, the private ECU is a better investment instrument. The same would hold for the nominal interest rate; the averaging effect is more pronounced.

The ECU's characteristic as a relatively stable currency with an average interest rate makes it attractive to borrowers, residents in a country with high-interest rates, and an equally attractive investment currency to residents of low-interest rates countries. The ECU's exchange rate is influenced by currencies that move closely in line with each other. In principle, the greater the number of currencies participants in the ERM with a narrow currency fluctuation margin, the greater the ECU's stability.

The freezing of the ECU's composition of the basket (Art. 109g) would reinforce the strong currency bias because it would ensure that the incremental effect on the ECU's strength, resulting from the increase in the weight of its stronger components (on the occasion of a realignment), is not undone by its weak components.

As to the *high confidence* criterion, traditional monetary theory argues that this stems, mainly but not wholly, from the institutional structure of a monetary system, including its banking component. Thus, advocates of an institutional approach to EMU argue that the ECU has not been endowed with a clearing system and an efficient payment system; thus little confidence is placed on the ECU. Today's ECU clearing system is a wholesale system based on low number, high value payments.

Such a complaint is not warranted because the wholesale payment system is appropriate for the international financial uses of the ECU as an investment asset, and is consistent with the Triffin postulate. In fact, for payment orders related to bank accounts, a privately run international clearing system has been in operation managed by the Ecu Banking Association (EBA), in association with the Society for World-wide Interbank Financial Telecommunication (SWIFT) and the Bank for International Settlements (BIS).

Further confidence in the ECU will be gained in the second stage of EMU, as the EMI will have the task of supervising the technical preparation of ECU bank notes, overseeing the development of the ECU clearing system and facilitating the functioning of the ECU-based payment system as an efficient and low cost retail system (bank transfers, cheque, credit-and payment cards, etc.).[44]

Concerning the political pillar of Cippola's third criterion, the active support by specific instruments for the development of the ECU is overwhelming. The EU support has been directed firstly, to the size and depth of the private ECU in financial markets, and secondly to providing very substantial governmental and institutional support. This is exactly what the State theory of money would have requested policy makers to do to a successful national financial market. The latest effort of the Commission (1992) concentrates on removing all legal obstacles to the use of the ECU in Member States in an effort to confer on it, as the State Theory of Money would suggest, the legal tender status.[45]

The three Cipolla criteria have been examined with conventional tools of monetary theory. In chapter 7, we return to them under a different conception of money considered as an 'externality'. There we identify the conditions that establish a currency as a means for the settlement of debts in a given money process (M-C-M*).

There is another reservation; neither confidence nor stability is gained unless the ECU satisfies our H5 on the Essentiality criterion. This is the core of our argument: *the origin, nature and functions of the ECU need to be shown to be consistent with an economic model.*

Advocates of the ECU who wish to establish it as an international currency before it becomes so in the EU, should be reminded of the Cipolla thesis that says that no currency ever was accepted by third parties prior to its establishment in the home market. This is the essence of our H3.

What procedure should one follow for the establishment of the ECU first in the EU and then in international markets? The Triffin postulate suggests a policy option.

3.5.H4 The Triffin postulate

Triffin, writing on *The Future of the EMS and the ECU* (1984: 5), stated the following postulate:

> *History teaches us that the most crucial reforms of the 'international' monetary system (as well as of 'national' systems) have always been determined, with very rare exceptions, by the private sector of the economy, rather than by the governments and their bureaucracies.*

Triffin's postulate finds support in Hicks (1969: 63): "In its origin, money was the creation of the Mercantile Economy; though it was the first of the creations of the Mercantile Economy which governments (even quite non-mercantile governments) learned to take over".

Triffin refers to historical instances in support of his postulate. For example, the nineteenth century development of notes and bank deposits to replace the gold and silver of national monetary systems should be credited to private initiatives and the market mechanisms. "By 1913, [notes and bank deposits] already constituted about 85% of world money supplies, but it took another 35 years for the French and Italian monetary authorities, for instance, to include checking deposits in their official monetary statistics" (1984: 5).

The same postulate applies to international monetary systems. Neither the gold standard nor Bretton Woods tried to minimise intrinsic flaws. Yet their official design enshrined contradictory features that led to their failure. For example, "...the 'gold standard' originated from a 1696 English law aiming to consolidate the 'silver standard', but at an official rate overvaluing gold in relation to silver, thereby making silver more attractive as a commodity than as circulating money" (Triffin, 1984: 5). The failure of the Bretton Woods resulted from the insistence on two features. "[Its proponents] unanimously regarded the stability of exchange rates and of the price of gold - at $35 per ounce - as the unshakable pillars of any international monetary system, present or future" (Triffin, 1984: 5).

A second element of this hypothesis is that the private sector is the source of money innovation in the way money is used and money instruments are developed. It is therefore difficult to draw the dividing line between money and non-monetary assets unless one devises a method that enables one to satisfy our Essentiality criterion (H2).

In the case of the ECU, the innovations brought about in commercial banking stem mainly from the private ECU. From such an aspect, the Triffin postulate is partly satisfied. "The private sectors of the economy are, as so often in the past, overtaking and stimulating the slow progress of the official authorities towards the development of the ECU, not only as a unit of account, but as a new 'parallel' currency in international settlements, investments, and working balances" (Triffin, 1984: 12).

Consistent with the Aristotelian suggestion (i.e. once the market has invented money, then the 'polis' puts on it a stamp), the EU, in establishing the EMS in December 1978, adopted the definition of the European Unit of Account (EUA), for the ECU. But the EUA had been established in June 1975 and from then the private use of the EUA increased slowly. Until mid-1980 both EUA and ECU markets were embryonic.

The driving force behind the Triffin postulate is that the behaviour of private investors in times of uncertainty cannot be predicted; shifts in the preferences have had important effects on exchange rates or interest rates. The relative weight of the private sector derives from its share of private international portfolios. The Commission (1990) constructed the world reference portfolio shown in Table 3.1.

Table 3.1
World reference portfolio
(in billion $)

	1981	1988
World external liabilities (assets)	3 745	8 505
+ Residents' deposits in foreign currencies	312	798
= World international portfolio	4 057	9 303
- Interbank assets	1 190	3 115
- Direct investment	700	1 227
- Official reserves	515	875
= World reference portfolio	1 652	4 086

Source: Commission (1990: Table 7.6)

We find that the world international portfolio in 1988 was $9 303 billion of which 44% (i.e. $4 086 billion) was held by the private international portfolios while the official reserves accounted for 9,4% (i.e. $875 billion) of the total. In other words, private international portfolios were about five times larger than the official foreign exchange reserves. This staggering statistic is confirmed in the G 10 Report (1993), which also points out that the institutional investors have assumed increasing importance.

However, acceptability of the private ECU rests on basic prerequisites described by Triffin (1986). The ECU must be made liquid, guarantee the convertibility of ECU assets and safeguard the stability of the system by institutional arrangements, all this because the co-existence of the ECU and national money, during the transitional period, might be explosive. The gradual extension of the legal rights to use the ECU in domestic and foreign transactions should be granted.

Once the private ECU is established in the private markets as a parallel currency, the official authorities responsible for the monetary unit of their system will be forced to adopt it as their means of settlements of debt in order to capture the seigniorage externalities we describe in chapter 6. In the interim, Triffin (1986: 19) proposed that the linkage between the official and private ECU should not encourage inflationary growth, and that should deal with the external shocks and disequilibria originating in the loose management of the paper dollar; a new Plaza accord involving the G 7 should be concluded, aiming at a stable international environment. As to the evolution of national currencies, "[t]he final stage of such a process, i.e. the total replacement of national currencies by the ECU, would undoubtedly be reached much earlier in some countries than in others".

3.5.a) H4 applied to the private use of the ECU

As we said in chapter 2, the private ECU originates with the private financial markets. The first issue of private ECU was made in 1981 in the form of ECU bonds, 223 million ECU. The breakthrough came in 1985 with 12.2 billion ECU while in 1992, it was 16.2 billion ECU bond issues. The total amount of ECU bonds, as Table 3.2 shows, is estimated to have reached 110.2 billion ECUs in February 1993.

Examining Table 3.2, two things should be noted. The first is the demand side of the ECU bond market. The Bundesbank (1992b: 31) holds the view that the growth of the ECU bond was "...mainly because some member states borrowed more in ECUs to help finance their budgets". The percentage accounted for by EC Member States for the entire period 1981 to Februry 1993 was 47,3% while that of the EC institutions 14,9%. About two-thirds of all international ECU bond issues have been launched by borrowers domiciled in the EC. Yet the role of institutions of the EU should be noted since their holdings of ECU bonds is about two fifths of the total.

Table 3.2
ECU bond market by nationality of issuer
(in ECU millions)

	1981-91	%	1981-Feb.93	%
EC Countries	42 760	47,5	52 105	47,3
Japan	6 067	6,7	6 637	6,0
USA	6 811	7,5	8 036	7,3
Other Countries	15 854	17,6	19 604	17,8
EC Institutions	13 133	14,6	16 378	14,9
International Institutions	5 488	6,1	7 453	6,7
Total	90 113	100,0	110 213	100,0

Source: Kredietbank statistics, April 1993

Capital controls have played a role in increasing the demand for the private ECU; the French and Italian authorities could overcome capital controls if the ECU were used. Political considerations (see Cipolla thesis) have also played a role. For Italy, France and the Benelux, the ECU was politically more acceptable than the DM. Institutions associated with the EC have seen in the ECU a means by which European integration can be advanced. This positive discrimination explains in part the European Investment Bank's regular bond issues in ECUs.

There is another aspect of the private use of the ECU in money markets which has assumed a certain role. "In the short end of the market, the ecu also scored successes as the banks' borrowing and lending operations in ecu continued to grow at a rapid pace...a particularly strong demand for ecu deposits by the non-bank sector brought the ecu assets and liability position of the banking sector in the new balance whereas, almost continuously up to now, a very sizeable excess asset position had prevailed..." (Commission, 1991c: 131-2).

It is of interest to note that once the market has developed an innovation, it is followed by Governments. "The Italian Government pursued its issue programme of ecu treasury notes initiated in 1987. The outstanding amount of these notes, which have a one-year maturity, is presently (June 1991) 4.7 billion. Early in 1989, the British Government also launched an issue programme of ecu treasury bills. Their maturities are one, three and six months which qualifies them more particularly as reserve instruments for central banks. The amount of outstanding ecu treasury bills is now (June 1991) 3.6 billion" (Commission, 1991c: 132).

The second thing has to do with the increasing significance of the private ECU as a long-term investment. This is particularly important if one takes account of the share of ECU bonds in total international issues. In terms of percentage, as Table 3.3 shows, in 1991, ECU bonds accounted for 10,6% of the total international bond issues, in third position after the US dollar with 30,2% and the yen with 13,7%. "As a result of this rapid development, the ecu increased its market share in the Eurobond market from 4,8% in 1988 to 7,3% in 1990 and 14% in the first six months of 1991. For that period, it also became, next to the dollar, the second widely used currency for straight bond issues" (Commission, 1991c: 130).

Table 3.3
International bond issues in 1991
(in%)

US$	Yen	ECU	UK£	CAN$	SF	DM	FF	AU$	Other	Total
30,2	13,7	10,6	8,7	7,6	6,8	6,7	5,9	1,5	8,3	100

Source: Deutsch Bundesbank (1992b)

Growth in banks' business in ECU should be seen in its context; it supports the statistical findings of Gros and Thygesen (1992) cited in chapter 2. The Bundesbank (1992b: 27-8) admits: "The fact that ECU business is subject to laws of its own, became particularly obvious last year, when, against the background of the economic recession in the industrial countries and a restrained lending policy on the part of certain categories of banks, aggregate foreign currency business contracted, whereas banks' ECU-denominated claims continued to expand".

The determinants of demand for private ECU have been the transaction costs, the size and depth of the market, the internalisation of the risk externality and economies of scale. Demand initially came from portfolio adjustment where the ECU was used as a convenient hedge against exchange rate variability. The private ECU has emerged as an efficient financial investment in the sense that there was no other national currency that offered a higher return for the same risk.

Even the market for the ECU derivatives has developed. It is possible to take forward positions in the ECU to cover interest rate exposure. Such a change in preference, though, will have consequences for management of risk because systemic risk will increase through the increasing interdependence of non-banking institutions in the traditional business of finance. Trust, insurance companies and life assurance investors are partly interlinked, via the development of new private ECU markets.

Consequently, the private ECU in the banking sector has followed a similar growth pattern. The share of the ECU in foreign currency positions of banks jumped from near zero in 1983 to 4% in 1990. At the end of 1991, the position of the ECU in banks' foreign currency business was in terms of claims, 5.4% and in terms of liabilities, 5.2% (see Table 3.4). In other words, the ECU has progressed to the position of the third most important lending currency, on equal standing with the yen (5%) after the US dollar (54%) and DM (14%).

Table 3.4
Banks' foreign currency business in 1991
(in %)

	ECU	US$	DM	Yen	SF	UK£	FF	Other
Claims	5,4	53,7	13,8	5,4	4,7	3,3	2,9	10,8
Liabilities	5.2	52,9	14,7	4,8	4,9	3,6	2,7	11,2

Source: Deutsch Bundesbank (1992b)

In fact, the banking sector has established the private ECU as a Eurocurrency with an autonomous status. The ECU's yield is not the weighted average of the yield curves of the component currencies, but reflects partly its semi-autonomous existence and the influence of the stronger currencies. This position is somewhat modified if one examines the currency turmoil of September 1992. The price of ECU bonds fell for the first time after 1987 although, until then, the actual yield on ECU securities had remained above the theoretical yield (which is obtainable by buying securities in each of the currencies making up the ECU). After the first Danish referendum, the actual yields fell to nearly 70 basis points below the theoretical. This trend was reversed in January 1993 with new issues of bonds by France (2.4 billion ECUs) and the UK (0.5 billion ECUs). In April 1993, the actual and theoretical yields were equalised, with a trend for the actual falling lower than the theoretical, thus reflecting the belief that the ECU has regained its earlier strength.

The structure of the ECU money market is interesting for a number of reasons. As Table 3.5 shows, at the end of September 1992, the ECU assets outstanding were 200 billion ECU and ECU liabilities outstanding, 201 billion ECU, with the private agents holding about 17,48% and banks 79,6% of liabilities; for assets, the percentages were: 29,8% and 70,2%. Both non-banks' claims and liabilities have inreased sixthfold in a period of less than six years. Should the trend continue, the money markets in Member States would change drastically.

Table 3.5
Structure of ECU money
(in ECU billion)

	1986	1991	Sep.1992
Total Claims of which	70.3	178.6	199.9
to non-banks	16.5	47.7	59.6
banks	53.8	130.9	140.3
Total Liabilities of which	60.4	176.4	200.9
to non-banks	6.4	29.4	35.0
banks	54.0	147.0	166.0
Official balances	2.9	28.8	n.a.

Source: BIS, International Banking and Financial Market
        Developments, February 1993

The strong expansion of interbank business can be explained by the following factors. The pegging of the Scandinavian and Austrian currencies to the ECU has allowed the private sector of these countries to convert their short-term Euro-market debt into ECUs. The use of the private ECU by central banks has had no precedent. National central banks have held ECU bonds and ECU Treasury bills. Their holdings in 1991 amounted to 28.8 billion ECUs but diminished during the currency turmoil of September 1992.

One may say that this growth in the ECU money market might have been a 'source of disruption' of monetary policy because national central banks have no direct control over banks' ECU liquidity creation in banking centres without minimum reserve requirements. Take the case of ECU holdings of non-banks of Table 3.5. These have taken the form of deposits of the non-bank sector with banks located in countries other than those in which the holders are residents, i.e. cross border holdings. "Despite their expansion in recent years, CBHs still represent a relatively small proportion of Community residents' monetary assets...However, as financial integration progresses further, CBHs may become increasingly important in the future" (Committee of Governors, 1993: 29).

Despite the success of the ECU in the bond, money and foreign reserve markets, the corporate sector has neither priced, nor invoiced, nor paid for trade in ECUs. "On average, less than 1% of the EC countries' total exports are invoiced in ecu. The figures are somewhat higher in Portugal and Spain but close to zero in Germany. They are also somewhat better for the current-account transactions as these include servicing payments on the financial transactions in ecus..." (Commission, 1991c: 132). This apparent reluctance was expressed by Lomax (1983b: 300) who had reviewed the literature of corporate consultants and arrived at this conclusion: "most authors point out that these composite units tend to suit companies only with somewhat unusual circumstances, and do not coincide with the normal range of risks with which companies need to deal".

On the other hand, the development of securities markets in private ECU has established it as a financing instrument for the business sector. This shift away from bank lending towards finance via securities issues is the result of market innovation brought about by the private sector aided by the process of globalisation. Crawford (1993: 233) recorded the trend: "A shift of this kind occurred in the USA in the 1980s and is still going on there; indeed, it has intensified since 1990 as companies have been repaying back debts and issuing bonds and equities. ... In future, securities will grow faster than bank credits in Europe, by a substantial margin".

Central bankers have interpreted the small percentage of ECU bank deposits by non-banks as posing no direct threat to monetary policy in Europe because such holdings do not account for more than 0,5% of the total money stock in the EC countries. Such an assumption is correct provided one assumes that money is still a commodity or paper with no serious near-money and that money supply is defined as M1. The efficiency of this old method becomes doubtful if, in the mean time, money has changed its character and has become credit or electronic money as we argue in chapter 7. Yet, even the Bundesbank (1992b: 25) admits that "...since the end of 1990 the market rates of interest have continuously fallen short of the respective 'basket parity'. On various occasions this had been interpreted as indicating that the private ECU has now detached itself from the basket definition and has become a currency in its own right".

How could one explain the autonomous existence of the private ECU while it lacks the traditional characteristics of money? An explanation may reside in an economic model that takes account of parallel currencies and their relationship in terms of determination of their prices. This is what we do in chapter 4 where Walras's paper money resembles the private ECU in terms of its monetary role in the *Elements*.

There has been a divergence of views between the Commission and some Member States, in particular Germany, as to the official promotion of the ECU. Why? It should be recalled that the European Council of December 1978 committed itself to creating the EMF which would mean the full utilization of the ECU as a reserve asset and a means of settlement within two years from the date of entry of the EMS. When March 1981 came, the initial enthusiasm had evaporated. "The path to joint official action on Monetary integration was effectively cut off and the Commission was left with no other choice than to try to propagate the ECU, the symbol of Community Monetary Integration, as a sui generis currency in the respective member states" (Moss 1984: 49).

Despite differences in aims, the promotion of private ECU by the

Commission falls squarely within the logic of the Triffin postulate: 'use the mechanisms of the market to bring about full integration on monetary matters'. Hence the Triffin postulate suggests a policy option: *The nature of a monetary institution will evolve as the nature of its monetary unit evolves.* So, if one wishes to change or modify a monetary institution, one could do it efficiently through the change or modification of its money. Causality runs from the nature of money to the nature of monetary institutions, not the other way.

This suggestion accords well with the Cipolla thesis that refers to independent monetary units, not composite currencies. Composite currencies have never served an 'own' monetary system for a long time. This implies that transforming the EMS into EMU will be effected more efficiently if one concentrates on the monetary 'nature' of the ECU.

However, the Triffin postulate, as a method by which money gets established, raises two important and unsettled monetary questions:

a) Under what conditions would the market mechanism establish the ECU as a parallel currency in the Community?

b) What consequences for national currencies, for fiscal and monetary policies and for national institutions would be envisaged, if the ECU were established as a parallel currency?

Question a) calls for the examination of H5, i.e. the Essentiality criterion, and its embodied suggestive capacity. If the ECU is considered essential as a parallel currency in the Community, it should meet the nexus of causality of H5 and be examined within the confines of a monetary theory. Question b) can only be settled provided that the co-existence of two currencies is consistent with H1 to H5.

3.6.H5 The Essentiality criterion

The Essentiality Criterion as a *hypothesis* is an economical way of stating *three* inseparable ideas:

a) the nexus of causality in monetary theory,
b) why money is essential in an economy, and
c) the welfare aspects of money.

These three inseparable ideas, in explaining the issues concerned with monetary institutions, seek to provide an answer to the question of 'what purpose, implicit or explicit, would EMU serve' *and* a reply to the priorities set by monetary theory.

Idea a) states the line of monetary causality and is specified in Table 3.6 as follows:

Table 3.6
Diagram on the nexus of causality

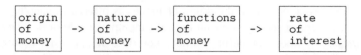

The nexus of causality states that it is the *origin of money which determines its nature.* The origin proper and its characteristics will also define the constraints on a proposed asset to be used as money or to cause an asset to fall into disuse. In other words, it is the economic process that defines money, not the other way.

When discussing the Aristotelian notion of evolving money, we found that pure exchange did not invent money. *It was the stage of economic development that had devised money to facilitate exchange.* In other words, the degree of the division of labour and specialisation, the level of technological advance and communication, economies of scale and size of the market as well as capital accumulation necessitated the invention of money to minimise the high transaction costs of alternative structures of exchange.

Under H5, we go further and say that it is of interest to know *whether* asset A or B will be chosen by the private sector, consistent with H4, to act as money and *why*. In providing an answer to the questions of *whether* and *why*, we can identify the origin of money. This will lead us to think of the relative costs and benefits of money A or B *and* will also tell us how money affects and is affected by the institutional structure.

It seems reasonable to argue that the origin of money is associated with the costs and benefits of a money economy and of the continued existence of money. Should the origin of money be found, it would also tell us the monetary links between three processes: exchange, production and distribution; or what the likely effects would be under full employment conditions or less-than-full employment; or how it may stimulate output in a slump and may alter relative prices.

The evolution of monetary institutions could be explained provided that we specify the likely origin of their money. Such an approach would also tells us something about the distributional effects of money and how these would change if money changes its character. Hence the welfare aspects are also addressed.

Traditional monetary theory identifies at least four doctrines on the origin of money: a) Chartalism, which claims that money originates in the will of the State; b) Nominalism, which asserts that money originates in social conventions; c) Commodity theory, which holds the view that money is one commodity amongst others, and d) Utility theory, which believes that money circulates only because of the utility, direct or indirect, of the money-stuff.

As we argue in chapter 4, doctrines c) and d) share common characteristics in their treatment of the role of money and thus are examined as one. In chapter 5, we treat doctrines a) and b) under the State theory of money.[46] An alternative approach to the origin of money is offered in chapter 6 and 7.

By the *nature* of money is meant the stuff money is made of or its *monetary character*. It does not define money, nor does it say what money does. Provided we explain *why* the nature of money changes as the Aristotelian stages unfold reflecting changes in technology, economies of scale, capital accumulation and division of labour, we may also explain the transformation of the character of money. Through its evolution, it would also suggest why the relevance and significance of the functions of money have changed over the years as the factors determining money's origin had changed.

Received monetary theory, either directly as in Hicks (1967) or indirectly through its properties as in Keynes (1936), defines money by its *functions*. Popper (1972: 20-21), by contrast, claims that functional definitions make no sense, since definitions "never give any factual knowledge about nature or about the nature of things". In fact, a definition is not and can never be an explanation. Furthermore, the argument of the functional definition is *circular* because it concentrates on the functions while, at the same time, it states that 'money is what money does'. The subject-matter is to explain *why money is what it is* and to describe *why money does what it does in that way*.

H5 on the nexus of causality differs from the nexus of received monetary theory. For example, Hicks's (1989) nexus of causality is:

functions of money ---> nature ---> rate of interest.[47]

In other words, Hicks disregards the origin of money as a causal factor although he does recognize that the market has invented money.

Our central argument concerns all monetary aspects. That is to say that the type of asset functioning as a means of settlement of debt or of exchange or of store of value, the type of monetary policy, the kind of power (economic, financial or political) that money entails, the substitutability of currencies or currency convertibility and the monetary institutions that should be created to accommodate the needs and requirements of the issue, control and distribution of money, all these aspects are related to one fundamental principle of monetary theory: *What is the monetary character of money?* It is this question which for us, should be the subject-matter of all monetary theory.

Idea b) of H5 on why money is essential in an economy, raises a simple question: *Is money neutral, non-neutral or super-non-neutral?*. We have followed Schumpeter's analysis in order to understand the monetary links. According to Schumpeter (1954: 277-8), whereas Real Analysis holds that "all essential phenomena of economic life are capable of being described in terms of goods and services, of decisions about them, and of relations between them", Monetary Analysis has a different analytic objective:

Monetary Analysis, in the first place, spells denial of the proposition that, with the exception of what may be called monetary disorders, the element of money is of secondary importance in the explanation of the economic process of reality. ... In the second place, then, Monetary Analysis introduces the element of money on the very ground floor of our analytic structure and abandons the idea that all essential features of economic life can be represented by a barter-economy model. Money prices, money incomes, and saving and investment decisions bearing upon these money incomes, no longer appear as expressions...of quantities of commodities and services and of exchange ratios between them: they acquire a life and an importance of their own, and it has to be recognized that essential features of the capitalist process may depend upon the 'veil' and that the 'face behind it' is incomplete without it.

Idea b) of H5 also states that a well specified economic model should be consistent with H1 to H5 and should be instrumental in *integrating the value and monetary theories*. This would require, inter alia, specifying the precise influence of money on production, exchange, distribution and consumption decisions and also the likely changes that would follow, if demand for or supply of money changed.[48]

In a money economy, the linkages between production, exchange and distribution are not always specified. Clower (1971: 24-5) identified the likely linkages resulting from a change in the quantity of money:

Such changes will also directly affect fixed investment decisions, via their effect upon security markets;... in a money economy all inventory decisions will be affected directly by changes in money flows that alter either the level or composition of the stock of money. Monetary influences will also affect real economic magnitudes via familiar channels - interest rates, wealth effects and so forth... .

As to the received monetary theories concentrating on idea b) of H5, Ellis (1934) contrasted the doctrines and identified four types of theory: a) the Utility theory, b) the Commodity theory, c) the State theory, d) the Credit theory.

For theoretical reasons, the four types of theory should be treated separately and contrasted on the basis of their details. In terms of fundamentals, explanations of the origin, nature and value of money still fall into two major schools: *nominalism* and *commodity theory*. In this respect, we have followed Ellis's (1934: 12) taxonomy: "Because of a natural kinship of ideas, those writers who attribute the existence of money to the adoption by trade usage of a certain 'unit of value' also believe that the value of money is not to be assimilated to that of goods; and those who trace the origin of money to the gradual growth in importance of one 'exchange commodity' are precisely those who would give to money the character of a commodity in its value".

Nominalism entails two wings: chartalism or state theory (to be treated in chapter 5) and credit theory. The commodity theory embraces the marginal utility and metallism (to be treated in chapter 4).[49]

Idea c) of H5 on the welfare aspects of money, could be explained by reference to the role assigned to money by received monetary theory. The distributional aspects of money have either been neglected or treated as an after-thought. The single most important aspect of H5 is that a money economy that differs qualitatively and quantitatively from models discussed in value theory, cannot separate *efficiency* from *equity*. This is the essence of idea c) of H5. It introduces the notion that money affects all the variables contributing to social welfare and the welfare of individuals comprising that society.

Such a statement implies a Social Welfare Function different from the one implicitly assumed by conventional monetary theory.[50] Received monetary theory concentrates on 'allocative efficiency or Pareto-optimality' (defined as a situation when at least, one person could be made better off while no-one else is made worse off), in exchange and to a lesser extent in investment decisions. Equity plays no role. Hence the social utility function is given by

$$W=W(U_a, U_b, ..., U_n)$$

where U_a, ..., U_n are ordinal utility indicators of individual a, b,..., n. We also need to make ethical judgements in comparing Us or to evaluate the contribution of a or b to social welfare.

Even if we disregard the fact that there is no objective measurement conceivable of Us, traditional monetary theory states that, once the three conditions for efficiency: efficient consumption (all individuals place the same relative value on all products), efficient production (marginal rate of substitution between factors should be the same in all industries) and product-mix efficiency (the subjective value of commodity x in terms of commodity y should be equal to its marginal cost), are satisfied, then the Pareto-optimal is attained.

However, we insist that monetary theory, in the sense of chapter 6 where money is an externality, necessarily introduces a different dimension to social welfare function, independent of the definition of the latter. In short, we argue in chapter 7 that the above function ought to be modified as follows:

$$W=W(U_a, U_b, ..., U_n, M_E)$$

where M_E is an index of externalities induced by the institution of money. M_E *is not real money balances.* The subjective nature of the Us is not solved. We only argue that efficiency and equity are *inseparable* because their interdependence is assured by M_E, inducing changes in the individual utilities derived from consumption, production and exchange.

M_E should not be confused with Patinkin's (1965: ch. IX) real money balances (M/P). Whereas Patinkin's M/P are quantifiable in the sense that they are stocks, as we argue in chapter 6, M_E are not since money externalities are unmeasurable and purely qualitative. Whereas Patinkin's M/P play the role of a variable in the excess demand functions of the goods and in bond or money demand functions via its induced real balance effect, M_E establish an endogenous money supply, which is contrary to Patinkin's exogenous supply of money. Whereas Patinkin's real balance effect is the integrating element for the real and monetary sectors, M_E act as the mechanism of redistribution of wealth and of distribution of income.

The important difference between our money externalities and Patinkin's real balance effect resides in the fact that, as we show in chapter 6, money is super-non-neutral while Patinkin's model simply assumes the absence of money illusion. Yet the question underlying the difference is *why money exists* in the two models.

It should be stressed that H5 is assumed in the context of three states of nature: a) uncertainty, b) the maximization principle, c) free entry.

Uncertainty and money are seen in the sense expressed by Rosenstein -Rodan (1936: 272): "Money (as cash balance) exists only and in so far as general foresight is not certain, it is a function of the individual's feeling of uncertainty, a means of meeting it: a good satisfying the want for certainty". Money and uncertainty are mutually compatible.

The maximization principle is borrowed from microeconomic analysis. It is used to express the idea that money holders are rational economic agents who prefer more to less, given the constraints of their budget and institutional structures.

The assumption of free entry is also borrowed from microeconomic analysis. It recognizes that the institutional setting could restrict the application of the principle of free entry but asserts that all agents or money are treated on a non-discriminatory basis.[51]

3.6.a) H5 applied to EMU and the ECU

In neither the Delors report nor the TEU, did they bother to ask whether their version of monetary union was welfare increasing. The case for EMU was made by the Commission's (1990) study on *One market, One money*, evaluating the potential benefits and costs of EMU. The underlying hypothesis is allocative efficiency as viewed by the theory of optimum currency areas; namely, that a single currency involves a trade-off between the benefits stemming from monetary integration and the costs associated with the loss of adjustment instruments. This approach was supplemented by analyses of imperfect markets, the optimal exchange rate policy, the economics of borrowed credibility, the effects of exchange rate instability and the gains of international currencies.[52]

The Commission (1990: 63) has estimated the *efficiency gains*, which arise from the elimination of transaction costs and uncertainty inherent in exchange rate regimes. If a single currency is assumed, the following are assumed to hold: a) savings resulting from the elimination of currency conversion are estimated at 'ECU 14 billion per annum, or about 0,4% of Community GDP'; b) transaction cost savings 'may be of the order of between 0,1% and 0,2% of GDP' for the large economies while a 'gain around 1% of GDP' for the small economies; c) elimination of 'transaction costs incurred by firms can be estimated to amount to some 15% of their profits'; d) reduction in banking costs associated with cross-border payments; e) a 'reduction in the risk premium of real exchange rate variability by 0,5 percentage point could raise income in the Community significantly, possibly up to 5.10%'. All these efficiency gains are expected to lead the Community to a new growth path. Yet Baldwin (1991) has quantified the one-time efficiency gains: 'a 1% efficiency gain could give rise to a permanent increase in growth rate of 0.1%'.

An element of double counting is involved. For example, findings b) and c) are shown as profits in national accounts. Finding e) solely depends on the formation of expectations about future profitability.

The efficiency gains have been variously assessed. Crockett (1991: 4) believed that the "conclusions surely exaggerate the benefits that would flow from a single currency. At the same time, the potential costs of adopting a single currency before adequate convergence is achieved have been understated". Emerson (1990: 37) stated the contrary: "New economic theory and particular features of the Community's actual structure and situation add six [borrowed price stability for small and open states, incidence of economic shocks, policy credibility, regime change, dynamic growth gains and international policy coordination] further major arguments, all pointing to benefits for EMU in the Community. On these grounds the economic case becomes strongly advantageous". A balanced view is expressed by Currie (1992: 238): "These calculations are pretty soft, and perhaps should not be taken seriously, but it is clear that the potential benefits could be significant".

The *benefits stemming from price stability* have been argued by the Commission (1990: 87) to be: i) an anticipated inflation of 10% leads to direct welfare losses that are of the same order of magnitude, about 0,3% of GDP; ii) high inflation countries have a higher unemployment rate and a lower per capita income and on average more unstable growth rates; iii) there is a strong link between central bank independence and inflation.

The *external dimension* of the ECU is found to be significant. The Commission's (1990: 178) main conclusions are: a) if the ECU is established as a vehicle currency in the Community, it will reduce transaction costs on the exchange market for the trade with non-EC countries 'up to 0,05% of Community GDP', reduce exchange rate risks due to the development of ECU invoicing and enlarge opportunities to European banks to work in their own currency; b) a saving on the exchange reserves of Member States is estimated to amount to USD 200 billion; c) seigniorage arising from foreign cash holdings of ECU are estimated to be of the order of '0,045% of Community GDP annually, corresponding to about USD 35 billion of foreign holding'.

These potential gains are set against the potential costs. The costs (loss of national monetary policy and of currency realignment) are studied under conditions where there would be no need for different monetary policies; such conditions are the economic circumstances of member states (convergent or divergent), the similarity of external shocks, the response of domestic economies to external stimuli and the consistency of fiscal policy and of other policies. The study argues that these conditions are relatively weak, due to the interdependence of the economies rendering both instruments inoperative.

Given the theoretical problems associated with the optimum currency areas, a more interesting appreciation of the EMU may be to examine the institutional case of EMU under H1 to H5 and concentrate on the institutional change of policy-making represented by the ECU. Such an approach, we argue in chapter 7, would lead to the conclusion that the institutional structure of EMU is inadequate and should be supplemented by a European Fiscal Authority, based not on federal-type arguments but on the internalisation of externalities arising from the monetary nature of the single currency of the system. In such a context, equity cannot be neglected because one man's gain is another man's loss in a zero-sum game and it is inequitable in a positive-sum game. Hence, Pareto-optimality cannot be defined purely on efficiency criteria.

3.7 Concluding remarks

The above considerations point to a direction different from those hitherto followed. They effectively imply a new approach based on H1 to H5, which constitute different priorities and alter the received theory's method of analysis. H1 to H5 as hypotheses define the methodology of this thesis in the same way as the assumptions of Keynes in the *General Theory*, which largely determine the argument . The same applies to Walras's assumptions in the *Elements*, which stipulate the theoretical setting of his general equilibrium.

H1 to H5 are meant to serve as partial premises for explaining and for suggesting. The overriding priority has been to identify the forces that explain *why* the EMU has been agreed to (H1), *when* its third stage would be sufficiently advanced to adopt a single currency (H2), *how* this monetary unit would be introduced (H3), *what* means would be needed to transform existing structures to facilitate the acceptance of the ECU (H4) and *what* purpose EMU and its anchor would serve (H5). The discussion boils down to one premise:

The origin, evolution and transformation of a monetary institution is the result of the origin, nature and role of its anchor.

Which theoretical model meets the logic of H1 to H5? In chapter 4, we review the Utility theory through a restatement of Walras's theory of money. In chapter 5, we survey the State theories via a review of Keynes's theory of money. The objective is to know whether these theories contain an explanation that can then suggest *how* the present status of the ECU should be developed or *what* further research is to be useful for the systematization of the final phase of EMU.

114

Notes

1. Holtfrerich (1989) discusses the German experience where Prussia had a dominant note-issuing authority before the establishment of the Reichsbank in 1876 and noted that before political unification, Germany was an integrated economic area with a currency based on a silver standard. The German experience would be comparable to EMU to the extent that the Bundesbank would be transformed into a European central bank, but he added: "This would certainly be unacceptable politically outside Germany" (p. 235).

2. Sannucci (1989) demonstrates that monetary unification in Italy was the result of political unification and had preceded economic integration. The issuance of paper money was at first made by a private bank, the Sardinian National Bank, later to become the National Bank which was merged with the Tuscan National Bank in 1893 and formed the 'Banca d'Italia'. Sannucci has arrived at some conclusions relevant to EMU. Currency competition did not result in a reverse Gresham-Law; it mainly fuelled instability. The independence of the Bank was never granted. Attempts at modifying the structure of monetary and financial markets were not always successful. Centralisation of monetary interventions took longer than in former times of decentralisation.

3. Miron's (1989) account of 'what had preceded the Federal Reserve Act of December 1913' is a fine example of a series of monetary disturbances (i.e. Hicksian proposition) leading to the creation of an institution. The underlying problem of the time was solved by the adoption of the Gold Standard; today, that solution has very little relevance to EMU faced with global markets. Yet the federal structure of the Federal Reserve System has many affinities to EMU.

4. Wittelsberger (1991) discusses the institutional aspects of the Bundesbank with respect to the statute of the ECB and draws attention to the constitutional rules and objectives that give rise to confidence externalities. Marsh (1993) gives an account of Bundesbank's struggle to gain independence and thus power.

5. See Hodgson (1988: ch. 2) for a critique of Friedman's and Popper's methodology. Blaug (1992) surveyed the literature on methodology and proposed a reformulation of Popper's falsificationism.

6. Robbins (1984: xiv) stated 'verification' as "the formation of hypotheses explaining and (possibly) predicting the outcome of the relationships concerned and the testing of such hypotheses by logic and by observation. This process of testing used to be called 'verification'". Hamouda and Price (1991) reformulated 'verification' to encompass the notions of 'confirmation, validation, falsification and modification'.

7. Kaldor (1985: 8-9) stated the *stylised facts* : "one should subordinate

115

deduction to induction, and discover the empirical regularities first, whether through a study of statistics or through special inquiring... One should also seek the most reasonable explanation capable of accounting for these "facts", independently of whether they fit into the general framework of received theory or not".

8. See Sheila C. Dow (1985: ch. 2) for a useful discussion on the modes of thought and their application to macroeconomics. Dow also elucidates how theories have been formulated and what are their basic differences in treating knowledge.

9. See Branson (1976) on why the instability of expectations causes high volatility and instability in short-run exchange rates.

10. According to Dornbusch (1976), under flexible exchange rates, uncoordinated monetary policies produce overshooting.

11. Thygesen (1986) applied the reasoning of misalignments to the EMS countries and argued that there is evidence to suppose that misalignments played a role in the decision of the EMS.

12. Artus and Young (1979) summarize the arguments about the inflationary risks associated with flexible rates; it is harder to maintain discipline of macroeconomic policies under flexible rates.

13. Tarshis (1984) looked into the debt problem and its dimension after the breakdown of Bretton Woods and warned that large scale defaults were still possible.

14. Scott (1986) cited instances in which overshooting was considered harmful and said: 'A major benefit of the EMS is to have reduced for its members the prospect of an overshooting exchange rate'.

15. These figures are given in Reading (1979).

16. See Williamson (1977) on the causes of collapse of Bretton Woods. Triffin's classic study (1960) on the gold standard is essential reading.

17. See Wallich (1972) for an interesting analysis of the *inconsistent trinity*, and for an analysis of the crisis of the Bretton Woods system. The term *logical inconsistency* was used instead by Padoa-Schioppa (1988). The EP report (A3-0294) proposes a reform of the EMS that would enable the inconsistent trinity to be managed during the second stage of EMU.

18. Masera (1989: 337) described the redundancy problem: "It should indeed be recognized that complete integration of national markets entails exchange rates remaining fixed. Otherwise, financial assets held in different currencies will not be perfectly substitutable, an indispensable condition for full integration. Financial integration itself calls for monetary convergence. In principle, sovereignty in monetary matters, which takes the form of autonomy in controlling the money supply and the exchange rate, is not compatible with the objective of creating by 1992 a 'single' European financial market".

19. Dornbusch (1991: 317-8) made a serious accusation on the loss of

independence of monetary policy: "In most European countries monetary policy has become powerless. Exchange-rate expectations are governed by accumulated imbalances and loss of competitiveness, and by political squabbles about who 'makes' inflation and who 'suffers' from it, not by short-run monetary policy...Once the ability to conduct any kind of independent monetary policy is so far gone one can ask why countries should not go ahead and abandon the pretence altogether".

20. See EP report (A3-0392) and the article by the President of Bundesbank, Tietmeyer (1993) on the implications for monetary policy brought about by the changing character of capital markets.

21. Former Chancellor of Germany, Helmut Schmidt appearing before the Monetary Subcommittee of the European Parliament on 2 December 1992, stated four motives that have given rise to EMU: security after the collapse of the USSR, fear of the dominance of the united Germany, monetary counterbalance with respect to the USA and Japan and the logical extension of the single market.

22. The case for the permanent importance of the Greek studies has been made by Skemp (1980).

23. As far as the sources consulted, we have not found any interpretation or statement of Aristotle's monetary theory of the kind developed in this section. The sources are: Trever [1916 (1978)], Houmanidis (1990), Gordon (1975), Reck (1935), Calhoun (1926), Laister (1923), Souchon (1898), Gomperz (1901), Schumpeter (1954), Berthoud (1981), Saint-Germes (1928), Lowry (1987), Langholm (1979).

24. The method by which food is procured is used by Aristotle to identify the stages of development (see Politics 1256a 40). Childe (1950) also defined 'savagery', 'barbarism' and 'civilization' by the criterion of the methods adopted for procuring food.

25. Support for this statement is found in Cipolla (1956: 12): "When a large part of the transactions are in the form of unilateral payments, when the society is at a rather primitive stage of economic development with slight division of labour, when shortages of commodities are frequent and dangerous, when because of the bad conditions of the market and an unbalanced distribution of income there are drastic and frequent shortages of coins, when, in a word, coins are not always available and not always desired, a society understandably moves toward a barter economy".

26. The role of capital accumulation or social surplus in the transformation of simple associations into later civilizations is paramount. Childe (1950) saw the social surplus as the moving and determinant factor in transforming savagery into civilization. In short social surplus initiated a new economic stage in the evolution of primitive societies into civil stage societies.

27. The word 'natural' had a special meaning for the pre-Socratic and

Socratic philosophers. For Aristotle, 'nature makes nothing idly or without purpose' (Politics, 1256b, 21). He does not deny that nature has her faults, simply he denies that nature is aimless.

28. Notice a difference between the *Ethics* and *Politics*. In the *Ethics*, Aristotle says that money originates as a social convention: "this is why money is called 'nomisma' (customary currency), because it does not exist by nature but by custom (nomos), and can be altered and rendered useless at will" (Ethics, 1133a 29). The same statement is repeated again in Ethics, 1133b 21. But in the *Politics*, money originated in the market when the Middle stage was attained.

29. Even Plato was in favour of credit provided it would take a particular form: 'no State guarantee and at lender's risk, if it exceeds the legal limit' (see Laws, book VIII 850).

30. See Niebyl (1946) and Green (1992) on the salient features of the classical theories of money.

31. Gordon (1975: 11) gives a lucid account of banking in the Athens of Pericles (461 to 430 B.C.): "Banking companies were formed and exercised a powerful influence. Their main business was money changing, since a wide variety of coinage was brought into the city by foreign trade. Nevertheless, they also received deposits, made payments for clients, undertook debt recovery, issued letters of credit, and invested in business ventures".

32. Cooper's analysis (1985) and Hamada's papers (1974, 1976, 1979) have become classic in their treatment of the reasons for economic interdependence and of the consequences for macroeconomic policy.

33. See Steinherr (1984) who sets the problem in the context of game theory.

34. The idea that the purchasing power of money is not fixed but more stable than any other commodity, as Chick (1978: 42-3) interpreted Keynes (1936), is not new. Aristotle had stated 2 360 years ago: "money is under the same law as other commodities, for its purchasing power fluctuates, but still its tendency is to remain more fixed than other commodities value" (Ethics, 1133b 15).

35. Support for changing 'high unitary value' for 'high confidence' in the monetary unit is found in Klein (1974, 1978a, 1978b).

36. All statistics referred to in this section are taken from the official publications of the Community.

37. Community GDP was 5 408,2 million ECU while the USA was second with 4 717,5 million ECU and Japan third with 3 024,1 million ECU.

38. In 1992, the Community population was 330 235 000. The USA and Japan had 255 045 000 and 124 650 000 inhabitants respectively.

39. In 1990, the Community's imports from the rest of the world accounted for about 10% of its GDP, while the USA's imports accounted for 9,2% of its GDP and Japan's imports accounted for 7,9% of its GDP.

40. The Community's IMF quota position stood at 27 981 million ECU while USA's was 18 901 million ECU and Japan's 4 454 million ECU.
41. See Mundell (1980: 379) for the term 'marketability'.
42. The ECU and the SDR are called 'composite currencies' because this definition accords with Hicks's definition of the 'composite commodity' in his *Value and Capital* (1939), which assumes fixed exchange rates. Aschheim and Park (1976) prefer the definition of artificial currency units (ACU).
43. Van den Boogoerde (1984) associated the growth of the private 'composite currencies' with the technical criterion of the inherent stability of the basket. The unsatisfactory performance of flexible exchange rates has offered a sure hedging to the private users.
44. See EP report (A3-0029/93) for proposals concerning the system of payments in the context of EMU,
45. See EP report (A3-0296/93) for an analysis of the consequences for national monetary policy if the legal obstacles to the use of the ECU are removed and for a method to promote the ECU in financial markets.
46. An extreme interpretation of the State theory of money might claim that the State is so coercive that it could impose 'its' money and enforce it. Even Plato, father of the State Theory of money, would have condemned such an interpretation. There might have been brief historical instances when a Ruler imposed his 'metallic' money; this would have been for 'domestic' exchange and could have never assumed an 'international' monetary function.
47. See Harris (1981: ch. 1) for a discussion of the fundamental questions of monetary theory and for an examination of the three functions of money: store of value, medium of exchange and unit of account. Whereas Wicksell (Lect.II) stresses mainly the medium of exchange function, Harris (1981: 10) believes that "Money is a Store of Value", which is of primary importance.
48. Harris (1979) and Chick (1991a) discuss money's role: remuneration of labour in money wages, synchronisation of exchanges, separation of purchase from sale and of production from consumption, storage of purchasing power, monetary profits and liability management. These roles make money essential in an economy.
49. For example, Walras's commodity money in the *Elements* is about the 'attributes of a commodity' (i.e. precious metals) and thus he traced the origin of money in its 'exchange commodity' nature. From the latter, he derived money's functions and consequently its value.
50. The approach preferred by Bergson (1938) and Graaff (1957) is followed in this section; we return to it in chapter 7.
51. A State theorist may claim that if one assumes free entry, one rules out the State theory by assumption. If that is true, then the State theory of

money is a special case applicable only to closed economies, which can say very little on the basic questions of monetary theory. In chapter 5, we demonstrate that this is not the case. Other defaults make this theory inappropriate for explaining the origin, development and transformation of monetary institutions.

52. See Baldwin (1991), Marston (1984), Giavazzi and Pagano (1988), Williamson (1985) and Alogoskoufis and Portes (1991) on these aspects.

4 Walras's theory of money and the ECU

4.1 Introduction[1]

The theoretical conceptualisation of the first and second stage of EMU fully resembles Walras's conceptualisation of monetary theory based on bimetallism supplemented by a paper money. All Neo-Walrasian proposals either to reform the EMS or to redefine the ECU, have derived their theoretical inspiration from Walras's monetary theory. The odd thing is that not a single proposal in this domain has admitted its indebtedness to Walras. However, one cannot understand the parallel currency proposals unless one grasps the theoretical foundations upon which they are based.

Walras's theory of money accords with the Kaldorian 'stylised facts' and hypotheses: H1 to H5 for the following reasons. First, Walras claims to have solved the problem of integration of value and money models as required by our H5 in the 'édition définitive' of his *Elements*[2]:

> There remains, then, only to find the price of circulating capital and to see what becomes of all these prices when the numéraire is also money. This is the object of the problem of circulation and money. We shall see in this fourth edition how the inclusion of the "desired cash balance" made it possible for me to state and solve this problem within this static framework in exactly the same terms and in precisely the same way as I solved the preceding problems (El.: 42).

Second, Walras's paper money resembles the ECU. Walras's paper money has no independent existence; it is based on a system of 100 per cent metallic coinage in which "money consist[s] of inconvertible 'paper francs', but where prices [are] quoted in 'metallic francs' of gold or silver" (El.: 325). Yet in Walras's bimetallic international system, paper money should be convertible for otherwise it has no meaning. The same applies to the ECU; its existence depends on a basket of twelve national currencies, and its convertibility remains a pure theoretical possibility. Walras's paper money and the ECU are also defined by their functions.

Third, Walras's international monetary system is bimetallic based on gold and silver; the EMCF in the first and EMI in the second stage of EMU are also based on gold and dollar reserves; the mixed system of EMU partly resembles bimetallism.

Fourth, Walras's theory of money belongs to the Aristotelian Middle Stage. Given the fact that his theory is static and applicable to one period analysis until effective equilibrium is attained, the Aristotelian notion of evolving money (H2) is not satisfied. Walras's money does not evolve. Yet H2 implies high interdependence of sectors and of countries, which is similar to the theoretical interdependence of Walras's system.

Fifth, Walras's theory of commodity money or paper money belongs to a period in which the monetary disturbance led him to adhere to bimetallism at the cost of the consistency of his assumptions; that might not fully resemble the monetary disturbance that gave birth to the EMS or EMU but both are consistent with the Hicksian proposition of historical contingency (H1).

Sixth, Walras's theory of money is free of institutional constraints and free of any central authority that could declare its monetary unit 'money' by law. Walras's model adheres to two theories of money: commodity and utility; both assume the market structure as a substitute for a central monetary authority. The development of central authorities until the third stage of EMU shall be absent.

Seventh, the properties and characteristics of Walras's money are the same ones recognised by the Cipolla thesis (H3) and criteria for its emergence as an international currency. This requires a demonstration of money's essentiality consistent with H5. The discussion on the origin, nature, functions and value of money as held by the utility and commodity theories of money and on the role of money in integrating the value and monetary theories are the criteria of H5.

Eighth, the Walras model is based on specific assumptions that glorify the market structure as a mechanism for the determination of equilibrium; it thus meets the Triffin postulate (H4) on the dominant role of the private sector in establishing the ECU in the market.

There is an essential difference between the Triffin postulate and the Neo-Walrasians on the parallel currency approach to EMU. The Triffin postulate concentrates on the dynamics created between the private sector across Member States and the official sector across Member States' monetary authorities. Shifts in the preference of private investors will determine the establishment of the currency most convenient to them in the market. Neo-Walrasian proposals concentrate on the dynamics created by competition between monetary authorities of Member States irrespective of the preference of the private sector. National currencies compete until the market selects the best.

4.2 Neo-Walrasians and the ECU

There are three versions of Neo-Walrasian thinking. The logic of the first rests with Walras's principle that competition is the best market structure. Von Hayek (1978, 1984), Vaubel (1978, 1984, 1990), Girto and Roper (1980), free banking advocates (Dowd, 1989 and Selgin, 1988) and the UK proposal of 1989 are representative of this version; they emphasise that the choice of money should be free private issuance. The second version concentrates on the dynamics of an additional currency, the ECU, issued by a new central authority. The All Saints' Day Manifesto (1975) and the UK proposal of 1991 or Fry (1991) are representative samples. The third version is established in Schmitt (1988), Riboud (1991, 1992) and Gnos (1989). This version concentrates on the forces behind the ECU that will make it a vehicle currency for external transactions.

Let us examine these proposals. Hayek's *Denationalisation of Money* is based on the idea that competition between private and official sectors in the field of money would ensure price stability; if not, their money would be driven out of the market and potential large seigniorage gains would be lost. A private money like the Swiss ducat, for example, should be entrusted to private institutions with money-issuing powers; their money should entail 'constant value' guarantees.

The first guarantee refers to a promise "to keep these ducats in circulation only if I fulfilled the expectation that their real value would be kept approximately constant" (p. 42). The constancy of value will be ensured by an index constructed by "a collection of raw material prices, such as has been suggested as the basis of a commodity reserve standard" (p. 44).

The second guarantee is legal: "the issuing bank legally commits itself to maintain the value of its unit, it should in its loan contracts specify that any loan could be repaid either at the nominal figure in its own currency, or by corresponding amounts of any other currency or currencies sufficient to buy in the market the commodity equivalent which at the time of making the loan it had used as its standard" (p. 43). The third guarantee specifies the method of money exchange: "These certificates or notes, and the equivalent book credits, would be made available to the public by short-term loans or sale against other currencies" (p. 43).

On the other hand, the 1989 UK proposal retains twelve official currencies plus the ECU and advocates currency substitution which would exert a force on national monetary policies with market forces thus ensuring that monetary policies converge to the best practice. In other words, the reverse Gresham Law would hold: 'good money shall drive out of the market bad money'. It advocates elimination of all barriers to the use of the ECU, promotion of cheaper cheque-clearing systems and elimination of anti-competitive practices by banks and financial institutions in charging for foreign exchange services. Hence all thirteen currencies become substitutable and competition between monetary policies at fixed exchange rates ensures low inflation. The ECU will be hardened because of the fixity of exchange rates. There is no need for an anchor or new institution.

With perfect currency substitution, all thirteen monies in the Community must yield the same explicit or implicit real return; otherwise individuals cannot be seen to be indifferent to which money to hold. Under these conditions the quantity of the currency of any individual country is *indeterminate* and hence monetary targeting is about the maintenance of the national currency's real yield. Hence the national central bank would have to buy its currency in unlimited amounts. However, equally indeterminate is the price level of Walras's paper money (see section 4.11).

Monetary unification might be achieved with little official action if private agents were to be induced to adopt a 'common' parallel currency, entailing high monetary quality. This is the essence of the second UK proposal (1991) in proposing the 'hard ECU'; it will be an entirely new currency (not a basket) and a common currency as a thirteenth Community currency 'parallel' to the others. It would be issued by a EMF and would have other functions: management of the ERM, co-ordination of intervention policies against non-EC currencies, management of medium-term balance of payments lending and co-ordination of national monetary policies.

The hard ECU would be an ERM member with a narrow band; it would never be devalued. At times of realignment, it would always be as strong as whatever EC currency was the strongest. The hard ECU would only be issued in exchange for EC currencies. The UK government believes that issuance of hard ECU could not add to aggregate inflationary pressure. As a parallel currency, it could add to demand in a particular country at the expense of demand elsewhere, making the running of national monetary policies difficult and possibly unstable.

Commenting on the chances of success of the hard ECU, Fry (1991: 451), said: "Unless huge subsidies were provided, the transaction costs of using more than one currency in any particular market would deter the adoption of ECUs as a means of payment... Indeed, the introduction of the ECU as a parallel currency may be advocated by those who do not want a single currency in Europe".

The difference between the 'hard ECU' and the proposals made by the All Saints' Manifesto (1975) or Fry (1991), which both advocate a 'constant value ECU', is that the latter is substitutable. These national currencies will resemble Walras's commodity money. For example, the All Saints' Day Manifesto (1975: 41) proposed "a parallel European money of constant purchasing power". The mechanism ensuring the inflation proof Europa is simple: "Its essence is to keep the price level of a representative commodity basket constant in terms of Europas. The commodity basket can be defined as the weighted sum of the national commodity baskets used to calculate the national consumer price indices" (p. 42).

Fry (1991: 497) proposed a 'commodity standard ECU' to be managed by the EuroFed: "Indeed, the EuroFed's role can be confined to publishing the prices of each item in the basket at regular intervals and promulgating acceptable convertibility arrangements. The actual supply of ECUs can be left to the private sector under the usual safeguards of prudential regulation and supervision. Alternatively, the EuroFed could issue official ECU notes and hold claims on a sufficient range of goods and services to maintain convertibility".

The proposals for a constant value ECU have one thing in common; their ECU is convertible as is Walras's paper money in his bimetallic standard if the latter is shown to be consistent with his assumptions. They introduce the Aristotelian commodity money process: C-M-C. Private money is obtained only if economic agents surrender goods and services with the private banks in exchange for private money.

The proponents of constant value ECU argue that its demand would be derived from the superior performance in the constancy of price stability generating lower trading costs. But the costs of switching currencies are ignored. The whole motive for holding constant value ECU is the expected capital loss incurred when the inflation rate between the ECU and national money is significant. Dowd (1991: 218) believes that "it seems very doubtful that a loss of 0.2 per cent would be enough to do the trick".

In terms of the reverse Gresham's Law, it has certain consequences. The circulation of weaker currencies would decrease because people would prefer the constant value ECU. The issuers of weak currencies would be faced with the option of either tighter monetary policies, so preserving the value of their currencies, or face devaluation. Hence the asymmetry inherent in the present arrangements of the first and second stages of EMU (the weak currency is faced with the option of devaluation or tighter monetary policy) while the strong currency could continue to pursue easier monetary policy.

The French version of the ECU as a 'vehicle currency' is about an ECU that will be used for transactions of the Member States with non-Community countries. Schmitt's (1988) ECU follows the logic of Keynes in proposing the 'bancor' for the Clearing Union. Schmitt's ECU is the n+1 currency and is the currency of foreign trade for Member States; the ECU will be the base for the exchange rates of all remaining n currencies but the ECU's value would be determined with reference to gold's value. Schmitt's ECU is Walras's paper money or Plato's metallic money intended for external transactions.

Riboud's (1991, 1992) 'constant external ECU' is about the purchasing power of money which arises from unconsumed production requiring an 'optimal' growth of money supply. Since this cannot be ensured for internal transactions, it can be satisfied by the external sector because there is neither production nor consumption but only exchange in the external sector. Hence money remains neutral and thus retains its purchasing power.

Schmitt's or Riboud's vehicle ECU does not conform to Cipolla's thesis which claims that the international status of a currency will follow only if this currency is first established as the anchor for a system. One may identify certain economies of scale to be internalised by a vehicle currency used for external trade. In this context, the legal tender status is not necessary either. Yet the constant external ECU needs to be shown consistent with the Essentiality criterion (H5).

4.3 What are the relevant issues?

The issues brought to the surface by the above proposals can be summarised in five themes. First, all proposals fall in the camp of the 'Leviathan government'; some have an explicit intention to break up the government monopoly of money; others have an indirect motive to break up the dominance of central banks to formulate and implement a single monetary policy. In both cases, an institutional structure for stage two of EMU, appropriately designed to introduce a second anchor currency, would allow some degree of monetary sovereignty to be retained by Member States. Hence the Neo-Walrasian ECU. The issue is whether the private ECU as a parallel currency is a better candidate.

The second theme is the relative cost. Efficient capital markets in Walras's are expected through arbitrage to induce changes in exchange rates; these changes will be reflected in the rate paid on interest-bearing assets. This implies that, if a currency is expected to depreciate against the parallel currency, there will be an incentive to use less cash of the currency concerned. In such an environment, the ECU as a parallel currency could only circulate side by side if it displaced national currencies whose depreciation is expected to be of the order of "...3 per cent per month, i.e. 40 per cent on an annual basis" (Gros and Thygesen, 1992: 33).

The third theme has to do with an explanation of *why* the private ECU has gained a relative independence in money, foreign exchange and capital markets to which we referred in chapter 3. Despite the recognition that the economies of scale are an important determinant of the demand for money and that the private ECU is at a disadvantage with respect to DM due to its small size market (the ECU money market is 3,5% while that of DM, 22,5%), even the

Bundesbank (1992b: 27-8) has recognised the autonomous existence of the private ECU:

> The fact that ECU business is subject to laws of its own became particularly obvious last year, when, against the background of the economic slowdown in the industrial countries and a restrained lending policy on the part of certain categories of banks, aggregate foreign currency business contracted, whereas banks' ECU-denominated claims continued to expand.

The question of interest is to know the forces that have established the private ECU in the market despite the fact that it lacks all the basic characteristics of money; neither is there a central bank to act as lender of last resort for it, nor does the private ECU have a currency area where it must be accepted as a legal tender. The answer given by Gros and Thygesen (1992: 221) that "the behaviour of the spot differential can therefore be explained only if the ecu and the basket are no longer equivalent" is characteristic of the literature but it is not an explanation. We attempt to give a more satisfactory explanation below by going back to Walras's *Elements*.

Essentially, our interpretation of the relative independence of the private ECU is based on the role of Walras's paper money. *Is it money or an investment instrument?* This is the fourth theme that interests us in this context. A satisfactory reply to the theme will also indicate the possible monetary role of the ECU. In the event that it does, this will impinge on macroeconomic processes and the effectiveness of monetary policy in two ways: a) by providing an alternative to the traditional payments and credits circuits, and b) by affecting the volume and geographical pattern of global capital and finance. This is the fifth theme to be developed in section 4.12.

The constant value ECU with its substitutability clause might weaken the link between the money supply of an anchor currency and nominal variables that it is to control. The DM role as the anchor for stage two might be checked. A system of two anchors: DM and the ECU, might be envisaged but the mechanics of such a system in the proposals referred to above have not been worked out. Walras's bimetallic system provides useful insights.

4.4 Assumptions of Walras's general equilibrium

Walras's theory of money consists of:

a) six assumptions which are basic to Walras's vision of economic processes
b) a three-phased equilibrium analysis that makes his system pass through preliminary groping to a static and then a dynamic phase.
c) four imaginary devices: tâtonnement, commodity (E), entrepreneurs and

numéraire which are essential for the establishment of the preliminary and effective equilibria.

Money enters the picture of the *Elements* in the static phase and is supposed to facilitate exchange and bring about 'effective equilibrium' by the end of the static phase. Money is supposed to render a 'service of availability' from which it derives its price and its role in a money economy. But essential to Walras's theory of money is his assumptions which constitute a methodology of their own. Walras assumed:

A1 Perfect competition in commodity, capital, labour and services markets (see El.: 40, 48, 84, 257; Harrod, 1956; Jaffé, 1980);
A2 Certainty (see El.: 222-5, 227, 273, 317; Jaffé, 1980; Perroux, 1991);
A3 Full knowledge (see El.: 93, 138, 161, 169, 175, 211, 222-5, 257, 301, 311 and Schumpeter, 1954); [3]
A4 Timeless, static analysis in the 'preliminary groping' and 'static' phases; a temporary equilibrium analysis in the 'dynamic' phase (see El.: 117, 242, 269, 282-3, 294, 378, 381; Hicks, 1934; Morishima, 1977);
A5 Fixed production coefficients in the static model, but variable coefficients in the progressive model (see El.: 240, 382, 527; Morishima, 1977; Jaffé, 1983); [4]
A6 Full employment (see Schumpeter, 1954; Emmanuel, 1972).

4.5 Walras's circulating fund

In order to introduce money as an intermediary in exchange, Walras envisaged, in his theory of production, a system composed of 13-items:
(1) landed capital, (2) personal capital and (3) capital goods proper which belong to the category of capital yielding consumers' services. The same items yield productive services and are numerated as (4), (5) and (6) respectively. Item (7): 'new capital goods' are newly constructed, 'unproductive of income for the moment' (El: 218), which are not treated until phase (3). For the remaining items capable of *acting as stocks*, Walras stated:

> With respect to income, we have:
> (8): stocks of 'income goods' consisting of 'consumers' goods', like bread, meat, wine, vegetable, fruit, oils, and firewood in the homes of consumers.
> (9): stocks of 'income goods' consisting of 'raw materials', like
> fertilizers, seeds, crude metals, lumber, textile fibres, cloth in bolts and industrial fuels in the bins and store-rooms of producers.
> (10): 'new income goods' consisting of 'consumers' goods' and 'raw materials' held for sale by their producers, like bread at the baker's,

meat at the butcher's, or metals, lumber, textile fibres, bolts of cloth which have been put into stock or placed on display by their producers. Finally, with respect to money, we have:
(11), (12) and (13): 'cash' holdings of consumers; 'cash' holdings of producers, and 'money savings' (El.: 218-9).

These six items constitute a *Fund of circulating or working capital* held by consumers and producers (El. 316-7). Money savings assume importance when one treats its monetary role.

Let us analyze the constituents of 'circulating capital' for they are the backbone of Walras's theory of money. In the theory of production, Walras postponed the discussion on three items: (11) (12) (13) that constitute money to Lessons 29 and 30 and gave a reason:

> We place money in a separate category, apart from capital and income, because of the mixed role it plays in production. From the social point of view, money is capital, since it is used in society more than once for making payments; from the individual point of view, money is income, for no individual can use it more than once, since he no longer has it after making a payment (El.: 219).

This dual facet that only money can have is not developed in the . Walras returns to it only once in his commodity money. It was Wicksell (Lec. II: 6) who made it clear what money can do to an economic system; for him, money's economic importance lies in its capacity to affect not only exchanges but capital accumulation.

What is developed in the is the idea that the Fund renders a 'service of availability'. This is possible because of Walras's vision that any element of the circulating capital can assume three roles. For example, take wheat as commodity (A); it can act as:
  a) a consumption good, call it (A_c),
  b) an inventory kept in the storage room, call it (A'),
  c) a means of production to produce flour, call it (M_a).

$A_c + A' + M_a = A$ make up the total endowment of the representative Walras individual at the beginning of phase (1) of which (A') and (M_a) constitute Walras's circulating capital. (A') and (M_a) may or may not be sold in the market, depending on the necessity to synchronize diverse activities. In the form of circulating capital, Walras gives it a price derived from the demand for a smooth functioning of deliveries and receipts. Yet $p_{a'}$ and $p_{m'}$ should be equal to the market price of wheat times the money rate of interest foregone $i_{m'}$, should the farmer decide to hold (A' + M_a) bushels as inventory; thus,

$$p_{a'} = p_a i_m \qquad \text{and} \qquad p_{m'} = p_m i_m \qquad\qquad (1)$$

$p_{a'}$ and $p_{m'}$ are called prices of the 'services of availability'. Given that the money rate of interest (i_m) is dependent on the rate of net income (i), we could express the above prices as

$$p_{a'} = p_a i \qquad \text{and} \qquad p_{m'} = p_m i \qquad\qquad (2)$$

For an economy as a whole, the fund of circulating or working capital could be separated into "pure capital" consisting of items: (9) raw materials and (10) stocks of inventories, *and* into "pure money" consisting of items: (11) cash holdings of consumers, (12) cash held by producers and (13) money savings. The separation is necessary because of the *dual role* of money, which is 'capital' from the social point of view and 'income' from the individual point of view.

Yet there is another reason. If money originates in the utility of the object, what kind of utility does money render? If money is capital, then capital goods do not yield direct utility of their own, but only *indirect* utility. Capital goods produce *two* types of indirect utility: the first due to its 'productive services', the second due to its 'service of availability'. Thus the pure capital fund renders two types of indirect utility.

On the other hand, the 'pure money' fund renders only a 'service of availability' and hence it yields only *one* type of indirect utility. Should the service of availability of money be shown to be unessential, the indirect utility of money would cease to exist.

4.6 Equations of circulation and money

The starting point of Walras in his theory of money is the consideration of the income side of an individual's budget when money is introduced. Money is defined as follows:

> Let (U) be money which shall first suppose to be an object without any utility of its own, but given in quantity, distinct from (A) [numéraire commodity], having a price of its own p_u and a price for its service of availability $p_{u'} = p_u i$" (El.: 320).

We can now define the *budget* or total purchasing power of Walras's representative individual as those quantities of land-capital (O_t), personal-capital (O_p) and capital-proper (O_k) as well as circulating capital: $O_{a'}$, $O_{b'}$, $O_{c'}$ ..., q_m including money (O_u). Walras (El.: 320) then states:

130

The quantities $O_{a'}$, $O_{b'}$, ..., positive or negative, of these services which he effectively offers at the prices $p_{a'}$, $p_{b'}$ ... will be determined at one and the same time by the equation of exchange

$$O_t p_t + O_p p_p + O_k p_k + ... + O_{a'} p_{a'} + O_{b'} p_{b'} + ... + q_m p_{m'} + ... + O_u p_{u'}$$

$$= d_a + d_b \ p_b + d_c \ p_c + d_d \ p_d + ... + d_e \ p_e \ ". \tag{3}$$

Equation (3) differs from the budget equation of the theory of capitalization only on the left-hand side where the value of the quantity of money: $O_u p_{u'}$ is added. Notice also that, in Walras's theory of capitalization, the term $d_e p_e$ represents the value of net savings which according to Walras will be expended on new capital goods. Hence whatever is saved takes the form of investment. Say's identity interpreted as ex ante investment equals planned saving holds.

The second step for Walras in developing his monetary theory was to apply the principle of maximum utility to the stock of money by stating:

And let $r = \Phi_\alpha(q)$, $r = \Phi_\beta(q)$ ... $r = \Phi_\varepsilon(q)$ be our individual's utility or want equations for the services of availability of products (A'), (B') ... and perpetual net income (E'), not 'in kind', but 'in money'. The quantities α, β, ... γ, positive or negative, of these services which he desires at the prices $p_{a'}$, $p_{b'}$, ... will be determined at one and the same time by the equation of exchange and by the following equations of maximum satisfaction:

$$\Phi_\alpha(\alpha) = p_{a'}\Phi_a(d_a)$$
$$\Phi_\beta(\beta) = p_{b'}\Phi_a(d_a)$$
$$.......$$
$$\Phi_\varepsilon(\varepsilon) = p_{a'}\Phi_a(d_a) \tag{4}$$

from which we obtain, first, the quantities desired of the services (A'), (B') ... (E') [in the form of money]

$$\alpha = f_\alpha(p_t, p_p, p_k \cdots p_b, p_c, p_d \cdots p_{a'}, p_{b'} \cdots p_{m'} \cdots p_{u'}, p_e)$$
$$\beta = f_\beta(p_t, p_p, p_k \cdots p_b, p_c, p_d \cdots p_{a'}, p_{b'} \cdots p_{m'} \cdots p_{u'}, p_e)$$
$$..$$
$$\varepsilon = f_\varepsilon(p_t, p_p, p_k \cdots p_b, p_c, p_d \cdots p_{a'}, p_{b'} \cdots p_{m'} \cdots p_{u'}, p_e) \tag{5}$$

secondly, the value of these quantities expressed in terms of numéraire

$$\alpha p_{a'} + \beta p_{b'} + ... + \varepsilon p_{a'} \tag{6}$$

and finally the quantity of money effectively offered

131

$$O_u = q_u - \frac{\alpha p_{a'} + \beta p_{b'} + \dots + \epsilon p_{a'}}{p_{u'}}. \tag{7}$$

In a similar manner, we could derive the quantities effectively offered by the other parties and, consequently, the total effective offer of money

$$O_u = Q_u - \frac{d_\alpha p_{a'} + d_\beta p_{b'} + \dots + d_\epsilon p_{a'}}{p_{u'}}. \tag{7a}$$

The value of all or part of the final products and perpetual net income which the parties to the exchange wish to purchase, and which they desire to keep in their possession in the form of cash or money savings, constitutes their *desired cash-balance* [*encaisse désirée*]" (El.: 320-1).

Equations (3) to (7a) raise more questions than they implicitly answer. First, in equation (4), the marginal utility of commodity (E) is equated with the price of the service of availability of commodity (A') taken as numéraire; this means $p_{e'} = p_{a'}$, which follows from the definition of $p_e = 1/i$ and definition of prices of availability, i.e. $p_{e'} = p_e i$ or $p_{e'} = 1 = p_{a'}$.

Second, as we argued earlier "Since O_u is by definition a quantity of money and $p_{u'}$ is really the price per unit of the service of availability of money, $O_u p_{u'}$ is the amount of interest received in terms of numéraire for the loan of O_u units of money and is obviously an item of expendable income" (Jaffé's note, El.: 543). In terms of equation (3), for a saver, the term: $O_u\, p_{u'}$ would be an income, and for a borrower an interest cost. The equivalent items of equation (3) is $d_e p_e$ which is the same as O_u in equation (7a). "O_u is the difference between the initial and optimum values of nominal money holdings... Walras conceives this difference as being invested in new capital goods to provide a yield equal to the rate of interest i"(Patinkin, 1965: 557).

Third, since O_u is the unused quantity of money that can earn interest if deposited with the banking system, O_u represents the *money savings* of the consumer which presupposes net saving and a progressive economy the moment net savings are transformed into new capital goods. New capital goods, though, do not enter the Walras system until phase (3).

Fourth, "...the 'equations of maximum satisfaction' [eq. (4)] show that the marginal utilities of the optimum quantities α, β,... like those of the optimum quantities of all other commodities - are proportionate to their respective prices, and that the factor of proportionality is the marginal utility of the numéraire (A)" (Patinkin, 1965: 555).

Fifth, Marget (1931: 580) believes that "...in the first edition of his "elements", Walras used a "Fisherian" equation of exchange, of the general form MV = p.Gv, ...and in the edition of the beginning with the second edition, Walras presented equations which are essentially identical with "real-balance" equations of the form of Keynes's equation n = pk".

Equations (3) to (7a) represent the supply side of the fund of circulating capital grounded in the consumers' desired cash balances.

4.7 Equation of the demand for money

The demand side of the fund of circulating capital is grounded in the requirements of 'production of one unit of commodity (A)'. It refers to the services rendered by the fund for the production of one unit (A). Walras believes that any quantity demanded of (A), like D_a would require certain quantities of *all* services of circulating capital for its production.

We can take the production of one unit of (A) requiring the services of (A'), (B') ... (M). These services of availability requirements can be expressed in the *coefficients of production*, $a_{a'}$, $b_{a'}$, ... Hence:

$$a_{a'}(D_a + D_{a'}) + b_{a'}(D_b + D_{b'}) +...+ m_a D_m +...+ k_{a'} D_k +...= D_{a'} \qquad (8)$$

Equation (8) shows the required services of the 'pure capital' of circulating capital (i.e. a_a, b_a, ..., m_a) necessary for the production of one unit of (A). $D_{a'}$ = $O_{a'}$ by necessity as well as a proportion of the other commodities: D_a, D_b,.... Equation (8) can be generalized for all components of the 'pure capital' of circulating capital.

Similarly, we can introduce the services of money (U) as *augmented* coefficients in the production of commodity (A) in the form of money. We can express the total demand for the services of availability of money (δ_α) required in the production of one unit (A) :

$$\alpha_{a'}(D_a + D_{a'}) + \beta_a'(D_b + D_{b'}) +...+ \mu_{a'} D_m +...+ \kappa_{a'} D_k +... = \delta_\alpha \qquad (9)$$

Equation (9) could equally be generalized to derive the δ_β, δ_γ ... δ_κ quantities of money demanded. If we multiply these by their respective prices, it would give us the individual values in terms of money of cash reserves that producers hold per unit of output. We can derive the total amount of the service of money for productive purposes as:

$$a_u(D_a + D_{a'}) + b_u(D_b + D_{b'}) +...+ m_u D_u +...+ k_u D_u +... =$$

$$= \delta_\alpha p_{a'} + \delta_\beta p_{b'} +...+ \delta_\mu p_{m'} +...+ \delta_\kappa p_k +... = p_{u'} O_u \qquad (9a)$$

Walras then stated: "...and finally the equation

$$\frac{\delta_a p_{a'} + \delta_\beta p_{b'} + \dots + \delta_\mu p_{u'} + \dots + \delta_k p_k + \dots}{p_{u'}} = O_u \tag{10}$$

expressing equality between the demand and offer of the services of money (U)" (El.: 323).

Equation (10) introduces a number of innovations to Walras's system. First, his system of production cost equations should include both the circulating capital and money as *cost*. The cost of production becomes:

$$a_t p_t + a_p p_p + a_k p_k + \dots + a_{a'} p_{a'} + \dots + a_m p_{m'} + \dots + a_u p_{u'} = 1$$
$$\dots\dots\dots\dots\dots\dots\dots\dots\dots\dots\dots\dots\dots\dots\dots\dots \tag{10a}$$
$$k_t p_t + k_p p_p + k_k p_k + \dots + k_{a'} p_{a'} + \dots + k_m p_{m'} + \dots + k_u p_{u'} = P_k$$

Equation (10a) should express equality between the selling prices of consumer and capital goods and their costs. Yet Morishima (1977: 144) found a 'careless technical slip'. The inclusion of the price of the service of money (p_u) and not the values in terms of 'cash balances' would create inconsistency. Mathematically, Morishima is correct because a_u, b_u ... of equation (9a) denote values in terms of 'cash balances' held by producers. If equation (9a) is substituted in equation (10), the price of the service of money (p_u) causes inconsistency. From the economic point of view, $a_u p_{u'}$, $b_u p_{u'}$.... express the opportunity cost of producers who hold cash instead of deposing it at the banks. Is this consistent with Walras's assumptions? Second, Walras's equation of net saving should also take account of both circulating capital and money:

$$D_k P_k + D_{k'} P_{k'} + \dots + D_{a'} + D_{b'} P_b + \dots + D_m P_m + \dots = E$$
or $\tag{10b}$
$$E = F_e(p_t, p_p, p_k\dots, p_b, p_c\dots, p_{a'}, p_{b'} \dots p_{m'}, \dots p_{u'}, i)$$

Third, we should add the equations relating to circulating capital:

$$1 = p_{a'} / i, \ P_b = p_{b'} / i, \ \dots, P_m = p_{m'} / i, \ \dots, P_u = p_{u'} / i. \tag{10c}$$

The last term of equation (10c) says that the price of one unit of money (p_u) today equals the discounted price of its stock-price $(p_{u'})$. This assumes importance in section 4.10, where we examine the role of money savings in Walras's general equilibrium.[5]

4.8 Walras's paper money

Walras in Lesson 30 considers two kinds of money: *paper* money (U) which "...is neither a commodity nor anything that can serve as the numéraire" (El.: 325) and *commodity* money which should be of metallic nature such as gold or silver (see El., § 280).

Paper money is a monetary unit of a country "...where money consisted of inconvertible 'paper francs', but where prices were quoted in 'metallic francs' of gold or silver... . We say, then, that $p_b,... p_m \cdots p_k \cdots p_{a'}, p_{b'}\cdots p_{m'} \cdots p_k \cdots p_{u'}$ are prices in terms of (A)" (El.: 325). But (A) cannot be anything else other than a precious metal. Hence the service price of paper money does not exist independently of gold or silver.

An interesting idea should be noted at this stage; it refers to the way Walras integrates paper money into his schema, by stating (El.: 325):

The circulating capital goods (A'), (B')... M)...render their service of availability in exactly the same way as the fixed capital goods (K), (K'), (K")...render their use services [stress added].

Because paper money renders a service of availability, (U) should be part of circulating capital. As soon as the equation of circulation is identified and solved, so would be the equation relating to (U). We explore the implications of such a method of integrating (U) into the model in the next section. The mathematical integration is correct but is there a role for paper money (U)?

Given the previously stated system of equations, Walras asserts:

Only the offer equation (7) of (U) and equation (10) expressing equality between the demand and offer of (U) remain outside [this solution]. Consequently, if price p'_u is cried at random and is held fixed during the process of groping in production and capital formation, we come to the last equation from which the equality between the price of the numéraire and unity is deduced at the same time as the equality between the demand and offer of the numéraire, so that there remains only to solve the equation

$$Q - \frac{d_\alpha p_{a'} + d_\beta p_{b'} + ... + d_\varepsilon p_{a'}}{p_{u'}} =$$

$$\frac{\delta_\alpha p_{a'} + \delta_\beta p_{b'} + ... + \delta_\mu p_{m'} + ... + \delta_\kappa p_k + ...}{p_{u'}} . \tag{11}$$

If we set: $d_\alpha p_{a'} + d_\beta p_{b'} + ... = D_\alpha$

135

$$\delta_\alpha p_{a'} + \delta_\beta p_{b'} + \ldots + \delta_\mu p_{m'} + \ldots + \delta_\kappa p_k + \ldots = \Delta_\alpha$$
$$d_\varepsilon p_e = E_\alpha, \text{ and}$$
$$D_\alpha + \Delta_\alpha + E_\alpha = {}^\circ H_\alpha$$

then the equation [(11)] ... becomes

$$Q_u = \frac{{}^\circ H_a}{p_{u'}} \tag{12}$$

The three terms $[D_\alpha / p_{u'}]$, $[\Delta_\alpha / p_{u'}]$, $[E_\alpha / p_{u'}]$ represent respectively *cash* in the hands of consumers, *cash* in the hands of producers and money savings (El.: 325-6).

This quotation raises at least three fundamental monetary questions:
a) What are the motives for holding 'cash'?
b) What role do 'money savings' play in a static model?
c) Do equilibrium prices established in phase (1) differ from those established when money is introduced in phase (2)?

Questions a) to c) refer to a single idea: *What is the monetary role of Walras's paper money?* This is equally fundamental for the *Elements* as it is for other monetary models which derive prices from costs or some variant of both cost-demand considerations. There seems to exists no rationale for the derivation of the price of money unless one first establishes its *raison d'être*.

4.9 Role of the circulating fund

Recall the circumstances that necessitate the introduction of the circulating fund. The tâtonnement process in phase (1), by means of tickets, establishes a vector of equilibrium prices in principle. Then Walras (El.: 316-7) states:

Once equilibrium has been achieved in principle, upon completion of the preliminary process of groping by means of 'tickets', the actual transfer of services will begin immediately and will continue in a given manner during the whole period of time considered. The payments for these services, evaluated in numéraire, will be made in money at fixed dates. The delivery of the products will also begin immediately and will continue in a given manner during the same period. And the payments for these products, evaluated in numéraire, will also be made in money at fixed dates. It is readily seen that the introduction of these conditions makes it necessary, first, so far as consumers are concerned, that they have on hand a fund of circulating or working capital ... and, secondly, so far as producers are concerned, that they have on hand a fund of circulating and working capital

In section 4.5, we separated the circulating fund into pure capital, consisting only of stocks of inventories, *and* pure money, consisting of cash and money savings. There we argued that commodity (A) could assume three roles: a consumption good, an inventory good and a means of production. As a consumption good, it has its own price (p_a) due to direct utility, but as an inventory good, it acquires another price $(p_{a'})$ because it renders a 'service of availability'. The two are related via the money interest rate (i_m): $p_{a'} = p_a i_m$.

We should stress that $p_{a'}$ is the result of Walras's conception relating to the role of inventories in his schema; these enable the smooth functioning of transfer and payments of services and delivery and payments of products as well as unforeseen accidents, as the above quotation states.

Coming to pure money of the circulating fund, our starting point is Schumpeter (1954: 1022): "With the stocks enters money. It is simply a particular item in the list of inventories and also renders a 'service d'approvisionnement', which acquires a price, like any other service, by virtue of its marginal utility functions". Schumpeter's insightful statement raises the fundamental question of 'how Walras integrates money in his schema'.

On the assumption that money renders a 'service of availability' and given the fact that his stocks render 'services d'availabilité', Walras found an ingenious way of integrating money into the logic of the . Just as commodity (E) renders a service by way of a method to aggregate heterogeneous sources of savings into a homogeneous commodity and thus acquires a price (p_e), so does money which forms part of circulating fund. One could concentrate on the service aspect of money and assert that it is just one additional service.

Given the fact that everything in the *Elements* - land, labour, capital proper, commodity (E) - renders a service and the price for each is set in a market of its own, so does money; it renders a service and its price would be determined in a special market called 'marché du capital'. In this money market, "...'money capital' is borrowed and lent, which is merely an annex to the service market" (El.: 270).

For any price to exist in the *Elements*, marginal utility should pre-exist. For all m commodities and s services, direct utility is essential for acquiring their prices. Yet in the case of paper money (U) - the s + 1 market - Walras assumes (U) to be "...an object without any utility of its own" (El.: 320).

Walrasians argue that marginal utility of the services of money is not the same as the marginal utility of bread. Paper money has an indirect utility and this indirect utility gives rise to $p_{u'}$. Where does this indirect utility come from? Walrasians say it comes from the role of money to 'synchronise' the transfer and payments of services, the delivery and payments of the products. Marget (1935: 160-1) states: "Even in a world in which everything were perfectly foreseen, a lack of synchronization between the receipt of income and its outlay would give rise to a need for cash-balances so long as there are not perfect facilities for the borrowing of money in anticipation of receipts and the investment of money during the period elapsing between receipt and outlay".

Despite the strict assumptions of Walras, Jaffé (1983: 363) believes that money has a role to play for purely technological reasons: "If, in the production process, the inflow of raw materials and intermediate products could be perfectly synchronized with the outflow of final output, there would be no need for a stand-by function of circulating capital". The same could be argued for the consumption process: "...for intractable physiological and technological reasons, the flow of products to the consumer's hands is rarely synchronized with the flow of these products".

Another explanation for the lack of synchronization was offered by Gilbert (1953: 152) based no the *time factor*: "Since human action takes time, complete synchronization between the receipt of wages and their expenditure is impossible. In fact, wages are paid weekly rather than at shorter intervals because of the administrative costs involved - an indivisibility. The time factor implies costs in exchange, and it is useful to develop equilibrium theory by not abstracting from such costs".

In other words, the 'cash' demanded by consumers and entrepreneurs in equation (10), is needed to bridge the time gap between fixed future dates as stated in the *Elements* (pp 316-7) and quoted at the start of this section. Marget (1966) identified Keynes's (1936: 170) "...transactions- motive, i.e. the need of cash for the current transaction of personal and business exchanges" with the motives of Walras's man to hold cash.

If the synchronisation interpretation of the *Elements* is correct, then the principle of maximisation that makes Walras's agents 'rational' in the theories of exchange, production and capitalization under the premises of maximum utility, does not hold in the theory of money.

What constitutes the 'rationality' of Walras's economic agents? It is his methodology defined by his assumptions and equilibrium phase, i.e. in phase (2) when money is introduced. Examine the relevant assumptions: A1, A2, A3, A4 in the context of the *Elements*. Walras endows his agents with "random quantities of circulating capital and money" (El.: 318) after phase (1) has come to completion by establishing a vector of equilibrium prices in principle. During the conditions for an equilibrium in principle hold in all markets, money enters the picture.

Under such stipulated conditions, either Walras's economic agent is 'irrational' because he forfeits maximising his utility or Walras's system of $m + s + 1$ equations is 'inconsistent' because the last equation is redundant.

If assumptions A1, A2, A3 and A4 hold in the theory of money, then Walras's economic agent is irrational since he holds cash balances and incurs a loss equal to the interest foregone. While he knows the equilibrium prices and the role of 'pure capital' goods of the Fund, he refrains from depositing his cash endowments with the banks. Equilibrium prices in the mean that "all commodities are equally and perfectly 'liquid'" which is the principle characteristic of a model in which "we can pass from indirect to direct prices at will simply by abstracting from the numéraire, so we can pass from indirect to direct exchange whenever it suits us, simply by abstracting from money" (El.: 191).[6]

Even if we relax Walras's assumption A2: certainty, in order to allow for a lack of synchronization due either to Marget's imperfect facilities, or Gilbert's time factor, or Jaffé's institutional and technological constraints, the problem of synchronization can be perfectly performed by the 'pure capital' goods held as inventories. *Pure capital goods are assumed to be held for that specific purpose* (see El.: 316-7). We allow for the relaxation of A2, despite the fact that the time factor may cause changes in the fixed data, i.e. changes in preferences and hence A4 would not hold.

As we argued in section 4.5, stocks differ from consumption goods because of their 'economic durability'. As long as the prices of stocks are derived from the prices of their services via the rate of interest, they can be integrated into the model. Yet economic durability allows the 'pure capital' of the circulating fund to be either capital or income. Hence while waiting to be paid for the products the entrepreneur has sold or the consumer waiting to receive income, the 'pure capital' performs a 'service of availability' by bridging unforeseen changes in the fixed data in the static phase of the . They could equally act as income if such stocks are consumed because of less-than-perfectly synchronized transactors.

This dual economic feature that only the 'pure capital' goods entail is stressed in the theory of production by Walras:

> When we come to the theory of circulation, attention will have to be drawn to the fact that stores of income goods, while being held for the eventual performance of their single act of 'use service', perform in the meantime a 'service of availability', which may be either a directly consumable service or a productive service (El.: 214).

In addition, the dual economic feature of stored income goods and raw materials in the equation of circulation meet both the criterion of 'rationality' and role of 'synchronization' in the schema of the *Elements*. It, however, renders the role of money *unessential* in the circulating fund. Thus, if the transactions motive is accepted as the sole economic reason for the demand for money, then the 'cash' terms of equation (12) are *without economic foundation*.

Being consistent with the stated assumptions, the peculiar equilibrium conditions and conceptual vision of the structure of the *Elements* strip cash balances of any essential role in establishing an effective equilibrium in the static model.[7]

139

4.10 Role of money savings

An economic rationale for including *money savings* in the circulating fund exists in the *Elements*. It is the structure of financing new capital goods or the investment opportunities for savers that makes room for money. Walras states:

> *Capital* being defined as the sum total of fixed and circulating capital goods *hired*, not in kind, but *in money*, by means of *credit*, it follows that every day in the operation of an economy a certain fraction of this capital becomes due and is repaid by the entrepreneur-borrowers to the capitalist-lenders. This quantity of repaid capital, to which land-owners, workers and capitalists add a certain excess of income over consumption...constitutes the day-to-day amount of savings available for lending in the form of money (El.: 317).

Hence, we have a perfect correlation between commodity (E) and money.[8] The very essence of net savings, in becoming a fixed new quantity via the instrumentality of money, necessitates a 'role' for money in the *Elements*.

However, there is problem: *do savings take the form of money or of investment instrument or of credit?* If savings take the form of money, they are held as cash balances. If they are lent directly to investors, savings are transformed into 'credit'. If they are held by the savers, because the Walras economic man can perform both roles, they are 'investment instrument'. In either of the three cases, the sequence of action and the phase of equilibrium play an important role.

It should be noted that, in the theory of capitalization, Walras argues that decisions over net savings to be transformed into new capital goods are taken during phase (1). The production of new capital goods occurs during phase (2). Yet new capital goods are not put to work until phase (3) (see El.: 319).

Who finances whom during phase (2)? Henderson and Quandt (1955: 629-30) identified Walras's money savings with 'credit' because there is not one group that is a creditor and another a debtor *and* because:

> The function of financing in this case is a function of credit, not a function of money. This can be illustrated by first showing how credit can perform this function, and then showing why money cannot. Debts are in existence during the period, but are zero at the end. Since credit performs the function of financing, it must enter the utility functions of the consumers. If they are debtors, credit allows them to consume when they derive the greatest amount of utility subject to the restrictions of the model, and on the margin they balance the interest charge for credit against the additional utility gained through its use. If they are creditors, they must balance the delay of consumption against the interest earned. Synchronization can take

place through the use of credit, and money is not necessary to perform this function. We need only a unit of account in which to express prices and debts.

Whenever Walras refers to savings, he talks of 'credit-in-abstract'. In his theory of production, he asserts: "At every moment, part of the money in circulation is absorbed by savings and part of the money in circulation is thrown back into circulation by credit" (El.: 220). In this and in all other instances, the time dimension is confined to one period; debts and credits are settled by the end of phase (2).

In the theory of capitalization, Walras talks only of credit and not of money (see El.: 306). If one sees the controversial section § 255 in the context of credit, it becomes clearer because the market for credit services is the market for numéraire-capital (see El.: 289).

There is another possibility open to Walras's economic man; *he can both save and invest*, which is consistent with equation (3) and follows from the assumption that he can perform any of the traditional functions of investor, saver or worker at the same time. Yet Walras recognises only three economic agents performing four roles. The three economic agents are: landowners, capitalists and workers. Any of those three can become 'entrepreneur'. Walras states:

It is undoubtedly true that, in real life, the same person may assume two, three, or even all four of the above-defined roles. In fact, the different ways in which these roles may be combined give rise to different types of enterprise (El.: 222).

Consequently, the capitalist who mainly saves has the option either of placing his savings in the 'services market' and thus receiving 'interest payments' or becoming himself (or lending to) an entrepreneur for a rate of profit. Thus, money savings can take any form: credit, commodity (E) or investment instrument. However, *what form of money savings is consistent in the logic of the Elements?*[9]

Given assumptions A1, A2, A3 and A4, together with the abstract analysis adopted and the static phase as well as the fact that cash balances have no rational existence, we favour the interpretation of an 'investment instrument' for Walras's money savings. This interpretation is consistent with the methodology of the *Elements* as well as Walras's theory of commodity money. Hence lending and borrowing of real capital goods take place in terms of 'an investment instrument' in a money capital market. This market establishes, given perfect competition, a money rate of interest (i_m) which is the same as the price of its service of availability $(p_{u'})$. At the end of phase (2), effective equilibrium would require the rate of net income (i), the money rate of interest

(i_m) and investment asset's service of availability $(p_{u'})$ to be equal: $p_{u'} = i_m = i$. Since cash balances are inconsistent with one period model, under certainty and maximisation principle, *an investment instrument, via the service sector of the Elements, gives a 'raison d'être' for the price of its service $(p_{u'})$*.

If Walras's money is only consistent in the structure of the *Elements* when it assumes the role of an investment instrument, then, it is *not any different from the ECU* in its present status, as we have argued in chapters 2 and 3. There, we found that the private sector has mainly used the ECU for hedging, financing and investment currency. Our argument is that the private ECU in its form of an investment currency is consistent with Walras's view of the anchor of his system (i.e. rate of net income, i) and with his assumptions. Our interpretation of Walras's money being essentially an investment instrument further gains support when one explains the tâtonnement of paper money.

4.11 Tâtonnement on money's service of availability

The section of the *Elements* that has tormented Walrasian scholars is the tâtonnement on money's services. *Is it on the circulating fund price $(p_{u'})$, on the price of money (p_u) or on the rate of net income (i)?* It all depends on the interpretation of the role of money and on this, Walras was not clear.

The equation of monetary circulation was given as equation (12). Walras then stated (El.: 326):

Hence, if perchance
$$Q_u \, p'_{u'} = {}^{\circ}H_{\alpha} \tag{13}$$
the question would be completely settled. Generally...we find that
$$Q_u \, p'_{u'} \gtrless {}^{\circ}H_{\alpha} \tag{14}$$
and the problem is to determine how equality between the demand and offer of money is reached by groping through adjustments in $p'_{u'}$.

The real then question is: *What does $p_{u'}$ do in the Elements?* Walras says:

On referring back to the various terms that enter into the composition of ${}^{\circ}H_{\alpha}$, we perceive that they are not absolutely independent of $p_{u'}$, since $p_{u'}$ figures in the term $o_u p_{u'}$ of the equation of exchange which, together with the equations of maximum satisfaction, enables us to deduce the quantities α, β, ..., ε for any one party to the exchange and, consequently, the aggregate quantities d_{α}, d_{β}, ..., d_{ε} for all parties together. We must admit, however, that the dependence of these items on $p_{u'}$ is very indirect and very weak. That being the case, the equation of monetary circulation, when money is not a commodity, comes very close, in reality, to falling outside the system of equations of [general] economic equilibrium (El.: 326-7).

The first sentence of the above quotation is a clear *demonstration of integration of value and money theories*. It is a demonstration grounded in the micro-foundations of individual rational behaviour. This integration is made possible through the income effect introduced with the term, $o_u p_{u'}$, in the budget equation (3). In a monetised economy, the income earned comes from three sources: (i) land, personal and capital-proper capital, (ii) circulating capital, and (iii) money interest earned $(o_u p_{u'})$.

The money interest earned during phase (2) through lending of one's savings can be expended on any item of equation (3) i.e. consumer goods, services or new capital goods. Hence the quantities: α, β, ..., ε of the services of availability of products: (A'), (B'), ..., (E'), which constitute the circulating fund and expressed in money, integrate the exchange model with the money model of Walras, as in equation (7).

The money service requirement for the production of goods integrates the production model with that of the money model, as shown in equation (9). This is rendered possible through the augmentation of the coefficients of production by the money service requirement. Thus any change in $p_{u'}$ would have repercussions on the δ_α, δ_β, ..., δ_ε, shown in equation (10), given the principle of minimum cost at the margin.

As to the theory of capitalization, attention should be drawn to equation (10b) which correctly includes both i and $p_{u'}$ as its independent variables. This could be explained by our argument money savings are transformed into investment assets.[10]

Does this interdependence of real and monetary sectors satisfy Walras? He himself denies it: "We must admit, however, that the dependence of these items on $p_{u'}$ is very indirect and very weak." (El.: 326). This is a formal contradiction and negation of the integration of value and money theories.[11]

Why does Walras negate his own achievement? Five reasons are given:
a) his adherence to the quantity theory of money,
b) dependence of $p_{u'}$ on i
c) absence of substitution effects
d) belief in bimetallism
e) non-autonomous existence of paper money.

For reason a), Schumpeter (1954: 1025) said: "The main motive seems to have been a wish to gain possession of a simple form of *quantity theory*". Walras (El.: 327) praised the simplicity of the quantity theory in Lesson 31 and derived equation (15) after an equilibrium price $p_{u'}$ had been established:

There is, then, an equilibrium price $p_{u'}$; and, if i is the equilibrium rate of net income, the unit quantity of money will be worth $p_u = p_{a'} / i$. Then also $p_{u'} / i = P_u / 1$; so that, if there is an agio, it is the same for the price of money as for the price of its service; that is to say, setting $°H_\alpha = H_\alpha i$, we have

$$Q_u = \frac{H_\alpha}{p_u} \ . \qquad (15)$$

Hence equations (12) and (15) become similar.

Equation (15) is important for a number of reasons. The same equation is derived when the *commodity* money is used. The quantity theory holds even when fiduciary money co-exists with metallic money. Walras asserts that "...the theorem of proportionality of prices to the quantity of money is not affected in any way by the existence of paper circulation and payments by offsets" (El.: 366). Therefore, *money is neutral at all times.* Equilibrium prices established in phase (1) differ from the equilibrium prices established in phase (2) only by a proportionality of the quantity of money. The method of obtaining the value of a unit quantity of money (p_u) is the same that Walras employs in his capitalization theory. That is to say p_u is equal to the price of the service of money ($p_{u'}$) capitalised on the rate of net income (i).

As to reason b), derivation of p_u presupposes a prior determination of $p_{u'}$. Walras recognises this by stating:

> If we first suppose [general] economic equilibrium to be established, then the equation of monetary circulation would be solved almost without any groping, simply by raising or lowering $p_{u'}$ according to
> $$Q_u \gtrless \{ \ ^{\circ}H_\alpha \ / \ p'_{u'} \ \}$$
> at a price $p'_{u'}$ which had been cried at random. If, however, this increase or decrease in $p_{u'}$ were to change $^{\circ}H_\alpha$ ever so slightly, it would only be necessary to continue the general process of adjustment by groping in order to be sure of reaching equilibrium. This is what actually takes place in the money market.
> Thus: *The price of the service of money is established through its rise or fall according as the 'desired cash balance' is greater or less than the quantity of money* (El.: 327).

This quotation clearly states that the equation of monetary circulation, in the money market, determines $p_{u'}$. However, *tâtonnement on p_u, means what?* Kuenne (1961: 100-1) faced the same dilemma and opted for the rate of net income (i) by arguing: "Walras, as in the case of the circulating and fixed capital analysis, had a choice: given $p_{u'}$, how is either i or p_u determined?"

Kuenne (1961: 196) proposed the solution of creating 'a separate market for money similar to commodity (E)': "The value of p_u is then determined by the necessity of the total demand for increased cash in the asset sense to be zero in equilibrium. The rate of interest, i, then follows identically as the ratio of $p_{u'}$ to p_u". Kuenne's option, however, relates to the function of money being a *store of value*. On this, Rosenstein-Rodan (1936: 261) noted: "The function of store of value and standard of deferred payments refers to the intertemporal contracts, and this fact alone explodes the framework of the timeless static equilibrium theory of the classical school; it could therefore not really be taken into account in this system".

Patinkin (1965: 566-7) opted for a different solution. His solution resides with the price level: "Walras could not have meant 'tâtonnement on i'. Instead, either he conceived of the tâtonnement as taking place on $p_{u'}$ as a whole; or, what seems more likely, he conceived of the tâtonnement as taking place on p_u - the reciprocal of the absolute price level - and, since he assumed the rate of interest to be already determined in the capital market, represented the movements of this variable by the directly proportionate $p_{u'}$.

When discussing the role of money savings, we opted for an alternative solution. We said that application of Walras's logic to understanding the function of money savings leads one to the conclusion that they take the form of an investment instrument, which is consistent with Walras's methodology. The $p_{u'}$ is determined in the banking sector or the money market (as Walras prefers to call it up to now but he adopts 'banks' in his bimetallic model) and $p_{u'}$ *represents the service of availability of an investment instrument*. This implies an identity between the money rate of interest (i_m) and the price of the service of credit: $i_m = p_{u'}$. Our solution then differs significantly from Walrasian interpretations.

Our solution says nothing of any deviation from the equilibrium or deviation from the rate of net income (i). During phase (2) when the tâtonnement on $p_{u'}$ takes place, i_m can depart from equilibrium i, which is already determined in the capital goods market. This is the essence of the Walras's cited quotation. When effective equilibrium is established at the end of phase (2), the equilibrium price of the investment instrument, $p_{u'}$, cannot deviate from the equilibrium rate of net income, i. Thus, $i = i_m$. Then logically,

$$p_u = p_{u'} /i = i_m / i = 1.$$

By necessity, *paper* money (U), if in equilibrium, is the numéraire as well. This demonstrates the Walras system consistent but contradicts the initial assumption that commodity (A) is the numéraire. Nevertheless, Walras had warned us at the beginning. "We reserve the right, however, later to identify (U) with (A), and then set $p_u = p_a = 1$ and $p_{u'} = p_a' = i$." (El.: 320). This solution comes later when Walras discusses his commodity money.

This inconsistency is trivial because it only holds while effective equilibrium is established. However, in the *Elements*, if the system is in equilibrium, it is *tautological*; it has no economic meaning. "Economically, p_u is indeterminate, even if mathematically it is determinate" (Kuenne, 1961: 102). This becomes apparent when Walras converts the quantity of the service ($°H_\alpha$) into the quantity of balances (H_α) as in equation (15) which gives us a simple form of the quantity theory. Given $p_u = 1$, we have a tautology: $H_\alpha = Q_u$.

What is not clear in the *Elements* is the definition of the price of (U). Walras arrived at a unitary definition of the value of (U). One could argue that, no matter whether paper money or commodity money is analyzed, the numéraire in the *Elements* is being analyzed. In terms of a monetary system, it is the anchor currency that is analyzed. This means that it is impossible, in a monetised economy, to use money and some other commodity as a standard of value in the same model and at the same time. The anchor of a system and the standard of value are one and the same thing (see § 148 in the *Elements*).

As for reason c), explaining Walras's negation of integrating value and monetary theories, Kuenne (1954: 121) stated: "In a simple exchange economy, the 'substitution' and income effects' are the paths of interdependence that give the system coherence". We have argued in this section that the income effect $(o_u p_u)$ is the integrating device in the *Elements*. The substitution effect is lacking because Walras does not explicitly consider paper money as an asset. Should (U) be an asset, then one could consider commodity (E) as being a substitute for (U) and the substitution effect is theoretically established.

However, a substitution effect is present in Walras's commodity money which should be seen in the context of a bimetallic system. This idea would take too long to develop in this book.[12]

4.12 Walras's bimetallic standard

For reason d), Walras expends two Lessons 31 and 32 to argue that the value and the relative stability of the bimetallic standard reinforced his thesis against the opponents of the quantity theory. First, he discusses the common errors made by Monometallists and by unrefined bimetallists. Then, Walras reworks equation (15) supplemented by a value ratio between the prices of gold and silver, and arrives at mathematical formula for both gold and silver that will preserve the stability of the system. He transforms these equations into a diagram of a price over time of both precious metals and derives the P-curve, showing the optimum quantities of both metals to preserve efficiency.

In doing so, Walras arrived at his first monetary rule:

> Bimetallism will work on condition that the price of the silver franc in the form of both bullion and coin is higher than the price of the gold franc in the form of bullion alone and on condition that the price of the gold franc in the form of both bullion and coin is higher than the price of the silver franc in the form of bullion alone (El.: 356).

The interesting aspect of the bimetallic standard is the co-existence of paper money with *two anchors*: gold and silver. Walras recognised that paper money had assumed importance: "Indeed, the expedients for performing exchange operations without the intervention of metallic money are steadily growing in importance" (El.: 362). Yet he could not be persuaded of the merits and efficiency of fiduciary money:

> Gold and silver, by reason of their exceptional qualities, are real, liquid wealth...they will always retain their value... Undoubtedly, the use of paper for transferring funds, in place of an equivalent amount of coin, releases additional precious metal for industry and ornament; but it still remains to be seen whether the pleasure that individuals get out of possessing impressive quantities of gold and silver plate and jewellery outweighs the inconvenience which the economy suffers from its inability to settle debts at any moment on however large or small a scale with complete security (El.: 365).

This prejudice of Walras has important consequences. First, he accommodates paper money in his commodity money model by stripping the former of any autonomous function. He reworks his equation of monetary circulation (equ.(15)) by inserting paper money (F) alongside the metallic money. Equation (15) becomes

$$(Q''_a + F)P_a = H \tag{16}$$

The coexistence is justified as follows: "...at any given moment the size of this cash balance is determined by settlements which have to be made in cash after making due allowance for offsets" (El.: 366). Yet this justification contradicts his earlier stand which said that debts are settled only by metallic money.

Second, Walras assumes that metallic money and paper money are substitutes in equation (16) and then states a *second* monetary rule:

> ...when the quantity Q''_a of the money commodity, on the one hand, and prices in terms of money, on the other hand, increase or decrease proportionately, the term F [paper money] will automatically increase or decrease in the same proportion and H will remain constant... . [A]fter a rise or fall in prices proportional to a given increase or decrease in the quantity of money, there is no reason why entrepreneurs and banks should not put the same quantity of capital into circulation for a proportionately greater or smaller nominal value of commercial paper and securities (El.: 366).

For the second monetary rule to hold, we need three conditions: a) the elasticity of substitution between F and Q''_a should have a value of infinity,

b) paper money should be fully convertible, and c) the price of fiduciary money should be higher than the value of metallic money by a small proportion taking account of the conversion charge.

These three conditions contradict his earlier position when Walras considered 'inconvertible paper francs' (see El:. 325); there the elasticity of substitution between F and Q''_a should have been zero. Another contradiction refers to the conversion charge; the theorem of maximum utility would require the rational consumer to prefer commodity money to paper money. Such behaviour would concentrate on Q''_a and thus would eliminate paper money as uneconomical; it may be saved only if some institutional restrictions are added giving rise to the conversion charge.[13]

4.13 A dual anchor for the second stage of EMU

The bimetallic standard of Walras resembles EMU in stage two. Walras's model has gold and silver as the anchor supplied by paper money. EMU has official reserves of gold and dollars (the latter once convertible into gold); its anchors are the DM established by the market and the ECU legally declared. The private ECU is its paper money.

Walrasian proposals have reincarnated the above system, without ever citing it. The hard ECU is inconvertible if used as a reserve. As Fry (1991: 490) says: "The hard ECU serves in lieu of gold and hence is an inconvertible managed currency on a paper standard. The EC Member States agree to convertibility of their national currencies into ECUs, just as gold standard countries converted their currencies into gold on demand. In this case, there is no automatic and passive substitution of national currencies for ECUs".

The hard ECU, being an 'inconvertible managed money', is Walras's bimetallic standard supplemented with paper money. The hard ECU is Walras's gold and the twelve national monies are Walras's paper money. The hard ECU would act as a gold standard. National currencies would be convertible into and out of ECUs on demand so that the hard ECU would never be allowed to depreciate against any EC currency. This would be ensured by a 'repurchasing obligation' to limit the ability of national monetary authorities to inflate at the expense of the EMF.

If the hard ECU is an inconvertible currency and establishes the standard, then its demand should be expected only from the official bodies such as central banks, which is the case of the official ECU today. However, the intention behind the hard ECU is to make it attractive to the private sector by ensuring a stability in value that would result in lower rates of interest.

If stage two of EMU is to make any qualitative contribution to the transition to the final stage, it may be envisaged that the EMI and the ECU assume a different role. The ECU, even in the existing legal framework, could become a co-anchor, with the DM, to EMU. For the time being, assume that it is. Then, equation (16), appropriately changed to reflect the DM and the ECU as co-anchors if supplied by Walras's first monetary rule over the anchors, might serve as the base for monetary cooperation until stage three.

The question addressed is to what extent the attribution to the EMI of the responsibility for monitoring the development of the ECU could become responsibility for issuing a co-anchor. This is the essence of Walras's equation (16). Under the hardened ECU or the hard ECU proposals, during the transitional period, new ECU issues will be made in exchange for national currencies. No net creation of money will be involved. The same, coupled with his second monetary rule, is argued by Walras for equation (16).

If the EMI's responsibilities are enlarged, it will be obliged to apply a monetary rule to any accumulation of the national currency held as counterpart to the ECUs issued. It may even suspend the convertibility of the ECU for national currencies. This discipline mechanism already exists today in the EMS; a country issuing its own currency faster than the anchor DM accumulates debt to another central bank or to the VSTF but, after three and a half months, it will have to repurchase its own currency. This repurchasing clause of the EMI, like Walras's second monetary rule requiring a stable price relationship between gold and silver, will be tied to the ECU and not to a national currency.

The problem at hand is to make the ECU attractive to the private sector so that, in equation (16), the ECU would replace the F term (paper money) both as a reserve and as a transactions currency. A positive step in this direction would be to make the EMI responsible for the last resort of managing risk. As we argue in the next chapter, this function arises from 'systemic risk' which concerns banks active in the private ECU market and is consistent with the role of the EMI in the payment and clearing systems, foreseen in Art. 109f of EMU. The objective is to help reduce systemic risk and thus costs in the private ECU markets. This is a strategy for linking the private and official ECU markets consistent with the Triffin postulate.[14]

All these reforms arising from Walras's bimetallic standard, are dependent on a single idea: 'the ECU is already established in the private sector'. Hence the interest in the relative autonomous existence in the private ECU markets as reflected in the increasing autonomy of the ECU interest rates from the rates of the component national currencies.

4.14 The ECU is Walras's paper money: the lessons

Where do all these ideas lead us? We have argued that cash balances play no role in the static model of Walras; money savings do if transformed into an investment instrument. We also argued that the money rate of interest of such an investment currency is regulated by the rate of net income determined in the capital goods market. The co-existence of convertible paper money with commodity money is contradictory. The case of 'inconvertible paper money' is examined in the context of prices of consumer and capital goods, which is quoted in metallic money of gold and silver, and hence redundant. Consequently, given assumptions: A1, A2, A3, A4, the two functions of money: standard of value (i.e. numéraire) and medium of exchange (i.e. monetary function), are not applicable to paper money in the static phase.

These considerations lead us to the conclusion that Walras's paper money has no independent existence, which is reason e) stated in section 4.11, and is redundant in the static model of the *Elements*. This explains the failure of Walras to integrate value and money theories. On the other hand, Walras's paper money resembles the non-autonomous existence of the ECU for almost the same reasons. There are other similarities between the ECU and Walras's paper money. Both derive their definition of money from their functions. Both are seen in an institutional arrangement which makes their development sub-existent and doubtful. Both fail the essentiality criterion (H5).

Does this functional approach to money answer the basic monetary question? Clower (1970: 609) finds it tautological: "Every durable commodity is, by its nature, a store of value. And every exchangeable commodity is necessarily a means of payments for any commodity that is exchanged for". The same sentiment is echoed in Chick (1978: 40): "Functional definitions of money do not suggest a unique mapping from money, the abstract concept, to any real-world counterpart. What is expected in final discharge of debt is largely determined at any point in history by social convention".

As we argue in chapter 3, the functions of money are derivatives of the 'nature' of money requiring to be shown consistent and essential in an economic model. Yet the nature of money stems from a demonstration of the 'origin' of money and its 'essentiality' in a system that analyses a money economy, not a barter economy.

The ECU, we said in chapter 2, is a composite monetary unit made up of twelve specified amounts of each currency. Yet the value of the ECU depends not only upon the number of units of twelve currencies but also on the respective values of these currencies, which are variable by definition. Hence, defining the ECU by its composition makes it a monetary unit fully dependent on the relative strength of the twelve currencies.

This non-autonomous existence of ECU is made clearer if one considers its supply side by the EMCF. The dollar reserves and gold of the EMU fully resemble the paper money of Walras's bimetallic standard. In this sense, Walras's paper money cannot be said to satisfy the Cipolla three criteria (H3).

Walrasian definitions of the ECU attempt to reverse the above handicap by redefining the ECU and by using the market in order to satisfy the Cipolla criteria: *highly stable value*, *high confidence* and *support by a strong economy*.

150

In terms of the first, it is not the ECU that is analyzed but its commodity standard. In terms of the second, is the State or the private sector more apt to generate it?.

The similarities between Walras's paper and the hardened ECU should be noted. Walras's paper money is supposed to be substitutable with his commodity money in his bimetallic model. If it is substitutable then it is also competitive. Through competition, the best monetary policy (stability in bimetallism for Walras, price stability for the hardened ECU) would emerge. Fair competition, though, would require that the same legal status should be given to all thirteen currencies. In the case of Walras, only one monetary authority pursues a policy mix of bimetallism whereas, in the hardened ECU case, we have twelve authorities pursuing price stability.

We have argued, in this chapter, that the utility theory applied to paper money, does not explain the origin or nature of money.[15]

On the other hand, our interpretation of Walras's money savings taking the form of an investment instrument:

a) reconciles the co-existence of Walras's paper money with a monetary system whose anchor is another currency;

b) makes the competitive model of Walras relevant to his monetary theory;

c) proposes a reconciliation for Walras's money savings.

Case c) is the more important because of the ECU's resemblance to Walras's paper money. The price of the latter via the tâtonnement is derived in conformity with the service of availability. We have shown in earlier chapters that the relative independence of the private ECU gained in global foreign exchange, money and capital markets. This has been achieved, not as a parallel or vehicle currency, but as a financing currency, a trading instrument, a hedging instrument or an investment currency.

The relative divergence between the market values of ECU-denominated sight balances and the theoretical values derived from the basket during 1991 (when the ECU was quoted on average 0,5% above its theoretical value), is explained by Walras's money rate of interest on paper money; this diverges, during tâtonnement, from the rate of net income, which is derived in the capital market.

We also demonstrated in section 4.8 that the interest rate of Walras's paper money is *indeterminate* if it is assumed as a parallel currency. Yet the determination of the value of an investment instrument is consistent with the tâtonnement process. The Bundesbank (1992b: 27) finds the same behaviour for the private ECU: "At any rate, without the basket definition and the exchange rate expectations for the ECU deriving therefrom, both the exchange rate and the interest rate of the private ECU would be completely indeterminate".

151

Given the fact that exchange rate changes are reflected in interest rate differentials, the question is whether the ECU's higher yield with respect to its anchor, DM, could induce the private sector to hold on to the ECU. For this to occur, the expected ECU interest rate would have to be lower than DM's, implying that the DMr would be expected to depreciate with respect to the ECU or the ECU to appreciate vis-à-vis the DM. Only then could an anchor be out-competed. Under what circumstances will this happen? Walras has no reply; the suggestive capacity of his monetary theory is constrained by the assumptions of his general equilibrium.

4.15 Conclusions

Walras's *Elements* as interpreted in this chapter, serve to understand the issues involved in the second stage of EMU and Neo-Walrasian proposals seeking to reform the EMS. Walras's bimetallic system may be appropriately reformulated to accommodate a dual anchor for the transitional phase of EMU. Yet this will not be a stable system for it will neither resist speculation, nor provide effective policy instruments in the face of global markets.

The Walras argument, if seen within H1 to H5, fails on grounds of consistency and of an inherent contradiction. The inconsistency resides with Walras's claim that the integration of value and money theories - idea b) of H5 - is made possible via the circulating capital encompassing paper money. Thus paper money is the integrating tool. The six assumptions of the *Elements* allow a price for paper money because the latter renders a service of availability or indirect utility. Yet the same assumptions strip paper money of any monetary role. The 'capital proper' of the circulating fund is assumed to be held for the same reasons since it performs two services: use service and service of availability. This dual feature of circulating fund fulfils the criterion of rationality and role of synchronisation. But it renders the economic foundation of paper money unessential.

There is another inconsistency. The Walras economic man when paper money enters into his schema in phase (2), ceases to be rational because he holds cash balances while he knows the equilibrium prices. He incurs a loss equal to the interest foregone while he knows the role of circulating capital in synchronising receipts and payments. This is the result of his assumptions: perfect competition, full knowledge of market opportunities, fixed data and certainty, which allow in the first place the inclusion of the paper money in the circulating fund and constitute the rationality of the *Elements*.

These two inconsistencies lead Walras to denounce the integration of value and money theories because paper money does not affect the equilibrium prices as his system unfolds from one phase to another. His paper money remains neutral at all times.

We give five reasons: adherence to the quantity theory of money, dependence of the price of paper money on the rate of net income, absence of substitution effects, belief in bimetallism and non-autonomous existence of paper money, which explain why Walras fails idea b) of H5. Yet we offer an interpretation that allows paper money to assume a monetary role in the *Elements*. This is dependent on a demonstration that its price represents the service of availability of an investment instrument.

Walras's contradiction resides with his conceptualisation of the *Elements* that adheres to the traditional nexus of monetary causality but is contrary to the evolution of phases of his equilibrium. Walras's phase (1) is effectuated by means of a numéraire to arrive at an equilibrium in principle; this is in accordance with the Aristotelian primary stage (H2). It is an asset of its own serving as the anchor to the system. As the system unfolds, effective equilibrium in phase (2) is effectuated via the intermediation of paper money, whose function is that of exchange, as in the Middle stage of H2.

However, paper money, as is the case of the ECU, looses both its anchor function and its independent derivation of its price. Recall the fact that Walras's paper money is defined by reference to its functions: standard of value and medium of exchange. The non-autonomous existence of paper money creates a contradiction. The two functions are rendered inapplicable in the static phase of the *Elements* because of the loss of independence in deriving the price of paper money. Walras's paper money is both inconvertible and quoted in gold or silver.

We have suggested a solution to the above contradiction. If Walras's paper money is considered in the context of his money savings, it can perform the role of an investment instrument. But could an investment instrument be transformed into money? Walras's theory would suggest 'possibly' and that 'possibly' would depend on the market which would have to assess it upon the functions of money. If we were to ask how Walras's monetary theory would explain the *evolution* of the functions in terms of their relative importance over time, no satisfactory answer could be given. Hence, the impasse with the utility theory of money and its inability to suggest a strategy for the transformation of the private ECU.

At a theoretical level, we are back to where we started from. What answers will the State theory of money give to the above questions? To the merits of the State theory, we next turn.

Notes

1.   Our reading of the *Elements* differs from the interpretation of Hicks (1933, 1934, 1939 and 1989), Schumpeter (1954), Kuenne (1956, 1961), Marget (1931 and 1935), Patinkin (1965), Morishima (1977) and Jaffé (1983). It could be summarized in the following propositions.

The *Elements* is not about the economics of equilibrium but about the economic forces that would move the system to an equilibrium. Walras did not work out the conditions which would bring his system back to a state of equilibrium, if the given endowments or preferences were to change. Walras did not consider non-zero prices but only 'positive' prices and he did not specify the conditions for a corner solution, although one might find sufficient evidence in the *Elements* to restate the Kuhn-Tucker solution.

The Walras system unfolds via three successive phases; each phase establishes an equilibrium: the first establishes the preliminary equilibrium, the second establishes the effective equilibrium and the third is supposed to establish a dynamic equilibrium.

Equilibrium could be attained only with the use of four imaginary devices: tâtonnement, numéraire, entrepreneur, and commodity (E), provided that two conditions are satisfied: constant returns and the elasticity of demand is equal or inferior to unity.

In a state of equilibrium, neither money, nor the entrepreneurs, nor the tâtonnement are 'essential'.

Profits are never realised in the *Elements*, unless false trading is assumed; but false trading will not establish a vector of equilibrium prices.

Walras's Law applies only if a state of equilibrium is attained, while Say's Law is true in all three phases.

Walras's money originates in the concept of the 'service of availability' and is part of the circulating capital fund whose prices are determined in the services market.

Walras considers two kinds of money: commodity and paper. His commodity money adheres to the theory of metallism. His paper money belongs to the utility theory. Both are assumed to be consistent with the quantity theory of money.

Walras's commodity money is consistent with his six assumptions designed to serve as partial premises for explaining its economic role. But his analysis necessarily requires both a 'stock' and a 'flow' equilibrium, which is not to be found in the *Elements*.

The *essentiality* of paper money is not shown to be consistent with Walras's assumptions, but is consistent with his flow equilibrium because it plays the role of a credit instrument.

If the constancy of the data is relaxed, Walras's money is asserted to become 'credit' in the dynamic phase; however, this is not shown either.

2. All references are made to the Edition Définitive (1926) titled "Elements of Pure Economics; or, The Theory of Social Wealth" translated by William Jaffé, first published in 1954 and reprinted in 1977 by A.M. Kelly, New York.

3. See Hamouda and Rowley (1988, ch. 3) for an interesting discussion on definitions, predictions and rationality, as developed over the years. Notice that Walras's A3, in their chapter 2, receives a different treatment from ours.

4. Robinson and Eatwell (1973: 38) think of variable production coefficients only and thus state: "No-fixed-factor of production coefficients. There is substitution between factors of production on the supply side and substitution on the demand side".

5. See the *Elements* pp. 323-4 for a lucid treatment on how the $3m + 2s + 3$ unknowns Walras system could be reduced to 1 unknown: "The equation relating to (U) is completely solved as soon as the equation of circulation is solved" (El.: 324).

6. With one important difference which concerns the interpretation of assumption A3: 'full knowledge' where Hicks assumes 'perfect foresight', Hicks (1933) dismissed Walras's effort to integrate money into his model on similar grounds: "Money as medium of indirect exchange plays no part in the Lausanne equilibrium. Money as standard of value does, of course, play a part; for if the $(n + 1)$ goods and services, one is chosen to act as standard (or 'numéraire') in terms of which the prices of the other n goods and services are measured. But this says nothing about the demand for money in its use as money; the tacit assumption of perfect foresight deprives the numéraire of any monetary function" (in his 1982: 33).

7. See Rosenstein- Rodan (1936: 271-2) for a similar result when A3 is interpreted as perfect foresight: "it is inconsistent to assume at the same time a state of general certain foresight and the existence of money: they are mutually incompatible".

8. Kuenne (1954: 329) was the first to correlate commodity (E) and money and argued as follows: "Walras assumes that consumers divide their inventory requirements into two accounts, those held in kind and those over which potential purchasing power in the form of cash balances is held (postponable inventories), each with separably calculable utility functions...".

9. The same dilemma was stated by Kuenne (1961: 96): "Upon this answer hinges the role of cash balances in the model as well as the manner in which the interest rate is determined. Unlike Wicksell whose adoption of the second wenpand was explicit...Walras is ambiguous".

10. Note Schumpeter's (1954: 1024) interpretation of the 'role' of money:

"This may be seen most easily by observing that variations in the price of the service of money - or, choosing money for numéraire, interest - affect directly the values of capital goods and stocks (inventories) and through these all the other prices and quantities in the system, including those of the productive services such as wages and the quantity of labour demanded and offered".

11. The consequences of this denial were exploited by Patinkin (1965: 561): "It follows that the equilibrium level of $p_{u'}$ is indeterminate ...so, then, is the level of p_u. Thus if Walras' assumptions are carried to their extreme...they imply the indeterminacy of money prices, and hence the impossibility of all monetary theory".

12. Walras's commodity money adheres to the quantity theory based on a bi-commodity money: gold and silver. Gold and silver are chosen because of their 'attributes' (El.:329). The objective is to prove the efficiency of the bimetallic system; in doing so it renders the existence of paper money 'subsidiary' (El.:330). A unitary elasticity of the demand for money is assumed and the price of commodity money varies directly with its utility and inversely with its quantity (El.: 330). Our interpretation that money savings take the form of an investment asset finds support in Walras's commodity money as well (El.: 332). Two of the thorniest issues of Walras's theory of money: tâtonnement on i_m or on p_u, and integration of real and monetary sectors are definitely settled in Walras's commodity money treatment (see El: 333).

No other writing, before Keynes's *General Theory*, had it so clearly described the role of the money rate of interest in integrating the real and monetary sectors. Why did he not do it? Because the demand for money in the is not autonomous but derived (a reflection of the demand for commodities, and not the source of that demand). As we argued in section 4.10, given assumptions: A1, A2, A3, and A4, the demand for money can only be justified by transforming money savings into investment instruments.

13. Support for our criticism can be found in Ellis (1934: 64): "With 'pure money...say irredeemable paper notes, the very valuelessness of the monetary material annihilates the meaning of 'extra-marginal use'. No limitation upon the employment of dollars here emanates from the shortness of supply of the social 'resources' used; no one goes without a medium of exchange by virtue of this limited supply".

14. These ideas are further developed in a report by the European Parliament (A3-0294/93). The EMI and Bundesbank are to assume joint responsibility for holding the ECU/DM parity. An interest rate indicator is to guide monetary co-ordination between the EMI and national central banks. Monetary discipline is to be maintained by modifying the existing reserve constraint of the EMS by denominating all reserves and new

public debt in ECUs. Total liquidity will be determined by the EMI and Bundesbank as a European monetary aggregate.

15. As to the Commodity theory of money, it describes the 'nature' of money but not its origin. Commodity money circulates because of the utility of its metallic content. Yet a commodity money cannot derive its value from the "demand side". Fisher (1911: 180) stated: "An increased demand for any individual commodity results in a greater consumption 'at a higher price', yet an increased general demand for goods will result in a greater trade (the Q's) 'at lower prices'".

5 State theory of money and the ECU

5.1 Introduction

The State theory of money claims, in terms of idea a) of H5 on the nexus of causality, that money originates with the State and that money's nature is whatever the State declares it to be. The value of money is its purchasing power and it circulates because it is legal tender. The father of the State theory is Plato (*Republic* and *Laws*), yet his contribution is hardly recognized. Monetary theorists recognise Knapp as its originator.[1]

Keynes is a State theorist par excellence. He defines money as "whatever is...legal tender on the spot" (1936: 167). In the *Treatise* (1930: 4-5), Keynes saw the monetary transformations that had occurred in the following sequence:

> Thus the Age of Money had succeeded to the Age of Barter as soon as men had adopted a money-of-account. And the Age of Chartalist or State Money was reached when the State claimed the right to declare what thing should answer as money to the current money-of-account - when it claimed the right not only to enforce the dictionary but also to write the dictionary. Today all civilised money is, beyond the possibility of dispute, chartalist.

Wicksell, according to Ellis (1934), is the representative of the orthodox nominalism. Yet Wicksell, as his views are stated in the *Lectures* (1906), paid little attention to the origin and nature of money,[2] concentrated a bit on the resultant functions but was mainly concerned with the value of money. Understanding Wicksell serves to understand why the TEU stresses that the primary objective of ESCB is to maintain price stability. It also serves to understand the causal relationship between rising prices and high interest rates or falling prices with low interest rates. These themes are relevant to EMU but Wicksell will not be examined in this book for it needs to be treated in depth if his theory is to be understood fully.

The modern version of the State theory is the institutional approach to EMU. There are two logically distinguishable aspects of this approach. The one refers to the *motives* for the creation of an institution and the other concerns the *means* for attaining an objective. If both are embodied in a study on the emergence of EMU, we have a theory of public choice.

According to our view, the basic premise of the institutional approach is that all human institutions have had a common feature: *they take the form that would serve the interests of the participants*; once this purpose is accomplished, or if the existing form of the institution is unable to further the interests of its members, they are either resolved or transformed.

In the context of the EU, *motives* take two forms: a) they are derivatives of the role assigned by the Treaty of Rome, as amended by the Maastricht Treaty, to the EU institutions: Commission, Parliament and Council, and b) they mainly stem from the national interests of Member States. For the former, there are two dominant motives: one economic, the other political. The economic motive is based on the same logic that has established the Single Market, i.e. allocative efficiency. The political motive is based on the view that economic integration is not only an end in itself but also a *means* for proceeding towards political union.

From a Member State's point of view, EMU presents an institutional case in which national interests have determined its technical aspect. EMU is seen as an instrument for the execution of their economic policies. This could be interpreted as a strength depending on the definition of the objectives of EMU but also as a weakness since there is nothing in EMU to prevent the withdrawal from or dissolution of the system.

There is not a priori reason why the forging of a single unit would necessarily be in a country's best interest than a second-best solution. An examination of bilateral circumstances and an assessment of the benefits and costs might well show that member countries, would support an institution for diametrically opposed reasons. This does not necessarily mean that vested interests do not play a role. On the other hand, such considerations do not yet constitute a coherent body of thinking.

In such a context, we first state Plato's theory of money (section 5.2) and reassess Knapp's chartalism (section 5.3); we then reconsider Keynes's version of the State Theory of money (section 5.4) and its extensions represented by the Post-Keynesians (section 5.5) and by the institutional approach (section 5.6). Finally, Keynes's *General Theory* is assessed under H1 to H5 (section 5.7). The end objective is to discover the underlying logic of the State theory of money, to find out what answers does this theory give to the basic questions of money and to assess both the explanatory power and suggestive capacity of Keynes's monetary theory.

5.2 Plato's theory of money

Nowhere is there to be found a chapter in Plato on monetary theory comparable to what we have been dealing with in this book. Laistner (1923: xli) was the first to differentiate the Greek economic thought from the economics of today: "The modern economist regards man, it is true, as a member of society, but begins his investigation with the individual, not with the whole of which the individual is a part".

However, there are two other aspects. The view of Plato on economic matters is predominantly ethical and should be seen within the institutions of the Polis (city-state) which confine the limits of the individual. The institutions of the polis and not the individual is their object for an analysis. Plato emphasised what the polis *should* do, while Aristotle stressed what the polis *could* do.

Plato considered an ideal state in its *civil stage* of development. The civil stage had resulted from the division of labour (Rep. 370 B-C, and 374 B-E), the accumulation of capital (Rep. bk II and 552B) and the advanced knowledge or technology (Rep. bk II).[3] The resulting interdependence of man (Rep. 371B) created the economic necessity to form associations and organise the exchange of goods. The growth of necessary exchange, which had resulted from the division of labour, necessitated the birth of money.[4] The State then would declare what the *token of exchange* should be (Rep. 371B).[5]

This *token of exchange*, which originates with the State and assumes the nature the State wishes to, is defined to assume two functions: a) it acts as a medium of exchange (*Laws*, bk V, 742 A-B) and b) it is a measure of value (*Laws*, bk XI, 918 B). No other function is it recognised.

The most interesting point in Plato's economy is his notion that in organized societies reaching their civil stage, there is only a *money exchange process* of the kind: Money - Commodities - Money (M-C-M). Plato described, in his *Laws*, bk VIII, 849, the details of the conduct of the market, the obligations of the Commissioners, commodities traded and then stated the (M-C-M) process:

> As for all other goods or manufactured articles of which various parties may be in need, they shall be brought to the general market, each article to the proper quarter, and there offered for sale on the site appointed for traffic, and furnished with convenient stalls by the Curators of Law and the Commissioners of Market and City. *The sale is to be by actual exchange of currency for goods and goods for currency, and neither party shall waive the receipt of a quid pro quo* [stress added].

There is yet another pioneering aspect in Plato; the treatment of a monetary system employing *two kinds of money* is stated in the *Laws* (bk V 742) where Plato proposes a dual anchor for his monetary system. For domestic trade, a

160

token money will do. For international trade and foreign expeditions, metallic money should be possessed by the State. Plato stated:

> As for a common Hellenic currency, to most the needs of campaigns and foreign expeditions, such as embassies or other necessary missions of State on which a man may be dispatched to serve these various purposes, the State must possess current Hellenic money.

The State theory of money was prominent among the Cynics and the Stoics in ancient Athens. When Aristotle, in his Politics (bk I, 1257b 10), refers to the fiat money established by law of the State, he refers to the Cynics[6] and to the Stoics.[7]

In short, Plato's economics deals with the satisfaction of human wants through exchange that is subject to a M-C-M process and subject to a regulation of production, distribution and exchange. Money originated in exchange but the latter had resulted from the increased division of labour and the complexity of the Polis. Yet the nature of money could not be other than what the Polis had wished to. The resulting functions of money were thought to be two: a medium of exchange and a common denominator of value. Speculation and usury were considered as practices contrary to the interest of the Polis, although both existed at Plato's time.

5.3 Knapp's chartalism[8]

The essence of Knapp's book on *The State Theory of Money* (1905) is stated in the author's preface to the first German edition of 1905 (1924: vii): "...the money of a State is not what is of compulsory general acceptance, but what is accepted at the public pay offices; and that the standard is not chosen for any properties of the metals, but for the deliberate purpose of influencing exchanges with the commercially important neighbouring States".

In three subsequent editions that followed his 1905 edition, Knapp endeavoured to prove the above statement. He maintained: "Money is a creature of law. A theory of money must therefore deal with legal history" (p. 1); by this he meant that the nominal value of money is a State affair. "The soul of currency is not in the material of the pieces, but in the legal ordinances which regulate their use" (p. 2). In this sense, the nature of money is irrelevant since money is a legal tender guaranteed by the State.

For Knapp, it is the State and its Offices that secure money's *validity*. But what is meant by *validity*? Is it money's material embodiment? Knapp's answer is no: "Hence the concept, means of payment, is freed from the actual nature of material" (p. 25).

One may say that *validity* stems from the fact that money assumes the function of being a means of payment and a means of settling debts. For Knapp, that will be secondary: "In legal history the concept of the means of payment is gradually evolved, beginning from simple forms and proceeding to the more complex. There are means of payment which are not yet money; then those which are money; later still those which have ceased to be money"(p. 2).

Is *validity* to be derived from the value of money? For Knapp this question is also secondary; the nominal character of money only exists by reference to the State and is a derivative of validity. "As soon as the State introduces a new means of payment in the place of the old, the law (1) should so describe the new means of payment that it should be immediately recognisable. (2) The law should settle a name for the new unit of value and call the new means of payment by it" (p. 21).

Is *validity* to be associated with a jurist's legal ordinance? Knapp replies in the negative: "The State, not the jurist, creates it. In all these cases the impulse comes from the political action of the State, jurisprudence only drawing its conclusions from the State's action as it needs them" (p. 40).

On the other hand, by *validity* Knapp implies the *power of the State*, and not of the jurist, to create the capacity to assign value on a chartal means of payment. "When Knapp imputes to the state the power of establishing validity for money, he means that the state creates money's *valuableness*, not that the state determines purchasing power" (Ellis, 1934: 15).

This is the *core* argument of Knapp and the rest of his book is the logical development of his conception of validity conferring on money the property to settle debts. Money is but a 'Chartal' creation of State authority stemming from history, tradition, custom and law which are the ingredients of the State.

Knapp was not a metallist, nor an advocate of paper money, nor a credit theorist. "Gresham's Law is to him a half-truth...paper does not displace metal because it is the worse driving out the better, but because the State has made it the better. It might be replied that the State chose it because it was the cheaper" (Bonar, 1922: 43). Nor was Knapp anti- bimetallist. He took bimetallism as an example to show that the metal chosen by the State to pay its own obligations or accept payments became sooner or later money.

Nor could one State superimpose its choice of money onto another State. Knapp went into lengthy discussions of monetary unions and historical instances to prove that the money of one State is prima facie not money of another State.

Both index numbers and the quantity theory of money were regarded by Knapp as having little value for he thought that 'what commodities should be included in a basket was an insolvable problem'. Both were considered belonging to politics not to monetary theory.

However, the critics of Knapp are many. Rist (1940: 362) criticised Knapp for his failure to explain the value of money: "Since he refuses to credit money with a value of its own, Knapp finds it impossible to understand that a money

162

can 'lose' its value". Schumpeter (1954: 1090)) charged Knapp with logical inconsistencies: "He explicitly denied that he was interested in the value of money. His theory was simply a theory of the 'nature' of money considered as the legally valid means of payment". Frankel (1977: 52) sees the state theories of money through the eyes of Simmel and argues that "...if we grant the basic assumption on which they all rest: that the State is all-powerful in monetary affairs, that it can and should 'decree' what money is and is to be, how it shall be used and who may and who may not use it, then we have in fact assumed away a free monetary order".

Not all these criticisms of Knapp are valid. The Rist-Schumpeter criticism is false for they criticised Knapp on false grounds; they misunderstood chartalism and interpreted Knapp's *validity* as meaning valuableness. Equally groundless is the criticism of Frankel. Knapp, in his 1905 edition, referred to Simmel's (1900) book and stated: "As it treats only of the sociological side of currency, I do not need to regard my work as competing with his" (p. vii).

A more valid criticism of Knapp is to say that his theory is incomplete. First, money existed amongst primitive societies when the state had little to say and played an insignificant role in economic affairs. Einzig (1948), in his numismatical and ethnological work on primitive societies, encountered forces other than the State - such as religion, custom and myth - that played a more important role in establishing means of payments. Second, the sovereignty of political states was not always strong. "In many parts of early medieval Europe they [monies] were at first undertaken by private individuals on their own initiative, not at the prompting of the state. The state did not possess the power to insist on the acceptance of its coin as legal tender and according to Cipolla [1956], 'probably did not even wish to do so'" (Congdon, 1981: 7). Third, state money might be rejected by private markets a case which would accord with the Triffin postulate (H4). Fourth, the instability of a system based on bimetallism and irredeemable paper. "In both instances the state gives two kinds of money the same "proclaimed validity"; in neither do the two moneys have the same validity in trade" (Ellis, 1934: 27). Fifth, private money has been accepted as means of payments. Sixth, if we see Knapp's chartalism through the spectrum of our five hypotheses, we come to the conclusion that it leaves unexplained the functions, the value of money or the theory of interest and above all its *essentiality* in a money economy.

5.4 Keynes's controlled monetary system

Whereas Keynes in the *Treatise* (1930) is concerned with the nature of money and with the value of money defined as a purchasing power of money, in the *General Theory* (1936), he is concerned with the nature of the monetary system and with his core thesis: 'the definition, determination and role of the rate of interest'.

It might be argued that there is a break between the two great books because the *Treatise* represents a marriage between Knapp's chartalism and Wicksell's forces that regulate the price level while the *General Theory* (hereafter GT) departs from such theorising and analyses the forces of money instability and the integration of the real and value models via the rate of interest or price of being liquid.

The Treatise reaffirms existing doctrines but the GT represents something *new*. This *new* is Keynes's view that the capitalist system is *inherently unstable*. The instability of the system stems from Keynes's vision based on eight assumptions, three of which are states of nature. Another *new* element is Keynes's method, which is macroeconomic.[9]

5.4.a) Keynes's assumptions

Keynes's argument about the monetary nature of production or about the capitalist system resulting in crises of confidence or about the inherent instability of unregulated economic systems is made plausible and persuasive provided that one accepts his assumptions. These are:

A1 Uncertainty (see GT: 145, 148, 168, 201, 208, 218, 231 and 316),
A2 Incomplete knowledge (see GT: chapter 12; Keynes, 1937a; Shackle, 1967; Frankel, 1977),
A3 Individual freedom (see GT: 154-64, 170-4, 314-6; Robinson, 1952; Shackle, 1967; Frankel, 1977),
A4 Broad price stability (see GT: 64, 239, 250-1, 270-1, 288-9, 328; Chick, 1992),
A5 Inelastic and exogenously given money supply (see GT: chapter 17, 247-8, 295-9, 303-9 and our chapter 7),
A6 Closed economy (see GT: chapter 6; Johnson, 1978; Assimakopulos, 1991; Chick, 1992),
A7 Short period analysis (see GT: 91-4, 114, 121-2, 270, 302-3, 328, 336; Robinson, 1952; Chick, 1983; Assimakopulos, 1991)
A8 Involuntary unemployment (see GT: 6, 15, 23-26, 128, 289 and Chick, 1992).

The three states of nature in the GT are assumptions: A1 on *uncertainty*, A2 on *incomplete knowledge* and A3 on *individual freedom*.[10]   They are instrumental in exposing the non-harmonious structures inherent in a capitalist system as well as in concentrating on what is decisively important.

As to *uncertainty*, Keynes (1937a: 214) considered it dominant in the conduct of economic decisions and stated:

164

The sense in which I am using the term is that in which the prospect of a European war is uncertain, or the price of copper and the rate of interest twenty year hence, or obsolescence of a new invention, or the position of private wealth owners in the social system in 1970. About these matters there is no scientific basis on which to form any calculable probability whatever.[11]

In Keynes's model, uncertainty gives rise to the role of money; uncertainty is held responsible for the speculative and precautionary motives; uncertainty causes expectations to be volatile and the equilibrium to be shifting; the role of a speculator depends on uncertainty; the volatility of liquidity preference and of marginal efficiency of capital is due to uncertainty; uncertainty conditions assumptions: A2, A3 and A8. "A monetary economy is a very complex system and is thus very likely to be characterized by structural instability...the economic agent has to face a disturbing amount of *structural uncertainty*..." (Vercelli, 1991: 71).

Incomplete knowledge in Keynes's sense is easily understood if it is compared to Walras's assumption of full knowledge. The latter's is gained because the market provides the necessary information on prices and quantities, given the assumptions of certainty and perfect competition hold. In the case of the GT, imperfect markets exist and uncertainty rules. The consequences are stated by Keynes (1937a: 213): "Thus the fact that our knowledge of the future is fluctuating, vague and uncertain, renders Wealth a peculiarly unsuitable subject for the methods of the classical economic theory".

This *incomplete knowledge* gives rise to money's function of store of value. As Keynes (1937a: 116) stated: "...our desire to hold money as a store of wealth is a barometer of the degree of our distrust of our own calculations and conventions concerning the future".[12]

As regards the individual freedom, Keynes stated a dilemma: "So long as it open to the individual to employ his wealth in hoarding or lending *money*, the alternative of purchasing actual capital assets cannot be rendered sufficiently attractive (especially to the man who does not manage the capital assets and knows very little about them) except by organising markets wherein these assets can be easily realised for money"(GT: 160-1).

Individual freedom stemming from unregulated markets, gives man the choice to hoard or lend money as speculative motives dictate. Then, socially desirable investment becomes subordinate to speculation. Such a situation, according to Keynes, raises a major question of welfare:

When the capital development of a country becomes a by-product of the activities of a casino, the job is likely to be ill-done. The measure of success attained by Wall Street, regarded as an institution of which the proper social purpose is to direct new investment into the most profitable

165

channels in terms of future yield, cannot be claimed as one of the outstanding triumphs of 'laissez-faire' capitalism... It is usually agreed that casinos should, in the public interest, be inaccessible and expensive (GT: 159).

Joan Robinson (1952: 154) drew attention to the undesirable effects of speculation: "The effect of speculation is then to speed up the movement of today's prices towards expected future prices. ... The market then becomes unstable. ... The operations of the speculators cast a thick fog over future prospects for the owners of wealth, increase uncertainty all around, and so raise the general level of interest rates".

In short, uncertainty, incomplete knowledge and speculation create crises of confidence, leading to structural instability. "The structural instability analyzed by Keynes is *pathological* in that it weakens and distorts the adaptive forces of the economic system. Since it depends on developed financial relations it may thus be called, more specifically, *financial fragility*" (Vercelli, 1991: 208).

How could one cure them? Keynes proposed two means. The first was about regulating the monetary system so that organised markets would allow no individual freedom for hoarding or lending money. Keynes stated:

> The only radical cure for the crises of confidence which affect the economic life of the modern world would be to allow the individual no choice between consuming his income and ordering the production of the specific capital-asset which, even though it be on precarious evidence, impresses him as the most promising investment available to him (GT: 161).

A second means was directed at curing "...the instability due to the characteristic of human nature that a large proportion of our positive activities depend on spontaneous optimism rather than on a mathematical expectation, whether moral or hedonistic or economic" (GT: 161). This is the condition identified by Keynes as *animal spirits*: "...a spontaneous urge to action rather than inaction, and not as the outcome of a weighted average of quantitative benefits multiplied by quantitative probabilities" (GT: 161).

Animal spirits in the GT is central to Keynes's theory of investment or what drives a capitalist to invest; investment determines the cyclical fluctuations and long run economic performance of economies. "Thus if the animal spirits are dimmed and the spontaneous optimism falters, leaving us to depend on nothing but a mathematical expectation, enterprise will fade and die" (GT: 162). However, animal spirits could flourish only if a stable macroeconomic environment existed.

In order to create stable conditions for the enterprises, Keynes proposed the control of the monetary system intended to influence long-term expectation by influencing the prospective yield of capital via the level of the rate of interest.

If this can be achieved, the result would be desirable. Keynes stated the causal nexus as follows:

> The expectation of a fall in the value of money stimulates investment, and hence employment generally, because it raises the schedule of marginal efficiency of capital, i.e. the investment demand-schedule; and the expectation of a rise in the value of money is depressing, because it lowers the schedule of the marginal efficiency of capital (GT: 141-2).

Hence, control of individual freedom and of the monetary system, where the rate of interest is determined, is the cure of Keynes so that neither speculation nor fluctuations of asset prices could dim animal spirits. The stable macroeconomic environment is of primary importance.

5.4.b) Keynes's interest rate

The important role of the rate of interest in determining effective demand becomes evident if we ask what determines the actual level of output and employment and what factors are prone to instability. Keynes (1937a: 221) raised the question and himself provided the following answer:

> More comprehensively, aggregate output depends on the propensity to hoard, on the policy of the monetary authority as it affects the quantity of money, on the state of confidence concerning the prospective yield of capital-assets, on the prospective to spend and on the social factors which influence the level of the money-usage. But of these several factors it is those which determine the rate of investment which are most unreliable, since it is they which are influenced by our views of the future about which we know so little.

The above quotation boils down to one factor: *influence of the rate of interest*. This is so because the propensity to hoard is dependent on the rate of interest. The monetary policy is about the capacity of a system to influence through its control of the money supply, the level of the rate of interest. The prospective yield of capital-assets could be changed, should the monetary authority be able to lower the rate of interest via its control of money supply and of credit; the prospective yield would be equally influenced if the fiscal authority undertook large scale investment that would influence *animal spirits*. The propensity to spend is also in part influenced by the level of the rate of interest. Because social factors that influence the level of money-wages could not be changed, an 'inflexible wage policy' could be substituted by a *flexible monetary policy*.
  The flexible monetary policy is analytically the same as the flexible wage policy because "...inasmuch as they are alternative means of changing the

quantity of money in terms of wage-units, in other respects there is, of course, a world of difference between them" (GT: 267). The relative efficiency of the monetary policy relies on its control by the government, on its speed in implementing it, on the money illusion externality it induces and an avoidance of a drag on the marginal efficiency of capital.

Given the important role of the rate of interest in determining effective demand by influencing the factors most sensitive to instability, Keynes's concern was first to define the rate of interest and then to show where it was determined. "The rate of interest is the reward for parting with liquidity for a specified period" (GT:167); hence it is *not* a reward of consumers' savings. In other words, the rate of interest is the price of being liquid. Secondly, the rate of interest is determined in the money markets and depends on a given supply of money at a point of time and on "the demand schedule for a present claim on money in terms of a deferred claim on money" (Keynes, 1937b: 241).[13]

Two aspects of Keynes's theory of interest rate should be stressed. First the rate of interest is determined in an organised money market. Second, hoarded money concerns *stocks*. Hence if an equilibrium is attained, it is a stock-equilibrium. This kind of an equilibrium implies a price-setting through the interaction of money stock-holders who can buy and sell amongst themselves. Such a price might be said to be an *inside price*.

The above might seem simple but they are not. If we ask the question: 'demand for money in terms of what?', the reply is not clear. Townshend (1937: 157) provided an answer:

> For it is an essential part of Mr. Keynes' theory of interest what the rate of interest - better envisaged as a simple function of the money-price of a monetary asset (a negotiable money-debt not payable at sight) - is not causally determined by the conditions of supply and demand (for new loans) at the margin. Rather are the demand and supply schedules for new loans determined by the value set by the market on existing loans (of similar types). That is to say, psychologically - determined changes in the latter influence largely, though they do not wholly determine, the former.[14]

The Townshend interpretation of Keynes's theory of the rate of interest suggests that the rate of interest can be considered as an *independent variable in the scheme of economic causation and it is psychological*. In fact, Keynes stressed this aspect as follows: "It is evident, then, that the rate of interest is a highly psychological phenomenon" (GT: 202). This is consistent with his view on the nature of a Monetary Economy: "...an Economy in which Money plays a part of its own and affects motives and decisions and is, in short, one of the operative factors in the situation, so that the course of events cannot be predicted, either in the long period or in the short, without a knowledge of the behaviour of money between the first state and the last" (CW, vol XIV: 408).

The psychological nature of the rate of interest relies heavily on the *monetary attributes* of an asset accepted as a means of exchange. One such property is money's unique potential power of being incorporated in any future use that its possessor may desire to put it. This property is not the only one. Chapter 17 of the GT is devoted to the unique properties of money and interest for it is the *core* of Keynes's view of why a monetary system cannot be left unregulated.

5.4.c) Keynes's properties of money

Three key properties are recognised: a) a *close to zero elasticity of production*, b) a *close to zero elasticity of substitution* and c) an *inelastic money rate of interest*.[15]

These three key properties of money imply certain consequences. The near zero elasticity of production implies that "Money...cannot be turned on at will by entrepreneurs to produce money in increasing quantities as its price rises in terms of the wage-unit" (GT: 230). Thus the money supply can be assumed exogenously given and, in terms of the ISLM model, LM is rather vertical. Lerner (1952: 184) stated two further consequences: "In the first place there is no direct increase in investment when there is an increase in demand for money, and in the second there are no increases in its stock to lower the marginal efficiency of holding it". It should be said that the inelasticity of supply is not only unique to money; Ricardian land, old masters and rare objects share this unique property; they are not easily reproducible.

The second property of money (low elasticity of substitution) gives rise to a confusion related to money's *derived utility*. It says that as the prices of non-monetary goods decline, it would cause the exchange value of money to rise and although the quantity of non- monetary goods would increase, there would be no increased demand for money. If this is so then Kahn's assertion (1954: 244) that "it is to the speculative motive that we must look as the source of interest- responsiveness and not at all to the precautionary motive" is contradictory. So is Lerner's view (1952: 184-5) that money's elasticity of substitution is not negligible but unitary: "In terms of liquidity, or purchasing power units, therefore, the total amount of liquidity yielded by a given stock of money increases 'in the same proportion' as the value of purchasing power of each unit. The elasticity of supply of liquidity is not zero but *unity*". Chick (1983: 303) offered an explanation to the confusion: "this is another example of Keynes's separation of money from the act of spending: consumption plans alter with income, not with available money, and the monetary preconditions of investment are not made explicit".

The zero elasticity of substitution implies no near-money and no parallel money. The high substitutability between money and financial assets calls for a theory that would explain the factors at work. In the next chapter, we make the case that once an asset has internalised sufficient externalities, the elasticity of substitution becomes high.

The third property of money is a derivative of the first and it was stated so by Keynes: "Thus the characteristic that money cannot be readily produced by labour gives at once some 'prima facie' presumption for the view that its own-rate of interest will be relatively reluctant to fall". This view of Keynes contradicts his position taken in chapter 15 of the GT where he argued that the phenomenon of a 'liquidity trap' is theoretically possible but "I know of no example of it hitherto. Indeed, owing to the unwillingness of most monetary authorities to deal boldly in debts of long term, there has not been much opportunity for a test" (p. 207). Yet in chapter 17, Keynes talks of compelling forces that give rise to the third property. These are: "...the money-wage being *more stable* than the real wage, tends to limit the readiness of the wage-unit to fall in terms of money" (GT: 232) [stress added] *and* "...the low (or negligible) carrying-costs of money play an essential part" (GT: 233).

There is another problem with the third property of money for it led Keynes to say: "The normal expectation that the value of output will be more stable in terms of money than in terms of any other commodity, depends of course, not on wages being arranged in terms of money, but on wages being relatively 'sticky' in terms of money" (GT: 237). Keynes tried to justify his assertion of *sticky wages* as follows: "In other words, the expectation of a relative stickiness of wages in terms of money is a corollary of the excess of liquidity-premium over carrying-cost being greater for money than for any other asset" (GT: 238). But then money's properties make *both* money's value stable and wages sticky.

Unless one explains *why money wages are sticky*, neither can they be taken as a common denominator nor the reasoning could it be other than circular. As to the circularity, Chick (1983: 306) stressed: "This seems on the face of it a peculiar way to argue, for the first condition [sticky money wages] makes the argument circular (sticky wages are both a corollary and a precondition for the liquidity-premium to attach to money) and the second [low carrying costs] blurs the attributes distinguishing l [liquidity-premium] and c [carrying costs]".

There is also a serious problem with Keynes's method. Chapter 17 is intended "...to discuss a process of long-run accumulation" (Joan Robinson in Eichner, 1978: xii), with tools similar to Walras's commodity E or money savings if transformed into investment assets. The whole discussion is centred on the process to find an equilibrium between three stocks: newly created money ($), stocks of bonds already existing (Y) and investments in new equipment (X). Each of these stocks has its 'own' rates. However, this is Walras's method in his theories of capitalization and of money. Keynes argues that for money, we have:

$$r_s = q_s - c_s + l_s$$

So an own rate such as r_s is equal to the worth of the direct use of \$ measured for a year of "\$" (q_s) less the depreciation that accompanies the use (c_s) plus the liquidity premium (l_s). The setting resembles Walras's circulating fund rendering a service of availability. In Keynes's GT, the liquidity premium exists because of the service rendered by having cash available arising from uncertainty while q_s and c_s are practically nil by assumption.

In principle, these three stocks could be candidates for *the* interest rate that will equilibrate with the marginal efficiency of capital. Yet as output increases, r_s falls less than either r_x or r_y and eventually becomes the *controlling* own rate. The r_s falls less because it is held in place by l_s. Why? First, because demand for money does not change its total (like in the *Elements*, quantities are held constant). Second, because money has no substitutes (like Walras's absence of substitutability stemming from the inconvertible paper money). Third, because the speculative motive due to uncertainty sets a floor (in the *Elements*, it is absent because of the certainty assumption). Hence

$$r_s = (c_x + r_x) = (c_y + r_y) = l_s$$

As quantities of X and Y are adjusted, possibly via arbitrage like in the *Elements*, the r_s is left as the highest while controlling its own rate. Liquidity preference sets a floor to which the yield on all other assets adapts. In the *Elements*, the rate of net income (i) sets the floor to which the price of money (p_u) adapts. The l_s sets the floor as long as the money wage remains sticky; Walras's i sets the floor as long as the numéraire is a commodity without money attributes. Both Walras's and Keynes's methods are alike; they differ in one assumption: certainty versus uncertainty.

Despite these theoretical difficulties with the three properties of money, Keynes argued that they are responsible for creating a *situation of rest* "...when the greatest amongst the own-rates of own-interest of all available assets is equal to the greatest amongst the marginal efficiencies of all assets" (GT: 236). The implication of such a state of affairs is that there would be no further increase in new investment. Although the equality between own-rates of own-interest and marginal efficiencies of all assets is satisfied under full employment conditions, Keynes believes that this is possible even under less than full-employment situations. This will occur, "...if there exists some asset, having zero (or relatively small) elasticities of production and substitution, whose rate of interest declines more slowly, as output increases, than the marginal efficiencies of capital-assets measured in terms of it" (GT: 236).

Commenting on the three properties of money, Dow (1985: 187) held the view the low degree of substitutability and low carrying costs are responsible for instability. Lerner (1952: 185) had stated it before:

> All this argument shows why 'money' can be the cause of depression if the monetary authorities do not create enough of it and why one cannot rely on the automatic working of the market to bring about the adjustment that may be needed to induce the investment required for full employment.

Money's instability is the cause of serious social consequences for Keynes because, according to Catephores (1991: 26), "[m]oney would...confer on its individual owner, an understandable feeling of omnipotence over goods, for as long...as his money lasted". "Therein lies the weakness of money-making as the driving force of capital accumulation; it is in the nature of money that it maintains the continuity of that process by continually interrupting it. The interruptions may become substantial, employment and accumulation may stop, a money panic may ensue among producers, without any improper behaviour on the part of financiers" (p. 29).

Keynes's cure to the above cause of depression was to bring under public control the authority responsible for monetary policy:

> Unemployment develops...because people want the moon; - men cannot be employed when the object of desire (i.e. money) is something which cannot produced and the demand for which cannot be readily choked off. There is no remedy but to persuade the public that green cheese is practically the same thing and to have a green cheese factory (i.e. central bank) under public control (GT: 235).

Wicksell had preceded Keynes by thirty years in diagnosing an 'inherent contradiction' in unregulated monetary systems: "Indeed, our modern monetary system is afflicted by an imperfection, an inherent contradiction. The development of credit aims at rendering the holding of cash reserves unnecessary, and yet these cash reserves are a necessary, though far from sufficient, guarantee of the stability of money values" (Lect. II: 126).

How could one correct the *inherent contradiction*? Wicksell's solution was similar to but had preceded by thirty years, the one proposed by Keynes:

> Only by completely divorcing the value of money from metal, or at any rate from its commodity function, by abolishing all free minting, and by making the minted coin or banknotes proper, or more generally the unit employed in the accounts of the credit institutions, both the medium of exchange and the measure of value - only in this way can the contradiction be overcome and the imperfection be remedied. It is only in this way that a logically coherent credit system, combining both economy of monetary

172

media and stability in the standard of value, becomes in any way conceivable (Lec. II: 126).[16]

Yet public control of the central bank, while leaving the individual free to employ his wealth in hoarding or lending in unorganised markets, would not necessarily mean full employment.   Full employment might be secured provided an active monetary policy would affect the motives of the individual that underlie the liquidity-preference.   The liquidity-preference is made expectational, unstable and unresponsive to changes in the money supply because "...expectations as to the future of the rate of interest as fixed by mass psychology have their reactions on liquidity-preference" (GT: 170).[17]

5.4.d) Determination of Keynes's interest rate

A necessary condition for the existence of liquidity preference is uncertainty as to the rate of interest ruling in future. Under such circumstances, bulls and bears and their expected purchases and sales of assets become operative. Given that the liquidity preference depends on the transactions, precautionary and speculative motives, it is of interest to know the relation between the three motives and changes in the money supply, in income and in the rate of interest.
    The total amount of cash (M) held is divided into two components: M_1 and M_2. Each of them is related to a liquidity function. M_1 is related to liquidity function L_1; and M_2 to L_2. L_1 corresponds to the function that would be relevant to the precautionary and transactions   motives and L_2 to the speculative motive. "L_1 mainly depends on the level of income, while L_2 mainly depends on the relation between the current rate of interest and the state of expectation. Thus

$$M = M_1 + M_2 = L_1(Y) + L_2(r), ... \text{"}   \text{(GT: 199).[18]}$$

As to $L_1(Y)$, Keynes (1937a), recognised that the precautionary motive has similarities to the speculative motive. $L_2(r)$ stands for the speculative which is "...the object of securing profit from knowing better than the market what the future will bring forth" (GT: 170). The demand for money is inversely related to the rate of interest, for given expectations and level of income.
    The equilibrium rate of interest is determined by two *stocks*: the stock demand for and the stock supply of money: "The rate of interest is not the "price" which brings into equilibrium the demand for resources to invest with the readiness to abstain from present consumption. It is the "price" which equilibrates the desire to hold wealth in the form of cash with the available quantity of cash" (GT: 167).
    Hence it is the *stock* of money in existence and the terms at which the public

is prepared to hold any 'new' stock with respect the stock of old securities that determine the rate of interest. It is *not* determined by the current 'flows' of investment and saving.

The composite nature of the liquidity preference as stated in the above formula has caused a number of theoretical objections.[19] One of them concerns Keynes's view that the rate of interest is independent of saving. In the GT: 165, Keynes stated: "The schedule of the marginal efficiency of capital may be said to govern the terms on which loanable funds are demanded for the purpose of new investment; whilst the rate of interest governs the terms on which funds are being currently supplied". In his Q.J.E. article (1937a: 222-3), Keynes repeated his GT thesis: "Thus instead of the marginal efficiency of capital determining the rate of interest, it is truer (though not a full statement of the case) to say that it is the rate of interest which determines the marginal efficiency of capital".

Yet assume an increase in income, then, according to the composite nature of the liquidity-preference, M_1 will increase to meet the increased demand for transactions. For a given supply of money such an increase would cause a rise in the rate of interest unless two assumptions are made: a) a liquidity trap exists, or b) the monetary authority exercises complete power to keep the rate of interest constant. The first option is categorically denied by Keynes in the GT (p. 207) where he asserts that the liquidity curve slopes downwards. The second option allows different interpretations. Robertson (1936: 182) pointed to an inconsistency:

> It seems clear that...Mr. Keynes' theory is simply readmitting by a back door the influence on the rate of interest of that factor, namely the shape and height of the productivity curve of funds devoted to investment uses, which in its cruder formulation is set out to exclude. For it is primarily upon that factor that the quantity $[M_1]$...depends.

In reply to Robertson (1938: 320), Keynes formally adopted the second option and conceded to the *loanable funds theory*: "The fact that 'any' increase in employment tends to increase the demand for liquid resources, and hence, if other factors are kept unchanged, raises the rate of interest, has always played an important part in my theory. If this effect is to be offset, there must be an increase in the quantity of money".

This back-door admission of the loanable funds in determining the rate of interest had been exposed by Ohlin (1937) who had argued that the rate of interest is regulated by the supply of *credit* and not by the supply of saving because the two are *not* identical. Credit contains dishoarding, particularly if the Aristotelian Modern stage is analyzed. But dishoarding cannot be accounted for by saving. In two articles, Keynes (1937b and 1937c) defended his GT position that the rate of interest is independent of saving but conceded to Ohlin the importance of *finance*.   Keynes (1937b: 246) stated the finance motive, which could regulate the pace of new investment, as follows:

> Planned investment - i.e. investment 'ex-ante' - may have to secure its 'financial provision' 'before' the investment takes place; that is to say, before the corresponding saving has taken place. ... This service may be provided either by the new issue market or by the banks; - which it is, makes no difference.

In the same article, Keynes defines this 'finance service' as a *revolving fund*: "Credit in the sense of 'finance' looks after a flow of investment. It is a revolving fund which can be used over and over again. It does not absorb or exhaust any resources" (1937b: 247).[20]

Given the fact that a period lapses between the date of arranging finance and the date of execution of investment, finance assumes importance. Would this factor affect the liquidity preference? Keynes answered in the affirmative but attached little importance to it for he believed that "'finance' is wholly supplied during the interregnum by the banks; and this is the explanation of why their policy is so important in determining the pace at which new investment can proceed" (1937c: 666). This is exactly what Wicksell (1906) and Ohlin (1937) had all along insisted on. Despite the spirited defense of Keynes's theory of the rate of interest from Joan Robinson (1952) and Kahn (1954), the debate between Keynes and his critics was not resolved.[21]

Asimakopulos (1984 and 1991: 113-4)) re-examined the relation of finance, investment and saving and concluded: "Keynes left matters in a muddle by intermingling statements about finance for working capital with those for fixed capital, and by his apparent failure to understand Robertson's question on the liquidity position of banks". The Robertson question was about banks being able to finance ex-ante investment without creating lack of liquidity. This might hold because the banking system's lack of liquidity is not restored until the repayment of the loan and therefore it takes time for an equilibrium to be re-established. "Keynes did not succeed in showing that investment is independent of the propensity to save under all circumstances" (Asimakopulos, 1991: 110). Furthermore if banks respond to demands for short-term loans to facilitate investment decisions, then an element of *endogeneity* in the determination of money supply is introduced by the 'revolving fund'.

By way of a summary, Keynes's monetary theory is the following. Money is preferred to interest-bearing securities because it is 'liquid'. It can be immediately exchanged for any other commodity; "its utility is solely derived from its exchange-value" (GT: 231). Yet the role of money depends on uncertainty and incomplete knowledge. Monetary policy mainly influences the incentives to hold wealth in non-liquid form via its effects on the rate of interest.[22] The rate of interest is a monetary phenomenon and to an extent

175

that current flows do not affect expectations, it does not depend on saving. It plays an important role in determining the level of effective demand and hence employment. Given that the properties of money and interest are in part responsible for creating structural instability resulting in unemployment, control of money and credit might be a solution. Given also the fact that, of the several factors affecting aggregate demand, the rate of interest is the most unreliable (or unstable), a monetary policy geared to influencing the perspective yield of capital-assets but operating under three states of nature: uncertainty, incomplete knowledge and individual freedom, might be impotent. Control of the monetary system through public ownership of the central bank and via it the organisation and regulation of money markets is attained.

5.5 Post Keynesians and world monetary system

No other economics text has stimulated so much research and on-going debate than Keynes's GT. A school of thought called Post Keynesian has developed further Keynes's ideas.[23] It takes off from the recognition that uncertainty undermines the traditional analysis of equilibrium and that all decisions are determined by expectations about the outcome. Monetary theory is set in historical time; its premises are endogeneity of money supply, investment precedes saving and financial instability.

Money comes into existence along with debts. For this to be operational, Keynes's view that money wages are more stable than the value of money is adopted by Post Keynesians (see essays in Eichner (1978)). In contrast to Keynes in the GT holding the view that the money supply is exogenous (assumption A5), Post Keynesians believe that the primary objective of central banks is to accommodate the supply of money to changes in the needs for economic activity. For Moore (1978: 126), "...post-Keynesian economists tend to regard the nominal money stock as endogenously governed by money wage levels" while for Chick (1992: 200), "...the theory of money supply must be a theory of banking policy with the authorities acting, if they act at all, through interest rates". Hence money is essentially *endogenous* because a credit money is analyzed. The liability management is equivalent to the monetisation of a newly issued debt. The effect is to change the total assets and liabilities of the private sector.

The endogeneity of money supply gains in a priori plausibility if Keynes's finance motive is adapted to the role played by credit instruments in the investment process. Credit permits investment to be carried out independently of current savings flows. Business cycles are viewed as an inherent feature of the capitalist system caused by the motives of producers and financial investors to accumulate money for its sake, the result of a failure to coordinate many individual economic activities.

176

The assumption of the endogeneity of money supply has consequences. Dow (1985: 188) summarised them in a single issue: "Endogeneity of the money supply also leaves interest rate determination even further in the air, particularly if that endogeneity is indeterminate (if bank lending practices are based on the same institutional and subjective factors as the demand for money-assets)". We offer a different interpretation of money supply endogeneity in chapter 7 which is based on financial innovations and the premise that money is an externality.

As long as money makes monetary debt possible, *financial instability* is endogenous to the capitalist system. Minsky (1978 and 1982) advanced the above hypothesis by grouping the financial actors into: 'hedge', 'speculative' and 'ponzi financing'. Hedge financing arises from a gap between expected gross profits and payment commitments. Bankruptcy is possible when realised profits are less than the contracted interest income to be paid out to a lender. Speculative financing is present when an investor can finance a long-term position in assets by short-term liabilities, the expected gross profit may be less than the payment commitments for some periods of time. Ponzi financing is generated by rising short-term interest rates over the full course of the investment project; outstanding debt grows because no new income-yielding assets are acquired and because new loans are borrowed at successively higher interest rates.

The relationship between the three categories of financing is not clear. For Minsky (1982), a shift of central bank monetary policy from targeting interest rates to the monetary base, will result in an increase in interest rates. Higher interest rates induce speculative at the expense of hedge financing and push speculative into ponzi financing. The same will happen if profits are expected to fall. "In either case, the overall debt structure of the economy could not be validated because payment commitments in their aggregate would far exceed aggregate expected cash flows, and a general debt deflation would follow leading to a rash of business bankruptcies and bank failures" (Rousseas, 1986: 25).

Can a major debt deflation be avoided? According to Minsky (1982), yes because of two mechanisms. First, central banks exercising the lender of last resort facility, they provide the necessary liquidity to prevent collapse. Second, government deficits "...sustain income or increase corporate profits and feed secure and negotiable financial instruments into portfolios hungry for safety and liquidity" (p. 71).

Rousseas (1986: 114-5), in his assessment of Minsky's thesis, stated:

Minsky's analysis reminds one, uncomfortably, of the artificial restoration of Say's law via the "skilful use of fiscal and monetary policy". It has the trappings of the neoclassical synthesis of "bastard" Keynesianism. ... Minsky's "hypothesis of financial instability" is a rather mechanical one and has the flavor of being designed 'ex post' to explain what was, and what already is, as interpreted by his basic theory. There is the strange feeling that Minsky's theory is a combination of Samuelson's fine tuning abilities and the central bank's ability to act as lender of last resort.

We argue in chapter 7 that the question is one of institutional financial instability and not Minsky's financial instability. This is so for two reasons. First, Minsky's groupings: hedge, speculative, ponzi have lost their significance in global markets. Institutional investors are the force behind globalisation today, as we said in chapter 2. Second, the lender of last resort bas become a last resort of *systemic risk* under the premise of money being an externality.

The GT is essentially about a closed economy (assumption A6). Post Keynesians, examining the international monetary system, have drawn inspiration from Keynes's 1944 vision of the Clearing Union while keeping the underlying principles of the GT. Keynes's (1940 in CW 1980) Clearing Union envisaged an international system based on the bancor as its monetary unit, negative interest rates on excessive bancor balances, a method of determining exchange rates and a policy assignment.

Davidson (1992-93: 158) elaborated on the above and proposed four rules designed:

> (1) to prevent a lack of global effective demand due to any nation(s) either holding excessive idle reserves or draining reserves from the system, (2) to provide an automatic mechanism for placing a major burden of payments adjustments on the surplus nations, (3) to provide each nation with the ability to monitor and, if desired, to control movements of flight capital, and finally (4) to expand the quantity of the liquid asset of ultimate international redemption as global capacity warrants.

Davidson's rules amount to two ideas. First, economic stagnation is caused by deficient global effective demand which is monetary in nature. In Keynes's GT, it is due to the uncontrolled monetary system; in Davidson's, it is rule (1). Second, capital mobility renders policy instruments ineffective, hence the imposition of capital controls is desirable. In Keynes's world of 1944 cited in chapter 3, the IMF article 7 regulating capital movements, was the essence of the Bretton Woods system; in Davidson's rule (3), capital controls are re-introduced and thus asset market equilibrium is assumed away. The globalisation of finance, capital, trade and foreign investment is not treated because it is believed that capital controls will deal with speculation and thus restore the effectiveness of policy instruments.

Both Keynes's (1940) and Davidson's present proposal boil down to one idea: 'create a supernational central bank with discretionary power supplemented with rules'. The anchor of Davidson's system will be the

International Money Clearing Unit (IMCU). "All IMCUs are held 'only' by central banks, not by the public" (Davidson, 1992-93: 159). Consequently, IMCU is not any different from the official ECU.

As regards the relationship of IMCUs with central banks of countries, the features of EMU in its first and second stages are adopted. Each nation's central bank is committed to guarantee one-way convertibility as it is with the official ECU when central banks borrow from each other in ECUs. The exchange rate of each nation will be set against the IMCU as it is with the ERM's official exchange rates of the ECU. The fixed exchange rates between a nations' currencies and the IMCU will be changed according to a rule: "...changes are to reflect permanent increases in efficiency wages" (Davidson, 1992-93: 161). A second rule governing changes in exchange rates relates to whether a poor or rich country is concerned: "If the deficit nation is a poor one,...the richer nations who are in surplus [will] transfer some of their credit balances to support the poor nation. If it is a relative rich country, then the deficit nation must alter its standard of living by reducing its relative terms of trade with its major trading partners" (Davidson, 1992-93: 163).

Davidson's proposal stands or falls provided his monetary system's IMCU would serve as an anchor. Whatever we have written so far and the subsequent two chapters on the ECU apply to Davidson's scheme and his IMCU. This institutional approach to the reform of the international monetary system presupposes fulfilment of H1 to H5 suggesting new answers to formerly unresolved basic questions of money.

5.6 Institutionalists and the ECU[24]

Four approaches are identified by Matthews (1986) that define the concept of institutions: 'property rights', 'conventions', 'types of contracts' and 'authority'. Each approach sets its own rights, rules and obligations that affect people in their economic lives. EMU belongs to 'authority'; it is an institutional setting of rules about 'who decides what and why'.

Yet the institutional approach to EMU boils down to one idea: What kind of institutions in the Community should be established so that the transfer of sovereignty to them should respect the principle of 'subsidiarity' and of 'efficiency'?. As to subsidiarity, Article 3b of TEU states the framework. As to efficiency, the alternative institutional set-up regulates both voluntary exchanges, where markets exist, and economic relations in areas where markets do not exist, would lead to a Pareto-improvement.

Institutionalists, echoing the views of State theorists, believe that EMU is the product of an agreement of the twelve States concerned. The State's role in the creation and evolution of institutions is paramount. "The state's involvement with institutions is inherent, in a way that it is not with technology... The range of its involvement is indicated by the titles on the standard shelf of legal textbooks; tort, bill of exchange, landlord and tenant, bankruptcy, company law, and so on. This responsibility remains even if the state tries to be non-interventionist as possible" (Matthews, 1986: 910).

All institutional approaches recognise that law, custom, trust, conventions and history play an important role in determining the internal structure of an institution. For example, confidence in the Bundesbank stems from its record to preserve the value of its money and from the trust inherent in the prudential control to prevent financial instability. Both are the product of 'history'. Keynes (1937a) outlined the *conventions* as major determinants of expectations and of relative stability in money wages. *Trust* is needed among Member States to renounce their right to manipulate their national currencies as a prerequisite for the establishment of the ECU as a currency of its own right.

New codes of conduct have to be established. These new rules limiting the discretionary decision-making power of central bankers and politicians as laid down in the TEU, are the reflection of 'custom' in some states where the independence of their central banks is recognised by 'law' while in others it is not. EMU requires under its Articles 108 and 109e(5), the independence of all national central banks.

The promotion of the ECU in the first and second stage of EMU would have required a different institutional setting (we have made a proposal to this effect in chapter 4). Yet the rules agreed reflect the culturally conditioned constraints of one State. The resistance of the Bundesbank to the emergence of the ECU as a parallel currency reflects Knapp's chartalism. Joeffre (1986) argues that the Bundesbank's reasons for the opposition to the private ECU are similar to the grounds on which Knapp would have opposed it: 'the ECU is not legal tender and has not a State to guarantee its *validity*'. The statutes of the Bundesbank and the German monetary law of 1948 stipulate that only the mark is the monetary unit of the German Sate; upon it the State has conferred the status of the legal means of payment. As long as the ECU is not recognised as the money of a State, its validity cannot be secured. Political union ought to proceed monetary union. This is what had happened in 1871 with the ancestor of Bundesbank: "The 'Reichsbank' was established after political unification had transferred the legislative authority in such matters from the member states to the central government" (Holtfrerich, 1989: 235). The fact that the TEU does not explicitly recognise parallel currencies is the logical corollary of the Bundesbank's monetary rules.

It is of interest to note that the ex-President of Bundesbank, Dr Pöhl (1990: 6) opposed the UK proposal on the 'hard ECU' on pure institutional grounds by arguing: "The main problem...is what role the [EMF] could assume and what conclusions are to be drawn therefrom for its institutional structure". He rejected the UK proposal because it would run the risk of being inflationary and because the main goal of the EMF will not be price stability: "the objective of stabilising exchange rates will be preferred to that of monetary stability...it is uncertain whether, as a Community institution, it will be able to exert any pressure towards an interest rate reduction on stability-conscious countries. ... Conflicts over these questions are by no means ruled out, and the 'indivisibility of monetary policy' is not assured" (p. 7).

Introducing a new currency requires a strategy or a theory. Pöhl (1990: 7-8) proposed a State-inducing strategy: "This can only be achieved if the decision-making power in the field of monetary policy is transferred to a supra-national institution which ensures a common, consistent monetary policy. After a transitional period with irreversibly fixed exchange rates, it could be empowered to issue a single currency".

What was decided at Maastricht? Article 109l(4) is a State theorist's statement and a strategy recommended by a Member State:

> At the starting date of the third stage, the Council shall, acting with the unanimity of the Member States without a derogation, on a proposal from the Commission and after consulting the ECB, adopt the conversion rates at which their currencies shall be irrevocably fixed and at which irrevocably fixed rate the ECU shall be substituted for these currencies, and the ECU will become a currency in its own right. This measure shall by itself not modify the external value of the ECU. The Council shall, acting according to the same procedure, also take the other measures necessary for the rapid introduction of the ECU as the single currency of those Member States.

As we argued in chapter 2, the two most important articles of EMU concerning the new system, are 109g and 109l(4). The first because the ECU links the EMS with the second stage via its 'hardened' character and the second because of the method chosen to introduce the single currency in a new institutional setting endowed with a single monetary authority. The responsibility for monetary policy is indivisible and assured by a statute.

The statute of the ECB follows Keynes's view that a money economy is inherently unstable; consequently, it has to be regulated. This new regulatory regime would create new relations because the change in institutions would induce a change in the conduct of economic performance similar to the relation between a change in transaction costs and a change in efficiency. The contribution of the new institutional setting to welfare would depend on the role of the ECU in the subsequent stages of EMU. This would be possible in areas where markets do not exist or in institutional arrangements that enable the transactor to co-operate more efficiently than they did before.

The presumption that appropriate institutional change is a source of economic growth has been the implicit idea of the Delors report, the hypothesis of the Commission (1990) study: *One market, one money* and the justification for the TEU. Matthews (1986: 915) discussed various features of institutions and concluded: "I have suggested a number of reasons why institutional change is not likely to be 'merely' a matter of Pareto-improving innovations and adaptations: the involvement of the state, non-voluntary interaction (externalities), and inertia and complexity, with their tendency to produce a random walk".

5.7 H1 to H5 applied to Keynes's GT

If Keynes's theory is seen through H1 to H5, we find that his GT satisfies fully H1 because, as we argue in chapter 3, it is the general depression (monetary disturbance) that has given rise to a theory and that is the GT.

Keynes's theory of money cannot predict the transformation of the monetary system for it partly fails H2 on evolving money. This is so because Keynes's money is whatever the State wishes it to be *and* because his theory of interest rate is developed independently of the evolution of financial institutions. As we argue in the next chapter, this is impossible for the integration of money in the economic system cannot be shown to be consistent beyond a Marshallian period. This argument merits emphasis for it is the 'core' of our alternative proposal envisaged to explain the evolution of monetary theory and institutions.

A similar point is made by Chick (1992: 193-4): "The theory of saving and the rate of interest can - or at any rate should - never be independent of the state of development of financial institutions...the reversal of causality in the saving-investment nexus proposed by Keynes (1936) should not be seen as correct theory in triumph over error but as a change in what constituted correct theory due to the development of the banking system".

A further problem is induced by H2. Contrary to the view of the theories surveyed in this thesis which have money acting as the 'standard' of the system, Keynes accepted the 'money-wage' as being more stable than the value of money. As we said earlier such kind of reasoning introduces circularity;[25] for an asset to be accepted as a means of exchange, its value must be more stable given that there are no institutional restrictions that raise the costs disproportionately.

Keynes's circular reasoning that money wages are more stable than the value of money introduces the following consequences. Keynes's money cannot meet fully Cipolla's second criterion of our H3 which requires a highly stable value of money; in the GT, it depends on the 'sticky' money wages. It is this property of money that enhances confidence in an asset to be accepted as money. It is characteristic of money that implies 'liquidity' as well. Although one may argue that the attribute of liquidity is a derivative of money's two zero elasticities of production and substitution, for this to occur, one needs a theory which demonstrates the origin and nature of money. This brings us back to idea a) of H5 on the nexus of causality, from where we begun our inquiry into the fundamentals of money.

The Triffin postulate (H4) is partly met by the GT if examined in the context of H5. Keynes states the mechanisms of the determination of the rate of interest. A case in point is Keynes's chapter 12 of the GT intended to show the causal link between the monetary policy and its influence on the factors affecting the rate of interest. Central to his argument is the level of the rate of interest and its effects on the supply price of capital assets, on the cost of finance and on the state of confidence. All three will influence the private sector's preference. However, Keynes came to a contrary conclusion:

> For my own part I am now somewhat sceptical of the success of a merely monetary policy directed towards influencing the rate of interest. I expect to see the State, which is in a position to calculate the marginal efficiency of capital-goods on long views and on the basis of the general social advantage, taking an ever greater responsibility for directly organising investment; since it seems likely that the fluctuations in the market estimation of the marginal efficiency of different types of capital, calculated on the principles I have described above, will be too great to be offset by any practicable changes in the rate of interest (GT: 164).

An explanation might be offered to the above conclusion. If the rate of interest is the reward paid to money hoarders for parting with liquidity *and* the liquidity preference is 'highly psychological', then, the liquidity preference can influence expectations and hence causally *influence* the determination of the rate of interest but cannot determine it.[26] This is explainable on two accounts. First, if the inactive demand of the composite nature of the liquidity preference due to the state of confidence and expectations on the part of the owners of wealth dominates the active demand due to the level of activity established by investment, then situations of rest such as implied in the third property of money cannot be changed by a monetary policy.[27]

Second, if situations of rest apply, the option left open to monetary authority to affect employment will be by an increase in the money supply as employed in the GT (see chapter 19, pp. 267-9). That is equivalent to inducing *price level externalities* and thus change proportionately the burden of debt. The *money-illusion externality* would cause changes in the value of existing loans leading to changes in the price of monetary assets.

There is another neglected aspect of the GT. As long as expectations are important determinants of the demand for 'new' stock of securities (money), they can be affected by current and expected 'flows' of investment and saving. If the resultant saving flows are judged to be smaller than the expected rates of planned investment, expectations of rising rates of interest will be reflected in higher current rates. Thus, Keynes's "fairly safe level of r" (GT: 201) becomes an *expectational r*, mainly influenced by *expectations externalities*.

If this interpretation is correct, then the L_2 should *not* correspond to the speculative motive of the GT but to the *externalities* generated by the monetary authority. The authority via its money supply, induces three externalities: *expectations, redistribution* and *money-illusion*. Then the exogeneity of money supply cannot be assumed.

As to idea b) of H5 on the integration of value and money theories, Keynes's theory of money is the only one that integrates the real and value models via his interest rate theory, which implies changes in quantities, and thus partly meets H5. This should not be interpreted that H5, once partly met, could predict the transformation of monetary systems and their monetary units. Our approach requires the fulfilment of all H1 to H5. Keynes gave us little direction as to how one could make, say, the ECU the money of the European Union.

5.8 Concluding remarks

We have inherited from Plato three monetary endowments: the genesis of money residing in the ideal Polis, a money exchange process, M-C-M and a dual anchor system. We have learned from Knapp that the role of the State is paramount in establishing the asset chosen by the State as a means of settlement of debt. His theory depends on the notion of *validity* which should be interpreted as the capacity of a State to create money's acceptability for the settlement of debt.

Had it not been for Keynes's *General Theory*, the State theory of money would not have taken the theoretical evolution it has. His theory is summarised in the preface of the GT: vii "A monetary economy...is essentially one in which changing views about the future are capable of influencing the quantity of employment and not merely its direction".

The central message of the GT is that the existence of money is a *source of instability* because paper money has particular properties which make a monetary economy fundamentally different from barter or from an economy based on commodity money. Money, as a store of value, is an act of individual saving. "Thus it depresses the business of preparing to-day's dinner without stimulating the business of making ready for some future act of consumption" (GT: 210).

Starting from the premise that unemployment is determined in the product, not in the labour, market, the GT is about what determines effective demand. Central to that is Keynes's theory of interest, which solves the old dichotomy between real and money theories via its functional relationships with all components of effective demand. In order to equate ex ante saving with investment, Keynes's theory of interest is instrumental for two reasons; first, by regulating the money market, it creates a stable macroeconomic environment for animal spirits to be realised; second, by using a flexible monetary policy as a substitute for flexible wage policy, it minimises uncertainty over the course of relative prices and level of demand. Both intended purposes are met by controlling the monetary sector of a capitalist economy.

Keynes's vision and its extension by the Post Keynesian or the institutional approach is only applicable to a closed economy where the central bank is able to control its money supply, capital controls are maintained and government is able to direct economic policy. In a highly interdependent world economy characterised by global markets in capital, trade, finance and direct investment, the *suggestive capacity* of the GT is limited, even insignificant save its notion of effective demand.

What really matters to a new monetary system is not the institutional change, nor the checks and balances that must be built in, nor the well designed rules. The point of interest is whether EMU would introduce an *innovation*. The structure of ECB is federal and does not break away from established conventions in monetary policy. The area that is not yet established is EMU's monetary unit, the ECU. For an *innovation* in this area, we need a fresh approach. The next chapter is an attempt at it.

Notes

1. The theories dating back to Hesiod up to Adam Smith have been treated by Gordon (1975) and Monroe (1923). The classical theories of money have been studied by Niebyl (1946) and Green (1992). A history of the monetary and credit theories from John Law up to mid-1930s has been completed by Rist (1940). Ellis (1934) has provided us with an indispensable study on the German monetary theory by concentrating on the period: 1905 to 1933 and on the origin, nature, functions and value of money. The economic history of deposit banking in the Mediterranean Europe by Usher (1943) stresses the importance of monetary institutions as clearing houses for the debts, as guarantors for payments and for confidence as well as it brings to the surface the legal aspects of such monetary arrangements.

2. Wicksell admitted: "We know nothing definite concerning the beginnings of the use of money" (Lec. II: 29-30).

3. Gordon (1975: 27-8) interpreted Plato's view on what constitutes the forces of economic growth: "A reader of Plato's 'Republic' might contest the view that the author was an advocate of the stationary state. At the opening of the second book of that work, the writer pays particular attention to elements of a growth process".

4. Trever (1916: 38) stated this point forcibly: "As Plato was the first of extant Greek thinkers to grasp the principle of the division of labor, he was the first to give any hint as to the origin of money. He states that it came into use by reason of the growth of necessary exchange, which in turn resulted from increased division of labor".

5. Trever (1916: 38-9) is explicit on this point: "The function of money he defines somewhat indefinitely by the term "token of exchange", an expression suggestive of Ruskin's definition "a ticket or token of right to goods". It seems to imply that money is not itself a commodity to be trafficked in".

6. See Trever (1916: 137) on the attitudes of the Cynics and the work: *Eryxias*. "This is suggestive of the cynic theory of fiat money, since the examples used are those of the worthless currency of Carthage, Sparta, and Ethiopia".

7. See Monroe (1924: 9) for an interesting discussion on how scholars of the Renaissance period viewed the Stoics.

8. All references to Knapp's *The State Theory of Money* in this section shall be taken from the English edition published in 1924 by Macmillan.

9. See Robinson (1978), Chick (1991b) and Assimakopulos (1992) on these matters.

10. Frankel (1977) devoted chapter V of his book to Keynes's morality of money and made references to the pre-GT to prove that Keynes's distrust

of money under uncertainty, incomplete knowledge and freedom of individual choice dated back to the conclusions of the report of the Royal Commission on Indian finance and currency in which Keynes had expressed doubts on the efficiency of a monetary system based on gold.

11. The consequences of economic decisions taken under uncertainty were pointed out by Shackle (1967: 133): "A theory of unemployment is, necessarily, inescapably, a theory of disorder. The disorder in question is the basic disorder of uncertain expectation, the essential disorder of the real, as contrasted with the conventionally pretended, human condition. It is the disorder of adventurous decision, of 'enterprise'. The work in which 'enterprise' is necessary and possible is a world of uncertainty".

12. This aspect of Keynes was explained by Shackle (1967: 132): "The deliberate self-deception of business, in supposing its investment decisions to be founded on knowledge and to be rationally justifiable; the insecurity of its faith in its own judgements, which the awareness of this self-deception engenders; the paralysis of decision and enterprise which can result when the structure of pretended knowledge is violently overthrown by events; this central core of the General Theory is to be found in Chapter 12...".

13. In his reply to his critics (Ohlin, Hicks, Robertson, Hawtry), Keynes (1937b: 250) reiterated: "The function of the rate of interest is to modify the money-prices of other capital assets in such a way as to equalise the attraction of holding them and of holding cash".

14. One may conceive a money market in which old and new bonds are traded for new stocks of money. Hence two prices are possible one referring to the old bonds and another to the new bonds. This implicit conflict can be resolved on the assumption that the new bonds dominate in the market. "Thus each increase in the quantity of money must raise the price of bonds sufficiently to exceed the expectations of some 'bull' and so influence him to sell his bonds for cash and join the 'bear' brigade" (GT: 171).

15. The relevant quotations from the GT are: "(i) The first characteristic...is the fact that money has, both in the long and in the short period, a zero, or at any rate a very small, elasticity of production, so far as the power of private enterprise is concerned, as distinct from the monetary authority" (p. 230). "The second 'differentiation' of money is that it has an elasticity of substitution equal, or nearly equal, to zero... This follows from the peculiarity of money that its utility is solely derived from its exchange-value, so that the two rise and fall pari passu..." (p. 231). The third property of money concerns the rate of interest and is associated with several reasons that explain "why in an economy of the type to which we are accustomed it is very probable that the money-rate of interest will often prove reluctant to decline adequately..." (p. 232).

16. This led Hicks (1977: 63) to declare: "It is that rate of interest which becomes the effective monetary regulator, not the Quantity of Money, in any sense".

17. Whereas the *Treatise* is firm on the instability of the demand for money, the GT is a mixed case. There are times when Keynes talks of 'unstable' and 'elastic' liquidity preference (see GT: 198). A page earlier Keynes had argued that the "speculative motive usually shows a continuous response to gradual changes in the rate of interest".

18. Notice in this context the important role of 'expectations' in the functional relation of $M_2 = L_2(r)$. Shackle's comment (1967: 221) should be noted: "A change of expectations, since its possible causes and its possible natures are infinitely diverse and beyond all survey, can have any effect we care to conceive. Thus the analyzable region of economic events consists in those chains of cause and effect, or those internal structures of situation, which exist in the presence of a given 'state of expectation'". Hence the function $M_2 = L_2(r)$ could be assumed stable as long as the state of expectation is unchanged.

19. Robertson (1936) raised a number of objections. First he argued that the liquidity preference formula obscured the dominant forces underlying the demand for money because it forces together "those who desire to 'hold' more money and those who desire to 'use' it" (p. 177). Second if an expansionary monetary policy leads to an increase in real income, any redistribution in favour of entrepreneurs will lead to higher hoarding implying that: "These two sets of forces are acting on the rate of interest in 'opposition' to the predominant set of forces, namely that which is raising the schedule of profitability of funds directed to investment" (p. 178). Third if the money wage and not money is accepted as a standard then in the long period money plays no special role.

20. Robertson (1938: 315) criticised Keynes's revolving fund for it corresponded to no banking practices, nor had it solid theoretical foundations and asked: "How is any revolving fund automatically released, any willingness to undergo illiquidity set free for further employment, by the mere act of the entrepreneur in spending his loan?".

21. Leijonhufvud (1986: 12) assessed the debate as follows: "The aspect of Keynes' theory which has created the most trouble for later interpreters, Keynesians and anti-Keynesians alike, is his theory of interest, which is rather a theory of short-run interest 'movements'. Even more to the point is Keynes' own obvious dissatisfactions with this aspect of the 'General Theory'. His repeated efforts at repairing this vital past of his theoretical structure were not only unsuccessful - they produced new contradictions and compounded the confusion".

22. The burden of adjustment which is placed on prices. Keynes (1937b: 25) recognised that: "The function of the rate of interest is to modify the

money-prices of other capital assets in such a way as to equalize the attraction of holding them and of holding cash".

23. A recently published book on the Post-Keynesian approach to economics by Arestis (1992) provides a comprehensive analysis of the micro-foundations of the Post-Keynesian paradigm.

24. We have been unable to find a book or an article coherent enough to describe, explain and predict by purely institutional tools, the origin, evolution and transformation of institutions. The economics of institutions has only recently become fashionable despite an early start of the institutionalist school by Veblen (1899). Hicks (1969) examined the emergence of the market. Barzel (1987) viewed the entrepreneur as the innovator of new markets via the introduction of new types of organisation or contract. Coase (1960) saw alternative systems based on tradeable 'property rights' capable of leading to a superior trading efficiency. Hodgson's (1988) critique of neoclassical economics is about the efficiency of its institutions. North (1981 and 1991) has combined economic history and tools of economics to view the institutional evolution. Dow (1985) attempts a methodological approach to money but leaves it at that. Matthews (1986) has systematised the economics of institutions. Eggertsson (1990: 13) attempts "...to extend and generaralize the theory of price and apply it to economic and political institutions". It is Coasean in its approach, rich in material and retains the essential elements of neoclassical economics. Its treatment of money is seen in a system of exchange rendering services of the kind we call 'transaction costs' and 'brand-name' externalities.

25. As Chick (1983: 306) says: "To 'be money', an asset must be widely acceptable. An asset becomes widely acceptable because it is believed to be liquid. It is liquid precisely because it is widely acceptable. The fact that the argument is circular does not make it less true".

26. Shackle (1967: 247) expressed another view: "The interest-rate depends on expectations of its own future. It is expectational, subjective, psychic, indeterminate. And so is the rest of the economic system. The stability of the system, while it lasts, rests upon a convention: the tacit general agreement to 'suppose' it stable. This stability, once doubted, is destroyed, and cascading disorder must intervene before the landslide grounds in a new fortuitous position".

27. Keynes (1936: 203) recognised this aspect of the monetary policy: "Thus a monetary policy which strikes public opinion as being experimental in character or easily liable to change may fail in its objective of greatly reducing the long-term rate of interest, because M_2 may tend to increase almost without limit in response to a reduction of r below a certain figure".

6 Money is an externality

6.1 Introduction

This chapter attempts to demonstrate idea a) of H5 concerning the nexus of monetary causality arising from money's:

origin ---> nature ---> functions ---> interest rate.

and idea b) of H5 on the role of money.

It is interlinked with H2 on the Aristotelian notion of evolving money, which asks *when* money becomes established. H2 also argues that money originates in the market, but the character of money will evolve as the stage of development progresses. We need a theoretic approach capable of explaining the monetary transformations of money from commodity to commodity money, to paper, to credit and, as we argue in chapter 7, to electronic money. We attempt this by concentrating on the 'nature' of money and we propose the premise: *money is an externality*.

The institution of money generates and internalises externalities. The asset, financial or not, that has been established as a means of settlements of debt in period t, had internalised a sufficient number of money externalities before period t-1. Money externalities can be classified under five categories: transaction, price level, confidence, learning and technological, and seigniorage.

The above premise is examined in the context of the literature on externalities.[1] A body of thinking on externalities and its salient features exists but "...one is left with the feeling that we still have not captured all its ramifications" (Baumol and Oates, 1988: 14). It should be recognised that Pigou's (1946) definition of externalities, which says that one person's activity influences the utility or production function of another, has been the backbone of all subsequent contributions. Pigou considered taxes and subsidies as necessary to induce the externality- generator to limit his activity with a view of attaining efficiency.

In a Pigouvian spirit, Scitovsky (1954) distinguished four types of direct and non-market interdependence, those of consumers' satisfaction, of producers' direct influence on personal satisfaction, of a producer's influence on another producer's output and of direct interdependence among producers' inputs.

Bator (1958) considered externalities as a variety of economic situations which illustrated cases of market failure. In his category of externalities, he included public goods as a special case. Market failure due to externalities required government intervention to re-establish the efficiency of the markets.

For Buchanan and Stubblebine (1962: 374), the only externality relevant to economic theory is that of Pareto-relevant: "An externality is defined to be Pareto-relevant when the extent of the activity may be modified in such a way that the externally affected party, A, can be made better off without the acting party, B, being made worse off".

Arrow (1970: 70) related his discussion of externalities to the perfectly competitive equilibrium and Pareto efficiency by stating two basic postulates: "(C), the convexity of household indifference maps and firm production possibility sets, and (M), the universality of markets". These two basic postulates allowed Arrow to derive the *duality theorem*: the universality of markets is a sufficient condition to lead to a competitive equilibrium which is Pareto-efficient *or* any Pareto-efficient allocation can be achieved as a competitive equilibrium by a suitable reallocation of initial resources.

The perfectly competitive model is used by Arrow (1970) and by Baumol and Oates (1988: 17-8), who defined an externality by reference to two conditions: I) "An externality is present whenever some individual's (say A's) 'utility' or 'production' relationships include real (that is, nonmonetary) variables, whose values are chosen by others (persons, corporations, governments) without particular attention to the effects on A's welfare"; II) "The decision maker, whose activity affects others' utility levels or enters their production functions, does not receive (pay) in compensation for this activity an amount equal in value to the resulting benefits (or costs) to others".

If the externalities generated by an 'institution' are the object of analysis, the above definitions are inappropriate because they concentrate on the 'individual' and are narrow in scope. Meade (1973) has provided us with a broader definition which is more appropriately adaptable to institutional externalities.

6.2 Meade's externalities[2]

Meade (1973: 15) offered the following definition: "An external economy (diseconomy) is an event which confers an appreciable benefit (inflicts an appreciable damage) on some person or persons who were not fully consenting parties in reaching the decision or decisions which led directly or indirectly to the event in question".

Commenting on Meade's definition, Cornes and Sandler (1986: 29) said: "First, it is not at all specific about the institutional framework within which social interactions take place. It simply suggests that, whatever that framework is, it places constraints on the ability of individuals to take steps to encourage (discourage) actions of others that confer benefits (costs) on them. ... Second, Meade's definition casts the net extremely widely, labelling as externalities situations that other writers prefer to call by some other name".

An important analytical point about externalities was stated by Meade:

> In a world of perfect markets in which there are no real effects (such as noise) which were not the subject of transaction in perfect markets, there would be no externalities. This would be so even if all decisions were taken by single decision-makers. In order that there should be perfectly competitive markets all decision-makers would have to operate on a small scale; otherwise a single decision-maker could influence market prices (p. 18).

Another notable feature of Meade's externalities is that he separates them into two classes: a) distributional externality, b) real income externality.

A *distributional externality* is realised through the price mechanism. If "...an external effect takes the form of a redistribution of income due to a price effect we may call it a "distributional externality" (p. 19). This price effect may be due to competitive forces or to a change of preference. This distributional externality is analogous to some of our *price level externalities*.

A *real-income externality* occurs if, without hurting himself, the action of an economic agent confers an appreciable benefit on others who were not a party to the initial decision. Take the case of a monopolist who decides to increase his output because he expects an increased demand for his product owing to new customers. The decision will result in two real-income effects; first, the price will fall so existing and any new customers will benefit; second, the increased output will increase the total revenue of the monopolist but may not maximise his profits. Meade's *real-income externality* is analogous to a number of externalities generated by the institution of money, which we shall refer to in the subsequent paragraphs.

There are certain types of externalities that are of mixed nature; they are partly distributional and partly real-income. We have already implicitly dealt with the sort of externality due to technological knowledge as the stage of economic development evolved under our H2. From our predecessors, we have inherited technical knowledge, a great stock of capital goods and efficient money markets. Meade's treatment of inheritance as an externality is justified on the grounds that: "This has certainly 'conferred upon us an appreciable benefit' through decisions in which, since we were not even born at the time, 'we were not fully consenting parties'" (p. 21).

What differentiates a *real-income externality* from a *distributional-externality* is that the former could occur if the system of perfect competition does not exist. A *distributional externality* might well occur even in perfectly competitive markets.

Real-income externalities play an important role. Meade separates them into six classes using the criterion of the technological and institutional conditions that have generated the externalities. These are:

a) the shared variable
b) the ill-defined ownership
c) the market organisation cost
d) the fiscal conditions
e) the monopolistic situations
f) the moulding-of-preference.

'Shared variable externalities' are the usual category dealt with in the literature; the same variable enters into the utility or the cost function of more than one independent individual. A case of shared variable externality par excellence is public goods. Meade summarised it as follows: "The decision to spend the money on defence and to raise the revenue by a particular set of taxes is in fact a decision of the government to which the individual citizens are not directly parties but which affects appreciably the welfare of every citizen. Public goods are clear examples of externalities" (pp. 31-2).

Weldon (1968, 1971, 1973) and Arrow (1970) were the first to apply public goods theory to money. Kindleberger (1983 and 1986) has now become the proponent. In setting the problem, Weldon (1973: 1) repeated his earlier position: "money should be regarded as an <u>essentially public</u> rather than a <u>purely private</u> good" [his underline].

The 'ill-defined ownership' externality arises from a situation "...where there is some scarce resource such that the more you use, the less there is for me, but where the resource has not been ascribed to the ownership of any specified economic agent" (Meade: 34). If applied to the institution of money, we have the following case: *in a money exchange process (M-C-M*), no one is excluded*. Then, "if exclusion is impossible or too costly to be privately profitable, an essential precondition for the establishment of effective property rights is absent" (Cornes and Sandler, 1986: 33). Without properly defined rights, who is going to decide: 'who owns a pool of oil lying under an area of land or who has the fishing rights in a disputed ocean?' This is an externality, analogous to the case if money is considered as a social institution to which no one has effective property rights.

The 'market organisation cost' externalities depend on cost conditions.

193

Meade gave an example drawing from monetary theory: "In dealing with monetary theory and with the closely connected problem of planning to meet an uncertain future, a basic element in the analysis is the fact that organising and using all the possible markets for all the possible contingent goods and services must be ruled out on grounds of cost. The question as to what limited number out of the infinite possible number of forward markets and of insurance markets it will pay to organise has become a central feature of monetary theory and of the theory of planning for the future" (p. 35).

It should be noted that organising a market of the kind we have, by our money process (M-C-M*) with its interwoven systems, alluded to is a costly business. In the absence of a market, the opportunity cost is higher. Suppose one is given property rights over a pool of oil, but there is no market for oil; such property rights are not worth the paper written on. The market organisation at a historical moment, could cause externalities of 'ill-defined ownership' to become relevant and give rise to 'shared variable' externalities where the Scitovsky-type externality is applicable. In either case, the structure of exchange would entail a cost.

Meade draws examples from public utilities services, such as postal services, public transport, supply of water and of electricity, to state: "In fact in every concern, both public and private, the operation of the pricing system will involve a cost. ... In every case there is a balance to be sought between the advantages of a more accurate pricing system and the costs of its administration. ... Everywhere there is some element of externality due to the 'market-organisation-cost'" (p. 40).

Our *transaction costs externalities* are market organisation cost. If one considers a money process (M-C-M*) as an interwoven system in which other systems such as telecommunications, information, etc., are essential parts for the efficient functioning of the market, then one should regard externalities of the market organisation cost as being induced by money. The 'fiscal set of conditions' are generated by the valuation of cost or benefit; it is described by Meade: "Where a tax or a subsidy is imposed on an activity in which there was no pre-existing other cause of divergence between marginal value and marginal cost, a tax will cause marginal value to remain above marginal cost and vice versa with a subsidy on the activity. This will give rise to externalities" (p. 40).

The essence of externalities due to taxation or subsidy is that "...by purchasing another unit of this taxed commodity I have given rise to an external economy which will be to someone's net benefit" (Meade, p. 41). The 'fiscal set' externalities correspond to some of our *price level externalities*. Money's ability to capture real resources either through inflationary finance or through its power to aid or hinder capital accumulation in the sense used by Wicksell (Lect. II), gives rise to externalities.

The 'monopolistic conditions' externalities arise because of institutional or legal impediments to the entry of competitors or because of economies of scale and indivisibilities. Then, there is a divergence between marginal cost and marginal benefit, or a divergence between private valuation and social valuation. This is the essence of Meade's monopolistic set of conditions: "An increase in the quantity bought by a monopsonist, just as an increase in the quantity sold by a monopolist, will lead to an external economy" (p. 42). *Seigniorage externalities*, identified with different forms of institutional structure, are identical in effects to Meade's monopolistic set of externalities.

The 'moulding of preferences' as generator of externalities is illustrated by Arrow (1970: 76): "What aspects of others' behavior do we consider as affecting a utility function? If we take a hard-boiled revealed preference attitude, then if an individual expends resources in supporting legislation regulating another's behaviour, it must be assumed that the behavior affects his utility". Meade added other examples: "There are many activities such as commercial advertising, to say nothing of political speeches, religious sermons, and university lectures, which alter citizens' tastes. Take the case of commercial advertisement. The advertiser takes a decision in which I play no part but which causes me to prefer commodity X to Y instead of Y to X. Am I better off or not?" (p. 76).

We refer to brand name externalities, to State instruments and policies, and to institutional arrangements in order to explain why different producers of money capture different *confidence externalities*. In our scheme, this category of externalities provide a solution to the Arrow-Meade puzzle over the role of 'moulding of preferences'; they act in a deliberate way so as to affect the utility function of the users of money. The choice of a trader in using one or another money as an intermediary in exchange, much depends on the confidence externalities engineered by producer X or Y of money.

6.3 Money externalities

We adapt Meade's (1970) definition to take account of the salient features of the institution of money, and state:

> *In a money process defined as Money-Commodity-Money (M-C-M*), a money economy (or diseconomy) - M_E - is an event realised in the market that confers an appreciable benefit (or inflicts an appreciable damage) on some person(s), transactor(s) or institution who were not fully consenting parties or active participants in reaching the decision(s) which led directly or indirectly to the event in question.*

A number of aspects of this definition should be noted. It differs from all the cited definitions. The latter have the individual as the base of their analysis and not the *institutions*. We find definitions of the kind referred to above both restrictive and inapplicable to analyzing externalities generated by institutions. For example, Buchanan's and Stubblebine's assumption that an externality 'may be measured' is at variance with our understanding that externalities, in general, *cannot be measured*.

Money externalities should not be considered new in economic literature. Adam Smith (1776), in his Chapter IV: Of the origin and use of money, advanced the hypothesis that money had existed in society because it had served to reduce the 'informational costs and inconveniences of exchange'. His discussion was set in a context similar to the one found in chapter 3 on the Aristotelian notion of evolving money.

Money externalities are *not tradable*, despite the fact that they are the products of the money process realised in the market. This notion is at variance with Coase's (1960) conception that, as long as property rights exist and transaction costs are low, there would be no externalities.[3] The institution of money may be subject to property rights and hence a system of transferable rights and enforceable contracts may be erected. Yet Coase's system says nothing on whether, under the states of nature of H5: uncertainty, free access and maximisation principle, it would lead to an institution being lawfully owned by a monopolist.

It should be recalled that Coase's solution to the problem of externalities is dependent on the assumption that the number of victims is small and transaction costs low. He argued that the mere existence of externalities was not a sufficient reason for government intervention. In our money externalities scheme, we are presented with the law of large numbers, which makes Coase's solution inapplicable. Baumol and Oates (1988) worked out the conditions that "'so long as the number of victims is large', the efficient treatment of victims prohibits compensation" (p.23) and "'the process of direct negotiation and agreement will generally be unmanageable'" (p. 10). Contrary to the perfectly competitive model of Coase, the internalisation of money externalities by an asset would establish a natural monopolist only if the Cipolla criteria are fully satisfied and the three states of nature of H5 hold.

Some money externalities of the type Viner (1931) had defined 'technological', i.e. generating a shift in production or consumption function, correspond to some of Meade's real-income externalities. Some are 'pecuniary', i.e. causing a movement along a production possibility curve, and have income distributional effects via changes in prices.

The Pigouvian correction of externalities via taxes or subsidies is not applicable to money externalities; the latter are capable either of conferring an appreciable benefit or inflicting an appreciable damage on the economy. The end result depends on the monetary policy pursued. The Pigouvian taxes or subsidies are replaced by *institutional rules and discretion* intended to improve resource allocation.

It should also be made clear that we analyze the money externalities present in an Aristotelian modern stage described in chapter 3.

We define a money exchange process as *money - commodities - money (M-C-M*)*. Clower (1969: 14) generalized the idea in an aphorism: "In every money economy, however, there are fairly precise rules: 'goods buy money, and money buys goods - but goods do not buy goods in any organized market'". Clower's money process is not new. It had been stated by Plato as we said in the previous chapter, and by Karl Marx in his *Capital*, as M-C-M'.

Our money process differs from Plato's and Marx's. Plato's M-C-M is neutral. Karl Marx's M-C-M' is non-neutral since M' is always greater than M. Yet our *M* could be equal to, or greater (or less) than M*. It all depends on monetary policy. As we demonstrate subsequently money is super-non-neutral because it gives rise to and internalises M_E.

Our money process (M-C-M*) is interwoven in an exchange system and interlinked with other systems such as a telephone system or satellite communications or information centres or security, etc.. In such a context, money generates and at the same time internalises different types of externality which we call *systems or institutional externalities*. Consequently, internalisation of such types of externality effectively establishes the *money economy*.

Whenever we refer to the *interwoven M-C-M* process*, it should be understood that the banking system, securities and futures markets, stock and money exchanges, payment and net settlement systems and everything else necessary to organize a money process, are integral parts of the institution of money. Otherwise monetary policy cannot be assumed to work, let alone have effects on key monetary variables such as the rate of interest.

We argue that the specific rules of M-C-M*, or the institution of money govern the *direction* of economic activity. The *direction* is of importance since money externalities cannot co-exist with the perfectly competitive model. The latter assumes that all exchangeable commodities are 'measurable'. In our scheme, money externalities are *non-quantitative, qualitative* and *unmeasurable*. Money externalities are *not priced*.

We identify five categories of money externalities (M_E), each entailing a number of sub-sets of M_E:

i   Transaction Costs Externalities
ii   Price Level Externalities
iii Confidence Externalities
iv   Learning and Technological Externalities
v   Seigniorage Externalities.

They are shown in detail in Table 6.1.

197

Table 6.1
Taxonomy of money externalities

i Transactions Costs Externalities

    a) Shared-Variable Externality
    b) Information: i)   Efficiency Externality (E_f)
                              . search and contract costs
                              . specialised services
                    ii) Organisational Externality (E_o)
                              . trading and waiting costs
                              . contract enforcement
                    iii) Expectations Externality (E_e)
                              . reduction of uncertainty
                              . linking the present with future
                              . institutional expectations

ii Price Level Externalities

    a) User Externality: i)   Distributional Externality
                            ii) Hoarding Externality
    b) Producer Externality: i)   Fiscal Set Externalities
                            ii) Redistribution Externality
                            iii) Money Illusion Externality

iii Confidence Externalities

    a) Commodity Clause or Constant PPP Guarantee
    b) Brand-Name Cost
    c) Government's Functions and Economic Background
    d) Symbol of Sovereignty
    e) Trust Externality
    f) Guarantees: i)   Constitutional Rules and Objectives
                            ii) Credibility and Reputation
                            iii) Endowments

iv Learning and Technological Externalities

    a) Technical Learning
    b) Social Economies
    c) Informational Content
    d) Public Good
    e) Technological Knowledge and Invention
    f) Capital Accumulation and Innovation
    g) Gains Externality

v Seigniorage Externalities

    a) Liability Management
    b) Risk Externalities
    c) Forced Saving and Revolving Fund
    d) Producer's Surplus and Resource Saving
    e) Reserve-Type: i)   Reserve management
                            ii) High-powered money
                            iii) Debt-reduction

6.3.i Transaction costs externalities

An ideally efficient trading should function without cost. If not, we have Meade's 'market organisation cost set of conditions' leading to real-income externalities. In a money economy in which the money process (M-C-M*) is interwoven, income effects are generated by the intermediation of money. The entire trading system is inseparable and interwoven; any externality generated in one system will enter into the utility or cost function of more than one independent decision maker, generating *shared variable externalities*.

A *shared variable externality* of this kind due to the existence of the monetary stock in a M-C-M* has to do with the fact that the possession of a real balance carried with by individual A affects not only the welfare of the holder but the welfare of everyone else in the system who gains from the fact that individual A is a participant in the exchange. This is illustrated by Weldon (1973: 20) as follows:

> When I am frustrated from completing a desired exchange by being short of adequate real balances, just as there is then a cost to my welfare so there is a cost to those who directly or indirectly would have benefited from the transaction being immediately consummated, and this would be true even if the barrier were a temporary one that could be passed by without much difficulty through some simple roundabout arrangement to accomplish what extra real balance would have facilitated even more simply.

Hence the decision of individual A to carry with him a real balance has led directly to the increase of welfare of everybody else participating in the trading who were not a fully consenting party to the decision taken by individual A. Weldon's (1973) externality is similar to Patinkin's (1965: 77) individual who runs out of cash and is faced with a temporary embarrassment: "The security which money balances provide against either of these types of inconvenience is what is assumed to invest them with utility".[4]

"Money has a comparative advantage in transmitting information and in reducing uncertainty" (All Saint's Day Manifesto (1978: 38-9)). This is not the only comparative advantage of money. Coordination seen as a mechanism for obtaining better policy performance as well as lower transaction costs and equalisation of marginal cost to price are realised via the intermediation of money. Money is a mechanism for internalising the externalities arising from spillover effects of policy actions or production, exchange and distribution activities that give rise to 'efficiency', 'organisational' and 'expectations' externalities.

Adam Smith (1776: ch. iv) made the case for the *efficiency externality*, E_f, by examining the monetary transformations as the Aristotelian stages unfolded. In the primitive stage, the market organisation was costly and unreliable and very inefficient, since "people must always have been liable to the grossest frauds and impositions" (Smith, 1776: 25). Such gross abuses and frauds necessitated a different market organisation and the internalisation of the money externalities led to the origin of coined money and to the establishment of public mints. "To prevent such abuses, to facilitate exchange, and thereby to encourage all sorts of industry and commerce, it had been found necessary, in all countries that have made any considerable advances towards improvement, to affix a public stamp upon certain quantities of such particular metals, as were in those countries commonly made use of to purchase goods" (Smith, 1776: 24).

This public stamp carried with it the informational requirement necessary and it was available to all participants in the trading process. The internalised externalities concerned with problems of moral hazard, reduced the transaction costs embodied in a market organisation based on weighing and fineness of metals.

If paper money is introduced, the transaction costs to society as a whole are further reduced for two reasons: first the informational requirement or characteristics of the intermediary of exchange is reduced and second it frees resources. Smith (1776: 276) is insistent:

> The substitution of paper in the room of gold and silver money, replaces a very expensive instrument of commerce with one much less costly, and sometimes equally convenient. Circulation comes to be carried on by a new wheel which it costs less both to erect and to maintain than the old one.[5]

Adam Smith's idea that knowledge of the characteristics of money reduces the informational requirement of transaction is analogous to a shared-variable externality stemming from the alternative market- organisation, having public goods characteristics. The consumption of this externality by consumer A diminishes neither the availability or usefulness of money, nor the informational knowledge money embodies for any other consumer.

Whereas Adam Smith concentrated mainly on the informational requirement of the monetary unit, Brunner and Meltzer (1971) concentrated on the institution of money, which would *reduce the lack of knowledge* of the characteristics and availability of consumer goods. They (1971: 786) rested their case on two postulates:

> 1) for each transactor in an exchange economy, the marginal cost of acquiring information, measured in units of consumption sacrificed, depends on the goods or services selected.
> 2) The marginal cost of acquiring information about the properties of any asset does not vary randomly within a social group and declines as the

frequency with which the group uses a particular asset increases.

The essence of postulates 1) and 2) is stated in Brunner and Meltzer (1971: 786): "The uneven distribution of information, and not the existence of an undifferentiated uncertainty...induces individuals to search for, and social groups to accept, alternatives to barter". This is another way of stating the market-organisation-cost set of conditions giving rise to externalities in the trading posts. Yet what services does money render to the transactors, which induce them to accept a money economy in favour of barter? Take an individual in a market place confronted with n commodities and a given budget. For Brunner and Meltzer (1971: 786), "Potential transactor possess very incomplete information about the location and identity of other transactor, about the quality of the goods offered or demanded, or about the range of prices at which exchanges can be made. Uncertainty about quality characteristics is a main reason for the dispersion of prices of any commodity".

Given the fact that acquiring information, averaging payments and scheduling purchases absorb resources, the use of money reduces uncertainty, expands trade and contributes to the efficiency of the market system in a number of ways: "One way is by providing a unit of account, or standard in which prices are expressed... The cost of acquiring, processing and storing information falls... A second and considerably more important way...is through service as a medium of exchange" (Brunner and Meltzer, 1971: 787).

We have a lot more to say on this increased knowledge and its derived externality in section 6.3.IV. However, the reduction of the informational cost about alternative market opportunities due to the use of money as an intermediary raises two *efficiency* questions. First, "...money as a medium of exchange, as a transaction dominating asset, results from the opportunities offered by the distribution of incomplete information and the search by potential transactor to develop transaction chains that save resources" (Brunner and Meltzer, 1971: 793). In this sense we have an *efficiency externality* engineered by the intermediation of money. This efficiency externality directly reduces the costs of inputs, either in the consumption or production function. All direct or indirect costs for search and chain transaction are substituted by the *informational content* that money carries with it. It is an external economy which confers an appreciable benefit on all participants in the exchange.

The informational content of money is related to Stigler's (1961) economics of information concerned with the distribution of price, the quality of commodities and inputs, the ease of bargaining and the making of contracts, the protection of property rights and its enforcement if money is declared legal tender. Money is a device designed to lower transaction and information costs.

An important aspect of money over the unfolding of the Aristotelian stages, has been its role in overcoming 'structural rigidity'. Money introduces flexibility. Vercelli (1991) encounters the following: avoidance of double

201

coincidence of wants, distributional flexibility induced by unexpected inflation rates, the allocation efficiency in the presence of stickiness of prices or inertia. These may be corrected by changes in money supply and technological change induced by the use of credit in reallocating resources in favour of innovations.

Clower (1967 and 1969) paid more attention to Adam Smith's thesis regarding the efficiency of the market-organisation. Clower's idea concerns the optimal transaction period for each transactor by considering total costs under different market organisations, such as isolated barter, fairground barter, trading-post barter and monetary exchange. Clower (1969: 9) defined total trading costs as transaction costs plus waiting costs. 'Transaction costs' include work devoted to search and bargaining activity and "...vary 'inversely' with the length of the transaction period". 'Waiting costs' include subjective and objective consequences of delayed trading, which "...vary 'directly' with the length of the transaction period...; some costs of delay are objective, for longer transaction periods involve larger costs of commodity storage and also larger costs of foregone income on earning assets whose purchase is delayed".

How do total trading costs fare under different market-organisations? Clower (1969: 11) believes that "Total trading costs would be enormous, of course, in an economy that had no institutional arrangements for organized trade". By comparing the total trading costs under the above mentioned market organisations, Clower (1969: 12) concluded: "...there is an absolute (and possibly enormous) gap between trading costs in highly organized as compared with moderately or unorganized markets". Niehans (1971) even argued that organisational costs in a M-C-M* process are reduced to zero and these lowest transaction costs explain the existence of money.

A second organisational question is related to the absence of money but with interwoven systems. The alternative would be the development of specialised trading and specialised services, accompanied by reputable middlemen with trademarks and brand names. All these additional costs can be avoided since the information-cost reducing factors are embodied in the asset used as an intermediary.[6]

Consistent with Meade's (1973: 40) postulate that "...in every concern, both public and private, the operation of the pricing system will involve a cost... . Everywhere there is some element of externality due to the 'market organisation-cost'", we may call the efficiency due to the organisation of a money economy, an *organisational externality*, E_o. Thus, E_o is the result of organised markets that follow a M-C-M* process. Goods do not buy goods, but only via money in any organised market.

An organized market, with money acceptable as an exchange intermediary, confers an appreciable benefit (external economy) on all economic agents who are either directly or indirectly participants in a trading activity. If we take one individual A, his utility would increase because an external economy, such as E_o, has diminished his total trading costs. Hence E_o stands for the externality due to organizational and trading efficiency as well as the reduced costs which would otherwise be devoted to search, bargaining and acquiring information about trading opportunities and for reduced waiting costs.

"The fundamental idea of transaction costs is that they consist of the cost of arranging a contract 'ex ante' and monitoring and enforcing it 'ex post', as opposed to production costs, which are the costs of executing the contract" (Matthews, 1986: 906). These opportunity costs are internalised in the unit used in the M-C-M* process for exchanging either ownership rights, or money for bonds, or futures for equity assets, etc. Furthermore, it is the institution of money that *enforces the newly acquired rights after exchange*. The M-C-M* confers appreciable benefits on the transactor by arranging a contract at lower costs. The institution of money assumes responsibility for enforcing the new titles by maintaining constant the purchasing power of money.

Assume for the moment that the origin of money is a historical datum and that we analyze an economy under uncertainty. What are the links between the present and the future? Keynes's (1936) links are mainly two in the *General Theory*: 'liquidity preference' and 'user cost'. Both links are based on expectations. Where expectations rule, they attribute to money a special status as a 'liquid asset':

> Just as we found that the marginal efficiency of capital is fixed, not by the 'best' opinion, but by the market valuation as determined by mass psychology, so also expectations as to the future of the rate of interest as fixed by mass psychology have their reactions on liquidity preference (GT: 170).

The induced role of money as a liquid asset assumes the role of a 'store of value' and helps to bridge the lack of knowledge about the ruling prices in the present with the uncertain future prices. In such a context, money confers an *expectations externality*, E_e, because it acts as a store of value by deferring consumption and payments and hence affects the intertemporal allocation of resources. Thus, through the reduction of the cost relating to imperfect information about ruling commodity prices and about the expected rate of interest, the *expectations externality* reduces uncertainty and costs associated with uncertainty.

Money, through its E_e, acts as a bridge between the present with the future and, thus assumes another function: 'coordination of investment decisions'. Being a store of value, money acts as a *signalling device*, which transmits information about present plans and future conditions as they are determined by the ruling expectations. Keynes's (1936: 69-70) user cost embodies that sense of the *expectations externality*:

> User cost constitutes one of the links between the present and the future for

203

in deciding his scale of production an entrepreneur has to exercise a choice between using up his equipment now and preserving it to be used later on. It is the expected sacrifice of future benefit involved in present use which determines the amount of the user cost, and it is the marginal amount of this sacrifice which, together with the marginal factor cost and the expectation of the marginal proceeds, determines his scale of production.

The important element, in this expectational world of Keynes, is that the expected course of economic activity and expected prices would condition and influence the economic behaviour of all transactors. The uncertain future adds its weight to the role of money, in becoming interwoven with money's store of value status as a 'liquid asset'. Arcelli (1975: 39) worked out this aspect of the interwoven nature of a money economy:

> ...instead of a known vector of intertemporal prices, the transactor is provided with expectations about marginal efficiency of capital and has a liquidity preference guiding him in the choice of his portfolio composition: money then besides satisfying his transaction needs, becomes one among many alternative assets to keep... . A keynesian model that keeps in due account the impact of expectations over the present state of the economy is...characterized by a complex information structure which expands beyond price and money flow signals.

Two other sources of E_e are due to the institutional aspects of a monetary system. Take the example of EMU. Lamfalussy (1989: 97-9) argues that "...expectations might arise that the union would tend to make assistance from other member governments more likely in the event of debt-servicing problems". A second source is present when "...expectations of monetization of an increase in government borrowing can lead to a depreciation of the currency, whereas a non-accommodative monetary stance could cause an appreciation by increasing the interest rate differential in favour of domestic assets".

When it comes to implementation, expectations as a desire for change are realised via the mechanism of money. Chick (1983: 22) has made this point: "when expectations are falsified there is a 'desire' for change. Where that desire is combined with the power to effect changes we have disequilibrium. Which expectations 'are' relevant 'depends on the activity'". This could be possible only because of the *expectations externality* embodied in an asset carrying with it the properties discussed by Keynes in chapter 17 of his *General Theory*, which we discussed in the previous chapter. Money and near-money embody the liquid attribute when expectations rule. We also argued that in Keynes's GT, expectations are important determinants of the demand for new stock of bonds; they could be affected by current and expected flows of investment and saving. A disappointment of such expectations will be reflected in higher current rates of interest; thus Keynes's interest rate becomes *expectational*.

In recapitulating, if we were to re-examine monetary theory in its historical context only by reference to the 'transaction costs externalities', we would find that coined money reduced the costs of fraud, moral hazards, the weighing of metallic money, etc. Paper money permitted society to have the same nominal stock of money while freeing resources for alternative use, thus, further reducing the cost of transaction. Acquiring information about the characteristics of commodities at lowest possible cost, permitted commodity prices to have the least possible dispersion.

Given a money economy, total trading costs declined as societies moved from the Aristotelian Primary stage to the Modern Stage via the internalisation of *efficiency* and *organisational* externalities. By bridging the future course of prices with the present via the *expectations externality*, not only money links the present course of economic activity with the future but it also acts as a surrogate for future anticipations. In this way, it constitutes a constraint on effective demand. Any withdrawal from circulation of the liquid asset would generate an external diseconomy and would inflict an appreciable damage on all participants in the trading process. In our modern stage, where money is a promise, credit cards embody transaction costs externalities.[7]

6.3.ii Price level externalities

Any act of a user of money or of a producer of money which affects, either directly or indirectly, the general level of prices, would cause a *price level externalities*. Call it E_p.

Price level externalities are examined under the three states of nature of H5: uncertainty, maximisation and free access. Hence, our methodology is at variance with Lucas's monetary theory.[8] According to Vercelli (1991: 4), Lucas's methodology puts emphasis on "substantive rationality, equilibrium, demonstrative methods and 'risk' (in the sense of Knight and Keynes)".

The case of *price level externalities* due to the *user* of money has been made by Wicksell (1906, Lec. II: 11) who stated:

> In reality, however, the economic significance of the change from hoarding to the modern forms of saving and (private) accumulation of capital is more fundamental than that. Any one who saves a part of his income and locks it away, thereby withdrawing it from circulation, to that extent *exercises a depressing influence on prices*, even though it may be infinitesimal as regards each individual. Other individuals thereby obtain more for their money; in other words they divide among themselves that

part of consumption which is renounced by those who save. The subsequent use of these savings, say in old age, involves sharing in the consumption of others [stress added].

Wicksell's *price level externality* gives rise to two other money externalities. The first has to do with the *distributional externality* in the sense that the individual decides at one moment in time, to hoard in the form of money with a view to the future. In doing so, he confers an appreciable effect on all other individuals who are not necessarily fully consenting parties to this decision. Any change in the price level would change the marginal valuation of their tangible goods and unless equi-proportional income distribution and wealth redistribution are assured, it would cause a divergence between private and social valuations.

A second type of an externality found in Wicksell's example is of the *shared variable* category. If one saves today, expecting to share in the consumption of the next generation, money is a coordinating device that internalises the *expectations externality*. This is reflected in liquidity preference and becomes operative in linking the present generation with the next. This act induces long-term effects on consumption, capital accumulation and savings and entails a *hoarding externality*.

The *hoarding externality* is better illustrated with an example taken from the resource allocation case. The use of money affects the intertemporal allocation of resources and, in this sense, bypasses the problem of synchronization of receipts and payments. It thus contributes to superior productivity since synchronization depends on the costs of acquiring information and of exchange. If the hoarding of today leads to superior techniques tomorrow then we confer an appreciable benefit on the next generation.

Samuelson (1968 and 1969) used a Wicksell-type argument to show that both Classical and Neoclassical monetary theories adhering to 'laissez-faire' entail too small real balances, so that anyone holding an extra dollar confers an infinitesimal benefit on the rest by affecting the level of prices in Wicksell's sense. Samuelson (1968: 9-10) stated:

Each man thinks of his cash balance of costing him forgone interest and as buying himself convenience. But for the community as a whole, the total M* [money endowment] is there and is quite costless to use. ... Yet if all were made to hold larger cash balances, which they turned over more slowly, the *resulting lowering of absolute price* would end up making everybody better off. Better off in what sense? In the sense of having a higher U, which comes from having to make fewer trips to the bank, fewer trips to the brokers, small printing and other costs of transaction whose only purpose is to provide cash when you have been holding too little cash. From society's viewpoint, the optimum occurs when people are satiated with cash and have:

dU/dM = 0 instead of r X (positive constant) > 0.

But this will not come about under laissez-faire, with stable prices"

[M is money demanded; r is interest rate; U is utility; stress added].

Samuelson's (1968) sub-optimality of laissez-faire gives rise to externalities of Meade's 'fiscal set type'; suboptimality will cause a divergence between private marginal value and social marginal cost. Johnson (1970) suggested a remedy: optimization would occur if private enterprise were allowed to compete with the monopolist state supplier. But this will not do as it will give rise to two additional externalities: *redistribution* and *seigniorage*.

A serious difference should be noted between Wicksell and Samuelson. Whereas Wicksell's price level externality would affect capitalization and social welfare of the next generation, Samuelson's externality affects only exchange.

The case of *price level externalities* due to the *producer* of money was made by Keynes in his *A Tract on Monetary Reform* (1923)[9] where he discussed systematically the 'consequences to society of changes in the value of money'. Keynes began with a statement:

> ...a change in the value of money, that is to say in the level of prices, is important to society only in so far as its incidence is unequal. ... Thus a change in prices and rewards, as measured in money, generally affects different classes unequally, transfers wealth from one to another, bestows affluence here and embarrassment there, and redistributes Fortune's favours so as to frustrate design and disappoint expectation (p. 1).

The above quotation refers to four externalities: *distributional, fiscal set, expectations* and *redistribution*.

Keynes assumes three classes: entrepreneurs who save and invest, producers, and workers *as well as* two great driving forces behind the changes in the value of money: "the impecuniosity of governments and the political influence of the debtor class" (Tract: 8). He also holds the view that: "The power of taxation by currency depreciation is one which has been inherent in the state since Rome discovered it "(Tract: 8). This is a pure case of a *fiscal set externality* since the event is not fully consenting and the divergence between marginal value and marginal cost widens as the power of taxation increases, causing marginal value to remain above marginal cost.[10]

A fiscal set externality induced by the power of a monopolist to tax entails unequal incidence. It gives rise to redistribution of *wealth*; call it a *redistribution externality*.[11] For example, Keynes's saving class who had invested heavily in Consols during the period 1815 to 1922, experienced a 'gain' due to a stable value of money and steady fall in the rate of interest

207

from 1815 to 1896. The purchasing power of the capital value of Consols in terms of an index rose from 56 to 208, but, as the Napoleonic wars were financed by inflation, "The owner of Consols in 1922 had a real income, one half of what he had in 1914 and one third of what he had in 1896" (Tract: 15).

Who gained from this experience? The business class because of a windfall profit induced by stock appreciation, and, via the *shared-variable externality*, the worker. Another source of windfall profit is induced whenever the 'money' rate of interest is not equal to the 'real'; "that is, the real rate of interest falls to a negative value, and the borrower reaps corresponding benefit" (Tract: 20). The windfall profits are shared between the business and wage earning classes because the latter have organised themselves and acquired power. "In fact, it was worth his while to pay ransom, and to share with his workmen the good fortune of the day" (Tract: 27).

If the *expectations externality* reigns, then production is expectational. "If, for any reason right or wrong, the business world 'expects' that prices will fall, the processes of production tend to be prohibited; and if it expects that prices will rise, they tend to be overstimulated" (Tract: 30). In addition, a *distributional externality* is induced via the changes in 'relative prices'; "that is to say of the comparative prices of different commodities, 'ought' to influence the character of production, because it is an indication that various commodities are not being produced in the exactly right proportions" (Tract: 30).

If inflation is a method of taxation giving rise to fiscal set externalities, then, on whom has the tax fallen? Is it an efficient method? "The burden of the tax is well spread, cannot be evaded, costs nothing to collect, and falls, in a rough sort of way, in proportion to the wealth of the victim" (Tract: 39). How could one deal with a high internal debt? Three methods are available: repudiation, capital levy and devaluation. Keynes preferred devaluation. The method is believed to be efficient and has been practised on a large scale. Keynes (1923: 54), drawing lessons from the period of slump, stated: "In the countries of Europe lately belligerent, this expedient has adopted already on a scale which reduces the real burden of the debt by from 50 to 100 per cent". Friedman and Schwartz (1986: 57) estimated this source of income for the USA: "At the end of World War II, the funded federal debt amounted to 6% more than a year's national income. By 1967 it was down to about 32% of national income despite repeated 'deficits' in the official federal budget. Since then it has risen as deficits have continued and increased, but even so only to about 36% currently".

If one enlarges the application of the price level externalities and places it in the context of Keynes's world of uncertainty, unemployment and 'inflexible money wages', then we have an explanation of the *money illusion externality*. As we argued in chapter 5, Keynes's money depends on uncertainty and incomplete knowledge. In the presence of uncertainty, the states of mind are overwhelmed by disquietude and insufficient knowledge. As a result of such states of mind, the individual hoards money as a store of value in the form of a 'liquid-asset', which is money.

However, the social dangers of hoarding money are further aggravated by social practices in the labour market where 'inflexible money wages' rule. How could one cure the disease of unemployment? Keynes answered his own question by using money as a means of escape from the evils of a monetary economy struck by confidence crises. He employed the money motives to generate *price level externalities* in order to influence saving, investment and the rate of interest:

> The method of increasing the quantity of money in terms of wage-units by decreasing the wage-unit increases proportionately the burden of debt; whereas the method of producing the same result by increasing the quantity of money whilst leaving the wage-unit unchanged has the opposite effect. Having regard to the excessive burden of many types of debt, it can only be an inexperienced person who would prefer the former (GT: 268-9) .

Keynes's preferred solution of *changing the burden of debt* via unexpected changes in the total stock of money would confer appreciable external economies or diseconomies on a number of social groups who are not necessarily fully consenting parties. Call this a *money-illusion externality*, perceived as a means to overcome the alleged inefficiency of labour markets, lack of knowledge and confidence crises. In a money economy, "The only radical cure for the crises of confidence which afflict the economic life of the modern world would be to allow the individual no choice between consuming his income and ordering the production of the specific capital asset" (GT: 161). Yet this can only happen if we analyze organised markets in our money process: M-C-M*, on the assumption that the *money-illusion externality* is operative.

Whereas Keynes worked out the incidence of inflation by assuming 'unanticipated' inflation, Bailey (1956: 93) made the case of considering the welfare cost of 'anticipated' inflation: "The welfare cost of open inflation, which, in effect, is a tax on the holding of cash balances, a cost which is fully analogous to the welfare cost (or 'excess burden') of an excise tax on a commodity or productive service."

How could one measure the welfare cost to society? Bailey (1956) measured it by integrating the area under the liquidity preference curve from the stock of real cash balances held at a zero rate of inflation to that held at the announced positive rate of inflation. This area measures the total loss of the productivity of real cash balances foregone. In order to measure the 'welfare loss' to society, one has to compare the ratio of the 'welfare cost' to the 'tax proceeds'. This ratio will provide a measure of the efficiency of this form of taxation or redistribution.

Bailey (1956: 108) even estimated the share of government tax receipts: "...the maximum desirable rate of inflation is 10 percent a year, at which rate the government will secure about 6 percent of national income". Marty (1967: 71) corrected this figure: "When 6 per cent of the national income goes to the government at a welfare cost of 7.04 percent of the amount collected, the annual rate of inflation should be 18 percent per annum, not 10 percent".

One may criticise the Bailey version of inflationary finance but one may not miss an essential aspect of money externalities. Consider an economy suffering from a triple disease: serious structural underdevelopment, inefficient and costly administration and a large underground economy. What would the efficient mechanism be in pursuing some objective? It seems that the most effective and efficient mechanism of redistribution of income is inflationary finance and the induced *price level externalities* become instrumental.

This solution should not be taken to mean that *confidence, transaction costs and technological externalities* would not suffer. Price level externalities may induce such kinds of external diseconomies that the first intended objective might not be attained. This conclusion finds support in what is supposed to be a divergence between a private overvaluation and a social under-valuation. This is what a *fiscal set externality* is about.

A mixed case (user's and producer's externalities) is induced when E_p are caused by the rules of an institution. We discussed in chapter 2 the criteria upon which a Member State would be judged to have satisfied, in order to pass to the third stage of EMU, are: price stability; upper limit on deficit/GDP: 3% and on debt/GDP: 60%; no devaluation for at least two years and low long-term interest rates. These criteria boil down to one factor: 'expected inflation rate'. The rules on excessive deficit and debt are designed to limit the effects of *price level externalities*. The financing of budget deficit by changes in money supply of a Member State would lead to higher inflation rate, allowing this country to levy an inflation tax on the rest. This is an act that confers an appreciable benefit on the producer of inflation country but inflicts a damage on the rest who are the users of inflationary debt. A situation of this kind will generate a *distributional externality* and a *shared-variable externality*.

The debt case is more complicated. If the debt of a Member State grows at a rate that does not compel monetization but leads to residents of one country buying the government debt of another, then we have a clear case of generating a *redistribution externality*. Suppose this redistribution of debt contributes to a higher rate of return on capital in one country than in another, then we experience an efficiency externality resulting in *seigniorage externalities*. However, for this to occur the internalisation of *confidence externalities* is a pre-requisite.

210

6.3.iii Confidence externalities

Confidence externalities are generated by the institutional structure necessary to support a monetary system and its money. They are mainly associated with the producer of money but are internalised and reflected in the choice of the users. Call them E_c.

An example of this type of externalities is given by Mundell (1980: 379) in his discussion of the EMF and of the ECU:

> Any new institution that is created is an attempt to internalize what used to be an externality in the system. The externality may be the filling of a gap that reflects a power vacuum or that reflects a monetary advantage. In the case of the ECU, there are two gaps. One is an economic gap and the other a political one.

Confidence externalities have to do with a set of conditions that 'mould the preferences' of the users of money. The question of interest is to know *how to create confidence in a currency*. This theoretical question takes us away from a purely economic issue and crosses the boundaries of sociology, psychology and philosophy. A manageable treatment, not exhaustive, is to concentrate on the economic forces that generate confidence or crises of confidence in a currency.

It was once thought that a national currency's convertibility into a specific amount (weight) of gold or another precious metal was a necessary condition for it to have value. In chapter 4, we demonstrated that this idea describes a C-M-C economy and not a money economy; as such, it does not explain the evolution of money and hence fails H2 (Aristotelian notion of evolving money); it does not conform to H3 (Cipolla's criteria); the essentiality of money (H5) is not demonstrated. Yet Walras's commodity theory of money points to a 'commodity guarantee' clause intended to generate confidence in a currency.

In chapter 4, we discussed various proposals that all share the same economic logic: 'introduce index-linked revaluations or constant purchasing power clauses to guarantee the *constant value of money*'. For example, Hayek's (1978) *Denationalisation of Money* is about entrusting private institutions with money-issuing powers to issue non-interest bearing Swiss ducats, under three guarantees: price index, legal clause, convertibility.

These three guarantees are meant to produce confidence in the private ducat. However, Hayek's first guarantee raises doubts about reliable price-indices and their construction as well as their timing or revaluations. Congdon (1981: 5) criticised the method by which an inflation-proofed ducat is proposed: "In the periods between the calculation dates no one would know by how much this value was to be changed".[12]

As to the legal clause, we may take the case of Knapp (1905); his money is essentially the creation of law and its value is regulated by the State. The primary importance is the validity of currency, not the value as such. A currency's power to discharge debt rests on its validity and hence its value is purely 'nominal' in the same sense conceived in Hayek's second guarantee. The State is instrumental in legally guaranteeing the private Swiss ducat.

Hayek's third guarantee introduces a commodity money process of the kind commodity-money-commodity (C-M-C). It entails a large *seigniorage externality*. This is so because private Swiss ducats can be obtained only if economic agents surrender other monies, goods and services with the private banks in exchange for ducats.[13]

The Hayek and similar schemes propose a system which would meet the Cipolla criterion: 'highly stable value of money'. These proposals consider *monetary stability* necessary for satisfying the second criterion: 'high confidence in the currency'.

However, 'high confidence' arises from the producer's side. Klein (1974, 1978a, 1978b) examined monetary stability in some detail. Klein's central theme is that monetary studies that have assumed away the costs of creating monetary confidence in money have missed an important element; unregulated competitive production of money cannot function unless a *product quality cost* is assumed. Otherwise private firms in a competitive world produce indistinguishable monies. "If buyers are unable to distinguish between the products of competing firms in an industry, competition will lead each firm to reduce the quality of the product it sells since the costs of such an action will be borne mainly by the other firms in the industry. ... But indistinguishability of the output of competing firms will lead to product quality depreciation in 'any' industry" (Klein, 1974: 430).

An argument that does not recognise the validity of judging the quality by reference to the technical characteristics of the product, would imply a dilemma: either a reliance on *brand name capital* which would entail a cost for the producer to engineer it or "consumers will not be able to distinguish between the output of different firms, and the quality of money sold will be destroyed. Hence brand-name differentiated output is necessary for the competitive production and sale of money" (Klein, 1974: 430). Between the two options Klein came out in favour of relying on brand-name capital because money users are provided with a reduction in costs when judging the credibility of fulfilment of a contract.

Who is more capable of creating monetary confidence? A government or a private firm? As we argued in chapter 5 on the State theory of money, the coercion of the State with its military power, its conception of a society or whatever other mechanism at its disposal, such as control of the media, would contribute to the power of the State and would make it a more effective *producer of moulding the preferences* of its citizens.

212

In general, confidence externalities arising from the functions of the State, are due to the *constitutional clauses* assigned to the State. In this sense the State as a producer of money generates both external economies as well as external diseconomies.

Two additional externalities could be identified: 'complementary nature' of government activities and command of governments on 'economic resources'. For the *complementary activities* of government, Klein (1974: 448-9) stated: "Another possible advantage for the government may be that the production of monetary confidence is highly complementary with the production of other goods that the government generally supplies. The production of national defense, for example, may be complementary with supplying monetary confidence. Positive technical externalities appear to go both ways; i.e. production of national defense not only yields some monetary confidence as a by-product, but production of monetary confidence also yields national defense activities".

For the government's *economic resources externality*, the twelve governments of the EU, directly or indirectly, account for about 50% of Community GNP. Their choice to set up their own bank would be a sufficient, but not a necessary, condition for the establishment of a Central Bank. This aspect of confidence externality is analogous to the third Cipolla criterion, i.e. the 'economic background' of a producer of currency. In chapter 3, we considered it as the single most effective factor in producing *confidence* in a currency. Using this criterion, we considered the reasons that explain why the ECU in its present status, does not create sufficient confidence in itself.

If we were to re-consider the third Cipolla criterion in the context of *confidence externalities*, we could safely say that - given the fact that the ECU neither has a natural home, nor backed by the goods, services and reserves of a single entity - it may not be able to internalise the C_e needed.

In at least one respect, money's convenience depends on acceptability for completing transactions. As a standard of deferred payment, its acceptability depends on the trust people have that it will retain its value over long periods of time. If 'trust' is abrogated, then both the credibility of the producer of money and the mutual respect of the users of money for each other are questioned. This is the core argument of Frankel (1977), who has pointed out two additional confidence externalities: *money is a symbol* and *money is trust*.

Frankel's (1977: 12)) symbolism of money and many aspects arise from a fact: "There is an intimate relationship between money and freedom; between the keeping of promises and the certainty of contracts; between social function and the rule of law". The more important aspect for Frankel (1977: 13) is Simmel's (1990) symbolic expression of economic relationships: "One of the basic facts of our subjective world was that we express social relations through symbolic images. Money was one of these. From being a functional it had become a symbolic expression of economic relationships. But Simmel warned

- and it is a warning of importance today - that such symbolic images could not be divorced from the circumstances which gave rise to them and to which they were bound".

The essence of Simmel's money is that there should be an ideology of money grounded in the *idea of trust*. If this premise is accepted, the logical conclusion is: "money contributed to the extension of individual personality and facilitates the development of an ever widening circle of economic interdependence based on trust. Under conditions of direct barter trust is confined to the parties immediately involved. The use of money extends it to the people of the village, of the tribe, of the nation, and finally, to vast areas of the world" (Frankel, 1977: 14).

If trust, custom and symbolism of money are interdependent concepts upon which monetary stability rests, then a new line of causality is identified. In order to be consistent with the aim of Simmel, which is the 'free monetary order' defined by Frankel (1977: 100) as "...a condition of civility, a code of civil monetary behaviour, an ideal - the pursuit of trust", it should show that it internalises more confidence externalities than any other alternative arrangement.

From the discussion of H2, it should be recalled that Aristotle's stages of development had been correlated with different forms of monetary arrangements creating confidence in the use of a currency. The Greek coinage of 650 B.C. carried with it a stamp as a 'guarantee' of weight, fineness, quantity and quality. The Cipolla story is about a State guarantee.[14] The paper money period has been about state institutions entrusted with the task of preserving confidence in three cases: in highly interdependent markets, in anchor currencies and in different exchange rate regimes.

By comparison to the EMS, EMU represents an 'institutional change' bound by specific rules relating to coordination among national central banks to help improve stabilisation, the balance between authority, control and independence, and an internal structure capable of internalising externalities that characterise monetary policy.

The two *constitutional features* of EMU related to the ECB intended to induce confidence externalities, are: independence and price stability objective. The independence of ECB and what that implied, were discussed in chapter 2 and is guaranteed by Article 107 of TEU. Independence in combination with the prime objective of the ESCB stated in Article 105: 'The primary objective of the ESCB shall be to maintain price stability' have constitutionally guaranteed the independence of EMU's monetary institution.

On paper, the ECB entails the only legally guaranteed clauses in the world. If compared to the Federal Reserve System, it fares better because the latter's main purpose is "...to regulate the supply, availability, and cost of money with a view to contributing to the maintenance of a high level of employment, stable values, and a rising standard of living" (FRS Board, 1947: 1).[15] The

ECB is partly comparable to the Bundesbank Law whose Article 3 states: "...shall regulate the note and coin circulation and the supply of credit to the economy with the aim of safe-guarding the currency and shall ensure appropriate payments through banks within the country as well as to and from foreign countries" (quoted in Wittelsberger, 1991: 36-7). It is not comparable to the Bank of Japan Law of 1942 as amended in 1949, which places the Bank of Japan under government control and gives the Minister of Finance the right to overrule the policy taken by the Policy Board.[16]

Why is guaranteed independence important? In chapter 2, we referred to studies that had established a close correlation between independence and inflation and the role of 'credibility' derived from independence. The Economist of 25.1.1992 summarised the evidence: "...central banks that are free from government interference do indeed tend to deliver lower rates of inflation. Nor is this achieved simply at the cost of jobs. Countries with independent central banks do not, on average, have higher unemployment than others; many have less. Workers and employers adjust their wage-setting more speedily to the climate of tight money if they believe that policy-makers have an unwavering commitment to low inflation" (p. 21).

Credibility arising from the consistency of monetary policy is not marketed and has no price. It is a 'reputation' won the hard way. Moreover, it is a shared-variable type. It enters into the utility function of every transactor that uses a money which had internalised this *credibility externality*; it also enters into the cost function of every producer who uses this money to conclude a contract. Credibility is a property of the system which is shared by all its members.

The credibility externality is not only related to the record of low inflation. It is earned from the experience of the conduct of monetary policy. It is about exchange rate stability and competitiveness, about ending or controlling speculative excesses; about preventing bank insolvencies or a potential source of financial instability. It is the institutional setting of EMU that promotes or destroys credibility.

Credibility feeds 'reputation' in monetary stability and this is important for creating confidence in the strength of the new institutional arrangement. However, EMU has not gained 'reputation' in monetary stability. The Fed has served the Bretton Woods System well, since the latter relied on the Fed's monetary constraint. The Bank of Japan has won its reputation in recent years because of its record concerning low inflation and growth. The Bundesbank's reputation has been won because its D-mark has served as an anchor currency for the EMS and the ERM has relied on Germany's monetary restraint. It has helped in creating an institutional setting in the Community where infrequent exchange rate realignments have led to the narrowing of nominal interest rate differentials. This *reputation externality* of the ERM has conferred appreciable benefits upon the EMS members, although so far, only the ERM members have borne the cost of monetary discipline.

The real problem for the ECB is that it has inherited this reputation naturally because of the evolution of a monetary system. Its task will be to preserve the inheritance intact. This inheritance is problematic for one reason: 'global markets have increased the interdependence of the world economy and with it the money externalities have multiplied'. The ECB would have to use one instrument, the expectational interest rate, to solve the 'conflicting quarter of globalisation' raised in chapter 3 *and* to maintain monetary stability and stable rates for ECU/Dollar and ECU/Yen.

As to the former, the task is herculean and under existing arrangements, the instruments do not suffice. As to the latter, an attempt could be made if, by inducing the expectations externality, it would influence the interest rate and if, by influencing the seigniorage and confidence externalities, it could control the money supply to which the price level externalities would adjust. Yet this method depends on two links: a) the link between the expectational interest rates and confidence-induced money supply, b) the link between the money supply and the price level. We are short of instruments. The only one available is monetary cooperation with the other two leaders: USA and Japan, with a view of establishing a world system of monetary stability in which every country would share. A *shared-variable externality* at world level.

The second test for the ECB in internalising the *reputation* and *credibility externalities*, would be the preferences of the public towards monetary stability. Bundesbank's internalisation of reputation and credibility externalities has been boosted by the historical aversion of the German public to inflation. The ECB would have to overcome the temptation to create unanticipated inflation so that it could induce price level externalities, such as fiscal set, distributional, redistribution and money illusion externalities.

At a micro level, confidence is correlated with *endowments*. In the banking sector, the set-up costs are substantial. For a new bank to start business in a new locality, it would need show that, at least, it could cover the substantial fixed costs. In a competitive setting, these substantial set up costs would give rise to losses or to a nonconvex production possibility set. The fact that a bank could use its liabilities as media of exchange gives rise to a series of *learning and technological externalities*.

6.3.iv Learning and technological externalities

Money is said to internalise all externalities induced by the 'use of the same currency unit', on the assumption that economic man is capable of learning and of communicating. Both learning and communicating contribute to the growth of knowledge and to the induced externalities. In forming his decisions, economic man applies reason in the context of accumulated experience. The greater the market and volume of transaction, the greater the social economies of scale, the greater the internalised external economies. *If this growth of knowledge is applied to a process, it is transformed into human capital.* We call the derived externalities from this transformation, *learning externalities,* E_l.

There are two kinds of information as the base of learning: market and technological. The former is associated with our money process (M-C-M*) and is about the market opportunities available to an individual. The internalisation of transaction costs externalities by money reduces uncertainty about market opportunities and, in part, replaces costly patterns of research.

The technological information is accumulated knowledge inherited from the past. Given that the process of learning is not purely economic but a social phenomenon, what form does it take in industry? "The process of learning associated with industry...implies a persistent movement, not a one-for-all change, but a 'rate of change' in time, a cumulative and indefinite movement" (Pasinetti, 1981: 4). However the question of 'how to explain progress and the role of money in it' remains unanswered. Pasinetti (1981: 22) equates growth in knowledge with technical progress and maintains:

> But we do not need any special hypothesis of evolution of the human species in order to explain technical and economic progress. A sufficient condition is to suppose that human beings are able to learn from past experience and to communicate among themselves the results of their learning activity. ... Therefore, as long as the intellectual abilities of mankind do not deteriorate, technical progress is an inherent characteristic of human history.

Mundell (1970) applied a similar reasoning to make the case for one European currency. He argued that each market transaction implies time, cost in research and cost in negotiations. However the existence of one money, given the learning capacity of man, would lead to a series of external economies associated with the human memory which acts as a factor of production and as an input in the utility function. The use of money reduces the need for the memory.

The *social economies* due to one money are not only a function of the width and the depth of the market. They also stem from the external economies due to 'new information' which only money carries with. Given that the production of information is costly and that it is cumulative, the introduction of money would capture all the external economies of the sectors of research and technology; these are interwoven with the growth of knowledge. Such money externalities would even establish a small number of currencies in a world characterised by a high degree of interdependence.[17]

A similar situation is described by Brunner and Meltzer (1971: 792) in their

217

discussion of the informational content that money carries. They believe that money reduces costs in two ways. The first, reduction in information costs about the quality of goods, was discussed earlier. The second has to do with the increased knowledge. They stated: "Second as the use of an asset in exchange increases, the transactor learns more about the asset's properties. With growing use of particular transaction chains and improved knowledge of the properties of the assets exchanged, uncertainty and the variances and covariances in the general covariance matrix describing the overall density $\pi(E)[\pi = \pi(E/P)$ where E is a matrix of exchange ratios, P summarises the information about market opportunities] decline".

Whereas Weldon (1968, 1971, 1973) argued that money is essentially a public good, because it entails *public attributes* by reference to its provision and its availability and because the distribution of real balances among individuals generates money externalities, Kindleberger (1983 and 1986) has argued that the public properties of money stem from its being a standard and that gains are generated in comparability and interchangeability. Given that money introduces standardisation, it leads to reduced transaction costs and to economies of scale. Both are external economies to the firm and to the user.

If we apply the standardisation function of money to production, we could say that it would generate physical economies and savings in transaction. "In production the saving may lie in economies of scale through repetitive production and in the reduction of down time for changing patterns and shifting materials" (Kindleberger, 1983: 384). To the extent that information is the reduction of uncertainty, the embodied information of money used in the market for exchange or production or contracts could be regarded as an input that reduces the cost of production.[18]

In the same spirit, Arrow (1970: 68) drew attention to the public characteristics of money creation: "Monetary theory, unlike value theory, is heavily dependent on the assumption of positive transaction costs; the recurrent complaint about the difficulty of integrating these two branches of theory is certainly governed by the contradictory assumptions about transaction costs. The creation of money is in many respects an example of a public good".

In other words, a body of knowledge is accumulated in the M-C-M* process via learning and communicating. Knowledge arises from the deliberate seeking and observing of markets or other activities. Such knowledge could be considered as a source of human capital capable of being transformed into *technological knowledge.*

We have treated information, learning and knowledge interchangeably and this implies two economic facts. First, that knowledge of the characteristics of an input of production or of a product is analogous to human capital. Second, knowledge is indivisible in the sense that there is no gain in acquiring the same information or knowledge twice.

In the first case, once the characteristics of an input or of a product are known and made public, then the individual consumption of this knowledge does not diminish the availability or usefulness of that knowledge to any other. This is the case of *learning externalities*. However, the producer of knowledge via the internalisation of E_1 cannot hope to recoup anything approximating its value for two reasons. First, the indivisible information can be transmitted easily from one person to another and there are social economies at work; this means that the optimal conditions require that the transmission should take place at a marginal cost close to zero. Second, a zero price implies the absence of a private producer of information; he has no incentive to produce the socially optimal information unless he sets a minimum cost to maximise profits. Even in this case, due to the social economies of scale, we would have an external economy of the type of shared variable driving the marginal cost of E_1 close of zero.

Given the informational content of money in the form of E_1, no legal protection can be made since it is intangible. In this sense, money is analogous to Arrow's (1962: 171) information being a commodity with uncomfortable properties:

> In the first place, the use of information is certainly subject to indivisibilities; the use of information about production possibilities, for example, need not depend on the rate of production. In the second place, there is a fundamental paradox in the determination of demand for information; its value for the purchaser is not known until he has the information, but then he has in effect acquired it without cost. Of course, if the seller can retain property rights in the use of the information, this would be no problem, but given incomplete appropriability, the potential buyer will base his decision to purchase information on less than optimal criteria.

Given that incomplete appropriability would give rise to price-level externalities of the type discussed earlier, what solution could be found? Arrow (1962: 171-2) favoured public ownership: "From the viewpoint of optimal allocation, the purchasing industry will be faced with the problems created by indivisibilities; and we still leave unsolved the problem of the purchaser's inability to judge in advance the value of the information he buys. There is a strong case for centralized decision making under these circumstances".

The implication of the existence of money in a money process (M-C-M*) with interdependent systems of banking, clearing houses, credit cards, communication networks etc., is that, if one analyses questions of equilibrium, that would move the interwoven system towards equilibrium, and that, then money becomes instrumental in this interwoven system in bringing the economy closer, say, to a production possibility frontier. In such a process, money induces and internalises *technological externalities*, (E$_t$).[19]

In such a context, Clower (1969b: 302) stated a technological externality:"From society's viewpoint, the effective amount of real cash balances can be altered only by devices that increase the technological efficiency of monetary institutions or by changes in existing parameters of production technology and personal taste". If this occurs, we have a technological externality due to the existence of money. It will confer an external economy on producers, thereby affecting positively the production possibility frontier.

In an interdependent monetary system, the role of money becomes one of a *technological innovation* in the sense that it coordinates and informs each producer or consumer of other people's economic decisions. It also transmits information reliably to the rest of the transactors, who respond accordingly. In this context, money eliminates socially wasteful resources by saving human time and energy required to acquire raw material and labour. Also, by promoting the transmission of information at zero marginal cost, money would save human and capital resources required to supervise and deliver payments to labour and to suppliers of raw material. In this sense, productivity gain will be higher and will shift the production possibility frontier to a higher level.

The role of monetary policy in promoting capital accumulation through the internalisation of *technological externalities* has often been cited. Yet the mechanism through which it is promoted has not been clearly stated. An example of this is Wicksell (Lec. II: 6), who recognises that, though the technological knowledge we have inherited from the past and captured by money is a source of growth, it does not necessarily mean a higher production possibility frontier. It mainly depends on monetary policy:

> The use - or the misuse - of money may, in fact, very actively influence actual exchange and capital transaction. By means of money (for example by state paper money) it is possible - and indeed this has frequently happened - to destroy large amounts of real capital and to bring the whole economic life of society into hopeless confusion. On the other hand, by a rational use of money, it is possible actively to promote the accumulation of real capital and production in general.

Schumpeter (1911) examined the link between technological change and capitalist development. The role of money in the process of development is fundamental because it affects the production possibility frontier via the realisation of innovations financed by credit creation; this induces a redistribution externality. Vercelli (1991: 205) summarised the Schumpeter argument: "...credit creation makes possible a rapid redistribution of resources in favour of innovations, 'enabling the entrepreneur to withdraw the producer' goods which he needs from their previous employments, by exercising a demand for them, and thereby to force the economic system into new channels'".[20]

The above activist monetary policy that promotes capital accumulation, necessitates an institutional arrangement and a money process in which credit could induce an *innovation externality* that is not appropriated. If one re-considers the banking system, as it has evolved through the Aristotelian stages, then, it has been a source of finance for the *innovation externality*. Chick (1992) argues that in stage 5 of the development of the banking system, the nexus of causality has changed. The banking system has gained an independence over saving and a capacity of redistributing 'credit' from borrowers to the banking system. But this is not all. In stage 5, the banking system has developed a 'liability management'. Hence the credit creation power of the banking system induces the financing of innovation externality. The incidence of banking does not stop here. If the innovation is applied to producing a commodity, the recipient of credit could, by purchasing the excess output or by bidding up the prices of resources, generate 'forced saving' externality conferred upon the depositors.

An interesting idea, concerning the capturing of values generated by unequal exchange but internalised by the institution of money, was given by Frankel (1977: 59): "From Plato and Aristotle onwards, and throughout the Middle Ages, there was little appreciation of the fact that trade is not the exchange of goods and services with 'equivalent' values but that every exchange transaction creates 'new' and additional gains over and above the values which existed before".

The idea of unequal exchange in a money economy where money captures the additional value is not new and dates back to Karl Marx's money process: M-C-M', with M' > M denoting the monetised profit. The study of Emmanuel (1972) substantiates the position that money as an intermediary would confer *new and additional gains* over and above the values which existed before.[21]

Assume that the new and additional gains are re-invested in inventions or in new capital goods that embody advanced technology. In doing so, we have transformed the learning and technological externalities into new forms of capital accumulation leading to a higher production possibility frontier. This idea can be illustrated if one compares the case of barter with that of a money economy.

What are the available means to transfer technology and capital? One may say there are two: either direct transfers or creation of an efficient money market. The latter would open the horizon to the flow of information and finance, since it would perform efficient financial services, create large scale liquidity and would allow the exploitation of economies of scale implicit in the knowledge industry. This is another *technological externality* captured by the money process.

Putting together these various *technological externalities*, E_t, we could argue that E_t are induced by the interwoven money process and affect the rest of the economic system but are affected by the technological innovation brought about by the inventories of money. The social economies captured by money give rise to new information transformed later into technological knowledge. Interdependence established by the M-C-M* is also influenced by the improvements of decentralised economic decisions which are rendered possible by the money process. Similarly, we could argue that the introduction of money results in superior productivity and promotes capital accumulation through the instrumentality of banking; this leads to economic growth via the generated forced saving. The gains of unequal exchange, if invested, lead to additional technological externalities.

Once technological externalities are transformed into 'invention' or 'information', then E_t are analogous to Arrow's invention as production of information. The consequences are stated by Arrow (1962: 172): "In the first place, any information obtained, say a new method of production, should, from the welfare point of view, be available free of charge (apart from the cost of transmitting information). This ensures optimal utilisation of the information but of course provides no incentive for investment in research... . In a free-enterprise economy, inventive activity is supported by using the invention to create property rights; precisely to the extent that it is successful, there is an underutilization of the information".

Arrow's underutilisation of information in a free-enterprise economy becomes clearer with an example. Assume that everybody else except myself pays for the information generated by a monetary system. However there is no exclusion mechanism to a money economy. If n-1 pay, then I shall be better off as a free rider; I enjoy the shared-variable externality when a public good is present. Yet suppose no one pays, then I shall not pay either and I shall equally be better off. In the absence of a decision, there will be a zero demand for obtaining information about the characteristics of intermediate inputs. The monetary system, unsupported, will disappear and, with it, all money externalities examined hitherto. Hence Pareto optimality would require intervention in order to overcome this *technological externality*.

6.3.v Seigniorage externalities

'Seigniorage' originated with the right of the State to charge a 'fee' for minting money on private account. The fact that in earlier times this change was higher than the actual cost of minting was a source of income to the State and was a profitable business for the individual, since he had his precious metals coined at a marginal cost lower than the average cost.

Neo-Walrasians and proponents of the quantity theory of money equate seigniorage with the monopoly of the State power to issue money. Hence

222

'seigniorage is the difference between the nominal and real rate of inflation'. We discussed this problem in chapter 2 and in section 6.3.III on price level externalities, where we argued that MV = PY is a tautology. All assumptions made for transforming the tautology into a theory have been met with difficulties.[22]

Today, *seigniorage has to do with the internalisation of externalities generated in the banking system* and with its incidence on and consequences for those who are participants in our M-C-M* process. The stage of development of the banking system is Chick's (1992) stage 5. In such a banking context, Mundell (1980) identified the sources of seigniorage of the US monetary system as stemming mainly from the unlicensed banking and the internalisation of the dollar.

However this is not the whole story. If banks develop, they induce a number of externalities. Two *liability externalities* are stated by McKenzie (1990: 364). The first arises when "By providing this facility and by acting as a clearing house for payments, banks reduce transaction costs and hence enable the real sector to operate more efficiently than otherwise". The second arises when "By transforming liabilities into assets possessing entirely different risk, return maturity and liquidity characteristics, they enable a more efficient allocation of investor funds than would occur if banks did not exist".

These two *liability externalities* procure to the banks profits. In exchange the latter through liability management, generate Meade's market organisation cost externality and the *efficiency externality*. McKenzie (1990: 364) put it in this way: "If asset and risks are known to a reasonable degree of accuracy, banks and non-monetary financial intermediaries (e.g. insurance and pension funds) enable real sector borrowing transaction to be undertaken on better terms than would be possible if primary securities markets were the sole mechanism for enabling savers to deploy their funds. The costs to borrowers and the risks by lenders are both reduced".

In principle, all contracts concluded in money-terms involve risk. A *risk externality* is present in our money process (M-C-M*) whenever a time element is involved. Paying out in money for wages and other expenses of production, separating purchase from sale, production from consumption or investment from saving induce a risk externality. All these acts involve a period; a contract is concluded in period t in the expectation of recouping the incurred expenses plus profit by disposing of the product or service for money at period t+1.

The most important source of risk externality is the banking system. Faced with global markets in finance, capital, trade and investment, the act of a bank at defining its task, managing deposits and pricing services involves risk. Banks and financial intermediaries exist because of risk. *Managing risk generates a risk externality*.

The act of managing risk by placing deposits in portfolios handled by a third party is an event realised in banking and financial markets and may confer an appreciable benefit on clients if successful or inflict an appreciable damage upon clients and third parties if a financial failure occurs. In either case, the depositors were not fully consenting parties when the decisions were made by the bank concerned. This money external economy or diseconomy becomes clearer if *four* risk externalities arising from differences in bank regulation are examined.

The first stems from the regulatory systems existing in different countries while the same bank is located in different countries, managing savings of depositors residing in different countries. A failure of this bank will confer an appreciable damage on residents in more than one country. A recent example of this is the failure of the Bank of Credit and Commerce International (BCCI); "so the cost of its failure are then borne either by overseas residents or by those who are required to pay deposit insurance" (CEPR report (1991: 72-3).

A second source of *risk externality* is present when the failure of one bank causes loss of confidence in other banks to survive. This kind of risk externality is prominent in global markets where market exposure increases as the banking activity in different countries or locations increases. This source of risk externality is due to the interbank market handling foreign assets in portfolios that are global.

A third source of *risk externality* arises in the payment systems. This is a cross-border externality that mainly depends on technology and regulation. The payment systems externality could be defined as the volatility of potential outcomes when the failure of one system inflicts an appreciable damage upon other systems connected with it.

The above three risk externalities are less important than the fourth: *systemic risk*. It is defined by the Committee of Governors (1992: 488) as "...the risk that the failure of one participant in an interbank funds transfer system or securities settlement system, as in financial markets generally, to meet his required obligations will cause other participants or financial firms to be unable to meet their obligations when due". In short, two overlapping aspects of *systemic risk* exist: a) payment systems and b) netting arrangements; both have a common origin: a counterpart may default on its side of a contract causing a series of failures. This is an event inflicting appreciable damage on third parties while the latter are not fully consenting parties in reaching the decision of default.

Systemic risk externality has increased as the globalisation of markets has accelerated. Looking at the two components of systemic risk, Freeman (1993: 41) found for payment systems that Japan alone in 1990 "...it took just two-and-a-half business days for Japan's interbank payment system to turn over the value of the country's GNP for the whole year. The increased volumes mean banks must routinely settle amounts far in excess of their capital. And because

224

they are constantly dealing with each other, a problem at one bank would have serious consequences for all the other banks in its system".

The second aspect of *systemic risk externality* is associated with managing large exposure and involves rules designed to minimise banks' exposures to markets via netting schemes. They are meant to secure settlement of interbank debt within a specified period. If a single net payment to a regular counterpart is made, the credit flow through payments and settlements systems will be reduced substantially. If a series of gross payments are made which only partly offset the overall debt, systemic risk will increase. Hence netting schemes are necessary to reduce systemic risk. The question addressed calls for a different approach that recognises that risk management cannot be ignored by central banks since it has changed its traditional function (see chapter 7).

Chick (1983), examining the role of banks in an interwoven system that we have been discussing in previous sections, discussed the terms of forced saving and revolving fund. Both occur when banks create credit implying a monetary act which confers an externality on some who are not fully consenting parties. Both generate 'seigniorage externalities' and are the result of the banking system falling within the confines stated above.

The idea of the *forced saving* becomes evident if seen in the context of Wicksell's credit money and if seen through the spectrum of a banking system which is not fully regulated but well-integrated with the rest of the markets. Then bank liabilities are not necessarily regarded as liabilities and the banking system internalises part of the confidence externalities. Bank liabilities are seen as means of payment. Banks develop 'liability management'. Hence, any bank lending in excess of saving shall result in unintended forced saving. Chick (1983: 237) stated the case in the following way: "No one asked the holders of the new deposits whether they wanted a larger aggregate money supply, nor does that question occur to the receiver. No one refuses payment for a sale just because the source of payment is an overdraft - otherwise granting overdrafts would be pretty futile. But in aggregate there is now a larger quantity of money than before which 'no one intended' to accumulate. In that sense it could be said to be 'forced'".

If Chick's (1983: 238) interpretation of forced saving due to the banking system "is about the possibility of 'forcing' saving so that investment may precede the 'intention' to save", then we have a classic case of an external economy which confers an appreciable benefit without the parties concerned being consenting to the event. This external economy would lead to the following consequences: unintended saving will increase because of bank credit which finances increased investment; this will lead to higher incomes and higher prices but the negative effect of higher prices on consumption has to be balanced against the positive effect of higher incomes.

Forced saving externality may be exercised in a monetary system like EMU, when excessive deficits of a Member State absorb a disproportionate share of savings of the other Member States. If markets do not work efficiently, Lamfalussy (1989: 96) remarked that: "excessive borrowing by one country would raise the interest rate level throughout the Community and crowd out investment in countries where the interest rate would otherwise have been lower. Finally, an 'exploitation' of savings might also occur if one country's borrowing either exerted pressure for a more accommodative monetary policy (resulting in a higher rate of inflation throughout the Community) or led to a depreciation of the Community's exchange rate vis-à-vis third currencies (entailing terms-of-trade losses for all Community residents)".

Another institutional source of *forced saving externality* is generated in EMU "if capital is borrowed by one country regardless of the rate or return it can earn. In that case the lending country ends up with a smaller 'domestic' capital stock (although one probably unchanged in the total) than it would otherwise have had, while the borrowing country must service more debt with no more capital" (Wood, 1990: 316). This is a pure case of shared-variable type giving rise to a *distributional externality*.

Whereas money constitutes a constraint on effective demand, the ability of banks to offer their liabilities as credit constitutes the case for a *revolving fund*. In this context, the constraint on effective demand will be broken. "The 'revolving fund' reflects the fact that the circular flow of income, consumption as well as investment, profits as well as wages, runs, almost in its entirety, through the banking system. That is even more true today, with the great diminution of payment of wages in cash" (Chick, 1983: 240).

The theoretical case for a revolving fund was first made by Keynes (1937b: 209) when "...investment is proceeding at a steady rate...one entrepreneur having his finance replenished for the purpose of a projected investment as another exhausts his on paying for his completed investment". However the underlying mechanism presupposes a banking system which can extend short-term loans of equal value to firms embarking on new projects without changing the overall liquidity position. This can only happen if the banking system has reached Chick's (1992) stage 5 where 'liability management on the part of banks' constitutes the core feature of banking.

The *seigniorage externality* captured under the revolving fund is conceptually related to the separation made by Gurley and Shaw (1960) between 'inside' and 'outside' money. Inside money is debt created by the private sector and resembling the revolving fund while outside money is supplied by government in response to anything other than private debt. This separation could be made if McKenzie's 'liability externalities' are not induced and money is not pure credit. If Chick's (1992) stage 5 is reached, it is incorrect to distinguish the 'inside' from the 'outside' money; the criterion that the former in contrast with the latter, does not entail any net wealth for the community, does not hold; both types of money constitute wealth.

The real sector of the economy will only benefit from such a liability externality, if the banking sector transforms this 'external gain' into a revolving fund. Johnson (1969a: 247), in discussing the role of money in growth models, referred to the 'producer's surplus' on the borrower's side as a welfare gain generated by the existence of credit money:

> In reality, the main importance of the development of banks and other financial intermediaries to the process of economic development may well lie in the gains in efficiency reflected in these surpluses, rather than in the implications of the presence of money for the possibility of influencing the growth process by monetary policy.

Johnson's specification of a money producer's surplus or a *money producer's seigniorage* is analogous to Meade's real income externality which stems from two related ideas; first, superior productivity is generated by the use of a money economy in contrast to barter, conferring external economies of the kind we analyzed in the previous two sections; second, an external diseconomy is caused and initially affects the non-banking sector, in the sense that the increased welfare gain is due to transformation from a commodity money to a credit money, mainly internalised by the banking sector.

Yet both Johnson (1969b: 326-7) and Grubel (1969: 271) believed that "In the long run, seigniorage persists only when competition is imperfect, either through collusion or, as is most frequent, as a result of legal or constitutional arrangements." The 'zero' seigniorage under perfect competition, was criticised by Klein (1978a: 5) who argued that "if all returns were competitively passed on to bank depositors in the payment of interest, seigniorage would be present in the system because of the government grant of the "privilege" to engage in fractional reserve banking". So, even under competitive conditions, seigniorage would exist; the difference between the exchange value of money and the cost of producing and maintaining it cannot be identified, unless one examines the supply side of money and consequently, *confidence externalities.*[23]

The most important category of seigniorage externality is *reserve-type externalities.* They will be generated by the holding, use, management and functions of reserves by the ECB. Pursuant to Article 30 of the ECB statute, an amount of ECU 50 000 million of foreign reserve assets will be transferred from national central banks to the ECB. This is additional to the capital of the ECB, an amount of ECU 5 000 million, which will be transferred from the national central banks on the base of a key for subscription, to the ECB, pursuant to Article 28 of the ECB statute.

The amount transferred raises the question of 'how' monetary unions should arrange their optimal level of reserves, provided that reserves act as *confidence-producing externalities.*[24] As to the optimum level of reserves, the ECB needs to hold foreign exchange reserves for two main reasons: a) foreign exchange intervention, and b) backing the ECU note issue. The *reserve-type externalities* are induced by Article 30 of the statute of the ECB: 'The ECB shall have the right to hold and manage the foreign reserves that are transferred to it and to use them for the purposes set out in this statute'. These reserve assets are meant to support the ECU in foreign exchange markets and the issue of ECU notes. Both would be managed by the ECB.

The reserve management by the ECB will create an externality. Article 33 of the statute obliges the ECB to allocate its net profits to its shareholders in proportion to their paid-up shares, which are the national central banks. Yet under Article 33.1(a), the Governing Council may decide to withhold an amount not exceeding 20% of the net profit and transfer it to the general reserve fund. If we assume that it is invested in alternative uses earning an income, the *management* of this fund is a potential source of seigniorage income. An event of that kind would induce a public good shared-variable externality.

This *reserve management externality* might become the instrument of monetary policy. Suppose the ECB pays interest on its reserve liabilities. This should be as attractive as other short-term government securities. The ECB could use the differential between the rate paid on reserve liabilities and open market rates on similar securities to influence demand for substitutable assets. "If the bank pays higher interest on reserves, the demand for reserves rises, and there is deflationary pressure. To stimulate the European economy and raise prices, the central bank would increase the differential and decrease the demand for reserves" (Hall in Giovannini, 1990: 283).

The more interesting case of a reserve-type externality would be generated if the ECU gained an international status. An international money would be held by third-country central banks as 'official reserves', by third-country residents as 'cash' and by third-country commercial banks as 'deposits'. If the estimates of the Commission (1990) are correct, at the start of the third stage of EMU, the ECU's international status would be significant. One should be cautious with the Commission's estimates because the underlying assumption is to estimate what the US dollar captures today, which could be alternatively captured by the ECU if it were established as an international currency.

There are three kinds of ECU liabilities that generate reserve-type externalities. First, if low-powered *ECUs become reserves* to other countries, any act by the ECB will not necessarily be in the interest of the latter; this would constitute an external act generating an economy or diseconomy. This is an act of sharing the same monetary unit. Take the case of the US dollar. Foreign official holdings of dollars consist primarily of holdings of Treasury securities or of interest-bearing Eurodollar deposits; they are essentially unbacked by high-powered dollar reserves. "International banking means the private creation of international or multinational money. Low-powered money in the United States becomes high-powered money in Europe. The European central banks have increasingly lost control over domestic money supply" (Mundell, 1973b: 152).

Suppose a third-country holds its official reserves in the form of interest bearing assets denominated in ECUs. All ECU denominated assets are issued by the ECU issuing country. The holding of these assets would mean a corresponding increase in demand for ECU denominated assets in the ECU issuing country. This would indirectly cause a fall in the interest rate of the ECU issuing country. This *interest rate externality* will induce all the incidence externalities that we discussed in the section on price level externalities. The most important effect, though, would be to *change its debt* with respect to third countries holding ECU-denominated assets.

A third reserve-type externality is induced by the holding of ECU-cash by non-residents. It would all depend on the motives for holding ECU-cash. Any change, say, in the exchange rate of ECU/Dollar or ECU/Yen would mean an induced *exchange rate externality* since the non-residents are not consenting parties.[25]

It should be noted that the primary cause of financial innovation has not been efficiency externalities but 'excessive' seigniorage externalities. In our M-C-M* process with interwoven systems, serious barriers to entry do not exist. Financial innovations are easily introduced and marketed. If so, competition would be intensified and institutional regulation would be overcome. The Euro-dollar market in the 1970s is an example that official regulations about capital controls, the need for reserves management, recycling of funds and liability management by US depository institutions, found an outlet in Euro-dollar deposits. The same story was repeated with the private ECU markets. We have reached the stage that *financial innovation has globalised* the international market for funds. Banking seigniorage, therefore, must be substantial, entailing important implications for the exercise of monetary policy and the control of money supply.

In short, seigniorage externalities stem from the fact that the marginal cost of an extra monetary unit tends to zero, irrespective of the fact that its average cost might be high. By average cost we refer to all those state or private institutions, i.e. central banks, regulated and non-regulated banking systems, financial institutions, etc., which are necessary for the support of issuing an extra unit of money without putting at risk the internalisation of confidence externalities.

In this case, seigniorage externalities have nothing to do with a legal enforcement of one kind of money or another for the settlement of debt. Or, we have a case of a tax arising from the fact that the issuer captures a monopolistic rent, which is due to the difference between money's exchange value and money's cost.

6.4 Two monetary conclusions

Two conclusions could be derived from our preceding sections:

A) Any asset, financial or not, that has the single property of internalising the money externalities generated in the economic spheres of exchange, of production, of accumulation and of distribution, is capable of becoming money.

B) The five categories of money externalities induced by the institution of money, causes money to be 'super-non-neutral'.

As to our first monetary conclusion, we could say that the internalisation of the categories of externalities associated with *transaction cost, learning and technological* and *seigniorage* by asset A would lead to the establishment of A as money. However, the continuance of A as money would depend on capturing *confidence* and *price level externalities*. We apply this monetary conclusion to the ECU in the next chapter to discover what money externalities it internalises in stage two of EMU.

Our second conclusion is a demonstration of idea b) of H5 on the role of money and is grounded in the notion that money is super-non-neutral with respect to Walras's neutral and Keynes's non-neutral money. It affects and is affected by all economic activities, monetary and real. Money is the integrating factor because production, consumption, exchange and distribution are interrelated through the 'money externalities' *and* because money externalities induce income, substitution and wealth effects.

The essence of the integrating property of money is brought to the surface when one considers its implications for: a) the perfectly competitive model, b) the traditional social welfare function, c) the IS-LM model, and d) the traditional functions of the central banks.

In the next chapter, we explore the above implications. We apply H1 to H5 to the premise: 'money is an externality'. The above two conclusions are applied to EMU and it is found that EMU's institutional structure is defective, in need of major modification. We are tempted to propose a solution in the next chapter.

Notes

1. Two excellent books on the theory of externalities survey the views expressed, analyze policy implications of externalities and apply the theory of externalities to environmental policy, such as Baumol and Oates (1988), and to public or club goods, such as Cornes and Sandler (1986). We shall be selective by making reference to those articles which are relevant to our purpose and, in particular, to Meade (1973).

2. All references made to Meade in this section, are taken from his (1973) book on *The Theory of Economic Externalities*.

3. Cornes and Sandler (1986: 5) summarised Coase's argument: "When, for example, few individuals were involved, participants could bargain with one another, thereby eliminating the potential inefficiency associated with the externality. Furthermore, Coase argued that any 'liability assignment' for the uncompensated costs, whether imposed on the externality-generator or the recipient, would achieve efficiency."

4. Weldon (1973: 22) believes that: "The use of the 'inventory in general form' benefits the individual in some extra degree over the advantage the particular inventories would provide, and not only that, extends to all those who are interested in easily completing the post-tâtonnement contracts on which all have agreed".

5. King and Plosser (1986) examined Adam Smith's informational externality of money against the model of Brunner and Meltzer (1971). Stein (1987) discussed the role of speculators as generators of informational externalities.

6. See Alchian (1977) and Alchian and Demsetz (1972) on why, in the absence of money, specialised firms would be created.

7. Brunner and Meltzer (1971: 802, fn. 21) made the case for credit cards: "Credit cards centralize information about deposit users, reduce a seller's cost of acquiring information, encourage the separation of payments and purchases and thereby increase (relatively) the use of deposits as a medium of exchange, lowering the ratio of currency to deposits".

8. Vercelli's (1991) chapters 8 and 9 on Lucas's scientific paradigm and model are the clearest statements on Lucas's monetary theory (1981 and 1984). To our view, Lucas has re-dressed Hayek's (1933) monetary theory in 'rational expectations hypothesis' language to prove that all business cycles are caused by a monetary shock.

9. Keynes's *A Tract on Monetary Reform* (1923) is taken from vol. IV of his 'Collected Writings'. The word 'Tract' will be used.

10. Neo-Walrasians prefer to regard the 'fiscal set externality' as 'seigniorage' (see section 2.6). We employ the notion of seigniorage in a different context and argue that these two notions are synonymous but with widely different implications (see section 6.V). Schmitt (1988)

dismisses 'seigniorage' as a 'phantasm'.

11. A *redistribution externality* applies to the event of *wealth* being redistributed among classes by a change in the value of assets brought about by changes in the money supply. A *distributional externality* applies to the distribution of income induced by a change in relative prices generated by changes in the money supply.

12. A related aspect concerning Hayek's first guarantee is that we are dealing with 'index-numbers'. If we base our calculations on anything other than a Sraffa-type 'standard- commodity', the welfare implications are considerable and consequently, price level externalities would be induced by the divergence between social and private valuations.

13. Congdon (1981: 4) commented on this aspect: "On the face of it, this would be a very profitable business. Anyone could set up a bank, print some paper and demand valuable products from the rest of the community in return. Why should the rest of the community endow the banking entrepreneurs with such massive seigniorage gains?"

14. About the State guarantee seen in historical context, Hicks (1989: 45-46) stated: "The chief thing which emerged from that discussion is that there can be no assurance that a guarantee will be kept if the guarantor has a monopoly position; the effort, often made by rulers, to prevent the export of the precious metals was an effort to protect their monopoly".

15. See Board of Governors of the Federal Reserve System (1947) and the articles by Miron (1989) and Eichengreen (1991).

16. See The Economist, 25.01.1992, on 'Central Banks: America v Japan' for an interesting discussion on the legally guaranteed clauses contained in the respective Laws of USA and Japan, and their post-war record on inflation and growth.

17. See Mundell (1970) for an interesting discussion.

18. Kindleberger (1983: 381) looked at 'standards', such as weights, measures, testing of drugs and food, standards of quality, etc. and argued: "where government lays down standards for the protection of ignorant consumers it may do so in the interest of producers...If this be true, an ostensible public good is effectively a collective good, although the two sorts of good can be complementary".

19. Weldon (1973: 16) believes that if such systems are interwoven, it would affect social welfare: "There now appears, from the social point of view, a production function in which, so to speak, increments of social welfare are produced by the interdependence of the monetary stock, the rest of the marketing system, (and any 'public finance' activities of the government)" [underline in original].

20. Pearson (1972: 387) also looked at the problem of growth and viewed money as 'a source of purchasing power' "that is independent of current and expected future resources...[because] the monetary authorities can

lend this purchasing power at will or supply the reserves for intermediaries to do so".

21. Emmanuel (1972) assumes a Marxian model characterised by differences in both wages and organic composition of capital. These two factors account for the 'non equivalence' in values. These two factors, also explain the long-term worsening of the terms of trade. The intermediation of money facilitates the monetary equivalence but not the equivalence in values.

22. Replacing the constancy of velocity (V) by the assumption of adjustable habits of business and of banking has meant unstable functions, not appropriate for econometric estimates. Assuming a given level and distribution of wealth has implied a stationary state with dull results. Amending the assumption of unitary elasticity of demand has been equivalent to saying that the V is not constant. Assuming full employment has produced uninteresting results. The assumption of full control of an exogenous M and of zero elasticity of substitution has meant ineffective monetary policy.

23. Klein (1974: 445) found: "The profit or 'seigniorage' currently being earned on foreign holdings of high-powered dollars should be thought of as payment by foreigners for the use of the U.S. confidence and as a normal return on the dollar brand-name capital".

24. On this question, (Mundell, 1973a: 122) stated: "Zero reserves 'and' floating exchange rates are suboptimal because of the externalities associated with the currency prices. It provides for no national cushion against shocks and forces upon the citizen the need to hold excessively large - socially non-optimal - holdings of foreign money. At the other extreme, however, a 100 or more per cent reserve system will be suboptimal except in countries where the state's need for emergency reserves exceeds the needs of individuals".

25. The Commission (1990: 186) estimated the international US dollar holdings to be about USD 100 billion in 1988 which corresponded to about 50% of the total cash circulation. The study estimates a potential shift towards ECUs, not to exceed USD 33 billion. The associated annual seigniorage revenue assuming a 7% nominal interest rate, would amount to 0,045% of Community GDP.

7 Money externalities and the ECU

7.1 Introduction

This chapter should be viewed as an application of the alternative approach advanced in chapter 6 to the unresolved monetary questions raised in preceding chapters. It links both the Walras and Keynes theories of money via our hypothesis: *money is an externality*, generated by the institution of money and internalised by the asset that serves as the unit for the settlement of debt in a monetary system, like EMU.

The implications of money externalities (M_E) for the perfectly competitive model and social welfare function are explored in section 7.2. The re-examination leads us to the conclusion that the money industry is essentially a natural monopoly and that the traditional social welfare function needs re-working to take account of the redistribution of income and wealth generated by M_E. The IS-LM model is reconsidered in section 7.3 and it is shown that its underlying assumptions cannot hold; we propose a number of reforms to it aimed at making it a more useful tool of monetary analysis.

The five hypotheses advanced in chapter 3 are reconsidered under the M_E in section 7.4; the discussion leads us to a third conclusion: *As money evolves so would its monetary system*. The most important aspect of the exercise is the one that applies the money externalities approach to the ECU in order to discover what M_E are internalised by the ECU (section 7.5).

The institutional aspects of the ECB considered under the traditional monetary theory in chapter 2, are reconsidered under our alternative approach in section 7.6. This reconsideration leads us to restate the Central Banks's traditional function of lender of last resort in terms of last resort of systemic risk (section 7.7). Our approach also explains *why* EMU should be endowed with a Fiscal Authority in order to partly remedy its defective institutional arrangement (section 7.8).

7.2 Implications of M_E for the perfectly competitive model

There is a *duality theorem* in welfare economics, which asserts a correspondence between Pareto efficiency and perfectly competitive equilibrium. Arrow (1970), as we said in section 6.1, translated this duality theorem into two postulates: a) convexity of household indifference maps and production function for each firm, which are twice differentiable, and b) universality of markets. Do these two postulates still hold if money is an externality?

These two postulates refer to three conditions:

$$MRS^A_{xy} = MRS^B_{xy} \tag{1}$$

Equation (1) states that efficient consumption means that all individuals (like A, B) place the same relative value on all products (like x, y);

$$MRTS^x_{KL} = MRTS^y_{KL} \tag{2}$$

Equation (2) states that efficient production is achieved when the marginal rate of technical substitution between factors (such as K and L) is the same in all industries (such as x and y); and

$$MRS_{xy} = MRT_{xy} \tag{3}$$

Equation (3) states that efficient product-mix is reached when the value of commodity x in terms of commodity y is equal to its marginal cost.

Under these conditions, we attain a Pareto optimal or efficient economic situation. If there is no change in policy or endowments, then 'it is impossible to make one person better off except by making someone else worse off'. A Pareto optimal situation corresponds to the conditions under which a perfectly competitive equilibrium is attained.

In short, any economic situation that does not respect the rule:

$$P_y = MC_y = AC_y = P_x MRTS_{yx} = P_x MRS_{yx} \tag{4}$$

would lead to market failure.[1]

The causes of *market failure*, according to Bator (1958) and Arrow (1970), are:
1) Ownership externalities,
2) Technical externalities,
3) Public good externalities.

These causes of market failure were examined by Bator (1958), Arrow (1970) and Cornes and Sandler (1986) with reference to the organisational, structural and institutional situations that induce *market failure* in the following instances:

a) failure of existence,
b) failure by incentive,
c) failure by structure,
d) failure by enforcement
e) absence of markets

In general the duality theorem will fail under these circumstances. We could relate the above causes of market failure to our money externalities.

The 'ownership externality' is similar to Meade's 'ill-defined ownership'. This is the case of the unpaid factor or free rider. There is no enforcement and no appropriation. Coase's (1960) property rights cannot be defined. There is lack of an incentive to define property rights (a precondition for voluntary exchange or Pareto efficiency) due to the presence of nonconvexities in feasible sets. Cornes and Sandler (1986: 34) discuss instances of nonconvexities, which become an important ingredient of externalities leading to failure by enforcement; they give the example of "...transactions technologies [which] tend to involve substantial set up costs and hence give rise to nonconvexity and consequent problems in attaining efficient decentralized allocations".

Our money process, M-C-M*, is analogous to the ownership externality causing a market failure: 'no one has effective property rights and no one is excluded from participating in the trading with money the intermediary'. Exclusion is too costly to be privately profitable and would lead to market failure by lack of enforcement.

The *indivisibility* of benefits and *nonexcludability* properties of pure public goods are also properties of our M-C-M* process. The benefits derived from a money process are not divisible; there is no rivalry of benefits. Those who participate in a M-C-M* process and benefit from it do not detract others from the opportunities to do so. Benefits available to all, due to the institution of money, shall be available to all as long as the money process is available.

Because the *transaction costs externalities* denote situations where some Paretian costs and benefits to the participants in the money process remain 'external' to decentralised cost-revenue calculations in terms of prices, these externalities violate the assumption of perfect divisibility. We have market failure by structure, since there is no way in which the question of appropriability could be settled by perfect divisible Paretian gains.

There is another cause that leads to failure of Arrow's universality of markets. There can be no efficient market for setting prices on externalities related to expectations, redistribution, money-illusion and organizational efficiency. Because of the divergence between private valuations and social

236

costs, there would be no private incentive to supply efficient markets for setting prices on such externalities. In this context, Arrow's second postulate on the universality of markets cannot hold which is Bator's failure by existence.

A crucial argument associated with failure by enforcement relates to money externalities captured under the categories of *transaction costs* and *price level externalities*. Social costs and benefits remain external to private valuation of profitability. Private valuations and social costs would diverge and there would be no correspondence at the margin. Furthermore, the externalities internalised by the institution of money are non-marketed commodities and are exogenous to participants in the money process. Any setting of prices on such externalities will cause monopolistic effects similar to Meade's monopolistic set of externalities. Once again, Arrow's second postulate of universal markets fails by reasons of structure and absence of appropriability.

The Cornes and Sandler example of high set-up costs giving rise to nonconvexity is similar to the substantial costs involved in the creation of *confidence externalities*. In this case, we have market failure by incentive and by structure because a competitive equilibrium would imply an equilibrium price vector, generating a 'loss'.

The case of loss is better explained by *technological externalities*. "The essential analytical consequence of indivisibility, whether in inputs, outputs or processes, as well as of smooth increasing returns to scale, is to render the set of feasible points in production (input-output space) nonconvex" (Bator, 1958: 467). Our *learning and technological* externalities cause both indivisibility and increasing returns to scale. The analogy is perfect; the perfectly competitive equilibrium fails for reasons of structure and of incentive. Hence, the first postulate on convexity of indifference maps and production function does not hold.

Learning externalities due to the existence of money entail two characteristics; they are indivisible and are subject to social economies of scale. Both create strong interdependence that leads to nonconvexity in production possibility sets. "Even if we have complete knowledge of the technologies of the interacting industries, we cannot infer anything from current equilibrium prices about whether an observed allocation is Pareto optimal" (Cornes and Sandler, 1986: 36). This is a pure case of market failure by structure. Given that *learning externalities* embody indivisible information, then, they can be easily transmitted from one person to another and thus the social economies of scale would imply: (i) a downward sloping average cost (AC), (ii) an associated marginal cost (MC) curve which will be falling will lie below the AC, and (iii) the input-output feasible set will be nonconvex. As the MC of money's learning externalities reaches zero, it would imply zero incentive of private producers to incur set up costs associated with the confidence externalities. Hence we have market failure by incentive.

The implications of a MC tending to zero were stated by Bator (1958: 471): "This case...is akin to where indivisibility or increasing returns to scale within a range allow profitable scope for one or a few efficient producers but for no more...if prices are not administered, oligopoly or monopoly will result". This shows that the money industry is essentially a *natural monopoly* and that it will be economically efficient for the establishment of one money within a trading area in which learning externalities are captured.

Further, the natural monopoly of money can be shown if instances of failures by existence are considered. In our M-C-M* process, money becomes instrumental in an interwoven technological system. Money then assumes the role of a technological innovation. This technological knowledge in part explains technical progress and economic growth. If the captured gains are re-invested in innovations, then production of information or invention entails external economies, which would cause MC to decline faster than AC.

We have argued that *transactions costs, learning and technological externalities* are the result of the generation of knowledge, information and efficiency which entail public attributes. The consumption and production involved are basically joint. This is a pure case of nonconvexity leading to market failure by existence. A second reason for failure by existence exists; money externalities cannot be traded and sub-optimality will result from perfectly competitive behaviour. "The real cause of externality is not the arbitrary rapaciousness of public authority but the indivisibility of the source of supply" (Bator 1958: 471).

Correcting market failure by existence would demand a social organization intended to induce the optimal production of money or optimal rate of money growth; on balance, it should internalise the optimum level of external economies and minimise diseconomies. This explains the monopolistic structure of the money industry from the point of view of 'public attributes' embodied in some M_E.

Money externalities internalised by the asset already established as money also defines the nature of the 'good'. However, if money is essentially an externality, money entails public attributes that establish a natural monopoly.[2] Consequently, it is an *essentially public* rather than a purely private good.

This proposition becomes apparent if one examines the traditional utility and production functions needed for deriving the social welfare function. However, it is not developed further except stating that both functions will not hold because money externalities violate the two assumptions of *homogeneity* and of *additivity* made by welfare economists.

If we were to re-consider idea c) of H5 on the welfare aspects of money referred to in section 3.6.H5, in the light of our two monetary conclusions, we would find that, in terms of equations (1) to (3), the three efficiency conditions would be violated. This violation could be demonstrated either because the perfectly competitive model does not hold when money enters the picture or because the traditional consumption and production functions fail under M_E. Consequently, the traditional social welfare function will be inappropriate.

The most we could say, at this level of our inquiry, is that Bergson's (1938) social welfare function referred to in chapter 3, calls for re-consideration if money is an externality. This necessary re-consideration ought to take into account that money externalities not only improve the consumption possibility and production possibility frontiers via the 'transactions costs', 'learning and technological externalities', but they also *generate redistribution of income and of wealth* via the 'price level externalities' of which, in particular, 'fiscal set externality'. *Transfers* between sectors via the seigniorage externalities are also induced. Consequently, M_E and the M-C-M* process introduce an alternative economic situation.

The re-consideration would have to concentrate on a social welfare function of the following type:

$$W = W (U_a, U_b, ..., U_n, M_E) \tag{5}$$

where U_a, ..., U_n are ordinal utility indicators of individual a,...n still needing to make ethical judgement in comparing Us, and M_E stands for money externalities as we argued in chapter 3.

7.3 The IS-LM model reconsidered[3]

We show, in chapter 2 while discussing monetary policy, that the economic logic of EMU resides in the premise that 'real income is wholly determined by whatever determines the stock of money'. For this premise to hold, two conditions should be satisfied: a) the ECB should be able to control the money supply, and b) the supply of money should be assumed to be an exogenous variable. The first condition is an attempt to regain control of money supply while faced with global markets. The second condition is justified on the principle of subsidiarity, which has meant the divorce of monetary policy from fiscal policy. Both the ability to control the money supply and the exogenously given supply of money are *challenged*.

Assume a short period in which the quantity of capital is taken as fixed; the money wages and the supply of money are exogenously determined. Assume also fixed prices, given preference schedules and a given distribution of income and wealth. Expectations are exogenously given.[4]

In a closed economy with no government sector, the behaviour of an economy 'during a period',[5] could be analyzed and would be "determined as an equilibrium performance, with respect to these data" (Hicks 1982: 319). Effective demand, made up of expenditure expected to be devoted to consumption and to new investment, would determine total income and the

239

level of employment. Hence,

$$Y = C + I \qquad (6)$$

Saving depends on total income and not on the rate of interest:

$$S = S(Y) \qquad (7)$$

"The rate of interest set against the schedule of the marginal efficiency of capital determines the value of investment; that determines income by the multiplier" (Hicks, 1937: 141). Thus,

$$I = I(r) \qquad (8)$$

For a given supply of money, liquidity preference which depends on income and interest rate would determine the rate of interest. Or,

$$M = L(Y, r) \qquad (9)$$

We have four equations to determine four unknowns: Y, S or C, I and r. If the money supply is *not* exogenous, the system is under-determined.

The essence of the model is stated by Hicks (1937: 141-2). In our scheme of *money being an externality*, the IS-LM model needs substantial change. The ideas needing change are:

a) the fixity of prices cannot be assumed;
b) the distribution of income and wealth cannot be maintained;
c) the fixity of an exogenous money supply is out of the question;
d) expectations are endogenous;
e) the demand for money needs a major revision;
f) the rate of interest is not the price of being liquid but expectational;
g) investment is not only determined by the rate of interest but also by money externalities.

The IS-LM as a fixprice model implies many uncomfortable things. It calls for the period to be fixed. Hicks (1982: 326) defines it as 'a year rather a week' and makes reference to Keynes's GT: 46, n. 1 in order to support his year. This period is needed because entrepreneurs could revise their decisions and a new equilibrium could be worked out. Yet, "...the exogenously fixed money wages and...the exogenously fixed prices of products must still be retained" (Hicks, 1982: 326).

The essential difference between the flexprice and the fixprice model is that the former is a full employment model, while the latter is consistent with unemployment during the specified period.[6] Hicks's 'year' is long enough for employment decisions to be revised but not relative prices and the price level. Otherwise, we have the Walras exchange model (see section 4.11 on tâtonnement on money savings), which only needs a circulating fund for the completion of the static equilibrium. Then, holding money as a price for being 'liquid' has no role to play.

Does the intersection of IS-LM determine income or output? If it determines income, it establishes a Walras-type static equilibrium. If it determines output, the price fixity assumption cannot be retained. Both relative prices and the price level will be changed during the year to establish a new equilibrium during the next year.

Is money supply exogenously given or endogenous in Hicks's IS-LM? If total quantity is changed, it will be erroneous to retain the fixity of the money supply assumption in equation (9). Either the exogenously given money supply accommodates to the new situation,[7] or the rate of interest rises, giving birth to the classical world. The IS-LM model is thus shown to be an apparatus of the classical theory.

In our scheme of *money being an externality*, the above contradictions do not arise. While discussing *price level externalities*, we made the point that in a M-C-M* process, both the user of and the producer of money exercise an influence, through their acts, on the price level. The former through the hoarding or dishoarding, the latter through its right to change the money supply. Changes in the level of prices would induce incidence effects that would give rise to distributional, fiscal set and redistribution externalities.

No matter whether the IS-LM model determines income or quantity, the *distribution of income will change*. Should the distribution of income be changed, it would give rise to a number of sequential changes depending on the cause of the change and on the accommodating monetary policy. If the entrepreneurial class is favoured, it may lead to the realisation of 'innovations' inducing the *technological externalities* which, in turn, will give rise to *seigniorage externalities*, etc.

The sequence could be identified if we knew the source of financing of new investment. This raises all the questions associated with the stage of development of the banking system assumed under the IS-LM model. As we argued in the section on the Aristotelian stages of development, the causality in Chick's (1992) scheme is very important. The exogenously given supply of money cannot be retained if new investment is not financed by own funds.

Keynes in the *General Theory* retains the exogenous money supply, a peculiar assumption to make, given his *Treatise* where he had assumed an endogenous money supply. The rate of interest in GT's chapter 13 is set on the assumption of an exogenously given supply. While discussing the liquidity preference (see GT: 171-2), its effects are illustrated with the use of an exogenous money supply. The causal nexus of money and the way the changes work their way out are illustrated with the use of an independent

241

monetary supply (see GT: 173).[8]

The reversal of Keynes's position on the matter in his 1937 papers in adopting the endogenous supply money version, we referred to in chapter 5, and his cautious treatment of money supply in the GT, point to another problem: "Keynes's theory of money, interest and investment is undermined if money is not exogenous. This fact has not, strangely enough, resulted in the presentation of an alternative fully worked-out theory" (Chick, 1983: 249, fn. 1).

An alternative formulation will be to take our confidence externalities (E_c) as the base. The discussion in chapter 6 showed that *confidence externalities* (E_c) are not independent but interrelated with the *seigniorage externalities* (E_s) and *price level externalities* (E_p). These considerations essentially make the case for considering a different specification of the money supply. It should be a function of *confidence externalities*, of *price-level externalities* and of *seigniorage externalities*. Hence money supply in equation (9) could be:

$$M^s = f(E_c, E_s, E_p) \tag{9*}$$

The 'independence' of these externalities cannot be assumed. We might specify at the extreme, a functional relationship such as

$$E_p = f(E_s).$$

This would imply that high *seigniorage externalities* are associated with high *price-level externalities* but we should be cautious in our interpretation of causality. The same caution should be exercised in stating a functional relationship between:

$$E_s = f(E_c).$$

It says that the higher the *confidence externalities*, the higher the *seigniorage* captured. Equally, the relationship:

$$E_c = f(E_p).$$

It implies that high *price level externalities* induce less confidence but should be interpreted with caution.[9]

An unsatisfactory treatment of the GT by Hicks (1937) is GT's chapter 5 on 'expectation as determining output and employment'. The original IS-LM article did not even refer to it. A correction was attempted by Hicks in his 'IS-LM-an explanation' article. Keynes distinguished two types of expectations: 'short-term and long-term expectation'. "The first type is concerned with the price which a manufacturer can expect to get for "finished"

242

output at the time when he commits himself to starting the process which produced it...The second type is concerned with what the entrepreneur can hope to earn in the shape of future returns if he purchases (or, perhaps, manufactures) "finished" output as an addition to his capital equipment".

In our scheme, Keynes's *current expectations*, as defined in the GT: 50, play a paramount role:

> Express reference to current long-term expectations can seldom be avoided. But it will often be safe to omit express reference to 'short-term' expectation, in view of the fact that in practice the process of revision of short-term expectation is a gradual and continuous one, carried on largely in the light of realised results; so that expected and realised results run into and overlap one another in their influence.

Our *expectations externality* (E_e) is set in historical time. It is the link between the past and the present because E_e is a function of our *learning externalities*. It is also the link between the present and the future because E_e is also a function of *technological knowledge*. Hence,

$$E_e = F(E_l, E_t) \qquad\qquad (10^*)$$

Keynes's *current expectations* are also in historical time because the process of revision of short-term expectation is set against realised sales, which are an event of the past. Our equation (10^*) is important because it implies that changes in the supply of money could affect the demand for money. This would occur because any revision of *current expectations* due to E_l or E_t, would have repercussions on the liquidity preference. They would help determine the position of the LM curve.

If the link between the money supply and the demand for money is made by our E_e, then an *expectations externality* is lurking beneath the surfaces of both liquidity preference and investment; and this because of expectations of an unknown future. This is recognised even by Keynes, who admits that, despite the fact that "the rate of interest is a highly psychological phenomenon" (GT: 202), long-term interest rates may be durable because of unchanged current expectations. A liquidity trap could be possible only if E_e is unchanged. "It might be more accurate, perhaps, to say that the rate of interest is a conventional, rather than a highly psychological, phenomenon. For its actual value is largely governed by the prevailing view as to what value is expected to be" (GT: 202).

As we pointed out in chapter 5, the GT gains in coherence if expectations are worked out as important determinants of liquidity preference. Since our E_e is affected by Keynes's 'current expectations', the demand for money is *expectational*.[10]

The expectational demand for money finds empirical support in the events of the early 1980s. We experienced substantial increases in the money supply, but they resulted, even after a short spell of time, in higher interest rates. Our E_e could explain the phenomenon in conjunction with the induced price level externalities. As the prices increased, expectations of higher prices, accompanied by higher interest rates, caused bond prices to fall until they reached lower levels at which fears of possible future capital loss were dulled by a slower rate of increase in the money supply. The act of increasing the money supply caused price level incidence, resulting in redistribution and fiscal set externalities.

We also said in chapter 5 that Keynes's rate of interest is the price of being 'liquid' but its level was determined by the speculative motive; the role of speculation is theoretically important because it is the speculators who hold varied expectations about whether the new rate of interest is below their 'expected normal rate'. In other words, the speculative motive works because there are speculators who hold the view that the current rate of interest in the market is mistaken; that is to say that it is lower than their 'expected' rate of interest which will be established in future. Hence, any new stock of money will be held by those speculators who hold expectations that the rate of interest will increase. If the interest rate is determined as an *inside price* by the expectations of speculators, then the rate of interest is *expectational*. This expectational inside price will affect the choice of assets held and efficiency of the control of money supply. Consequently, the assumption of the exogeneity of money supply cannot hold.[11]

If we take account of the above considerations, then the right-hand side of equation (9) needs modification. E_e would have to stand for the *expectational* rate of interest and will determine the shape of the liquidity preference. E_p would have to be included because of the induced distribution of income, the generated redistribution of wealth and resulting fiscal incidence. A suggested form is:

$$M^d = L(E_e, E_p, Y) \qquad\qquad (11*)$$

E_p stands for any changes in the redistribution of wealth. E_e is a surrogate for the speculators' active role in holding active money balances or bonds. The M^s and M^d functions will determine the rate of interest in money and bonds markets. The methodological foundation is still macroeconomic.[12]

In our money externalities world, it is the banking system that makes investment independent of saving, but this does not hold under all circumstances. If investment were to be greater than normal saving, the *expectations externality* about the 'normal' rate of interest would be induced; this may act as a break on investment plans. Yet the *liability, forced saving* and *revolving fund externalities* establish a credit creation mechanism which

244

makes possible the financing of 'new' investment. In our scheme, any change in the expectations of entrepreneurs about future profits to be derived via an investment project would find the appropriate extension of credit by banks. The new investment, depending whether it is labour or capital intensive, would increase effective demand, which would in turn increase income and employment, resulting in increased saving. In this context, all five categories of externalities would be induced. Consequently, equation (12) requires adaptation. We propose it to be:

$$I = I(E_e, E_s, E_p, r) \qquad\qquad (12^*)$$

The revised view of Hicks on his IS-LM model resides with his treatment of expectations. It is expectations that make possible the coexistence of a 'stock' and of a 'flow' equilibrium. "Expectations must be kept self-consistent; so there can be no revision of expectations at the injunction between one 'short' period and its successor. The system is in stock equilibrium at each of these junctions... That can only be possible if expectations - with respect to demands that accrue within the 'long' period - are 'right'" (Hicks, 1982: 329).

Our E_e, being a function of E_l and of E_t as in equation (10*), does not allow Hicks's constancy. The movement inherent in the M-C-M* process, is due to equation (10*). Assuming constant expectations is equivalent to Walras's assumptions: A3 on full knowledge and A4 on constancy of the date, which establish the 'static phase' equilibrium. Our assumption of uncertainty implies not only a role for money but also conditions the revision of the *expectations externality*. Only then could we assume the existence of the liquidity preference.

Hence either the equilibrium method is inconsistent or expectations take a value. Hicks's (1982: 330) opted for the second:

Suppose we make them expectations that the values that are expected, of the variables affecting decisions, will fall within a particular range. This leaves room for liquidity, since there are no certain expectations of what is going to happen; but it also makes it possible for there to be an equilibrium, in the sense that what happens falls within the expected range.

Hicks's imposition of values on expectations strips liquidity preference of any theoretical relevance. Shackle (1982: 438), instead, rejected the equilibrium method: "...the elemental core of Keynes' conception of economic society is uncertain expectation, and uncertain expectation is wholly incompatible and in conflict with the notion of equilibrium." In fact, Hicks's expectational range of values is another phrase for Walras's expected constancy of his data, i.e. Walras's A4 on certainty. As we demonstrated in chapter 4, one does not need money for an exchange model of which the data are held constant by assumption. Walras's circulating fund can do the job. The IS-LM model, in its new Hicksian version (1982), is Walras's theory of money.

7.4 Money externalities and H1 to H5

Schematically, the Hicksian proposition (H1) suggests the following nexus: Monetary disturbance --> Monetary theory --> Monetary institution --> Monetary policy. Our money externalities approach suggests that the Hicksian proposition is relevant to the extent that one should examine the historical circumstances that have given rise to the internalisation of one type or another of money externalities. This internalisation has evolved according to the Aristotelian notion of evolving money, and has influenced the development of monetary theory and institutions capable of translating the resultant theory into monetary policy.

The case for Keynes has been made by Hicks (1967 and 1977) and by our treatment of his monetary system in chapter 5. The case for Walras (1834-1910), a contemporary of Jevons (1835-1882), Menger (1840-1921), partly Clark (1847-1938) (all of the same liberal school) and of Wicksell (1851-1926), partly J. S. Mill (1806-1873), and of Knapp (1842-1926) (all three representatives of the State theory of money) was briefly made in chapter 3.[13]

The Aristotelian notion of evolving money (H2) suggests that it is the stage of development that generates certain money externalities, and it is the stage of development that would determine which asset would be established as money. As we argued in chapter 3, Aristotle's causal factors of change are: division of labour and specialisation, level of technological advance and communications, economies of scale (social and economic) and capital accumulation. It is these factors that set an economy in motion and its stages of development; it is these factors that determine the nature of the M-C-M* process.

The *money externalities approach* advances an alternative premise. Factors such as social economies of scale, size and depth of the market, proper social and economic institutions or conventions and customs are all relevant in enhancing one category of externalities or another. Hence it is the stage of economic development that determines *which category of money externalities* plays a more important role. This is the core argument of the Aristotelian notion of evolving money.

In the Autarky stage, there are no money externalities and hence no asset could emerge as money, since there is hardly any exchange.

In the Primary stage, barter is well developed and *transaction costs externalities* would begin emerging. Commodity money began appearing towards the end of the period. It had little monetary use (i.e. its medium of exchange value was practically non-existent). It was mainly used as a store of value for creating *confidence externalities*. It captured few of seigniorage externalities save the seigniorage charge and would not create price level externalities. It could hardly internalise the learning and technology externalities, though as the market expanded, the social economies and unequal values externalities became operational. The efficiency and organisational externalities were partly internalised. Some resource saving externalities concerned with the money supplier, were captured by the commodity money.

The Aristotelian Middle stage coincides with the most important monetary developments. As we pointed out in chapter 3, Aristotle's causal factors revolutionised markets, trade and changed the nature of money: *it evolved*. The interdependence of man was increased. In the early middle stage, we had the C-M-C process where the M internalised some *transaction costs externalities*, except the expectations externality, the fiscal set and some confidence and a few *learning externalities* coupled with some *seigniorage externalities*. In the late middle stage, we had Walras's paper money, similar in nature to the ECU in stage one and two of EMU.

The Aristotelian Modern stage and its associated money externalities, are those described in chapter 6. The Cipolla thesis and his three criteria - high confidence, highly stable value and economic background - *correspond to different degrees of internalisation of money externalities*. The asset that internalises all five categories of money externalities would satisfy all Cipolla criteria. This is the essence of our H3.

We devoted section 3.4.a) to analyzing the ECU in its present status against the Cipolla criteria and arrived at a provisional conclusion that the high confidence and highly stable value criteria were partly satisfied. In the next section we return to it to discover why the ECU internalises certain types of externalities and not other.

As to the Triffin postulate (H4), we argued in section 3.5.H4 that institutional reforms are necessary in order to give a new impetus to the private sector, *and* that a new monetary innovation in the nature of the ECU is necessary.

Our H4 suggests that the evolution of EMU from its first stage to its third implies the evolution of its monetary unit. But according to chapter 6 and the Essentiality criterion (H5), the *nature of the ECU would be changed* if it were to internalise more money externalities than it does today. Secondly, H4 implies the co-existence of the ECU and national monies in stage two of EMU. This essentially means a different institutional set up resembling Walras's bimetallic system. The EMU in its second stage could have the ECU and the D-Mark as anchor currencies. For this to happen, we would need to know the money externalities internalised by these two currencies. They should, also, need to satisfy the nexus of causality of our H5.

As we stated in section 3.6.H5, the Essentiality criterion hypothesis (H5)

entails three inseparable ideas: a) the nexus of monetary theory, origin -->
nature --> functions --> rate of interest, b) the demonstration that money is
essential in an economy, and c) the welfare aspects entailed in a money
economy.

Our money externalities approach has shown that the *origin of money* should
be sought in the *property of an asset to internalise the five categories of
externalities* stated in chapter 6. That was our first monetary conclusion.
Contrary to the theories reviewed, our approach, by explaining the origin of
money, would also suggest its evolution.

If the nature of internalised externalities evolves, *so will the nature of asset
established as money*. It was a pure commodity in the primitive stage but a
commodity money in the middle stage, with paper money in the late middle
stage. The modern stage has experienced paper and credit monies.

Equally, because the nature of money evolved over the years, *so has the
significance attached to the functions of money*. In the primitive stage, the
store of value was more important than its unit of account function. In the
middle stage, the standard of value and medium of exchange functions
assumed paramount importance. In the modern stage, the three traditional
functions amount to one: 'a settlement of debt'. This would become clearer
in the next section where we argue that the internalisation of all five categories
of money externalities would transform credit money into *electronic
money*.[14]

The discussion on H1 to H5 leads us to state a third monetary conclusion:

> *The origin, evolution and transformation of a monetary institution is the
> 'result' of the origin, nature and role of its monetary unit. As money
> evolves so will its monetary system.*

7.5 Money externalities internalised by the ECU

What types of money externalities does the ECU internalise in the first stage
of EMU? Since the first stage of EMU fits well the givens of the Aristotelian
Middle Stage, it is unlikely that the ECU will internalise more than a few
transaction costs externalities.

At a time when the money process (M-C-M*) is interwoven with the most
sophisticated communications and information centres, the ECU circuit belongs
to the Middle stage. In its present status, the ECU does not affect a
possessor's welfare, nor that of anybody else who participates in the trading
process, because daily transactions are concluded on national monies. Hence,
it cannot internalise the *shared-variable externality*. Adam Smith's idea that
knowledge of the characteristics of money reduces the informational
requirements of transactions and moral hazard does not apply to ECU because,

as a composite currency, unbundling its components implies higher informational cost.

The *efficiency externality* arises from the fact that the distribution of information is uneven and that an undifferentiated uncertainty exists. Money with its medium of exchange function reduces both direct or indirect costs associated with search and chain transactions. It further reduces the cost arising from the specialised services by reputable middlemen with trademarks and brand names. These costs are substituted or internalised by the informational content that money carries with it. As we argued in chapters 2 and 3, although the growth of the private ECU is striking, it is not more than a Eurocurrency.[15]

As a Eurocurrency, the ECU falls within the determinants of financial innovation, which arise to exploit profit opportunities due to inefficiencies but not to exploit an incomplete market. As we said in section 3.5.a), among the determinants accounting for the growth of the private ECU have been the positive discrimination on the part of the Community institutions as well as the restrictions of capital movements in certain Member States that have given rise to higher demand for ECU loans and ECU bonds. Hence the private ECU partly internalises the *organizational externality* but hardly captures the *efficiency externality*.

The *expectations externality*, which is generated by uncertainty and imperfect information about ruling commodity prices and expected rates of interest, cannot be captured by the ECU because it has not assumed the role of a store of value based on liquidity. Nor can it act as a signalling device about investment decisions carrying with it its own rate of interest via which investment (potential or actual) might be realised. The ECU partially internalises the portfolio requirements in acting as a 'investment instrument', which is similar to Walras's money savings.

As to the *price level externalities*, one has to distinguish between the official ECU, which causes symmetrical[16] monetary base changes between Central Banks and also redistribution of reserves, and the private ECU, which might affect either directly or indirectly the general level of prices. Yet there is a link between the two, provided that one shows that the Eurocurrency market affects the volume and geographical pattern of international capital flows.[17] This would occur when the ECU reaches the stage of a fully developed parallel currency in Europe,[18] or when private ECUs are held by central banks as official reserves.[19]

"'Symmetric monetary-base interventions' occur whenever the intervening central bank uses reserves held at the central bank of the country whose currency is being used, thereby causing simultaneous opposite movements in the monetary bases of the two countries" (Masera, 1987: 4). In other words, if the Banca d'Italia uses DM to support the lira when it reaches the lower limit of its divergence threshold, it will cause a contraction of the Italian monetary base but an equivalent expansion in the German money supply. Then, what are the likely effects? Under the traditional theories, the price level in Italy will diminish while that of Germany will increase and their respective exchange rates will change proportionately.

Under our money externalities approach, there is *no symmetrical* monetary base change. The action of the Banca d'Italia is analogous to Wicksell's individual who saves a part of his income by withdrawing it from circulation, thus causing a depressing influence on prices. Such an action will lead to a *distributional externality* because the depression of prices in Italy will confer an appreciable effect on German residents who hold Italian tangible goods and assets without being fully consenting parties to the Italian decision. Such an effect will have consequences because it directly causes redistribution of wealth and income. In turn, it will affect not only the demand for money but its supply as well if our money supply equation (9*) is accepted; such a change will lead to further changes in price levels.

However, we cannot assume that an action causing changes in price level will not cause a divergence between private marginal value and social marginal cost. This is the case of Samuelson's suboptimality of laissez-faire. In addition, we cannot assume away the *expectations externality* because it would affect present consumption plans with consequent effects on next generation's welfare.

The more interesting case presented here is the *redistribution externality* generated by the act of the Banca d'Italia. Any government act that produces deflation will increase the welfare gain to society at the expense of government tax proceeds. This will induce a *redistribution externality* in the sense that although it has conferred upon third parties an appreciable benefit, they were not fully consenting parties.

There is a second type of *redistribution externality* due to the obligations of the exchange and intervention mechanism of the EMS. In chapter 2, we briefly referred to the intervention measures available to national authorities when a currency crosses its bilateral margins and we argued that under existing rules symmetrical measures do not necessarily lead to symmetrical effects but more often to asymmetries. One such asymmetry is present whenever the DM is revalued and reaches its upper limit because of external pressure, such as devaluation of the dollar. The immediate effect has been to cause weak currencies to reach their lower bilateral margins. The authorities concerned are obliged to intervene so as to keep their currencies within the prescribed limits by selling DM reserves and by buying their own currencies.[20]

The asymmetrical effects of reserve gains and reserve losses not only constitute a clear case of *redistribution externality* since the authorities of the weak currencies were not consenting parties to the event in question, but also such redistribution externality would put differential pressure on Germany vis-à-vis weak currency countries to make internal adjustments.

None of the above externalities is captured by the ECU. The partial internalisation of *price level externalities* effected by the present status of the ECU is only possible because of its constituent components. Furthermore, it fails to generate the money *illusion externality* perceived as a means to overcome the alleged inefficiency of the labour market, lack of knowledge and confidence crisis.

As to the *confidence externalities* generated by the institutional structure supporting a monetary system and its currency, the ECU derives confidence from its components. In chapters 2 and 3, we referred to technical, institutional and economic factors that 'create confidence in the ECU'. All are derived from the structure of a composite currency which nets out both the exchange and interest rate changes and which, consequently, it is more stable and predictable than individual currencies. Despite the spectacular growth of the private ECU, "The ECU still has to make a breakthrough in the non-financial sphere; its use as an invoicing currency and as a means of settlement of non-financial transactions remains very limited" (Committee of Governors, 1992: 43). Hence the basic feature of the private ECU is the interbank business in Eurocurrency markets. This is a clear demonstration of lack of 'monetary confidence' on the part of the users. This is so despite the selective promotion accorded by EEC institutions and by individual EEC Member States to create the *brand-name externality* necessary for the backing of a composite currency.

Central to creating monetary confidence is the economic background of the issuing authority of the currency in question. We found that, for the ECU, this is yet unattainable. An explanation for this failure is given by the ex-President of Bundesbank, Pöhl (1990: 6): "So it is no surprise that the ECU's role in the EMS has remained marginal, because, as a basket, and lacking a central bank with full responsibility for it, it could not be expected to assume a central role".

Yet EMU so far has created some monetary stability. Not only have the Member States, participants in the ERM, have they benefited from this externality but also the remaining states who have acted as 'free riders', have internalised it. They have reaped the fruit of monetary stability while pursuing an independent monetary policy and without being consenting parties to the ERM discipline. The *shared-variable externality* is present in this case.

Two extra externalities internalised by the ECU are: ECU as symbol and ECU as trust. As a *symbol*, the ECU is viewed as a means to advance towards the goal of European Union. ECU as *trust* could mean the widening circle of economic interdependence in the EU through which the social and economic cohesion is advanced. The stable value of the ECU reinforces the idea that acceptability of and demand for any means of payments rests on 'faith'. This means that it will be accepted by others as payment of a predictable value. Both a *symbol* and *trust* are based on faith, but this faith is generated by all associated externalities.

The single most important source of confidence externalities is the institutional *guarantee externalities*. We spent a large part of section 6.3.III on this subject and have made the case for EMU when endowed by its own money, the ECU. But this important category of confidence externalities is generated only at the third stage of EMU.

As to the *learning externalities*, the ECU internalises a few because its market and volume of transactions are small. As long as the ECU remains a composite currency, it cannot capture social economies generated by the utilisation of a single money which lead to reducing time and costs in search and negotiations.

The informational content of the ECU is not substantial because it carries with it information regarding the monetary policies of the Member States, the development of economic aggregates, the management of the ERM and the economic environment in the Community. Hence, it cannot internalise the knowledge externality associated with the money properties, because it is a composite currency and not a means of settlement of debt, arising from the exchange of goods and services.

Nor does the ECU act as a standard of value to the non-bank transactor; such a role would reduce transaction costs shared by all and thus meet the non-excludability and non-exhaustiveness criteria of a public good. These public properties of money are assumed by established common monies which have their medium of exchange function well developed.

As to the *technological externalities*, the relevant question to ask is whether the official or private ECU reduces the cost of production of services and of goods. We could associate financial innovation with the sector of services and informational invention with the sector of goods. Both would lead to higher total productivity and thus would shift the technocratic frontier to a higher level.

Yet what causes financial innovation to occur? Van Horne (1986: 456) believes that five factors account for it: "(1) Regulatory change; (2) tax law changes; (3) technological advances; (4) changing interest rate and currency levels as well as volatility; and (5) changes in the level of economic activity. With a change in one or more of these factors the equilibrium is upset". To the extent that a financial innovation would confer an appreciable benefit to a producer who had not been a consenting party to the cause, this would be an external economy to him. If this financial innovation is demonstrated in or introduced by a specific currency, it is reasonable to say that this currency carries with it the financial innovation in question.

An example taken from today's financial system based on advanced technology will illustrate the above *technological externality*. Credit money implies the application of new technology in computer-based information to the transfer of funds and settlement of debts. But such fund transfers prompt changes in the delivery and in the cost of financial services. In a competitive market, those who do not adapt to new technology would be inefficient in exploiting an incomplete market. And to remain competitive means that a financial intermediary must be cost-effective in processing transactions.

Has the ECU introduced a financial innovation? The official ECU might have been the off-spring of Van Horne's fourth factor (currency and interest rate volatility), but it introduces no serious technological innovation in the sense of promoting coordination or defusing information about producers' and consumers' economic decisions. This limited applicability finds an explanation in the fact that the official ECU is not interwoven with the rest of the economic system. On the other hand, the private ECU owes its existence to the regulatory change and to the 'infant currency argument'.[21] The private ECU and its derivatives, such as futures, options and bonds, can be said to constitute a financial innovation that enlarges the domain for risk externality. To this limited extent, it internalises some *technological externality*.

Neither the official nor the private ECU could capture the gains externality derived from nonequivalent values which result in unequal commodity exchange. We have argued that, due to the money process (M-C-M*), money carries with it the single property which captures the 'new and additional gain above value in every exchange transaction'. This presupposes invoicing and pricing in ECUs as well as trade financing particularly in international transactions. The ECU is far from having reached this status.

As to the *seigniorage externalities*, the official ECU cannot internalise either the *forced saving* or the *revolving fund externality*. This is so because the two are generated by commercial banks when they extend credit upon the assumption that bank liabilities are acceptable means of payment. On the other hand, the private ECU, in theory, captures both but the extent is limited. Given the unregulated nature of Eurocurrency markets, any interbank lending in excess of saving (i.e. liabilities exceeding assets) would result in unintended force, saving via the liability management externality. In practice, this has not occurred. Equally there is no evidence that the revolving fund externality has been captured by the private ECU.

Theoretically, a money *producer's surplus externality* exists for both the official and private ECU. The EMCF is responsible for the creation of official ECU and it might have captured this externality once and for all. This might have occurred when it issued the equivalent amount of ECUs in exchange of 20% of dollar and 20% of gold reserves and when third countries, such as Sweden, Norway, etc. decided to hold ECUs. The same principle applies to the private ECU created by commercial banks participants in the Eurocurrency markets. Yet the total of ECU deposits by non-banks is tiny compared with the domestic aggregates of Member States.

The resource saving seigniorage generated with the major monetary transformations, which involved the adoption and establishment of new monetary units, cannot have been internalised by the ECU. This is so because the ECU, as a composite currency, introduced no monetary transformation and its system is designed to answer the monetary questions of the Aristotelian middle stage and not of today.

Neither can the ECU capture the *reserve-type externality*. For this externality to be seized the currency in question must have reached its international status; this endows it with the privilege of financing the issuer's external deficit with its own domestic currency.

In order for the ECU of the third stage EMU to internalise the uncaptured externalities we have referred to above, it would not suffice to endow it with an institution like the ECB. It essentially demands that it will introduce a technological innovation. The complexity of banking, capital mobility, rapid dispersion of information and globalisation of markets point to a different ECU from the one adopted by the Treaty on European Union. Our money externalities approach suggests an *electronic ECU*.[22]

The electronic ECU, by itself, will not suffice. The organisation of money requires an institutional setting, which would induce the optimal production of money aiming at internalising the optimal level of external economies and at minimising diseconomies. Our second monetary conclusion says that, not only does money internalise the five categories externalities but, because money is super-non-neutral, it also generates externalities of the categories considered under the real income and distributional externalities. This makes the case for the organisation of the ECU needing two institutions: a ECB and a European Fiscal Authority.

7.6 The ECB reconsidered

The two traditional functions of Central Banks: a) lender of last resort, and b) prudential supervision were discussed in chapter 2. If money is an externality, will these traditional functions retain their presumed strength? We argue below that the answer will depend on the degree of money externalities the ECB will capture or generate.

What sort of externalities would the ECB capture or generate at the third stage of EMU? First, it will capture and create the *efficiency externality*, because it will solve the present problem of free riding. That is to say, it will solve the present insufficiency of information about the producers of money in the Community and the quality of their monetary policy. As a result, costly information will be diffused by this central body to both national Central Banks and commercial banks. National Central Banks that have offered cheaper quality monetary policy, and yet have benefited from a better reputation than deserved, having internalised the externality due to monetary stability induced by third parties, will not be able to continue to be free riders.

The organisation of markets would be more important because trading has necessitated specialist information concerning the availability of goods and services in the market-place, the reputation of producers, the quality of goods and services and the credit-worthiness of buyers. We also argued in chapter 6 that leaving the provision of such specialised information to the market is not satisfactory because of market failures, which arise from the limited appropriability and non-exhaustiveness induced by *learning and technological externalities*. Yet the ECB will internalise the *organisational externality* for another reason. In its role as the manager of depositors' wealth and saving, it creates a *distributional externality* through its *reserve management externality*.[23]

There is another aspect of Central banking that creates organisational externality; this concerns the nature of assets and the solvency function of Central Banks. As to the nature of assets, Goodhart (1986a: 15) argues that "...unlike unit trusts, banks' assets are primarily non-marketable, or at least non-marketed, taking the form of loans and overdrafts". As to the solvency function, in principle, the ECB will be more efficient because it will generate and internalise the public properties associated with clubs and shared by their members which, in the Community context, will be national Central Banks. However, as we argue below, the solvency function has changed.

The early proponents of the creation of the ECB have followed the institutionalist school and proposed its creation for reasons different from ours. Triffin (1986: 11), for example, argues that "The merging of national currencies into a single currency would, of course, eliminate forever any risks of exchange-rate instability, and enable therefore interest-rate differentials to elicit stabilizing capital movements from surplus countries to deficit countries". The ECB will not only eliminate risks of exchange rates by the creation of a common currency and stabilise capital movements; it generates confidence, causes price-level externalities and captures seigniorage.

Take the case of reserves held by Central Banks. The main purpose of reserves is to maintain confidence in Central Banks' ability to defend their rates. The creation of the ECB will be associated with three additional external economies by extending the domain of risk-sharing concerned with reserves, by creating conditions for reserve-saving, by minimising overhead costs of transactions and by capturing all reserve externalities associated with third countries holding ECUs as their reserves. The risk-sharing externality adds support to the ability of this institution to maintain confidence in its defence of its rate; the reserve-saving associated with our *transaction costs externalities* will produce a lower optimal level of reserves and provide for lower holdings of foreign reserves. On the other hand, spreading set-up costs over a larger population makes the law of large numbers and the economies of scale involved become operative.

The capital and exchange reserves (gold and dollar assets) of the ECB shall meet the guarantee clause intended to generate confidence in the ECU. It should be pointed out that the total level of reserves (gold and dollar) of Member States was about ECU 368 billion in April 1991 (of which about ECU 113 was in gold and the rest in foreign currencies). The gold reserves of the EEC meet the community guarantee clause as a prerequisite to generate confidence in the reserve centre.

The externalities induced by risk-sharing, commodity guarantee and spreading of overhead costs point to resource savings. All suggest considerable resource savings enlarging thus the gains to be accrued from the creation of the ECB. An own monetary unit of the ECB will induce transactions costs, learning and technological externalities. They are closely related to the nature of the transmission of information discussed earlier. The ECB will constitute information both with respect to the intention to manage a single currency reducing risk and vis-à-vis the quotation of prices on one currency instead of several; hence, it will yield resource saving.

It is the existence of uncertainty that imparts economic value to information embodied in a currency. Money's informational property makes it a unique; money is indivisible both for the supplier and the user; it is of limited appropriability; it could be transmitted at very low cost; its value is not known until the holder puts it to use. Furthermore, the production of money differs from the production of goods in one basic characteristic; once the information embodied in a currency is acquired, there is no gain in acquiring the same information twice. It becomes knowledge that has arisen from deliberate seeking in money markets and from observing the activities related to them.

If the new monetary unit of the ECB acts as an efficient communication system, two kinds of information: market and technological, will be captured. The market information has to do with capital markets. We have said earlier that the role of capital markets is to allocate savings to users of investment in real assets. Yet capital markets entail costs which are associated with information, pooling of savings, administrative and diversification costs. In the absence of money, the divergence between the expected return and the risk involved in lending would have been substantial. A money invention that would reduce the divergence would also assume the role of the technological innovation and consequently would generate external economies to the market. This *technological externality* is mainly captured by the medium of exchange established in the market, given the stage of economic development. The less the cost to the capital market, the more efficient the allocation of savings, and the less the input cost for the production of services and of goods.

The technological information captured by an efficient capital market based on a new monetary unit will be associated with the state of nature related to the size of an individual's own endowments and to the returns attainable from an investment. If the new monetary unit spurs discovery of hidden market opportunities and also knowledge about improvements in production, then it

256

will serve as an incentive for investors to stimulate technical knowledge, promote the allocation of additional resources to invention and coordinate inventive research in Member States. The result will be internalisation of economies of information yielding resource saving, risk sharing and integration of national financial markets.

It is the above considerations that make the case for the *electronic ECU*. The whole idea is to introduce a monetary innovation consistent with our third monetary conclusion: *as money's nature evolves so would its monetary system*, in order to capture more money externalities that paper or credit money at present internalise.

7.7 Last resort of managing risk

As long as the ECB internalises the four-type of *reserve externalities*, it becomes responsible for the supervision of the banking and financial systems. The question of interest is to know whether the traditional function of *lender of last resort* is appropriate when faced with global markets and when money is an externality. Freeman (1993: 41) summarised the findings of the Promisel report commissioned by the Basle Committee: "The report's main observation was that banks increasingly have dealings with non-banks such as trust and insurance companies, so traditional measures of interbank dealings are potentially misleading. Banks and non-banks alike need proper contingency plans for disasters".

If the interdependence of banking and financial intermediaries has increased to an extent that casts doubt on the ability of monetary authorities to devise contingency plans for disasters, then the traditional function of lender of last resort is redundant. This becomes clearer if we examine the source of financial instability in global markets.

In section 6.3.V, we made the point that *liability management* and *risk externalities* have increased systemic risk disporpotionately. Given the global activities of banks and financial intermediaries in managing their portfolios, payment systems and netting schemes have become global. The fact that both these externalities are internalised by banks and financial intermediaries and not by Central Banks, renders the traditional function of lender of last resort *inoperative*. Financial instability caused by unmanaged systemic risk cannot be handled by Minsky's remedy of providing the necessary liquidity to prevent collapse.

To the extent that global markets are not regulated at a global level, the three institutional prerequisites: a) netting schemes, b) uniform accounting methods and c) disclosure rules, which could minimise systemic risk, are *not effective*. Central Banks, therefore, will have to face systemic risk as their principle function. Systemic risk mainly stems from an institutional setting designed in

1944 to deal with a different scale of finance, capital and investment movements. Globalisation has caused a change in the traditional function of central banks; it calls for a new institutional arrangement to deal with liability and risk externalities.

It is the *management of systemic risk* that necessitates the supervisory role of a Central Bank, not the old function of lender of last resort. The principle source of financial instability is the *risk externality* generated by the failure of one institution interlinked with a chain of financial markets and systems. Hence it is institutional in nature. The risk externality is the more important source because the settlement systems are part and parcel of the money process (M-C-M*), which is interwoven with advanced information technology and interdependent payment systems linked via the intermediation of money externalities. Failure to manage liability and risk externalities will expose EMU to *financial instability*.

Institutional financial instability could be remedied by conferring on national central banks the task of 'last resort of systemic risk'. In this way, the moral hazard (induced by the same institution that authorises the establishment of a bank and also rescues it from failure) partly disappears because the two roles are divorced. The ECB is responsible for authorization while national central banks for supervision and closures of insolvent institutions.

If sufficient money externalities are internalised by the ECU to establish it as a single currency, for a period, institutional instability will increase because of adjustment costs and netting settlements which threaten the entire system. In order to manage the institutional financial instability, the ECB should assume formal legislative power in prudential supervision although not implementation power. The latter could be delegated to national central banks as formal agents of the ECB, consistent with the principle of subsidiarity. It would be the national central banks responsible, as the second Banking Directive under the 'home-rule' requires, for the closure of insolvent banks. Separation of authority between two bodies concerning *decision* and *execution* respectively is a means of checks and balances.

7.8 A European Fiscal Authority (EFA)

There is another aspect which is even more important and which has not been discussed. It concerns the capturing of seigniorage externalities and the generating of price level externalities by the ECB. It is mainly the nature of its monetary unit that will spur and internalise learning and technological externalities. The internalisation of these four categories of externalities effectively calls for the creation of a Fiscal Authority in the Community. In addition, given the fact that there can be no effective monetary policy not supported by a fiscal policy, when money is considered as super-non-neutral, shared responsibility managed by a European Fiscal Authority (EFA) for enhanced cooperation, becomes imperative.

Our argument for a EFA has nothing to do with the Federal-camp proposal. The Federal-camp argument is about a Community mechanism of redistribution of income in order to correct regional disparities.[24] Our argument is twofold: about the categories of money externalities captured by the ECB which are at the expense of national central banks and of national banking systems, and about *why* EMU is defective in its present institutional setting.

We have identified seigniorage as the internalisation of externalities generated in the banking system. This means revenue or a surplus generated by the banking system which is derived from two components of demand for money; the first is a direct demand for currency, the second is an indirect demand for bank reserves related to the demand for deposits and reserve requirements. In our scheme of a money process (M-C-M*), the exchange of money (M) for real resources or commodities (C) will be a loan carrying with it interest which is free and permanent but captured by M*.

In other words, in our oligopolistic money market which is due to the generation or internalisation of money externalities, not only does the producer of a currency capture seigniorage but the latter also confers appreciable benefit to the banking system, should it choose to place its reserves on money markets, generating additional income via the *reserve liability externality*. Hence our second monetary conclusion induced by our money process, in which the monetary stock exists only by reference to its interwoven nature with interdependent systems, is satisfied because *seigniorage externalities* are captured by the ECB. In addition seigniorage externalities could be generated through the interdependent economic system and active role of the ECB.

Theoretically, a EFA will be functioning as a body whose primary objective will be to 'redistribute' the *seigniorage externalities* captured by the ECB. However, there is no way to estimate what is the amount of seigniorage accrued or generated. This is so because certain *seigniorage externalities* are not quantifiable and some others exist on account of the interdependent nature of the monetary system. Hence, the EFA is born out of the necessity to complete the institutional structure that would extract the optimum level of seigniorage and distribute it equitably. For this to occur, one needs to know the sources of seigniorage.

An important source of seigniorage externalities is the *reserve-type*. National central banks are to hold as their reserve the monetary unit of the ECB. Any creation of reserve assets entails a *reserve-type externality* in the sense that a low-powered money for the national central bank becomes the reserve component of the national money supplies generating either an external economy or diseconomy and a *distributional externality* since both share the same monetary unit. The same will occur if third countries accept to hold as reserves the ECU as we have argued in section 3.6.V. Then any reserve creation will create benefits and costs similar to the ones experienced under the dollar standard.

Assume that the new monetary unit of the ECB is *electronic ECU*; that is to say a fully fledged credit money. Then the *resource saving* seigniorage will be substantial. It will be analogous to the major monetary transformations discussed earlier. Any resource-saving seigniorage will lead to a greater producer's surplus on the borrower's side because the cost involved in fulfilling the function of a reserve centre or of a technological innovation in settlement of debts will be less. This results from the size of the European market and from the depth of a unified financial markets. Consequently two sources of *gains-externality* will be born. First the superior productivity which is induced by a superior technocratic frontier and second the *technological externality* internalised by the banking system because it will use advanced technology for the transmission of payments and of settlement of debts.

It should be noted that in the case of resource-saving seigniorage the *gains-externality* captured by the ECB via its 'electronic ECU' system might act as an external economy to all other national central banks. If the ECB were to use a paper money, then only the domain of risk-sharing is extended. On the other hand, if the *gains-externality* entails a high seigniorage, it will lead to financial innovation which would lower set-up costs and thus attract new comers.

We have used the term *forced saving externality* to denote the power of the banking system to extend credit in excess of saving either because banking liabilities are accepted as means of payment or because of a not-fully regulated banking system. Similarly, the *revolving fund externality* was used to denote the power of commercial banks to use the flow of income, consumption, investment, profits and wages in order to create private debt or inside money. Both notions are integrated into the power of the banking system to distribute savings via their *liability and risk management externalities* but the two differ in their effects. Whereas the *forced saving externality* will be operational when credit overdraft is extended to finance investment and thus, investment precedes saving without causing inflationary finance, the *revolving fund externality* will be effective only if it leads to redistribution of income via a price increase. For this to occur private debt should be considered as a net worth.

With the creation of the ECB, national banking systems would be obliged either to give up their activities in this area or they would transfer part of such seigniorage to the ECB. The first option will depend upon the regulatory framework agreed to while the second option will depend on the reserve management of the new system.

The most important aspect of the ECB is the effective transfer of national monetary sovereignty to a Community institution whose capacity of creating the *price level externalities* is associated with the producer of a single currency. Yet a producer of money, even when inflation is anticipated, could impose an excise tax on the holders of real balances whenever he decides to increase its money supply. This effectively means a *redistribution externality* capturing real national resources and transferring them to the European budget.

However, capturing the *redistribution externality* implies a Fiscal Authority which sets a taxation system favouring indirect transfers. Should this redistribution externality be captured, it would lead to a second externality, identified in section 6.3.II as *fiscal set externality* which is caused by the divergence between the national marginal value attached by Member States; the latter would be above the marginal cost of an extra monetary unit issued by the ECB.

The *money-illusion externality* will be operative if the ECB uses its monetary policy to generate price level changes to modify the burden of debt proportionately. Keynes's concern with high unemployment, uncertainty and inflexible labour markets[25] reflects the concerns of today. However, they possibly differ in degree. Yet Keynes's method to use the money supply, instead of changes in wages, will induce changes in the burden of debt through the operation of the *money illusion externality*. In this case, the act of the ECB would be an external economy to the national economies, though a number of social groups might not be consenting parties.

This brings us to another pressing problem. If the ECB assumed responsibility for monetary policy, its objectives might be in conflict with the economic policies of Member States. This separation of responsibilities reflects the economic logic of EMU but might lead to monetary instability. In chapter 2, we referred to Meade's (1990) argument that EMU is unstable. His explanation rests on the interdependence of monetary and fiscal policies *and* the elasticities of demand and supply coupled by multiplier effects, which would cause the following situation. Monetary policy might reduce the price level by less than it might affect the budget deficit while fiscal policy might affect the price level by more than the budget deficit. Meade's example of EMU being unstable equally applies to a national context; it is not only the property of EMU.

On the other hand, our money externalities approach throws new light on the notion of monetary instability. Our second conclusion relating to the super-non-neutral money, rejects both the economic logic of EMU, which assumes that real income is determined by whatever determines the money supply, and the separation of monetary from fiscal policy. The interdependence assured by our money externalities, cannot be managed by two entities having divergent objectives. The only safety clause is the rule on excessive deficits, which, if applied strictly, might lead to permanent depression.

A permanent depression is possible because of the inherent 'monetary instability' due to the nature of money. Let us consider the reformulated IS-LM model. Equations (9*) to (12*) are relevant. Assume the ECB raises the interest rate by y% in order to cause an x% fall in inflation. This would only occur if the *expectational demand* for money and *expectational rate of interest* react according to traditional theory. In our model, the situation is 'ambiguous' and would depend on the *expectations externality* (equation 10*) and on *price level externalities*, causing fiscal set, redistribution and money illusion externalities. These two categories of externalities would cause a continuous shift in IS-LM curves without establishing or tending to establish, an equilibrium. The end result might be lower or higher inflation rate depending on the new level of income that corresponds to the new rate of interest.

A EFA would have to assume the above 'coordinating role'. A well functioning monetary system needs an 'automatic mechanism' that allows monetary disturbances to be corrected without producing inequitable effects and without aggravating existing structural weaknesses. The solution to this automatic mechanism lies in the technical characteristics of the monetary system and in the institutional setting-up to support it.

7.9 Overall conclusion

The ECU, with the inception of the EMS and in conformity with the State theory of money, has been conceived to be the 'anchor' currency of the system. The birth of the EMS and EMU conforms fully to the Hicksian proposition. So does the growth of the private ECU, which is consistent with the Triffin postulate and has assumed the characteristics of Walras's paper money in its status as an investment instrument where Walras's money savings and inter-banking investments are placed. This development accords with the nature of the Aristotelian middle stage that establishes a monetary unit like the official ECU or Walras's paper money, both of whose existence and status are non-autonomous.

Our *money externalities approach* explains why, since the mid-1980s, the market has established the Deutsch-mark as the anchor to the EMS. It also explains why the institutional arrangements of EMU, originally conceived to raise credibility of the enterprise undertaken by the Treaty on European Union, will not be able to establish the ECU as the anchor to EMU while at the same time satisfying our five hypotheses.

Our *money externalities approach*, in accordance with the requirements of the Aristotelian modern stage and the hypothesis on the nexus of monetary causality, makes the case for an innovation: 'introduction of the *electronic ECU*' that markets would establish as the anchor for EMU. The electronic ECU will even satisfy the Cipolla criteria because it would capture the greatest possible number of money externalities.

On the other hand, the three monetary conclusions derived from our approach that 'Money is an Externality', explain why the European Central Bank, which entails all the institutional guarantees necessary to enhance its independence, should be endowed with a European Fiscal Authority.

The ECB would capture the *seigniorage* and *price level externalities*; it would internalise the *transaction costs*, *learning and technological externalities* and would induce *confidence externalities*. Consequently, the traditional function of Central Banks' lender of last resort will become a *last resort of managing risk*. The ECB will have to assume responsibility for it.

A EFA originates in the need to compensate for the loss of national monetary autonomy and the capturing of national real resources; it will coordinate the structural policies of the European Union with national fiscal policies consistent with the objectives of monetary policy set by the ECB; it would promote economic integration via the transfer of resources; it would aim at eliminating asymmetries via the convergence of performance which, if not addressed, would be accentuated because of the gradual liberalisation of capital movements and financial integration.

The EFA would tackle the redistribution of wealth and income induced by the establishment of the ECB and would deal with the monetary instability inherent in the economic logic of EMU.

Notes

1. A host of implicit assumptions are made by the perfectly competitive model: no conflict over the initial endowments, full knowledge of prices, property rights clearly defined and costlessly enforced, mobility of factors and full employment, homogeneous commodities, costless exchange, etc.

2. Arrow (1970: 68) discussing the case of public goods, stated: "Typically, at least in allocation theory, we mean the failure of a more or less idealized system of price-market institutions to sustain 'desirable' activities or to stop 'undesirable' activities".

3. We have chosen Hicks's (1937) 'Mr Keynes and the Classics' as the base because we share his view that: "The IS-LM diagram, which is widely, though not universally accepted, as a convenient synopsis of Keynesian theory..." (Hicks, 1982: 318).

4. Hicks (1982: 319) restated the above assumptions but explicitly said that "IS-LM was in fact a translation of Keynes's non-flexprice model into my terms" and "expectations, in our models, were strictly exogenous".

5. See Chick's (1982) comment on Hicks's 'IS-LM- an Explanation' for the meaning of the 'period'.

6. This point is made by Weintraub (1982: 446): "Hicks fostered, that the unemployment that Keynes discerned was attributable just to an analytic gimmick, namely, of Keynes 'assuming a "rigid" wage so that the "underemployment equilibrium" automatically ensued."

7. To be fair to Hicks (1937: 144), he admitted: "Instead of assuming, as before, that the supply of money is given, we can assume that there is a monetary system - that up to a point, but only up to a point, monetary authorities will prefer to create new money rather than allow interest rates to rise". Thus the fixity of the rate of interest assumption that is retained.

8. There is a contradiction in the GT. Whereas chapter 13 of the GT is on an exogenously given supply of money, Keynes (GT: 173) favoured an accommodating money supply to keep the rate of interest constant: "Finally, if employment increases, prices will rise in a degree partly governed by the shapes of the physical supply functions, and partly by the liability of the wage-unit to rise in terms of money. And when output has increased and prices have risen, the effect of this on liquidity-preference will be to increase the quantity of money necessary to maintain a given rate of interest".

9. As we argued earlier, information about future performance is costly and consumer confidence is not a free good; it carries with it 'confidence-creating-expenditures' on the part of producers. Klein (1978a: 7) argued that "the real market value of the brand-name capital (or 'backing'), ß, of the fiduciary money supplier's output is:

$$ß = \{[i - r_m]/ \rho\} [M/P]$$

where ρ is the real rate of discount of the money supplier's gross profit stream, [i is the nominal market rate of interest on bonds and r_m is the nominal rate of interest paid on money], and (M/P) is the value of real balances".

10. Asimakopulos (1991: 100) is at last persuaded of the expectational demand for money: "If, given the propensity to save, and expected income levels, the resulting saving flows are seen to be smaller than the expected rates of planned investment (as indicated, for example, by national surveys) at specified interest rates, then expectations of rising rates of interest will be reflected in higher current rates".

11. We find support for our view that 'the rate of interest is an expectations externality' in Dow (1985: 192): "The actual rate of interest is thus determined by the state of expectations about asset prices, and the confidence with which they are held on the one hand, and the willingness and capacity of financial institutions to supply credit on the other, all in the light of conventional interpretations of past history".

12. See Chick's (1991) criticism of Hicks (1989) who attempted to integrate Keynes's liquidity preference with the loanable funds theory.

13. The literature on these great thinkers is voluminous. The historical, economic and social background of the Walras period is documented in Schumpeter (1956). The history of money in Galbraith (1975). Valuable insights are given in Ellis (1934). A short treatment of Walras's followers is Brémond (1989). For Walras, the collection of essays by Jaffé edited by Walker (1988), is a necessity. Schumpeter's (1956: 827) appraisal of Walras is to an extent, true: "However, so far as pure theory is concerned, Walras is in my opinion the greatest of all economists."

14. See Minehan's (1986) article on how the 'U.S. electronic payments system' works and what it does. The mechanisms of control necessary for the reduction of risks are also discussed. Borio and van der Bergh (1993) discuss the globalisation incurred by the electronic payment instruments and systems.

15. Several articles treating the private ECU as a Eurocurrency exist. See Abraham et al (1984), Moss (1984), Masera (1986), Mayer (1986), Allen (1986) and Levich (1986).

16. We refer to the official view as expressed in the Resolution on the EMS as well as to Masera's (1986) position.

17. See Mayer (1985) and IMF study (1987) on this point.

18. See Moss (1984) and Allen (1988) for further discussion.

19. See Committee of Governors (1993) for an analysis of private ECUs held by central banks as a reserve asset.

20. This is what happened with the thirteenth realignment and the turbulence of 13-16 September 1992. Our 'money externalities' approach explains the turmoil on different grounds. The analysis begins with equation (10*)

that defines the 'expectations externality' in conjunction with equation (9*) definition of money supply, and equation (11*) that defines demand for money. In a world characterised by global markets and capital mobility, the organisational and efficiency externalities are instrumental in the transmission of information. The three currencies today that internalise the greater number of money externalities are: DM, Yen and $. The DM has been established as the anchor currency for the first stage of EMU. It therefore captures more money externalities than any other European currency. In this sense, it can use effectively the liability management and reserve-type externalities to the maximum degree as long as confidence externalities are internalised by the DM. Being the anchor currency, it can determine the extent of price level externalists and can set the level of the expectational interest rate.

21. See Collignon (1990) and Thygesen (1988) who both justify the positive discrimination for the ECU on grounds of the 'infant industry' argument.

22. We have arrived at the epoch of 'electronic payment system' in the USA. Two networks are in full operation: Fedwire (owned and operated by the Federal Reserve System) and CHIPS (Clearing House Interbank Payments System) operated by the commercial banks (see Borio and van der Bergh, 1993). Both systems have reduced Meade's market-organisation-cost substantially.

23. See Fama (1980) who has generalised the functions of banking into two distinct services: a) provision of payments and transmission of services, and b) portfolio management of depositors' savings. The question of distributional externalities was not addressed.

24. The conflict between "equity" and "efficiency" was raised in ch. 2 and 5 but Kaldor's (1970) article is classic; Goodhart (1975: 298-9) devoted ch. 14 and 15 to argue that "a single-currency area requires a strong centralised fiscal authority, ready and able to ease regional adjustment problems, and also that it will be difficult to establish any effective centralised fiscal authority covering areas with independent, separate currencies".

25. The phrase: 'inflexible labour markets' summarises the essence of Keynes's GT: chapter 19 and refers to the characteristics of labour markets that make ineffective a flexible money-wage policy in reducing unemployment. See GT: 263-268 where Keynes discusses the similarities between the inflexible labour market and the flexible monetary policy; in our section 6.3.II, we discuss the efficiency of monetary policy stemming from the fact that it creates a *money-illusion externality* leading to "...a gradual and automatic lowering of real wages as a result of rising prices" (GT: 264).

Bibliography

Abraham, F., Abraham, J-P. and Lacroix-Destrée, Y. (1984), 'EMS, ECU and Commercial Banking', *Revue de la Banque*, No 2, pp. 5-35.

Aizenmann, J. and Frenkel, J.A. (1982), 'Aspects of the Optimal Management of Exchange Rates', *Journal of International Economics*, Vol. 13, pp. 231-256.

Akhtar, M.A. and Hilton, R.S. (1984), 'Effects of Exchange Rate Uncertainty on German and U.S. Trade', *Federal Reserve Bank of New York*, Quarterly Review, Spring.

Alchian, A.A. (1977), 'Why Money?', *Journal of Money, Credit and Banking*, No 9, pp. 133-140.

Alchian, A.A. and Demsetz, H. (1972), 'Production, Information Costs and Economic Organisation', *American Economic Review*, Vol. 62, No 5, pp. 777-798.

Alesina, A. (1989), 'Political and business Cycles in Industrial Democracies', *Economic Policy*, No 8, pp. 57-89.

Alesina, A. and Grilli, V. (1991), 'The European Central Bank: Reshaping Monetary Politics in Europe', *National Bureau of Economic Research*, Working Paper No 3860.

Alesina, A. and Summers, L. (1990), 'Central Bank Independence and Macroeconomic Performance: Some Comparative Evidence', *Harvard Institute of Economic Research*, Discussion Paper No 1496.

All Saints' Day Manifesto (1975), 'The All Saints' Day Manifesto for European Monetary Union', *Economist*, 1 November, reprinted in Fratiani, M. and Peeters, T. (eds.) (1978), *One Money for Europe*, London: Macmillan.

Allen, P.R. (1986),'Birth of a New Euro-Currency: The ECU', *N.Y.: Group of Thirty, Occasional Paper*, No 20.

Allen, P. R. (1988), 'The ECU and Monetary Management in Europe' in P. de Grauwe and T. Peeters (eds.) *The ECU and European Monetary*

Integration, London: Macmillan.

Allsopp, C. and Chrystal, K. Alec (1989), 'Exchange Rate Policy in the 1990s', *Oxford Review of Economic Policy*, Vol. 5, No 3, pp. 1-23.

Alogoskoufis, G. and Portes, R. (1991b), 'International Costs and Benefits from EMU' in Commission, *The Economics of EMU: Background Studies for European Economy No 44, One Market, One Money*, Brussels: European Economy, Special Edition No 1.

Altvater, E. (1993), *The Future of the Market: An Essay on the Regulation of Money and Nature after the Collapse of 'Actually Existing Socialism'*, London: Verso.

Arcelli, M. (1975), 'Some Thoughts on the Foundations of Money', *Metroeconomica*, Vol. XXVII, pp. 22-43.

Arestis, P. (1992), *The Post-Keynesian Approach to Economics: An Alternative Analysis of Economic Theory and Policy. New Directions in Modern Economics*, Edward Elgar, London.

Aristotle (1934), *Politics*, Rackham, H. (trans.) The Loeb Classical Library, Heinemann, London.

Aristotle (1931), *The Nicomachean Ethics*, Rackham, H. (trans.), The Loeb Classical Library, Heinemann, London.

Arrow, K.J. (1970), 'The Organization of Economic Activity: Issues Pertinent to the Choice of Market versus Non-Market Allocation' in R.H. Howeman and J. Margolis (eds.), *Public Expenditures and Policy Analysis*, Chicago: Markham.

Arrow, K. (1971), 'Economic Welfare and the Allocation of Resources for Invention' in N. Rosenberg (ed.), *The Economics of Technological Change*, Middlesex: Penguin Books.

Arrow, K.J. and Hahn, F.H. (1971), *General Competitive Analysis*, San Francisco: Holden-Day.

Artis, M. J. and Taylor, M. P. (1988), 'Exchange Rates, Interest Rates, Capital Controls and the European Monetary System: Assessing the Track Record' in F. Giavazzi, S. Micossi and M. Miller (eds) The European Monetary System, Cambridge: Cambridge University Press.

Artus, J.R. and Young, J.H. (1979), 'Fixed and Flexible Exchange Rates: A Renewal of the Debate', *IMF Staff Papers*, Vol. 26, pp. 654-698.

Aschheim, J. and Park, Y.S. (1976), 'Artificial Currency Units: the Formation of Functional Currency Areas', *Princeton Essays in International Finance*, No 114.

Asimakopulos, A. (1983), 'Kalecki and Keynes on Finance, Investment and Saving', *Cambridge Journal of Economics*, September, pp. 221-233.

Asimakopulos, A. (1991), *Keynes's General Theory and Accumulation*, Cambridge: Cambridge University Press.

Association for the Monetary Union of Europe (AMUE) (1990), *A Strategy for the ECU*, London: Kogan Page.

Association for the Monetary Union of Europe (AMUE) (1993) 'The First Stage of EMU: Lessons from the EMS and Policy Options for the Future', *European Parliament Working Papers*, Economic Series, W-9, 7-1993.

Atkinson, A. B.; Blachard, O.; Fitoussi, J-P.; Malinvaud, E.; Phelps, E. and Solow, R. (1992), *La Désinflation Compétitive, le Mark et les Politiques Budgétaires en Europe*, Paris: Seuil.

Aupetit, A. (1901), *Essai sur la Théorie Générale de la Monnaie*, Paris.

Baer, G. D. and Padoa-Schioppa, T. (1989), 'The Werner Report Revisited' in Delors Committee for the Study of Economic and Monetary Union, *Report on Economic and Monetary Union in the European Community*, Luxembourg: Office for Official Publications of the EC.

Bailey, M. J. (1956), 'The Welfare Cost of Inflationary Finance', *Journal of Political Economy*, April, pp. 93-110.

Balassa, B. (1964), 'The Purchasing Power Parity Doctrine: A Reappraisal', *Journal of Political Economy*, Vol. 72, pp. 584-596.

Baldwin, R. (1991b), 'On the Microeconomics of the European Monetary Union' Commission of the EC, (1991b), *The Economics of EMU: Background Studies for European Economy No 44, One Market, One Money*, Brussels: European Economy, Special Edition No 1.

Bank of England (1979), 'Intervention Arrangements in the European Monetary System', *Quarterly Bulletin*, Vol. 19, No 2.

Bank of England (1992), 'The Case for Price Stability', *Quarterly Bulletin*, Vol. 32, No 4.

Bank for International Settlements (1988), *International Convergence of Capital Measurement and Capital Standards*, Basle: BIS, July.

Bank for International Settlements (1990), *Survey of Foreign Exchange Market Activity*, Basle: BIS, February.

Bank for International Settlements (1991), *International Banking and Financial Market Developments*, Basle: BIS, November.

Bank for International Settlements (1992), *Banking Activity and International Finance*, Basle: BIS, February.

Baquiast, H. (1979), 'The European Monetary System and International Monetary Relations', in Ph. H. Trezise (ed.) *The European Monetary System: Its Promise and Prospects*, Washington D.C.: The Brookings Institution.

Barre Plan (1969), 'Mémorandum de la Commission au Conseil sur la Co-ordination des Politiques Economiques et la Coopération Monétaire au sein de la Communauté', *Supplement au Bulletin*, No 3.

Barrell, R. (ed.) (1992), *Economic Convergence and Monetary Union in Europe*, London: Sage Publications.

Barro, R.J. (1974), 'Are Government Bonds Net Wealth?', *Journal of Political Economy*, November-December.

Barro, R. J. (1986), 'Recent Developments in the Theory of Rules versus Discretion', *Economic Journal*, Vol. 96, pp. 23-36.

Barzel, Y. (1987), 'The Entrepreneur's Reward for Self-Policing', *Economic Inquiry*, No 25, pp. 103-116.

Bator, F. M. (1957), 'The Simple Analytics of Welfare Maximization', *American Economic Review*, March, pp. 22-59.

Bator, F. M. (1958), 'The Anatomy of Market Failure', *Quarterly Journal of Economics*, August, pp. 351-379 reprinted in W. Breit and H.M. Hochman (eds) (1968), *Readings in Microeconomics*, N.Y.: Holf, Rinehart and Winston.

Baumol, W. J. and Oates, W. E. (1988), *The Theory of Environmental Policy*, 2nd Edition, Cambridge: Cambridge University Press.

Bean, Ch. R. (1992), 'Economic and Monetary Union in Europe', *Journal of Economic Perspectives*, Vol. 6, No 4, pp. 31-52.

Békerman, G. et Saint-Marc, M. (1991), *L' écu*, Paris: Presses universitaires de France.

Begg, D. 1989, 'Floating Exchange Rates in Theory and Practice', *Oxford Review of Economic Policy*, Vol. 5, pp. 24-39.

Bergson, A. (1938), 'A Reformulation of Certain Aspects of Welfare Economics', *Quarterly Journal of Economics*, Vol. L 11, pp. 310-34.

Bernholz, P. (1982),'Flexible Exchange Rates in Historical Perspective', *Princeton Studies in International Finance*, No 49.

Berthoud, A. (1981), *Aristotle et l'Argent*, Paris: Burt Franklin.

Bevan, T. (1985), 'The ECU - Europe's New Currency', *Barclays Review*, November, pp. 62-86.

Bishop, G. (1991), 'The EC's Public Debt Disease: Discipline with Credit Spreads and Cure with Price Stability', London: *Salomon Brothers*.

Bini Smaghi, L. and Vori, S. (1992), 'Rating the EC as an Optimal Currency Area: Is it Worse than the US? in R. O'Brien (ed.) *Finance and the International Economy: The AMEX Bank Review Prize Essays*, Oxford: Oxford University Press.

Blackburn, K. and Christensen, M. (1989), 'Monetary Policy and Policy Credibility: Theories and Evidence', *Journal of Economic Literature*, Vol. XXVII, March pp. 1-45.

Blaug, M. (1992), *The Methodology of Economics or How Economists Explain*, 2nd edition, Cambridge: Cambridge University Press.

Blinder, A. and Solow, R.M. (1973), 'Does Fiscal Policy Matter?', *Journal of Public Economics*, 2, November, pp. 319-38.

Bonar, J. (1922), 'Knapp's Theory of Money', *Economic Journal*, March, pp. 39-47.

Borio, C. E. V. and van der Bergh, P. (1993), 'The Nature and Management of Payment System Risks: An International Perspective', *BIS Economic Papers*, No 36.

Branson, W. H. (1976), 'Asset Markets and Relative Prices in Exchange Rate Determination', *University of Stockholm Seminar*, Paper 66.

Brémond, J. (1989), *Les Economistes néo-classiques: de L. Walras à M. Allais, de F. von Hayek à M. Friedman*, Paris: Hatier.

Bresciani-Turroni, C. (1936), 'The Theory of Saving', *Economica*, February and May, pp. 1-23 and 162-181.

Brittan, S. (1979), 'EMS: a Compromise that Could be Worse than Either Extreme', *World Economy*, Vol. 2, pp. 1-30.

Britton, A. and Mayes, D. (1990), 'Obstacles to the Use of the ECU: Macroeconomic Aspects', *Economic Journal*, 100, pp. 947-958.

Britton, A. and Mayes, D. (1992), *Achieving Monetary Union in Europe*, London: Sage Publications.

Broder, E-G. (1985), 'The ECU in Perspective', *European Investment Bank*, Information No 46, October.

Brunner, K. (1979), 'Reflections on the State of International Monetary Policy', *Banca National del Lavoro*, December, pp. 513-535.

Brunner, K., and Meltzer, A. H. (1971), 'The Uses of Money: Money in the Theory of an Exchange Economy', *American Economic Review*, 61, pp. 784-805.

Bryan, D. (1992), 'International Accumulation and the Contradictions of National Monetary Policy', *Science and Society*, Vol. 56, No 3, pp. 324-352.

Buchanan, J.M. and Stubblebine, C.W. (1962), 'Externality', *Economica*, Vol. 29, pp. 371-84.

Buchanan, J. M. (1965), 'An Economic Theory of Clubs', *Economica*, Vol. 32, pp. 1-14.

Burdeking, C.K., Wihlborg, C. and Willett, T.D. (1992), 'A Monetary Constitution: Case for an Independent European Capital Bank', *World Economy*, Vol. 15, No 2, pp. 231-249.

Business Week (1981), 'A Return to the Gold Standard', *No 2706*, 21 September.

Calhoun, G.M. (1926), *The Business Life of Ancient Athens*, Boston: Houghton.

Cannan, E., Ross, W.R., Bonar, J. and Wicksteed P.H. (1922), 'Who said 'Barren Metal'?, *Economica*, No 5, pp. 105-110.

Castoriadis, K. (1975), *L'Institution Imaginaire de la Société*, Paris: Seuil.

Catephores, G. (1991), 'Keynes as a Bourgeois Marxist', *University College London*, Discussion Papers in Economics, No 91-23.

Centre for Economic Policy Research Report (1991), *Monitoring European Integration: The Making of Monetary Union*, London: CEPR.

Chick, V. (1978), 'Unresolved Questions in Monetary Theory: A Critical Review', *De Economist*, 126, No. 1, pp. 37-60, reprinted in Chick (1992) as Essay 9.

Chick, V. (1982), 'A Comment on 'IS-LM: An Explanation', *Journal of Post Keynesian Economics*, Vol. IV, No 3, reprinted in Chick (1992) as Essay 5.

Chick, V. (1983), 'A Question of Relevance: The 'General Theory' in Keynes's Time and Ours', *South African Journal of Economics*, vol. 51, no

3, reprinted in Chick (1992) as Essay 1.

Chick, V. (1983), *Macroeconomics After Keynes: A Reconsideration of the General Theory*, Oxford: Philip Allan.

Chick, V. (1986), 'The Evolution of the Banking System and the Theory of Saving, Investment and Interest', *Cahiers de l'I.S.N.E.A., Economies et Sociétés*, Serie MP, No 3; revised and reprinted in Chick (1992) as Essay 12.

Chick, V. (1991a), 'Two Essays on Keynes: A Biographical Sketch and A 'Partial Survey' of his Monetary Theory', *University College London, Discussion Papers in Economics*, 91-05.

Chick, V. (1991b), 'Hicks and Keynes on Liquidity Preference: a Methodological Approach', *Review of Political Economy*, Vol. 3, No 3, pp. 309-319.

Chick, V. (1992), *On Money, Method and Keynes, Selected Essays*, (eds.) by P. Arestis and S.C. Dow, London: Macmillan.

Childe, V. G. (1950), 'The Urban Revolution', *The Town Planning Review, Quarterly*, vol. XXI, No 1, pp. 1-13.

Ciampi, C.A. (1989), 'An Operational Framework for an Integrated Monetary Policy in Europe' in Delors Committee for the Study of Economic and Monetary Union, *Report on Economic and Monetary Union in the European Community*, Luxembourg: Office for Official Publications of EEC.

Cipolla, C.M. (1956), *Money, Prices and Civilization in the Mediterranean World; fifth to seventeenth century, Princeton*: Princeton University Press.

Clower, R.W. (1965), 'The Keynesian Counter-Revolution: A Theoretical Appraisal' in F.H. Hahn and F. Brechling (eds.), *The Theory of Interest Rates*, London: Macmillan.

Clower, R.W. (1967), 'A Reconsideration of the Micro-foundations of Monetary Theory' *Western Economic Journal*, Vol. 6, pp. 1-9.

Clower, R.W. (1969a), (ed.), *Monetary Theory: Selected Readings*, Middlesex: Penguin Books, Introduction by R.W. Clover, pp. 7-21.

Clower, R.W. (1969b), 'What Traditional Monetary That Really Wasn't', *Journal of Economic and Political Science*, May, pp. 299-302.

Clower, R.W. (1970), 'Review of J. Hicks' 'Critical Essays' in Monetary Theory', *Journal of Political Economy*, pp. 608-611.

Clower, R.W. (1977), 'The Anatomy of Monetary Theory', *American Economic Review*, Papers and Proceedings, 67, pp. 206-12.

Coase, R. (1960), 'The Problem of Social Cost', *Journal of Law and Economics*, Vol. 3, pp. 1-44.

Coats, W.L. (1982), 'The SDR as a Means of Payment', *IMF Staff Papers*, September, pp. 422-669.

Cobham, D. (1991), 'European Monetary Integration: A Survey of Recent Literature', *Journal of Common Market Studies*, Vol, XXIX, No 4, pp. 363-383.

Cohen, J. (1984), 'The Money Supply Process: How Much Progress since

C.A. Phillips' Bank Credit?', *Kredit und Kapital*, 3, pp. 333-354.

Collignon, S. (1990), 'The EMU Debate: a Common or a Single Currency?', *EIU European Trends*, No 3.

Collignon, S. (1990), 'The Economic Consequences of a Single European Currency on Centre-Periphery Relations within the Community' in Association for the Monetary Union of Europe (AMUE), *A Strategy for the ECU*, London: Kogan Page.

Collignon, S. (1992), 'An ECU Zone for Central and Eastern Europe: a Supportive Framework for Convergence' in R. Barrell (ed.) (1992), *Economic Convergence and Monetary Union in Europe*, London: Sage Publications.

Collin, F. (1964), *The Formation of a European Capital Market and Other Lectures*, Brussels: Kredietbank.

Commission of the EC, (1979), *The European Monetary System: Commentary, Documents*, Brussels: European Economy, No 3.

Commission of the EC, (1982), *Documents relating to the European Monetary System*, Brussels: European Economy, No 12.

Commission of the EC, (1983), *On the Promotion of the International Role of the ECU*, Brussels: COM(83) 274 final, 24 May.

Commission of the EC, (1984), *On Developing the European Monetary System*, Brussels: COM(84) 678 final, 29 November.

Commission of the EC, (1985), *Completing the Internal Market*, Brussels: COM(85) 310 final, 14 June.

Commission of the EC, (1987), *Creation of a European Financial Area*, Brussels: COM(87) 550 final, 4 November.

Commission of the EC, (1988), *The Economics of 1992*, Brussels: European Economy, No 35.

Commission of the EC, (1989), *The EMS Ten Years On*, Brussels: Communication of Commission to Council, DG II, March.

Commission of the EC, (1990), *One Market, One Money: An Evaluation of the Potential Benefits and Costs of Forming an EMU*, Brussels: European Economy, No 44.

Commission of the EC, (1991a), *Main Features of Community Trade*, Brussels: European Economy, No 50 (Special Edition).

Commission of the EC, (1991b), *The Economics of EMU: Background Studies for European Economy No 44, One Market, One Money*, Brussels: European Economy, Special Edition No 1.

Commission of the EC, (1991c) *The ECU and its Role in the Process Towards Monetary Union*, Brussels: European Economy, No 52.

Commission of the EC, (1992), *Removal of the Legal Obstacles to the Use of the ECU*, Brussels: SEC(92) 2472.

Commission of the EC, (1993a), *Annual Economic Report for 1993*, Brussels: European Economy, 54.

Commission of the EC, (1993b), *Report: Progress with regard to*

Economic and Monetary Convergence and with Implementation of Community Law concerning the Internal Market, Brussesls: COM (93) 1755.

Committee of Governors of the Central Banks of the Member States of the EEC, (1992a), *Recent Developments in the Use of the Private ECU: Statistical Review*, Basle: CGCB.

Committee of Governors of the Central Banks of the Member States of the EEC, (1992b), *Blue Book: A Description of the Payment Systems in the Member States of the EEC*, Basle: CGCB.

Committee of Governors of the Central Banks of the Member States of the EEC, (1993), *Annual Report 1992*, Basle: CGCB.

Congdon, T.G. (1980), 'The Monetary Base Debate: Another Instalment in the Currency School vs. Banking School Controversy?', *National Westminster Bank*, August, pp. 2-13.

Congdon, T. (1981), 'Is the Provision of a Sound Currency a Necessary Function of the State?', *National Westminster Bank*, August, pp. 2-21.

Cooper, R.N. (1968), *The Economics of Interdependence*, N.Y.: McGraw - Hill.

Cooper, R.N. (1982), 'The Gold Standard: Historical Facts and Future Prospects', *Brookings Papers on Economic Activity*, Vol. I.

Cooper, R.N. (1984), 'A Monetary System for the Future', *Foreign Affairs*, May.

Cooper, R.N. (1985), 'Economic Interdependence and Coordination of Economic Policies' in R. Jones and P.B. Kenen (eds.) *Handbook of International Economics*, N.Y.: North-Holland.

Cooper, R.N. (1990), 'Comments and Discussion on Giovannini's Paper on 'European Monetary Reform': Progress and Prospects', *Brookings Papers on Economic Activity*, 2, pp. 211-291.

Cornes, R. and Sandler, T. (1986), *The Theory of Externalities, Public Goods and Club Goods*, Cambridge: Cambridge University Press.

Crawford, M. (1993), *One Money for Europe? The Economics and Politics of Maastricht*, London: Macmillan.

Crockett, A. D. (1991), 'Great Britain and the European Monetary Union', *Vortrag vor der Kommission 'Konjunktur und Wahrung' des Wirtschaftsrates der CDU* e.V. Am 22, April.

Crook, C. (1992), 'Fear of Finance: A Survey of the World Economy', *The Economist*, 19 September.

Cukierman, A., Webb, B. and Neyapti, B. (1992), 'Measuring the Independence of Central Banks and its Effects on Policy Outcomes', *World Bank Economic Review*, Vol. 6, No 3, pp. 353-398.

Currie, D. and Hall, S. (1986), 'The Exchange Rate and the Balance of Payments', *National Institute Economic Review*, February, pp. 74-99.

Currie, D. (1992), 'European Monetary Union: Institutional Structure and Economic Performance', *Economic Journal*, 102, pp. 233-44.

Currie, D. (1993), 'International Cooperation in Monetary Policy: Has it a Future?', *Economic Journal*, 103, pp. 178-187.

Dalton, G. (ed.) (1968), *Primitive Archaic and Modern Economics: Essays of K. Polanyi*, N.Y.: Anchor Books.

Davidson, P. (1965), 'Keynes' Finance Motive', *Oxford Economic Papers*, No 17, pp. 47-65.

Davidson, P. (1992-93), 'Reforming the World's Money', *Journal of Post Keynesian Economics*, Vol. 15, No 2, pp. 153-179.

Davidson, P. and Weintraub, S. (1973), 'Money as Cause and Effect', *Economic Journal*, Vol. 83, No 332, pp. 1117-1132.

Davies, G. (1982), 'The EMS, its Achievements and Failures', London: *Simon and Coates Special Analysis*, 11 May.

Davis, O.A. and Kamien, M.I. (1970), 'Externalities, Information and Alternative Collective Action' in R.H. Haveman and J. Margolis (eds.), *Public Expenditure and Public Analysis*, Chicago: Markham.

De Brunhoff, S. (1976), *Marx on Money*, N.Y.: Urizen Books.

De Cecco, M. (ed.) (1983), *International Economic Adjustment: Small Countries and the EMS*, Oxford: Blackwell.

De Cecco, M. and Fitoussi, J-P., (1987), 'From the Use to the Production of Money: Monetary Theory and Economic Institutions - Theme and Outline of the Conference' in M. De Cecco and J-P. Fitoussi (eds) *Monetary Theory and Economic Institutions*, London: Macmillan.

De Cecco, M. and Giovannini, A. (eds.) (1989), *A European Central Bank? Perspectives on Monetary Unification after Ten Years of the EMS*, *Cambridge*: Cambridge University Press.

De Grauwe, P. (1989), 'Is the European Monetary System a DM-zone?', *CEPS Working Document*, No 39.

De Grauwe, P. (1992), *The Economics of Monetary Integration*, Oxford: Oxford University Press.

De Grauwe, P. and Peeters, T. (1979), 'The EMS, Europe and the dollar', *The Banker*, April, pp. 39-45.

De Grauwe, P., Gros, D., Steinherr, A. and Thygesen, N. (1992), 'In Reply to Felstein', *The Economist*, July 4th.

De Haan, J. (1987), 'The (Un)Importance of Public Debt: A Review Essay', *De Economist*, 135, No 3, pp. 367-384.

De Roover, R. (1955), 'Scholastic Economics: Survival and Lasting Influence from the 16th century to Adam Smith', *Quarterly Journal of Economics*, Vol. LXIX, pp. 161-175.

Delors Committee for the Study of Economic and Monetary Union (1989), *Report on Economic and Monetary Union in the European Community*, Luxembourg: Office for Official Publications of the EC.

Dempsey, B.W. (1943), *Interest and Usury*, Washington: American Council in Public Affairs.

Deputies of the Group of Ten, (1985), 'Report on the Functioning of the

International Monetary System', IMF Survey, July.

Deutsche Bundesbank, (1979), 'The European Monetary System. Structure and Operation', *Monthly Bulletin*, March.

Deutsche Bundesbank, (1992a), 'The Maastricht Decisions on the European Economic and Monetary Union', *Monthly Report*, February.

Deutsche Bundesbank, (1992b), 'Markets for private ECUs', *Monthly Report*, May.

Dooge Ad Hoc Committee, (1985), *Interim Report to the European Council on Institutional Affairs*, Brussels: Commission Document, June.

Dornbusch, R. (1976), 'Expectations and Exchange Rate Dynamics', *Journal of Political Economy*, 6, pp. 231-244.

Dornbusch, R. (1988), 'The European Monetary System, the Dollar and the Yen' in F. Giavazzi, S. Micossi and M. Miller (eds.) *The European Monetary System*, Cambridge: Cambridge University Press.

Dornbusch, R. (1991), 'Problems of European Monetary Integration' in A. Giovannini and C. Mayer (eds.), *European Financial Integration*, London: Cambridge University Press.

Dow, S. C. (1985), *Macroeconomic Thought: A Methodological Approach*, Oxford: Basil blackwell.

Dow, S. C. (1987a), 'The Money Supply as a Theoretical Variable and as Policy Variable', *University of Sterling Discussion Paper in Economics, Finance and Investments*, No 128.

Dow, S. C. (1993), *Money and the Economic Process*, London: Edward Elgar.

Dowd, K. (1989), *The State and the Monetary System*, London: Philip Allan.

Dowd, K. (1991), 'Evaluating the Hard ECU', *The World Economy*, Vol. 14, No 2, pp. 215-225.

Doyle, M. (1991), 'Implications of Economic and Monetary Union for Ireland', *Central Bank of Ireland*, April.

Drazen, A. (1989), 'Monetary Policy, Capital Controls and Seigniorage in an Open Economy' in M. de Cecco and A. Giovannini (eds.) (1989), *A European Central Bank? Perspectives on Monetary Unification after Ten Years of the EMS, Cambridge*: Cambridge University Press.

Duisenberg, W.F. (1989), 'The ECU as a Parallel Currency' in Delors Committee for the Study of Economic and Monetary Union, *Report on Economic and Monetary Union in the European Community*, Luxembourg: Office for Official Publications of the EC.

Dwyer, G.P. and Saving, T.R. (1986), 'Government Revenue from Money Creation with Government and Private Money', *Journal of Monetary Economics*, 17, pp. 239-49.

Eagly, R. V. (1974), *The Structure of Classical Economic Theory*, N.Y. Oxford University Press.

The Economist, (1989), *European Monetary Union: from A to EMU*,

24 June.

The Economist, (1990), *Currency Reform: A Brief History of Funny Monney*, 6 January.

The Economist, (1992), *Central Banks: America v. Japan, The Rewards of Independence*, 25 January.

Edmonds, K. and Shea, M. (1991), 'EMU and the ECU: the Practitioners' Viewpoint', *National Westminster Bank*, November, pp. 23-38.

Eggertsson, T. (1990), *Economic Behaviour and Institutions*, Cambridge University Press.

Eichner, A.S. (1978) (ed.) *A Guide to Post-Keynesian Economics*, N.Y.: M.E. Sharpe, Inc.

Eichengreen, B. (1990), 'Is Europe an Optimum Currency Area?', *CERP Discussion Paper* No 478, November.

Eichengreen, B. (1990), 'One Money for Europe? Lessons from the US Currency Union', *Economic Policy*, 10, pp. 117-87.

Eichengreen, B. (1991), 'Designing a Central Bank for Europe: A Cautionary Tale from the Early Years of the Federal Reserve System', *CEPR Discussion Paper*, No 585, October.

Einzig, P. (1948), *Primitive Money*, Oxford: Oxford University Press.

Ellis, H. S. (1934), *German Monetary Theory (1905-1933)*, Cambridge, Mass.: Harvard University Press.

Eltis, W. (1989), 'The Obstacles to European Monetary Union', *International Currency Review*, Vol. 20, August-September, pp. 17-28.

Emerson, M. (1979), 'The EMS in the Broader Setting of the Community's Economic and Political Development' in Ph. H. Trezise (ed.) *The EMS: its Promise and Prospects*, The Brookings Institution, Washington, D.C.

Emerson, M. R. (1990), 'The Economics of EMU' in Centre for Economic Performance of LSE (eds.), *Britain and EMU*, London: London School of Economics.

Emmanuel, A. (1972), *Unequal Exchange: A Study of the Imperialism of Trade*, N.Y.: Monthly Review Press.

Estrup, H. (1966), 'Oresme and Monetary Theory', *The Scandinavian Economic History Review*, XIV 2, p. 97.

European Parliament (1986), *US-EC Monetary Relations*, Economic Series, No 8.

European Parliament (1992), *Maastricht: The Treaty on European Union; the position of the European Parliament*, Rapporteurs: D. Martin and F. Herman, Luxembourg: Official Publications of the EC.

European Parliament (1993a), *On the System of Payments in the Context of Economic and Monetary Union*, Rapporteur: P. Bofill Abeilhe, A3-0029/93

European Parliament (1993b), *EMS plus 1992 Programme: Lessons to be drawn for the Implementation of EMU*, Rapporteur: J. Cravinho, A3-0294/93.

European Parliament (1993c), *Removing the Legal Obstacles to the Use of the ECU*, Rapporteur: K. Riskaer Pedersen, A3-0296/93

European Parliament (1993d) *International Monetary Cooperation within the Framework of the Easing of Restrictions on Capital Markets*, Rapporteur: P. Roumeliotis, A3-0392/93

European Parliament (1994), *Role, Independence and Accountability of the EMU Institutions*, Rapporteur: G. Saridakis, PE 205.541, 24.2.1994.

Fama, E. (1980), 'Banking in the Theory of Finance', *Journal of Monetary Economics*, pp. 39-57.

Federal Reserve System, (1947) *The Federal Reserve System: Its Purposes and Functions*, Washington D.C.: Board of Governors, 25.

Federal Reserve System (1984), *Purposes and Functions*, Washington D.C.: Board of Governors.

Feldstein, M. (1992), 'The Case against EMU', *The Economist*, 13 June, pp. 19-22.

Fisher, I. (1911), *The Purchasing Power of Money*, (2nd ed. 1931, 3rd ed. 1963) N.Y.: Augustus Kelley.

Fisher, I. (1930), *The Theory of Interest*, London: Macmillan.

Fisher, S. (1981), 'Towards an Understanding of the Costs of Inflation: II', *Carnegie-Rochester Conference Series on Public Policy*, 15, pp. 5-42.

Fischer, S. (1982), 'Seigniorage and the Case for a National Money', *Journal of Political Economy*, Vol. 90, pp. 295-313.

Fisher, S. (1986), 'Friedman versus Hayek on Private Money', *Journal of Monetary Economics*, 17, No 3, pp. 433-439.

Fleming, J.M. (1971), 'On Exchange Rate Unification', *Economic Journal*, Vol. 81, pp. 467-88.

Folkerts-Landau, D. and Nathieson, D.J. (1989), *The European Monetary System in the Context of the Integration of European Financial Markets*, Washington: IMF, Occasional Paper No 66.

Folterts-Landau, D. and Garber, P.M. (1991), *The ECB: A Bank or a Monetary Policy Rule*, Washington: IMF Mimeo.

Fotopoulos, T. (1990), 'Monetary Union and its Cost for US' (in Greek), *Eleftherotypia*, 17 November.

Fotopoulos, T. (1991), 'Maastricht: Damnation of the Periphery' (in Greek), *Eleftherotypia*, 21 December.

Frankel, S.H. (1977), *Two Philosophies of Money: the Conflict of Trust and Authority*, N.Y.: St Martin's Press.

Frankel, J.A. and Goldstein, M. (1991), 'Monetary Policy in an Emerging European Economic and Monetary Union', *IMF Staff Papers*, Vol. 38, No 2, pp. 356-373.

Franz, O. (1989), *European Currrency in the Making*, Sintelfingen: Libertas.

Fratiani, M. and Peeters, T. (eds.) (1978), *One Money for Europe*, London: Macmillan.

Friedman, M. (1948), 'A Monetary and Fiscal Framework for Economic

Stability', *American Economic Review*, Vol. 38, pp. 245-264.

Friedman, M. (1953), 'The Case for Flexible Exchange Rates' in his *Essays in Positive Economics*, Chicago: University of Chicago Press.

Friedman, M. (1953), 'The Methodology of Positive Economics' in his *Essays in Positive Economics*, Chicago: University of Chicago Press.

Friedman, M. (1968) 'The Role of Monetary Policy', *American Economic Review*, March, pp. 1-17.

Friedman, M. and Schwartz, A.J. (1963), *A Monetary History of the United States 1867-1960*, N.Y.: Princeton.

Friedman, M. and Schwartz, A.J. (1986), 'Has Government any Role in Money?', *Journal of Monetary Economics*, 17, pp. 37-62.

Fry, M. J. (1991), 'Choosing a Money for Europe', *Journal of Common Market Studies*, Vol. XXIX, No 5, pp. 481-504.

Fustel de Coulanges, H.D. (1901), '*La Cité Antique*' W. Small (trans.) , Boston: Lee and Shepard, 10th ed. 1921.

Galbraith, J. K. (1975), *Money: Whence it Came, Where it Went*, London: Andre Deutsch.

Garnier, Le Marquis, (1819), *Histoire de la monnaie, depuis les temps de la plus haute antiquité jusqu'au Règne de Charlemagne*, N.Y.: Burt Frankling, originally published, Reprinted: 1970.

Georgescu-Roegen, N. (1971), *The Entropy Law and the Economic Process*, Cambridge, Mass.: Harvard University Press.

The German Proposal, (1991), 'Overall Proposal to Amend the EEC Treaty', *Europe Documents*, No 1700, 20 March.

Giavazzi, F. and Pagano, M. (1985), 'Capital Controls and Foreign Exchange Legislation', *Euromobiliaire, Occasional Paper*, June.

Giavazzi, F. and Giovannini, A. (1986), 'The EMS and the Dollar', *Economic Policy*, No 2, pp. 455-485.

Giavazzi, F. (1989), 'The European Monetary System: Lessons from Europe and Perspectives in Europe', *Economic and Social Review*, Vol. 20, p. 73-90.

Giavazzi, F., Micossi, S. and Miller, M. (eds.), (1988), *The European Monetary System*, Cambridge: Cambridge University Press.

Giavazzi, F. and Pagano, M. (1988), 'The Advantages of Tying One's Hands: EMS Discipline and Central Bank Credibility', *European Economic Review*, 32, pp. 1055-1082.

Giersch, H. (1989), 'EC 1992: Competition is the Clue', *European Affairs*, Vol. 3, pp. 10-17.

Gilbert, J.C. (1953), 'The Demand of Money: The Development of an Economic Concept', *Journal of Political Economy*, April, pp. 144-59.

Giovannini, A. (1990), 'European Monetary Reform: Progress and Prospects', *Brookings Papers on Economic Activity*, 2, pp. 211-291.

Giovannini, A. and Mayer, C. (eds.), (1991), *European Financial Integration*, Cambridge: Cambridge University Press.

Girard, J., and Steinherr, A. (1991), 'ECU Financial Markets: Recent Evolution and Perspectives' in A. Steinherr and D. Weiserbs (eds.) *Evolution of the International and Regional Monetary Systems*, London: Macmillan.

Girton, L. and Roper, D. (1988), 'The Theory of Currency Substitution and Monetary Unification', *Economie Appliquée*, 33, pp. 135-160.

Gnos, C. (1989), 'Faut-il abstraire l'ECU de ses monnaies composantes?', *Revue du Marché Commun*, No 330, pp. 465-468.

Gnos, C. (1991), '*La transition vers l'Union économique et monétaire européenne: L'émission d'un ECU central*', Université de Bourgogne, Mimeo.

Gnos, C. (1992), *Production, Répartition et Monnaie*, Dijon: Editions Universitaires de Dijon.

Goldstein, M., Folkerts-Landau, D., Garber, P., Rojas-Suarez, L. and Spencer, M. (1993), *International Capital Markets; Par I. Exchange Rate Management and International Capital Flows*, Washington, D.C.: IMF, April.

Gomperz, T. (1921), '*Griechische Deuker*', Small, W. (trans.), 12th ed. Berlin.

Goodhart, C.A.E. (1975), *Money, Information and Uncertainty*, London: Macmillan.

Goodhart, C. (1986a), 'Why do we need a Central Bank?', *Banca d'Italia, Temi di Discussione*, No 57, January.

Goodhart, C.A.E. (1986b), 'Has the Time Come for the UK to Join the EMS?', *The Banker*, February.

Goodhart, C.A.E. (1991), 'Fiscal Policy and EMU' in J. Driffill and M. Beber (eds.) *A Currency for Europe*, London: Lothian Foundation Press.

Goodhart, C. (1991a), 'The Draft Statute of the European System of Central Banks: A Commentary', *Special Paper, 37, Financial Markets Group, LSE*.

Gorden, W.M. (1972), 'Monetary Integration', *Princeton University Essays in International Finance*, No 93.

Gordon, B. (1975), *Economic Analysis before Adam Smith: Hesiod to Lessius*, London: Macmillan.

Graaf, J. de V. (1957), *Theoretical Welfare Economics*, Cambridge: Cambridge University Press.

Grandmont, J.M. and Younes, Y. (1972), 'On the Role of Money and the Existence of a Monetary Equilibrium', *Review of Economic Studies*, 39, pp. 355-372.

Grantham, G., Velk, T. and Fraas, A. (1977), 'On the Microeconomics of the Supply of Money', *Oxford Economic Papers*, Vol. 29, No 3, pp. 339-356.

Green, R. (1992), *Classical Theories of Money, Output and Inflation: A Study in Historical Economics*, Macmillan, London.

Greenwald, B. and Stiglitz, J.E. (1991), 'Towards a Reformulation of Monetary Theory: Competitive Banking', *The Economic and Social Review*,

Vol. 23, pp. 1-34.

Grice, J. (1990), 'The UK proposal for a European Monetary Fund and a 'Hard ECU', London: Treasury Bulletin, Autumn.

Gros, D. (1988), 'Seigniorage versus EMS Discipline: Some Welfare Considerations', CEPS Working Document, No 38.

Gros, D. (1989), 'Seigniorage in the EC: the Implications for the EMS and Financial Market Integration', Washington: IMF, Working Paper WP/89/7.

Gros, D. and Thygesen, N. (1988), 'The EMS, Achievements, Current Issues and Directions for the Future', CEPS Paper, No 35.

Gros, D. and Thygesen, N. (1990), 'The Institutional Approach to Monetary Union in Europe', Economic Journal, 100, pp. 925-35.

Gros, D. and Thygesen, N. (1992), European Monetary Integration: From the European Monetary System to European Monetary Union, London: Longman.

Group of Ten, (1993) International Capital Movements and Foreign Exchange Markets, Washington: Mimeo, April.

Group of Thirty, (1993), Derivatives: Practices and Principles, Washington DC: Group of 30, Global Derivatives Study Group, No 30, July.

Grubel, H.G. (1969), 'The Distribution of Seigniorage from International Liquidity Creation' in R.A. Mundell and A.K. Swobota (eds.) Monetary Problems of the International Economy, Chicago: University of Chicago Press.

Guimbretiere, P. (1982), 'Les conditions d'un marché de l'ECU', Revue du Marché Commun, Novembre.

Gurley, J.G. and Shaw, E.S. (1960), Money in a Theory of Finance, Washington: The Brookings Institution.

Haberler, G. (1949), 'The Market for Foreign Exchange and the Stability of the Balance of Payments: a Theoretical Analysis', Kyklos, Vol. 3, pp. 193-218.

Hagemann, H. and Hamouda, O.F. (1991), 'Hicks on the European Monetary System', Kyklos, Vol. 44, pp. 411-429.

Hahn, F.H. (1982), Money and Inflation, Oxford: Blackwell.

Hahn, F. and M. Hollis (eds.) (1979), Philosophy and Economic Theory, N.Y.: Oxford University Press.

Hall, R.E. (1982), 'Optimal Fiduciary Monetary Systems' in 'Conference on Alternative Monetary Standards', University of Rochester, 15-16 October.

Hall, R. E. (1990), 'Comments and Discussion on Giovannini's Paper on 'European Monetary Reform: Progress and Prospects', Brookings Papers on Economic Activity, 2, pp. 211-291.

Hamada, K. (1974), 'Alternative Exchange Rate Systems and the Interdependence of Monetary Policies' in R.Z. Aliber (ed.) National Monetary Policies and the International Financial System, Chicago: University of Chicago Press.

Hamada, K. (1976), 'A Strategic Analysis on Monetary Interdependence', *Journal of Political Economy*, August, pp. 677-700.

Hamada, K. (1979), 'Macroeconomic Strategy and Coordination under Alternative Exchange Rates' in R. Dornbusch and J. A. Frenkel (eds.) *International Economic Policy*, Baltimore: John Hopkins University Press.

Hamouda, O. (1992), *John R. Hicks: An Intellectual Biography*, London: Blackwell Publishing.

Hamouda, O.F. and Price, B.B. (1991), *Verification in Economics and History: A Sequel to 'Scientification'*, London: Routledge.

Hamouda, O. and Rowley, R. (1988), *Expectations, Equilibrium and Dynamics: A History of Recent Economic Ideas and Practices*, Hertfordshire: Harvester-Wheatsheof.

Harcourt, G. C. (1972), *Some Cambridge Controversies in the Theory of Capital*, Cambridge: Cambridge University Press.

Harris, L. (1979), 'The Role of Money in the Economy', in F. Green and P. Nore (eds.) *Issues in Political Economy: A Critical Approach*, London: Macmillan.

Harris, L. (1981), *Monetary Theory*, London: McGraw-Hill.

Harrod, R.F. (1956), 'Walras: A Re-appraisal', *Economic Journal*, June, pp. 307-316.

Havelock, E.A. (1957), *'The Liberal Temper of Greek Politics'* (2nd printing), London: Cape.

Hawtrey, R.G. (1919), *'Currency and Credit'*, London: 2nd Edition, 1923, 3rd Edition, 1928.

Hawtrey, R.G. (1925), 'The State Theory of Money', *Economic Journal*, Vol. 35, pp. 251-255.

Head, J.G. (1962), 'Public Goods and Public Policy', *Public Finance*, XVII, No 3, pp. 197-219.

Healey, H.M. and Levine, P. (1992), 'Unpleasant Monetarist Arithmetic Revisited: Central Bank Independence, Fiscal Policy and European Monetary Union', *National Westminster Bank*, August, pp. 23-37.

Heinsohn, G. and Steiger, O. (1981), 'Money, Productivity and Uncertainty in Capitalism and Socialism', *Metroeconomica*, Vol.XXXIII, pp. 41-77.

Heinsohn, G. and Steiger, O. (1984), 'Marx and Keynes - Private Property and Money', *Economies et Sociétés*, Cahiers de l'ISMEA, Tome 29, No 4.

Heinsohn, G. and Steiger, O. (1986), 'Marx and Keynes - Private Property and Money', *University of Bremen, Economics Department*, Mimeo.

Heller, W.P. and Starrett, D.A. (1976), 'On the Nature of Externalities' in S.A.Y. Lin (ed.) *Theory and Measurement of Economic Externalities*, N.Y.: Academic Press.

Hellermann, R. (1979), *Gold, the Dollar, and the European Currency Systems: the Seven Year Monetary War*, N.Y.: Praeger Publishers.

Henderson, J.M. and Quandt, R.E. (1955), 'Walras, Leontief, and the

Interdependence of Economic Activities: Comment', *Quarterly Journal of Economics*, October, pp. 621-635.

Henning, C. R. (1991), 'Wake Up America!', *The International Economy*, March/April, pp. 63-66.

Hicks, J.R. (1933), 'Equilibrium and the Cycle', Zeitschrift fur Nationalokonomie, No 4, reprinted in his Essays No 3.

Hicks, J.R. (1934), 'Léon Walras', *Econometrica*, October, reprinted in his Essays No 7.

Hicks, J.R. (1937), 'Mr Keynes and the 'Classics'; A Suggested Interpretation', *Econometrica*, Vol. 5, April, pp. 147-159, reprinted in M.G. Muller (ed.) *Readings in Macroeconomics*, London: Holt, 1970.

Hicks, J.R. (1939), *Value and Capital. An Inquiry into some Fundamental Principles of Economic Theory*, Oxford: Oxford University Press, Second Edition, 1946.

Hicks, J. (1967), *Critical Essays in Monetary Theory*, Oxford: Clareton Press.

Hicks, J. (1969), *A Theory of Economic History*, Oxford: Clarendon Press.

Hicks, J. (1977), *Economic Perspectives, Further Essays on Money and Growth*, Oxford: Clarendon Press.

Hicks, J. (1982), *Money, Interest and Wages: Collected Essays on Economic Theory*', Vol. II, Oxford: Blackwell.

Hicks, J. (1989), *A Market Theory of Money*, Oxford: Clarendon Press.

Hochreither, E. and Knobl, A. (1991), 'Exchange Rate Policy of Austria and Finland, Two Examples of a Peg', *Pecunia*, October, pp. 33-61.

Hodgson, G. M. (1988), *Economics and Institutions: a Manifesto for a Modern Institutional Economics*, London: Polity Press.

Hollander, J.H. (1911), 'The Development of the Theory of Money from Adam Smith to David Ricardo', *Quarterly Journal of Economics*, Vol. 25, pp. 429-70.

Holtfrerich, C-L. (1989), 'The Monetary Unification Process in Nineteenth - Century Germany: Relevance and Lessons for Europe Today' in M. De Cecco and A. Giovannini (eds.) *A European Central Bank? Perspectives on Monetary Unification after Ten Years of the EMS, Cambridge*: Cambridge University Press.

Houmanidis, L.O. (1990), *Economic History of Greece* (in Greek), Athens: Papazisis.

House of Commons, (1985), *The EMS: the Financial and Economic Consequences of UK Membership of the EC*, 13th Report from the Treasury and Civil Service Committee, Vol. I and II, London: HMSO, 29 October.

Howitt, P.W. (1973), 'Walras and Monetary Theory', *Western Economic Journal*, December, pp. 487-499.

Hume, D., 'On Money' in his Political Discourses, 1752 (ed.) by E. Rotwein, *David Hume's Writings on Economics*, London: Nelson, 1955.

Ingram, C. J. (1973), 'The Case for European Monetary Integration', *Princeton Essays in International Finance*, No 98.

International Monetary Fund, (1987), *The Role of the SDR in the International Monetary System*, Washington: IMF Occasional Paper 51.

International Monetary Fund, (1993a), *A Note on Macroeconomic Causes of Recent Exchange Market Turbulance*, Washington: Document SM/93/16.

International Monetary Fund, (1993b), *International Capital Markets - Developments and Prospects, and Key Policy Issues, Part I - Background Material*, Washington: Document SM/93/38.

Isard, P. (1978), 'Exchange-rate Determination', *Princeton Studies in International Finance*, No 42.

Ishiyama, Y. (1975), 'The Theory of Optimum Currency Areas: A Survey', *IMF Staff Papers*, Vol. 22, pp. 344-383.

Jaffé, W. (1967), 'Walras' Theory of Tatonnement: A Critique of Recent Interpretations', *Journal of Political Economy*, 75, pp. 1-19, reprinted in Jaffé (1983).

Jaffé, W. (1972), 'Léon Walras' Role in the 'Marginal Revolution' of the 1870's', *History of Political Economy*, 4, Fall, pp. 379-405, reprinted in Jaffé (1983).

Jaffé, W. (1980), 'Walras' Economics as Others See it', *Journal of Economic Literature*, June, pp. 528-549 reprinted in Jaffé (1983).

Jaffé, W. (1942), 'Léon Walras' Theory of Capital Accumulation' in O. Lange (ed.), *Studies in Mathematical Economics and Econometrics*, Chicago University of Chicago Press, reprinted in Jaffé (1983).

Jaffé, W. (1983), *Essays on Walras* edited by D. A. Walker, Cambridge: Cambridge University Press.

Jenkins, R. (1978), 'European Monetary Union', *Lloyds Bank Review*, January, pp. 1-15.

Jevons, W. S. (1871), *The Theory of Political Economy*, London.

Joachim, H.H. (1951), 'Aristotle: The Nicomachean Ethics; A Commentary', in D.A. Rees (ed.), London: Oxford.

Jeoffre, A. (1986), 'G.F. Knapp et l'ECU', *Economie et Humanisme*, janvier, pp. 33-41.

Johnson, C. (1980), 'Slow Progress in Adopting the ECU', *The Banker*, November, pp. 29-32.

Johnson, H.G. (1969a), 'Inside Money, Outside Money, Income, Wealth and Welfare in Monetary Theory', *Journal of Money, Credit and Banking*, February, pp. 30-45, reprinted in Johnson (1978).

Johnson, H.G. (1969b), 'The Case for Flexible Exchange Rates, 1969', *Federal Reserve Bank of St. Louis Review*, June.

Johnson, H.G. (1970), 'Is there an Optimal Money Supply?', *Journal of Finance*, Vol. XXV, No 2, pp. 435-42, reprinted in Johnson (1978).

Johnson, H.G. (1978), *Selected Essays in Monetary Economics*, London:

Allen and Unwin.

Jones, R. (1976), 'The Origin and Development of Media of Exchange', *Journal of Political Economy*, August, pp. 757-76.

Kahn, R.F. (1954), 'Some Notes on Liquidity Preference', *The Manchester School of Economics and Social Studies*, Vol. XXII, pp. 229-257.

Kaldor, N. (1970), 'The Case for Regional Policies', *Scottish Journal of Political Economy*, Vol. 17, pp. 337-347.

Kaldor, N. (1972), 'The Irrelevance of Equilibrium Economics', *Economic Journal*, Vol. 82, reprinted in his *Further Essays on Economic Theory*, London: Duckworth, 1978.

Kaldor, N. (1985), *Economics without Equilibrium, The A.M. Okun Memorial Lectures*, Cardiff: University College Cardiff Press.

Kalecki, M. (1935), 'A Macrodynamic Theory of Business Cycles', *Econometrica*, 3, pp. 327-344.

Kanta, H. (1992), 'Systemic Risk and International Finance Markets' in F.R. Edwards and H.T. Patrick (eds.), *Regulating International Financial Markets: Issues and Policies*, Boston: Kluner.

Kaufmann, H.M. (1985), 'The Deutsche Mark between the Dollar and the European Monetary System', *Kredit und Kapital*, Jahrg., pp. 188-212.

Kees, A. (1987), 'The Monetary Committee of the European Community', *Kredit und Kapital*, 20, Heff 2, pp. 258-267.

Kenen, P. B. (1969), 'The Theory of Optimum Currency Areas: An Eclectic View' in R.A. Mundell and A.K. Swobota (eds.), *Monetary Problems of the International Economy*, Chicago: University of Chicago Press.

Keynes, J. M. (1923), *A Tract on Monetary Reform*, London: Macmillan, 3rd edition reprinted in his CW, Vol. IV., London: Macmillan.

Keynes, J. M. (1926), *The End of Laissez-Faire*, London: Hogarth.

Keynes, J. M. (1930), *A Treatise on Money*, Vol. I: The Pure Theory of Money, Vol. II: The Applied Theory of Money, London: Macmillan.

Keynes, J. M. (1936), *The General Theory of Employment, Interest and Money*, London: Macmillan.

Keynes, J. M. (1937a), *The General Theory of Employment*, Quarterly Journal of Economics, February, pp. 209-223.

Keynes, J. M. (1937b), 'Alternative Theories of the Rate of Interest', *Economic Journal*, June, pp. 241-252.

Keynes, J. M. (1937c), 'The 'Ex-Ante' Theory of the Rate of Interest', *Economic Journal*, December, pp. 663-669.

Keynes, J. M. (1980), *Activities 1940-4: Shaping the Post-War World: The Clearing Union*' in his CW, Vol. XXV, London: Macmillan.

Keynes, J. M. (1980), *Speech at the House of Lords on the Clearing Union on 23 May 1944* in his CW, Vol. XXVI, London: Macmillan.

Khan, W. and Willen, T.D. (1984), 'The Monetary Approach to Exchange Rates: A Review of Recent Empirical Studies', *Kredit and Kapital*, January, pp. 199-222.

Kindleberger, C. P. (1983), 'Standards as Public, Collective and Private Goods', *Kyklos*, Vol. 36, Fasc. 3,, pp. 377-396.

Kindleberger, C. P. (1986), 'International Public Goods without International Government', *American Economic Review*, March, pp. 1-13.

King, R. G. (1983), 'On the Economics of Private Money', *Journal of Monetary Economics*, 12, No 1, pp. 127-158.

King, R. G. and Plosser, C. I. (1986), 'Money as the Mechanism of Exchange', *Journal of Monetary Economics*, 17, pp. 93-115.

Kiyokaki, N. and Wright, R. (1989), 'On Money as a Medium of Exchange', *Journal of Political Economy*, Vol. 97, No. 4, pp. 927-954.

Klein, B. (1974), 'The Competitive Supply of Money', *Journal of Money, Credit and Banking*, November, pp. 243-253.

Klein, B. (1978a), 'Money, Wealth and Seigniorage' in K. Boulding and T.F. Wilson (eds.), *Redistribution through the Financial System: the Grants Economics of Money and Credit*, N.Y.: Praeger.

Klein, B. (1978b), 'Competing Monies, European Monetary Union and the Dollar' in M. Fratianni and T. Peeters (eds.), *One Money for Europe*, London: MacMillan.

Klein, M. and Neumann, M. J. M. (1990), 'Seigniorage: What Is It and Who Gets It?', *Weltwirtschaftliches Archiv*, Band 126, pp. 205-221.

Kloten, N. (1989), 'The Delors Report: A Blueprint for European Integration?', *World Today*, Vol. 45, pp. 191-194.

Knapp, G. P. (1905), *The State Theory of Money*, 2nd edition in 1918; 3rd edition in 1921; 4th edition in 1923 and translated by H. M. Lucas and J. Bonar, London: Macmillan, 1924.

Kolm, S-C. (1972), 'External Liquidity - A Study in Monetary Welfare Economics' in G. P. Szego and K. Shell (eds.), *Mathematical Methods in Investment and Finance*, London.

Krause, L. B. and Salant W. S. (1973) (eds.), *European Monetary Unification and its Meaning for the U.S.*, Washington: Brookings Institution.

Krause, U. (1982), *Money and Abstract Labour*, London: Verso.

Kregel, J. A. (1976), 'Economic Methodology in the Face of Uncertainty: the Modelling Methods of Keynes and the Post Keynesians', *Economic Journal*, 86, pp. 209-225.

Kregel, J. A. (1982), 'Microfoundations and Hicksian Monetary Theory', *De Economist*, 130, N.R. 4, pp. 463-492.

Kregel, J. (1990), 'The Formation of Fix and Flex Prices and Monetary Theory: An Appraisal of John Hick's 'A Market Theory of Money", *Banca Nazionale del Lavoro*, No 175, pp. 475-486.

Krugman, P. (1984), 'The International Role of the Dollar: Theory and Prospect' in J.F.O. Bilson and R.C. Marston (eds.) *'Exchange Rate Theory and Practice'*, Chicago: University of Chicago Press.

Krugman, P. (1989), 'Policy Problems of a Monetary Union', MIT *Mimeo*.

Kruse, D.C. (1980), *Monetary Integration in Western Europe: EMU, EMS and Beyond*, London: Butterworths.

Kuenne, R. E. (1954), 'Walras, Leontief and the Interdependence of Economic Activities', *Quarterly Journal of Economics*, August, pp. 323-354.

Kuenne, R. E. (1956), 'The Architectonics of Léon Walras', *Kyklos*, Vol. IX, pp. 241-249.

Kuenne, R. E. (1958), 'On the Existence and Role of Money in a Stationary System', *Southern Economic Journal*, XXV, pp. 1-10.

Kuenne, R. E. (1961), 'The Walrasian Theory of Money: An Interpretation and a Reconstruction', *Metroeconomica*, August, pp. 94-105.

Kuenne, R. E. (1963), *The Theory of General Economic Equilibrium*, Princeton: Princeton University Press.

Kuhne, K. (1979), *Economics and Marxism*, London: Macmillan.

Kuhn, T.S. (1970), *The Structure of Scientific Revolutions*, Chicago: Chicago University Press, 1962.

Kydland, F. and Prescott, E. (1977), 'Rules rather than Discretion: the Inconsistency of Optimal Plans', *Journal of Political Economy*, Vol. 85, No 3, pp. 473-491.

Laistner, M.L.W. (1923), *Greek Economics*, London and Toronto: Dent.

Laidler, D. (1969), 'The Definition of Money: Theoretical and Empirical Problems', *Journal of Money, Credit and Banking*, Vol. 1, pp. 508-525.

Lamfalussy, A. (1979), 'The Failure of Global Flexibility?' in R. Triffin (ed.), *'EMS: the Emerging European Monetary System'*, Bulletin of the National Bank of Belgium, April.

Lamfalussy, A. (1989), 'Macro-coordination of Fiscal Policies in an Economic and Monetary Union in Europe' in Delors Committee for the Study of Economic and Monetary Union *Report on Economic and Monetary Union in the European Community, Luxembourg*: Office for Official Publications of the EC.

Lange, O. (1938), 'The Rate of Interest and the Optimum Propensity to Consume', *Economica*, V, pp. 169-192.

Lange, O. (1942), 'Say's Law: A Restatement and Criticism' in O. Lange et al. (ed.) *Studies in Mathematical Economics and Econometrics*, Chicago: Chicago University Press.

Langholm, O. (1979), *Price and Value in the Aristotelian Tradition*, Bergen, Norway: Universitetsforlaget.

Laursen, S. and Metzler, L.A. (1950), 'Flexible Exchange Rates and the Theory of Employment', *Review of Economics and Statistics*, 32, pp. 281-99.

Le Cacheux, J; Mathieu, C. and Sterdyniak, H. (1990), 'The Private ECU: A Step towards the Single European Currency?', in Association for the Monetary Union of Europe (AMUE), *A Strategy for the ECU*, London: Kogan Page.

Leduc, G. (1950), 'Schumpeter, Disciple de Walras', *Economie Appliquee*, III, pp. 450-453.

Leijonhufrud, A. (1968), *On Keynesian Economics and the Economics of Keynes - A Study in Monetary Theory*, N.Y.: Oxford University Press.

Leijonhufrud, A. (1981), 'The Wicksell Connection: Variations on a Theme' in his *Information and Coordination: Essays in Macroeconomic Theory*, Oxford: Oxford University Press.

Lerner, A. P. (1952), 'The Essential Properties of Interest and Money', *Quarterly Journal of Economics*, May, pp. 172-193.

Lomax, D.F. (1983a), 'Prospects for the European Monetary System', *National Westminster Bank Quarterly Review*, May.

Lomax, D.F. (1983), 'International Moneys and Monetary Arrangements' in G.M. von Furstenberg (ed.) *International Money and Credit: the Policy Roles*, Washington, D.C.: IMF.

Louis, J-V. et al. (1989), *Vers un système européen de banques centrales*, Bruxelles: Editions de l'Université de Bruxelles.

Lowry, S. T. (1965), 'The Classical Greek Theory of Natural Resource Economics', *Land Economics*, XLI, No 3, pp. 208-219.

Lowry, S. T. (1987), *The Archeology of Economic Ideas. The Classical Greek Traditions*, Durham: Duke University Press.

Lucas, R.E. (1972), 'Expectations and the Neutrality of Money', *Journal of Economic Theory*, 4, pp. 103-24.

Lucas, R.E. (1981), *Studies in Business-Cycle Theory*, Cambridge, Mass.: MIT Press.

Lucas, R.E. (1984), 'Money in a Theory of Finance' in K. Brunner and A.H. Meltzer (eds.) *Essays on Macroeconomic Implications of Financial and Labour Markets and Political Processes*, Amsterdam: North-Holland.

Ludlow, P. (1982), *The Making of the European System*, Toronto: Butterworths.

MacDougall Report, (1975), *The Role of Public Finances in European Integration: Vol. I and II*, Brussels: Commission of EC.

Magnifico, G. and Williamson, J.H. (1972), *European Monetary Integration*, London: Federal Trust Report.

Marget, A. W. (1931), 'Leon Walras and the 'Cash-Balance Approach' to the Problem of the Value of Money', *Journal of Political Economy*, October, pp. 569-600.

Marget, A. W. (1935), 'The Monetary Aspects of the Walrasian System', *Journal of Political Economy*, April, pp. 145-186.

Marget, A. W. (1966), The Theory of Prices', 2 Vols., N.Y., A.M. Kelley Publishers.

Marjolin Study Group, (1974), *On Economic and Monetary Union 1980*, Brussels: Commission of the EC: II/675/3/74-E fin.

Marston, R.C. (1984), 'Exchange Rate Unions as an Alternative to Flexible

Exchange Rates' in J.F.O. Bilson and R.C. Marston (eds.) *Exchange Rate Theory and Practice*, Cambridge, Mass.: MBER.

Marsh, D. (1993), *The Bundesbank: The Bank that Rules Europe*, London: Mandarin Paperback.

Marty, A. (1967), 'Growth and the Welfare Cost of Inflationary Finance', *Journal of Political Economy*, February, pp. 71-76.

Marx, K. (1971), *A Contribution to the Critique of Political Economy* with an Introduction by Maurice Dobb, London: Lawrence and Wishart.

Marx, K. (1974), *Capital*, Vol: I-III, London: Lawrence and Wishart.

Masera, R.S. (1981), 'The First Two Years of the EMS: the Exchange Rate Experience', *Banca Nazionale del Lavoro*, September.

Masera, R. S. (1982), *Determinants of the Growth of the Euro-Currency Markets*, Basel: BIS., September.

Masera, R. S. (1987), 'An Increasing Role for the ECU: A Character in Search of a Script', *Princeton Essays in International Finance*, No 167.

Masera, R. S. (1989), 'Panel Discussion: The Prospects for a European Central Bank' in De Cecco, M. and Giovannini, A. (eds.) *A European Central Bank? Perspectives on Monetary Unification after Ten Years of the EMS*, Cambridge: Cambridge University Press.

Matthes, H. (1987), 'Toughest Test for the EMS', *European Affairs*, No 2, pp. 52-63.

Matthews, R.C.O. (1986), 'The Economics of Institutions and the Sources of Growth', *Economic Journal*, 96, pp. 903-910.

Mayer, H. W. (1985), *Interaction between the Euro-Currency Markets and the Exchange Markets*, Basle: BIS Economic Papers, No 15.

Mayer, H. W. (1986), *Private ECUs Potential Macro-Economic Policy Dimensions*, Basle: BIS Economic Papers No 16.

Mazas, C. and Santini, J-J. (1988), 'L'Entrée de la livre dans le SME après les accords de Nyborg: quelques éléments de réflexions', *Revue d'économie politique*, No 6.

McCallum, B. T. (1984), 'Are Bond-Financed Deficits Inflationary? A Ricardian Analysis', *Journal of Political Economy*, Vol. 92, N 1, pp. 123-35.

McDonough, W.J. (1993), 'The Global Derivatives Market', *Federal Reserve Bank of New York Quarterly Review*, Vol. 18, No 3, pp.1-5.

McKenzie, G. (1990), 'Capital Adequacy Requirements, Deposit Insurance and Bank Behaviour', *Economic and Social Review*, Vol 21, N 4, pp. 363-75.

McKinnon R.I. (1963), 'Optimum Currency Areas', *American Economic Review*, Vol. 53, pp. 718-25.

McKinnon, R.I. (1969), 'Private and Official International Money: The Case for the Dollar', *Princeton Essays in International Finance*, No 74.

McKinnon, R.I. (1982), 'Currency Substitution and Instability in the World Dollar Standard', *American Economic Review*, June, pp. 320-333.

McKinnon, R.I. (1984), '*An International Standard for Monetary*

Stabilization', Washington, D.C., Institute for International Economics.

McKinnon, R.I. (1986), 'The Case for Internationalizing American Monetary Policy' in L. Tsoukalis (ed.), *Europe, America and the World Economy*, London: Blackwell.

Meade, J.E. (1951), *The Balance of Payments - The Theory of International Economic Policy*, London: Oxford University Press.

Meade, J. E. (1952), 'External Economies and Diseconomies in a Competitive Situation', *Economic Journal*, March, pp. 54-67.

Meade, J.E. (1955), 'The Case for Variable Exchange Rates', *Three Banks Review*, September, pp. 3-27.

Meade, J.E. (1973), *The Theory of Economic Externalities - The Control of Environmental Pollution and Similar Social Costs*, Geneve: Institut Universitaire de Hautes Etudes Internationales.

Meade, J.E. (1989), 'The International Application of National Macroeconomic Control Rules: A Note', *Department of Applied Economics*, Cambridge University, Working Paper, 8911.

Meade, J.E. (1990), 'The EMU and the Control of Inflation', *Oxford Review of Economic Policy*, Vol. 6, No 4, pp. 100-107.

Melvin, M. (1985), 'Currency Substitution and Western Monetary Unification', *Economica*, 52, pp. 79-91.

Menger, C. (1892), 'On the Origin of Money', *Economic Journal*, Vol. II, pp. 239-55.

Micossi, S. and Padoa-Schioppa, (1984), 'Short-Term Interest Rates Linkages Between the U.S. and Europe', *Banca d'Italia, Temi di Discussione*, No 33, Agosto.

Micossi, S. (1985), 'The Intervention and Financing Mechanisms of the EMS and the Role of the ECU', *Banca Nazionale del Lavoro*, No 155, pp. 327-345.

Mill, J. S. (1848), *Principles of Political Economy with Some of their Applications to Social Philosophy*, Vol. II, London: First edition; fifth edition in 1895.

Miller, M.H. and Williamson, J. (1988), 'The International Monetary System: An Analysis of Alternative Regimes', *European Economic Review*, Vol. 32, pp. 1031-54.

Minehan, C.E. (1986), *Remarks on US Large Dollar Payment Systems*, Paris: ECU Banking Association, No 1.

Minsky, H.P. (1975), *John Maynard Keynes*, N.Y.: Columbia University Press.

Minsky, H.P. (1978), 'The Financial Instability Hypothesis: A Restatement', *Thames Papers in Political Economy*.

Minsky, H.P. (1982), *Can 'It' Happen Again? Essays on Instability and Finance*, N.Y.: M.E. Sharpe, Inc.

Minsky, H.P. (1983), 'The Legacy of Keynes', *Metroeconomica*, Vol.

290

XXXV, pp. 87-103.

Miron, J.A. (1989), 'The Founding of the Fed and the Destabilization of the post-1914 US Economy' in M. de Cecco and A. Giovannini (eds.) *A European Central Bank? Perspectives on Monetary Unification after Ten Years of the EMS*, Cambridge: Cambridge University Press.

Mitchell, J. (1991), *Banker's Racket or Consumer Benefit? A Consumer View of the Single European Market for Financial Services*, London: Policy Studies Institute.

Modigliani, F. (1944), 'Liquidity Preference and the Theory of Interest and Money', *Econometrica*, January, pp. 79.

Monroe, A.E., (1923), *Monetary Theory before Adam Smith*, Cambridge: Harvard University Press.

Monroe, A.E. (ed.), (1924) *'Early Economic Thought: Selections from Econ. Literature prior to A. Smith'*, Cambridge: Harvard University Press.

Moore, B.J. (1978), 'Monetary Factors' in A.S. Eichner (ed.) *A Guide to Post-Keynesian Economics*, N.Y.: M.E. Sharpe, Inc.

Morishima, M. (1976), *The Economic Theory of Modern Society*, Cambridge: Cambridge University Press.

Morishima, M. (1977), *Walras' Economics - A pure theory of capital and money*, Cambridge: Cambridge University Press.

Moss, F. (1984), 'The Private Use of the ECU: its Implications for National Monetary Authorities in EEC Member States', *Revue de la Banque*, No 2, February, pp. 41-64.

Mundell, R.A. (1961), 'A Theory of Optimum Currency Areas', *American Economic Review*, Vol. 51, pp. 657-665.

Mundell, R.A. (1962), 'The Appropriate Use of Monetary and Fiscal Policy under Fixed Exchange Rates', *IMF Staff Papers*, March, pp. 70-77.

Mundell, R.A. (1968), *International Economics*, N.Y. Macmillan.

Mundell, R. (1970), 'Plan pour une monnaie européenne' in P. Salin (ed.) *L'Unification monétaire européenne*, Paris: Calmann-Levy.

Mundell, R. A. (1973a), 'Uncommon Arguments for Common currencies' in H.G. Johnson and A.K. Swoboda (eds.) *The Economics of Common Currencies*, London: Allen and Unwin, pp. 114-132.

Mundell, R. A. (1973b), 'A Plan for a European Currency' in H. Johnson and A. Swoboda (eds.) *The Economics of Common Currencies*, London: Allen and Unwin, pp. 143-172.

Mundell, R. (1980), 'Comments on J.J. Polak's Paper on the EMF: External Relations', *Banca Nazionale del Lavoro*, September, pp. 376-381.

Mussa, M. (1984), 'The Theory of Exchange Rate Theory' in J.F.O. Bilson and R.C. Marston *Exchange Rate Theory and Practice*, Chicago: University of Chicago Press.

Myrdal, G. (1931), *Monetary Equilibrium*, Original Swedish text, German translation by F.A. Hayek; English text translated from German, London: W.

Hodge and Co., 1939.

Myrdal, G. (1958), *Economic Theory and Underdeveloped Regions*, Bombay: Vora and Co.

Nagel, E. (1963), 'Assumptions in Economic Theory', *American Economic Review, Papers and Proceedings*, May, pp. 211-9.

Narassiguin, P. (1992), 'La problématique de la monnaie unique et son application au cas de l'Europe', *Revue d'Economie Politique*, Novembre-Decembre, pp. 799-842.

Neumann, M.J.M. (1991), 'Central Bank Independence as a Prerequisite of Price stability', *European Economy, Special Edition*, No 1.

Niebyl, K.H. (1946), *Studies in the Classical Theories of Money*, N.Y.: Columbia University Press

Niehans, J. (1971), 'Money and Barter in General Equilibrium with Transactions Costs' *American Economic Review*, December, pp. 773-783.

Niehans, J. (1987), 'Classical Monetary Theory, New and Old', *Journal of Money, Credit and Banking*, Vol. 19, No 4, pp. 409-424.

Nooman, J.T. (1957), *The Scholastic Analysis of Usury*, Cambridge: Harvard University Press.

North, D. C. (1981), *Structure and Change in Economic History*, N.Y.: Norton.

North, D. C. (1990), *Institutions, Institutional Change and Economic Performance*, Cambridge: Cambridge University Press.

North, D. C. (1991), 'Institutions', *The Journal of Economic Perspectives*, Vol. 5, No 1, pp. 97-112.

North, R. (1981), Ike, N. and Triska, J., *The World of Superpowers*, Stanford: Notrik Press.

Obstfeld, M. (1985), 'Floating Exchange Rates: Experience and Prospects', *Brookings Papers on Economic Activity*, 2.

O'Connell, T. (1992), 'Do Regions Naturally Converge or Diverge in an Economic and Monetary Union?', *Central Bank of Ireland*, Spring.

Ohlin, B. (1937), 'Some Notes on the Stockholm Theory of Savings and Investment', *Economic Journal*, March and June, pp. 53-69 and 221-240.

Optical Report 1975, (1976), *Towards Economic Equilibrium and Monetary Unification in Europe*, Brussels: Commission: II/909/75-E final, January.

Optical Report 1976, (1977), *Inflation and Exchange Rates: Evidence and Policy Guidelines for the EC*, Brussels, Commission: February.

Organisation for Economic Cooperation and Development, (1987), *Prudential Supervision in Banking*, Paris: OECD.

Ostroy, J.M. (1973), 'The Informational Efficiency of Monetary Exchange', *American Economic Review*, 63, No 4, pp. 597-610.

Padoa-Schioppa, T. (1980), 'The EMF: Topics for Discussion', *Banca Nazionale del Lavoro*, No 134, pp. 317-343.

Padoa-Schioppa, T. (1986), 'Lessons from the European Monetary System', *Bank of Italy, Economic Bulletin*, No 2, pp. 63-72.

292

Padoa-Schioppa Study Group Report, (1987), *Efficiency Stability and Equity, Strategy for the Evolution of the Economic System of the European Community, Brussels*: Commission, DG II, April.

Padoa-Schioppa, (1988), 'The European Monetary System: a Long-Term View' in F. Giavazzi, S. Micossi and M. Miller (eds) *The European Monetary System*, Cambridge: Cambridge University Press.

Page, S.A. (1981), 'The Choice of Invoicing Currency in Merchandise Trade', *National Institute Economic Review*, November.

Pasinetti, L. L. (1981), *Structural Change and Economic Growth: A Theoretical Essay on the Dynamics of the Wealth of Nations*, Cambridge: Cambridge University Press.

Patinkin, D. (1965), *Money, Interest and Prices - An Integration of Monetary and Value Theory*, Second Edition, N.Y.: Harper and Row.

Patinkin, D. (1976), 'Keynes' Monetary Thought: A Study of its Development', *History of Political Economy*, 8, Spring, pp. 1-150.

Pearson, G. (1972), 'The Role of Money in Economic Growth', *Quarterly Journal of Economics*, Vol. 86, pp. 381-394.

Perroux, F. (1991), *L'Economie du XXe siècle*, Grenoble: Presses Universitaires de Grenoble.

Pesek, J.G. and Saving, T.R. (1967), *Money, Wealth and Economic Theory*, N.Y.: Macmillan.

Phelps, E. E. (1973), 'Inflation in the Theory of Public Finance', *Swedish Journal of Economics*, Vol. 75, pp. 67-82.

Pigou, A. C. (1946), *The Economics of Welfare*, 4th Edition, London: Macmillan.

Plato, (1926), *The Laws*, Vol. I and II translated by R.G. Bury, Loeb Classical Library, London: W. Heinemann Ltd.

Plato, (1930), *Republic*, Vol. I and II translated by Paul Shorey, Loeb Classical Library, London: W. Heinemann Ltd.

Pöhl, K. (1989), 'The Further Development of the European Monetary System' in Delors Committee for the Study of Economic and Monetary Union *Report on Economic and Monetary Union in the European Community, Luxembourg*: Office for Official Publications of the EC.

Pöhl, K. O. (1990), 'Prospects of the European Monetary Union' in Centre for Economic Performance of LSE (eds.), *Britain and EMU*, London: London School of Economics.

Pöhl, K.O. (1993), 'How to Save the European Monetary System', *The Wall Street Journal*, 1 February.

Polak, J. J. (1979), 'The SDR as a Basket of Currencies', *IMF Staff Papers*, December, pp. 627-53.

Polak, J. J. (1980), 'The EMF: External Relations', *Banca Nazionale del Lavoro*, September, pp. 359-381.

Polanyi, K. (1944), *The Great Transformation*, N.Y.: Rinehart.

Polanyi, K. (1957), 'Aristotle Discovers the Economy' in K. Polanyi, C.M. Arensberg, H.W. Pearson (eds.) *Trade and Market in the Early Empires*, N.Y.: Free Press

Polanyi, M. (1967), *The Tacit Dimension*, London: Routledge and Kegan P.

Popper, K. R. (1972), *Conjectures and Refutations: the Growth of Scientific Knowledge*, London: Routledge and Kegan Paul.

Prate, A. (1992), 'Prudential Supervision within EMU', *The ECU today*, Special Issue, November.

Rachline, F. (1982), 'La Nature de la Monnaie', *Revue Economique*, Vol. 33, pp. 446-475.

Radford, R.A. (1945), 'The Economic Organisation of a P.O.W. Camp', *Economica*, Vol. 12, pp. 189-201.

Reading, B. (1979), 'The Long Road to EMS', *Euromoney*, January, pp. 38-55.

Reck, H. (1935), *Economic Thought and its Institutional Background*, London: Macmillan.

Rey, J-J. (1982), 'Some Comments on the Merits and Limits of the Indicator of Divergence in the EMS', *Revue de la Banque*, No 1, pp. 11-25.

Riboud, J. (1991), *The Mechanics of Money*, London: Macmillan.

Riboud, J. (1992), 'The ECU: an Uncomplete Currency', *ECU No 21*, IV.

Ricardo, D. (1971), *On the Principles of Political Economy and Taxation*, London: Pelican Books (based on the 3rd edition published in 1821; first edition in 1817).

Rist, C. (1940), *History of Monetary and Credit Theory from John Law and the Present Day*, London: Allen and Unwin.

Robbins, L. (1984), *An Essay on the Nature and Significance of Economic Science*, London: Macmillan, 1st Edition, 1932, 2nd Edition, 1935, 3rd Edition.

Robbins, L. (1981), 'Economics and Political Economy', *American Economic Review*, Vol. 71, reprinted in his *An Essay on the Nature and Significance of Economic Science*, London: Macmillan 3rd Edition, 1984.

Robertson, D. H. (1922), *Money*, London: Nisbet and Co. Ltd.

Robertson, D. H. (1936), 'Some Notes on Mr. Keynes' General Theory of Employment', *Quarterly Journal of Economics*, November, pp. 168-191.

Robertson, D. H. (1938), 'Mr Keynes and 'Finance', *Economic Journal*, June, pp. 314-322.

Robinson, J. (1952), *The Generalisation of the General Theory and Other Essays*, First Edition as 'The Rate of Interest and Other Essays' Second Edition 1979, London: Macmillan, 1979.

Robinson, J. (1964), *Economic Philosophy*, London: Penguin Books, first published by C.A. Watts in 1962.

Robinson, J. (1971), *Economic Heresies, Some Old-Fashioned Questions in Economic Theory*, London: Macmillan.

Robinson, J. and Eatwell, J. (1973), *In Introduction to Modern Economics*,

London: McGraw-Hill.

Robson, P. (1982), *The Economics of International Integration*, London: Allen and Unwin.

Rogers, C. (1989), *Money, Interest and Capital: A Study in the Foundations of Monetary Theory*, Cambridge: Cambridge University Press.

Rogoff, K. (985), 'Can Exchange Rate Predicability be Achieved without Monetary Convergence?' *European Economic Review*, Vol 28, pp. 93-115.

Rosenstein-Rodan, P.N. (1936), 'The Co-ordination of the General Theories of Money and Price', *Economica*, Vol. 3, pp. 257-280.

Rousseas, S. (1986), *Post Keynesian Monetary Economics*, London: Macmillan.

Rowthorn, R.E. (1977), 'Conflict, Inflation and Money', *Cambridge Journal of Economics*, 1, pp. 215-240.

Russo, M. and Tullio, G. (1988), *Monetary Coordination within the European Monetary System: Is there a Rule?* Washington: IMF, Occasional Paper No 61.

Sachs, J. and Sala-i-Martin, X. (1989), *Federal Fiscal Policy and Optimum Currency Areas*, Cambridge, Mass.: Harvard University Mimeo.

Saint-Germes, (1928), 'Les Théories Monétaires de la Grèce Antique', *Revue d'Histoire Economique et Sociale*.

Salin, P. (1979), *L'Unité Monétaire Européenne: Au Profit de Qui?*, Brussels: Institution Européenne.

Salin, P. (1984), (ed.), *Currency Competition and Monetary Union*, Amsterdam: Martinus Mijhoff Publishers.

Salop, J. (1981), 'The Divergence Indicator: Technical Note', *IMF Staff Papers*, December, pp. 682-697.

Samuelson, P. A. 'The Pure Theory of Public Expenditure', *Review of Economics and Statistics*, 36, pp. 387-89.

Samuelson, P. A. (1955), 'A Diagrammatic Exposition of a Theory of Public Expenditure', *Review of Economics and Statistics*, 37, pp. 350-56.

Samuelson, P.A. (1958), 'An Exact Consumption-Loan Model of Interest With and Without the Social Contrivance of Money', *Journal of Political Economy*, December, pp. 467-482.

Samuelson, P. A. (1968), 'What Classical and Neoclassical Monetary Theory Really Was', *Canadian Journal of Economics and Political Science*, February, pp. 1-15.

Samuelson, P. A. (1969), 'Non-Optimality of Money Holding under Laissez Faire', *Canadian Journal of Political Science*, May, pp. 301-308.

Sannucci, V. (1989), 'The Establishment of a Central Bank: Italy in the Nineteenth Century' in M. de Cecco and A. Giovanninni (eds.) *European Central Bank?*, Cambridge: Cambridge University Press.

Sarcinelli, M. (1986), 'The EMS and the International Monetary System: Towards Greater Stability', *Banca Nazionale del Lavoro*, No 156, pp. 57-83.

Sarcinelli, M. (1992), 'The European Central Bank: A Full-Fledged Scheme or Just a 'Fledgling'?, *Banca Nazionale del Lavoro*, No 181, pp. 119-144.

Sargent, T.J. (1973), 'Rational Expectations, the Real Rate of Interest, and the Natural Rate of Unemployment', *Brookings Papers on Economic Activity*, 2, pp. 429-472.

Sargent, T. and Wallace, N. (1976), 'Rational Expectations and the Theory of Economic Policy', *Journal of Monetary Economics*, April, pp. 221-250.

Sargent, T. J. and Wallace, N. (1981), 'Some Unpleasant Monetarist Arithmetic', *Federal Reserve Bank of Minneapolis, Quarterly Review*, Vol. 5, No 3.

Say, J. B. (1803), *A Treatise on Political Economy*, translated by C.C. Biddle, Philadelphia: Grigg and Elliot, reprinted in 1834.

Scharrer, H-E. (1991), 'European Monetary Union: No Field for Political Compromise', *Intereconomics*, November/December, pp. 259-264.

Schinasi, G. J. (1989), 'European Integration, Exchange Rates and Monetary Reform', *The World Economy*, Vol. 12, pp. 389-414.

Schmitt, B. (1975), *Monnaie, Salaires et Profit*, Paris: Castella.

Schmitt, B. (1977), *L'Or, le Dollar et la Monnaie supra-nationale*, Paris: Calmann-Levy.

Schmitt, B. (1988), *L'ECU et les souverainetés nationales en Europe*, Paris: Dumod.

Schumpeter, J. A. (1934), *The Theory of Economic Development*, Oxford: Oxford University Press.

Schumpeter, J. A. (1939), *Business Cycles: a Theoretical, Historical and Statistical Analysis of the Capitalist Process*, N.Y.: McGraw-Hill.

Schumpeter, J. A. (1954), *History of Economic Analysis*, N.Y.: Oxford University Press.

Scitorsky, T. (1954), 'Two Concepts of External Economies', *Journal of Political Economics*, 62, pp. 143-151.

Scitorsky, T. (1958), *Economic Theory and Western European Integration*, London: Unwin University Books.

Scott, A. (1986), 'Britain and the EMS: An Appraisal of the Report of the Treasury and Civil Service Committee', *Journal of Common Market Studies*, March, pp. 157-168.

Selgin, G. A. (1988), *The Theory of Free Banking*, New Jersey: Rowman and Littlefield.

Senior, N. W. (1840), *Three Lectures on the Value of Money* delivered before the University of Oxford, London: LSE reprint series in 1829, No 4 in series of Reprints of Scarce Tracts in Economic and Political Science by London School of Economics and Political Science, London: B. Fellowes.

Shackle, G.L.S. (1945), 'Myrdal's analysis of Monetary Equilibrium', *Oxford Economic Papers*, March, pp. 47-66.

Shackle, G.L.S. (1967), *The Years of High Theory - Invention and Tradition in Economic Thought, 1926-1939*, London: Cambridge University Press.

Shackle, G.L.S. (1982), 'Sir John Hicks' 'IS-LM: An Explanation': A Comment', *Journal of Post Keynesian Economics*, Vol. IV, pp. 435-438.

Simmel, G. (1900), *The Philosophy of Money*, 2nd enlarged edition in 1907 which runs up to six editions in 1958. 2nd enlarged edition was translated by T. Bottomore and D. Frisby, London: Routledge and Kegan Paul, 1978.

Simons, H. C. (1936), 'Rule versus Authorities in Monetary Policy', *Journal of Political Economy*, No 44, pp. 1-30.

Skemp, J. B. (1980), 'The Permanent Importance of Greek Studies', *The Durham University Journal*, Vol. LXXIII 1, pp. 1-7.

Smith, A. (1776), *An Inquiry into the Nature and Causes of the Wealth of Nations*, Edited, with an introduction, notes, marginal summary and an enlarged index by Edwin Cannan, N.Y.: Modern Library, 1937.

Smithin, J. N. (1984), 'Financial Innovation and Monetary Theory', *The Three Banks Review*, No 144, pp. 26-38.

Souchon, A. (1898), *Les Théories Economiques dans la Grèce Antique*, Paris: L. Larosse.

Soudek, J. (1952), 'Aristotle's Theory of Exchange. An Inquiry into the Origin of Economic Analysis', *Proceedings of the American Philosophical Society*, Vol. 96, No 1, pp. 64-68.

Spanish Ministry of Economics and Finance, (1991) 'The ECU and the ESCB during Stage Two', *Mimeo*, 24 January.

Spaventa, L. (1987), 'The Growth of Public Debt: Sustainability, Fiscal Rules, and Monetary Rules', *IMF Staff Papers*, Vol. 34, No 2, pp. 374-99.

Spaventa, L. (1989), 'Seigniorage: Old and New Policy Issues', *European Economic Review*, Vol 33, pp. 557-563.

Spengler, J. J. (1955), 'Aristotle on Economic Imputation and Related Matters', *Southern Economics Journal*, XXI, pp. 371-389.

Sraffa, P. (1932), 'Dr Hayek on Money and Capital', *Economic Journal*, Vol. XLII, pp. 42-53.

Sraffa, P. (1960), *Production of Commodities by Means of Commodities: Prelude to a Critique of Economic Theory*, Cambridge: Cambridge University Press.

Steil, B. (1992), 'Regulatory Foundations for Global Capital Markets' in R. O'Brien *Finance and the International Economy 6: the AMEX Bank Review Prize Essays*, Oxford: Oxford University Press.

Stein, J. (1987), 'Informational Externalities and Welfare-reducing Speculation', *Journal of Political Economy*, Vol. 95, pp. 1123-1145.

Steinherr, A. (1984), 'Convergence and Coordination of Macroeconomic Policies: some Basic Issues', *European Economy*, No 20.

Stigler, G. (1961), 'The Economics of Information', *Journal of Political Economy*, 66, pp. 213-25.

Summers, L.H. and Summers, V.P. (1990), 'When Financial Markets Work

Too Well: A Case for a Securities Transaction Tax' in D. R. Siegel (ed.) *Innovation and Technology in the Markets*, Chicago: Probus.

Tarshis, L. (1984), World Economy in Crisis: Unemployment, Inflation and International Debt', Toronto: Canadian Institute for Economic Policy.

Tavlas, G. S. (1990), 'On the International Use Currencies: The Case of the Deutsch Mark', *IMF Working Paper*, WP/90/3.

Tavlas, G.S. and Ozeki, Y. (1991), 'The Japanese Yen as an International Currency', *IMF Working Paper*, WP/91/2.

Thornton, H. (1939), *An Enquiry into the Nature of the Paper Credit of Great Britain*, London: First Publication, 1802 Allen and Unwin, reprinted.

Thygesen, N. (1980), 'Problems for the European Currency Unit in the Private Sector', *The World Economy*, Vol. 3, No 2, pp. 235-264.

Thygesen, N. (1986), 'Flexible Exchange Rates and National Monetary Policies' in L. Tsoukalis (ed.), *Europe, America and the World Economy*, London: Blackwell.

Thygesen, N. (1988), 'Decentralization and Accountability within the Central Bank: Any Lessons from the U.S. Experience for the Potential Organization of a European Central Banking Institution?' in P. de Grauwe and T. Peeters (eds.), *The ECU and European Monetary Integration*, London: Macmillan.

Thygesen, N. (1989), 'A European Central Banking System - Some analytical and operational considerations' in Delors Report Delors Committee for the Study of Economic and Monetary Union *Report on Economic and Monetary Union in the European Community, Luxembourg*: Office for Official Publications of the EC.

Tinbergen, J. (1952), *On the Theory of Economic Policy*, Amsterdam: North-Holland.

Tietmeyer, H. (1993), 'Changing Capital Markets: Implications for Monetary Policy', *Deutsche Bundesbank Auszüge aus Presseartikeln*, Nr. 58, 25 August

Tobin, J. (1958), 'Liquidity Preference as Behaviour towards Risk', *Review of Economic Studies*, 25, pp. 65-86.

Tobin, J. (1963), 'Commercial Banks as Creators of Money in D. Carson (ed.) *Banking and Monetary Studies*, N.Y.: Irwin, Homewood, III.

Tobin, J. (1980), *Asset Accumulation and Economic Activity*, Oxford: Basil Blackwell.

Tobin, J. (1983), 'Monetary Policy: Rules, Targets and Shocks', *Journal of Money, Credit and Banking*, No 15, pp. 509-518.

Tobin, J. (1984), 'On the Efficiency of the Financial System', *Lloyds Bank Review*, 153, pp. 1-15.

Tobin, J. (1986), 'On the Welfare Macroeconomics of Government Financial Policy', *Scandinavian Journal of Economics*, Vol. 88, pp. 9-24.

Tobin, J. and Brainard, W.C. (1963), 'Financial Intermediaries and the

Effectiveness of Monetary Controls', *American Economic Review*, 53, pp. 383-400.

Tovias, A. (1991), 'A Survey of the Theory of Economic Integration', *Revue d'Intégration Européenne*, Vol. XV, No 1, pp. 5-23.

Tower, E. and Willett, T.D. (1975), 'The Theory of Optimum Currency Areas and Exchange Rate Flexibility: A More General Framework', *U.S. Department of the Treasury Discussing Paper*.

Townshend, H. (1937), 'Liquidity-Premium and the Theory of Value', *Economic Journal*, March, pp. 157-169.

Trades Union Congress (TUC), (1988) *Report on Europe 1992: Maximising the Benefits, Minimising the Costs*, London: TUC Publications, August.

Trever, A. A. (1916), *A History of Greek Economic Thought*, (Reprint of the 1916 ed. published by University of Chicago Press), Pennsylvania: Poruipine Press in 1978.

Triffin, R. (1940), *Monopolistic Competition and General Equilibrium Theory*, Cambridge, Mass.: Harvard University Press.

Triffin, R. (1960), *Gold and the Dollar Crisis*, Yale: Yale University Press.

Triffin, R. (1975), 'A European Monetary Area in World Trade', *Banca Nationale del Lavoro*, March, pp. 3-35.

Triffin, R. (1977), 'A European Parallel Currency as a Shelter Against Exchange Rate Instability', *Bulletin del' Ires*, No 45, Louvain-la-Neuve, December.

Triffin, R. (1979), 'The American Response to the European Monetary System' in P.H. Trezie (ed.) *The European Monetary System: Its Promise and Prospects*, Washington, D.C.: Brookings Institution.

Triffin, R. (1980), 'The Private Use of the ECU', *Instituto Bancario San Paolo di Torino*, Rome, December.

Triffin, R. (1984), 'The Future of the European Monetary System and the ECU?', *CEPS Papers*, No 3.

Triffin, R. (1985a), 'The International Accounts of the U.S. and their Impact Upon the Rest of the World', *Cahiers Economiques*, BIL.

Triffin, R. (1985b), 'Proposals for the Strengthening of the European Monetary System - A discussion of Germany's Objections', *Ifo-digest*, 3/85.

Triffin, R. (1989), 'A European Monetary Bank with Central Bank Functions', in O. Franz (ed.) *European Currency in the Making*, Hinter Gasse: libertas.

Triffin, R. (1991), 'The IMS (International Monetary System or Scandal?) and the EMS (European Monetary System ... or Success?), *Banca Nationale del Lavoro Quarterly Review*, No 179, pp. 399-436.

Triffin, R. and Swings, A.A.L. (eds.), (1980), *The Private Use of the ECU*, Brussels, Kredietbank.

Tsiang, S.C. (1959), 'The Theory of Forward Exchange and Effects of Government Intervention in the Forward Market', *IMF Staff Papers*, 7 April, pp. 75-106.

Tsiang, S.G. (1966), 'Walras' Law, Say's Law and Liquidity Preference in General Equilibrium Analysis', *International Economic Review*, 7, pp. 329-345.

Tsoukalis, L. (1977), *The Politics and Economics of European Monetary Integration* London: Allen and Unwin.

UK Treasury, (1989), *An Evolutionary Approach to Economic and Monetary Union*, London: HMSO, November.

UK Treasury, (1991), *Economic and Monetary Union Beyond Stage I: Possible Treaty Provisions and Statute for a European Monetary Fund, London*: HM Treasury, January.

Ungerer, H., Evans, O., Nyberg, P. (1983), *The European Monetary System: the Experience, 1979-82*, IMF, Washington, D.C., May.

Ungerer, H. (1990), 'The EMS, 1979-1990: Policies - Evolution - Outlook', *Konjunkturpolitik*, 36, Jahrg. H.G.

U.S. Congress/Gold Commission, (1982), *Report to Congress of the Commission on the Role of Gold in the Domestic and International Monetary Systems'*, Government Printing Office.

Usher, A.P. (1943), *The Early History of Deposit Banking in Mediterranean Europe*, Cambridge, Mass., Harvard.

Vaciago, G. (1986), 'Financial Innovation in Italy and its Implications for Monetary Policy', *Greek Economic Review*, Vol. 8, No 2, pp. 167-186.

Vaciago, G. (1993), 'Public versus Private Debt', *Banca Nazionale del Lavoro Quarterly Review*, No 186, pp. 339-353.

Van den Boogaerde, P. (1984), 'The Private SDR: An Assessment of Its Risk and Return', *IMF Staff Papers*, March, pp. 25-61.

Van der Knoop, H. (1990), 'The Potential Money Character of Assets', *Kredit und Kapital*, Heft 2, pp. 204-214.

Van Horne, J. C. (1986), 'An Inquiry into Recent Financial Innovation', *Kredit und Kapital*, No 4, pp. 446-460.

Van Ypersele, J. and Koeune, J-C. (1985), *The European Monetary System: Origin, Operation and Outlook*, Brussels: The European Perspectives Series, revised edition, 1989.

Vaubel, R. (1977), 'Free Currency Competition', *Weltwirtschaftliches Archiv*, Kiel: September, pp. 435-59.

Vaubel, R. (1978), *Strategies for Currency Unification*, Tubingen: J.C.B. Mohr.

Vaubel, R. (1984), 'The Government's Money Monopoly: Externalities or Natural Monopoly?', *Kyklos*, Vol. 37, pp. 27-58.

Vaubel, R. (1990), 'Currency Competition and European Monetary Integration', *Economic Journal*, 100, pp. 936-946.

Veblen, T. (1899), *The Theory of the Leisure Class*, London: Macmillan, reprinted by Mentor Book, 1953.

Vercelli, A. (1991), *Methodological Foundations of Macroeconomics: Keynes, Lucas*, Cambridge: Cambridge University Press.

Vinals, J. (1990), 'The EMS, Spain and Macroeconomic Policy', *CERP Discussion Paper*, No 389, March.

Viner, J. (1931), 'Cost Curves and Supply Curves', *Zeitschrift für Nationalokonomie*, 111, pp. 23-46.

Von Hayek, F. A. (1931), *Prices and Production*, London: Routledge.

Von Hayek, F. A. (1933), *Monetary Theory and the Trade Cycle*, London: J. Cape.

Von Hayek, F. A. (1978), *Denationalisation of Money - The Argument Refined*, London: The Institute of Economic Affairs, Second Edition.

Von Hayek, F. A. (1984), 'The Theory of Currency Competition' in P. Salin (ed.) *Currency Competition and Monetary Union*, The Hague: Martinus Nijhoff.

Von Neuman, J. (1945-46), 'A Model of General Equilibrium', *Review of Economic Studies*, XIII, 1-9.

Walker, D. A. (1981), 'William Jaffe, Historian of Economic Thought, 1898-1980', *American Economic Review*, Vol. 71, No 5, December, pp. 1012-1019.

Wallich, H.C. (1972), *The Monetary Crisis of 1971 - The Lessons to Be Learned*, Washington, DC: The Per Jacobsson Foundation.

Walras, L. (1969), *Elements of Pure Economics; or The Theory of Social Wealth* translated by Jaffé, William, N.Y.: A.N. Kelley, [1954 ed.]. A translation of the 'Edition Definitive' (1926) of the 'Elements d'Economie Politique Pure'.

Walras, L. (1896), *Etudes d'Economie Sociale*, Lausanne: F. Rouge, 1896.

Walras, L. (1898), *'Etudes d'Economie Politique Appliquée'*, Lausanne: F. Rouge.

Walsh, C.M. (1903), *The Fundamental Problem in Monetary Science*, N.Y.: MacMillan.

Walsh, V. and Gram, H. (1980), *Classical and Neo-Classical Theories of General Equilibrium: Historical Origins and Mathematical Structure*, N.Y.: Oxford University Press.

Walters, A. (1986), *Britain's Economic Renaissance: Margaret Thatcher's Reforms 1979-84*, Oxford: Oxford University Press.

Weintraub, S. (1978), *Keynes, Keynesians and Monetarists*, Philadelphia: University of Pennsylvania.

Weintraub, S. (1982), 'Hicks on IS-LM: more explanation?', *Journal of Post Keynesian Economics*, Vol. IV, No 3, pp. 445-452.

Weldon, J.C. (1966), 'Public Goods (And Federalism)', *Canadian Journal of Economics and Political Science*, May, pp. 230-37.

Weldon, J. C. (1968), 'On Money as a Public Good', Ottawa: Carleton University, *Mimeo*.

Weldon, J. C. (1971), 'Theoretical Penalties of Inflation' in M. Swan and D. Wilton (eds.) *Inflation and the Canadian Experience*, Toronto: Queen's University, July .

Weldon, J. C. (1973), 'On Money as a Public Good', Montreal: McGill University, *Mimeo*, 2 June, or Canadian Economic Association, Annual Meeting, Kingston: Queen's University, June 1973.

Weldon, J. C. (1984), *A History of Economic Thought, Various Working Notes*, McGill University: Mimeo.

Werner Report (1970), *Report to the Council and the Commission on the Realisation by Stages of Economic and Monetary Union in the Community*, Brussels: EC Bulletin, Supplement 11, October 1970.

Whitman, M. v N. (1975), 'Global Monetarism and the Monetary Approach to the Balance of Payments', *Brookings Papers of Economic Activity*, 3.

Wicksell, K. (1893), *Value, Capital and Rent*, (Uber Wert, Kapital und Rente), First Published in, Reprinted by A.M. Kelley, 1970.

Wicksell, K. (1898), *[Geldzins und Guterpreise], Interest and Prices - A Study of the Causes Regulating the Value of Money*, translated by R.F. Kahn, London: Macmillan, 1936.

Wicksell, K. (1901), *Lectures on Political Economy*, [Vorlesungen uber Nationalokonomie], Volume One: General Theory, 2nd edition in 1911, 3rd edition in 1927 and translated from the Swedish by E. Classen, London: Macmillan, 1934.

Wicksell, K. (1906), *Lectures on Political Economy*, [Vorlesungen uber Nationalokonomie], Volume Two: Money [and Credit] [Geld und Kredit], 2nd edition in 1911, 3rd edition, JENA, in 1928 and translated from the Swedish by E. Classen, London: Macmillan, 1935.

Wicksell, K. (1907), 'The Influence of the Rate of Interest on Prices', *Economic Journal*, June, pp. 213-220.

Willett, T.D. and Tower, E. (1970), 'Currency Areas and Exchange-Rate Flexibility', *Weltwirtschaftliches Archiv*, 105, No 1, pp. 48-63.

Williamson, J. (1975), 'The Implications of European Monetary Integration for Peripheral Areas' in Vaizey, J. (ed.) *Economic Sovereignty and Regional Policy*, London: MacMillan.

Williamson, J. (1977), *The Failure of World Monetary Reform*, 1971-74, London Nelson.

Williamson, J. (1983), *The Exchange Rate System*, Washington, D.C.: Institute for International Economics.

Williamson, J. (1985), 'More on Choosing the Right Rules for Exchange-rate Management', *The World Economy*, September, pp. 81-84.

Williamson, J. (1986), 'Target Zones and the Management of the Dollar', *Brookings Papers on Economic Activity*, 1, Washington.

Wittelsberger, H. (1991), 'The Bundesbank: History and Lessons for European Monetary Unification', *De Pecunia*, Vol. III, pp. 31-44.

Wood, G. E. (1983), 'The European Monetary System - past developments, future prospects and economic rationale' in Roy Jenkins (ed.) *Britain and the EEC*, London, MacMillan.

Yeager, L.b. (eds.) (1962), *In Search of a Monetary Constitution*, Cambridge, Mass.: Harvard University Press.

Yeager, L. B. (1968), 'Essential Properties of the Medium of Exchange', *Kyklos*, XXI, No 1, pp. 45-69.

Yeager, L. B. (1976), *International Monetary Relations: Theory, History and Policy*, Second Edition, N.Y. Harper and Row.

Young, R. A. (1973), *Instruments of Monetary Policy in the United States: The Role of the Federal Reserve System*, Washington, D.C.: IMF.

Zavvos, G. S. (1989), *Banking Policy of the EEC in the context of 1992 - Strategic Options for the Greek Banking System* (in Greek), Athens: Association of Greek Banks.

Zavvos, G. S. (1990), 'Banking Integration and 1992: Legal Issues and Policy Implications', *Harvard International Law Journal*, Vol. 31, No 2, pp. 463-505.